**A Freedomways
Reader**

20 $ 2.25 511

INTERNATIONAL PUBLISHERS
381 Park Avenue South NEW YORK, N. Y. 10016

A Freedomways Reader
Afro-America in the Seventies

Editor: Ernest Kaiser

International
Publishers
New York

A Freedomways Reader

Afro-America in the Seventies

Ernest Kaiser
Editor

James Baldwin
Foreword

Published simultaneously by
International Publishers, New York
and Seven Seas Books, Berlin, 1977

Library of Congress Cataloging in Publication Data
Main entry under title:

A Freedomways reader.

1. Afro-Americans–Addresses, essays, lectures.
2. United States–Race relations–Addresses, essays,
lectures. I. Kaiser, Ernest. II. Freedomways,
III. Title: Afro-America in the seventies.
E185.F845   973'.04'96073   77-5319
ISBN 0-7178-0493-3 pbk.

Contents

Foreword

Freedomways, for me, is rather like that friend you have known so long that neither of you can remember exactly where, or when, you met. All that's clear, now, is that a friend came along when you needed one.

I certainly needed *Freedomways,* and I was not alone.

If the advent of *Freedomways* was a much needed, much longed for event, the circumstances which brought it into existence were – and are – exceedingly strenuous.

Freedomways appeared about five years after Mrs. Rosa Parks refused to stand up on that bus, in Montgomery, Alabama, and give her seat to a white man. Mrs. Parks thus entered history, and so did, among others, Martin Luther King, Jr.: but I have always wondered about that so critically weary white man, so anxious to take a load off his feet, for whom history appears to have reserved not the smallest footnote. Did his neighbors rally round him as the Blacks marched and the townspeople gritted their teeth and the bus company went bankrupt and segregation on the buses was finally outlawed? or did they drive him out of town? or push him in front of a bus? However – let me not be frivolous.

Five years after the crucial events in Montgomery, the Black students of the deep South challenged the southern "folkways" on the level of apple pie and coffee – refused, in other words, to be treated as inferior on any level whatever.

But many a white student, after all, and many a white soldier, loathed the kind of gratuitous emasculation he was expected to endure by doing and saying nothing while the buddy with whom he played football, or the buddy with whom he had faced death, was forced to eat, and fulfill the most basic human functions in quarters, which, however boastfully "equal" were yet more certainly and demeaningly "separate": separate because meant to be demeaning, and demeaning, furthermore, for both Black and white. The white student did not have to know the difference between segregation de jure and segregation de facto to sit down beside a Black person at a lunch counter. From which lunch counter both Black and white were carried off to jail, of course: for this "apple-pie and coffee" stratagem brought into question the self-serving legal labyrinth in which the South attempted to defend its "folkways," and in which the entire nation defended and justified its murderous treatment of the Black population.

The key to this legal labyrinth is the American concept of private and public property: the means taken by Americans to prevent the government from invading the private sector. In principle this concern for human liberty seems admirable, but reveals itself, in action, as being motivated by nothing more complex than greed. A man's home may or may not be his castle, depending on his standing in the community or the real needs of the state. If he is isolated – that is defenceless – in the community, and has no possibility of calling on aid of the state, he not only has no castle, he may soon have no life. You and I both have the right, for example, to eat with whom we please, in the privacy of "our" castles. But, once I have decided to cook, not merely for my family and friends, but for a public which will pay me for cooking and serving meals, I have made my private property public, and can have no legal basis, then, for discrimination, which clearly is, or ought to be, a private matter.

But that the American concern for human liberty is thoroughly compromised by concerns far less noble began to be revealed as the "apple-pie and coffee" challenge brought under scrutiny a positive cat's cradle of dubious laws designed with the single intention of protecting white status, property, and profit.

And, perhaps, no single detail of the ensuing, grim, and on-going struggle is more revelatory of his single intention than the fact that, in the deep South, when a Black man or woman attempted to register to vote, his, or her, name and address were posted on the court-house door for thirty days. Nor could this presumed citizen of a hypothetically free country hope for any help from the federal government – as the melancholy record proves. The concept of "states rights" made him isolated and defenceless in the community, and this same concept tied the hands of the state, which was – hypothetically – sworn to defend his rights as a citizen.

Freedomways perceived this as collusion, and addressed itself to the task of re-interpreting the American reality: which, in the middle of the twentieth century, had global reverberations. No other black American periodical saw this as early, or as clearly, as *Freedomways*. We have not always seen eye to eye, my old friend and I, which must be taken as natural: on the other hand, we have never had any profound, wrenching disagreements, either, which must be taken as rare. In any case, the *Freedomways* record, or that portion of it contained in this book, a record which stretches from the backwoods of the American south, through the ghettos of the American north, and Latin America, and Africa – the troubled globe, in short – will also give you cause for argument, cause for wonder, cause for hope.

Saint-Paul-de-Vence
November 29, 1977   James Baldwin

Introduction

The Black people have a long and militant tradition of struggle for freedom here in America. From the slave revolts through the early convention movement and the Abolitionist crusade against chattel slavery to the present day.

They have also understood the value of the printed word as a potent weapon in their freedom fight. From the early slave petitions through *Freedom's Journal*, David Walker's *Appeal*, Frederick Douglass's *The North Star*, the hundreds of published slave narratives, *The Anglo-African* (newspaper and magazine), *The Christian Recorder*, *The AME Church Review*, William Monroe Trotter's *The Guardian* newspaper, the W.E.B. Du Bois-edited *Crisis* of the NAACP, Carter G. Woodson's *Journal of Negro History*, Marcus Garvey's *The Negro World* newspaper, A. Philip Randolph and Chandler Owen's *The Messenger* magazine and the hundreds of other black newspapers and magazines, the many thousands of pamphlets and books of black history, fiction, poetry and social protest written and edited by Blacks over the past 130 years—almost all have played some part in advancing the black struggle for full citizenship rights.

The militance of the Black people reached a high level during World War II both in protest action and in the black press when the paradox of fighting for democracy against fascism while Jim-Crowing and denying democracy to civilian Blacks at home and to Blacks in the armed forces at home and abroad was especially galling.

After the war, three organizations concerned with rights of the Black people presented petitions to the United Nations in behalf of U.S. Blacks: the National Negro Congress in 1946, the NAACP's Du Bois-edited *Appeal to the World* in 1947 and the Civil Rights Congress's *We Charge Genocide* in 1951. During this period Black war veterans in the South staged dramatic marches for the right to vote and against lynchings and mistreatment. There were also the great struggles and protests around such cases as the Trenton (N.J.) Six, the Martinsville (Va.) Seven, Willie McGee (Miss.), Walter Lee Irvin (Fla.), Willie Earle (S.C.) and the Rosa Lee Ingram (Ga.) case of the late 1940's and the early 1950's. There was also a militant struggle against the segregated armed services at this time resulting in considerable armed services desegregation in the 1950's.

The Montgomery (Ala.) Bus Boycott of 1955-56 led by Rev. Martin Luther King, Jr. and others was the beginning of the great black revolt. There were other bus boycotts in Tallahassee, Fla., Birmingham, Ala., and in other cities in South Carolina and other states. The Southern Christian Leadership Conference was formed in 1957 after the Montgomery boycott by Rev. King and other southern Black ministers.

The Black student sit-ins, started in February 1960, spread rapidly over the South. They were aided by the Congress of Racial Equality (another direct-action, non-violent, interracial organization founded by James Farmer and others in 1942 during World War II), the NAACP and SCLC. The sit-ins and the non-buying boycotts which often accompanied them desegregated hundreds of restaurants in about 200 southern cities.

The Negro American Labor Council, founded in 1960 by A. Philip Randolph and headed by him, represented, with its 10,000 or more Black union members, a separate organization to fight discrimination in various locals as well as in the organizational structure of the AFL-CIO.

The Black Muslims and other Black nationalist groups also came into prominence at this time, voicing their extreme disillusionment with America and calling on Blacks to separate themselves from Jim-Crow-ridden white America. These nationalist groups were stimulated by and tied in with the great independence and revolutionary movements of Africa, Asia, Latin America and the Caribbean, bringing many new nations into the UN and helping U.S. Blacks to accept, like and be proud of their history, culture and physical characteristics in a society that rejects everything but the attributes, the history, culture and physical characteristics of white people.

The National Urban League, an interracial social work organization, whose executive secretary was the late Whitney Young, and the Southern Conference Educational Fund, an interracial organization which grew out of the Southern Conference for Human Welfare, were also doing yeoman work in helping school desegregation and other civil rights causes in the southern states.

Into this militant, maturing Black Freedom Movement, with hundreds of thousands of Black people in organized struggle against segregation, came the African-American magazine that had to come: *Freedomways* in the spring of 1961. This magazine, subtitled A Quarterly Review of the Negro Freedom Movement, was edited by two very knowledgeable and capable Black women, the late Shirley Graham and Esther Jackson. *Freedomways* aimed to speak not only for the struggling Afro-Americans but also for the African, Caribbean and Latin American peoples fighting for freedom and independence against colonialism. This would strengthen the relationship among people of African descent everywhere. A magazine was needed to mirror the developments in the Black people's struggles as well as provide a public forum for the review, examination and debate of all problems faced by Blacks in the U.S. and elsewhere.

A magazine was needed to examine, in terms of black freedom as well as the nation as a whole, the new forms of economic, political and social systems now existing or emerging in the world.

A magazine was needed to provide a medium of expression for serious and talented writers—those with established reputations and the young developing writers on various levels of craftsmanship.

All of these functions and roles the magazine *Freedomways* assumed and it invited historians, sociologists, economists, artists, workers, students and especially activists in the Movement to contribute constructively to its search for truth. The magazine had no special political, organizational or institutional interests to serve other than the aims stated above, and it was to provide an open forum for the free expression of ideas which might or might not agree with those of the editors.

This was the preamble and credo of *Freedomways* and it proceeded to try to live up to its lofty aims.

The Winter 1965 number of *Freedomways* was the W.E.B. Du Bois Memorial Issue. This issue was a landmark and was published as a book with many additions and some deletions in hardback and paperback in 1970. Other special issues were on Harlem, the South, the Caribbean, Africa and Mississippi. The Harlem number was also published as a hardcover and paperback book.

How does the magazine *Freedomways* measure up in carrying out its multiple aims in terms of the freedom movement in the U.S., in Africa and in the Caribbean and in publishing young and established Black writers? John N. Berry in "Demand for Dissent?" (*Library Journal*, Oct. 15, 1964) called *Freedomways* a high quality quarterly of the Black Freedom Movement. Sterling A. Brown, the distinguished Black professor, critic and poet then at Howard University, in "A Century of Negro Portraiture in American Literature" (*The Massachusetts Review*, Winter 1966) ends his long survey by calling the Mississippi issue of *Freedomways* a good anthology of the developing, healthy literature of the freedom movement and an assurance that after the tracts, pamphlets, satires and autobiographical narratives of the movement's Black activists in a worthy historical tradition will come the good novels, poems and plays by Black writers about the current freedom struggle. Ann Allen Shockley's "Black Book Reviewing: A Case for Library Action" (*College and Research Libraries*, Jan. 1974) calls the outstanding feature of *Freedomways* of special interest to librarians its extensive, annotated list of recent books in all subject areas with full bibliographic information and with additional titles on similar subjects or themes pointed out in the annotations.

Freedomways has continued and even improved from

1966 to 1976 as a critical review, a stimulus and direction-giver of the freedom movement and, within its physical limitations, as a publishing outlet for young and developing and reputable Black writers. Innumerable essays and short stories published in *Freedomways* have been reprinted later in books. The three possible criticisms of 1966 that not enough young, unknown Black writers had found their way into the magazine; that the language of the magazine was too sanitary, not earthy enough as a fighting people's organ; and that there was not much humor, one of the mainstays of the Black people, have been overcome somewhat. Contributing editor Brumsic Brandon, Jr.'s humorous cartoons have been appearing regularly for years in *Freedomways*.

Freedomways has continued to publish scores of important critiques and critical book reviews in its battle with the distorters and defilers of black history, struggle and culture. There have been special issues on The Crisis in Education and the Changing Afro-American Community, American Indians and Mexican Americans, The African-Asian struggle, Paul Robeson: The Great Forerunner, The Black Image in the Mass Media and Afro-American Youth–The Road Ahead. Back in 1966, we called for a *Freedomways Reader*. Here is that book. We have covered literature, history, music, theater; racism's new face; the black image in the mass media and people, politics and movements including Africa. Poetry and short stories have been omitted because of space limitations.

Ernest Kaiser

I. Literature, History, Music, Theater

Is Black Writing American Literature?

Loyle Hairston

Ernest J. Gaines is one of the best fiction writers in the United States today; Alice Walker's *The Third Life of Grange Copeland* was one of the better novels published in the United States in recent years. And yet these two fine writers are practically unknown because their respective publishers have failed to acknowledge the importance of their work. These same publishers have spent generous sums of money to publicize many white writers of far less talent. Can this be ascribed wholly to commercial considerations? How explain the fact that the Pulitzer Prize and National Book Award judges rarely find black writing worthy of critical attention.

If Eudora Welty rather than Ernest Gaines had written *The Autobiography of Miss Jane Pittman*, imagine the acclaim the book would have received. It would have been an immediate book club selection. On the other hand if Paule Marshall, one of our meticulous novelists, had written *Them*–Joyce Carol Oates' excellent novel–would she have received the National Book Award? I don't think so for one simple reason–Ms. Marshall is Black.

Less critical observers will say that one shouldn't make such severe charges against the literary establishment at a time when black writing is receiving so much commercial attention. At a time when practically every bookseller has a stall of black writing on prominent display; when publishers are hustling everything about the "black experience" into print, however mediocre or badly written it is; when even a few Black editors have been hired to help sift this bonanza of literary ore–at the beginning of the millennium one shouldn't be such an ingrate.

My concern however is not with the quantity of black writing being published (this "quantity" amounts to less than .001 percent of titles published) but with the literary establishment's peculiar attitude towards serious black writing. The term "literary establishment" is appropriate because the social views of many influential critics, editors, and publishers are institutional in the way they reflect traditional American racial sentiments. Racism? Indeed, but the word itself tends to oversimplify the deeper implications of this persisting irrationality. We must look further than the traditional attitudes of whites towards Blacks in American society and examine certain "impulses" inherent in our social order. When Dickens's young hero in *Martin Chuzzlewit* journeyed to America to seek his fortune, he found a country more immersed in greed, double-dealing, self-righteousness, pious hypocrisy, violence, slavery, racism, and just plain rudeness than he thought humanly possible. This scathing satire of life in nineteenth-century America seems hardly exaggerated for, indeed, all of the remarkable qualities discerned by that great writer are flourishing still. Although the slaveholders have been routed, racism and assorted aberrations have been judiciously integrated into our corporate culture.

The business of America is *business*, someone once said in summing up the ethos of our social system, a system so committed to that lofty end that the value of any endeavor is measured by its capacity to increase private wealth. Even culture is reduced to a commodity but its marketability depends less upon artistic excellence than whether its content offends or flatters those in control of the marketplace. The titles on most "best seller" lists, for instance, indicate that a writer's success tends to improve with the shallowness of his work. Such is the "aesthetic" judgment of the literary establishment's sponsorship. But it could hardly be otherwise when we realize that publishers, editors, critics function as a kind of conduit to many of society's cultural, intellectual needs. Keeping certain ideas, social habits, myths, moral conventions, prejudices, hobgoblins, alive in the public mind becomes a primary obligation of those presiding over literary taste. Racism then, as a centerpiece in American mores, is incorporated in mainstream literature and criticism because it serves the rulers of our social order.

In a sense genuine humanism in American literature scarcely survived the nineteenth century. With the exception of such "radicals" as Mark Twain, Jack London, Upton Sinclair, John Dos Passos, Theodore Dreiser, twentieth-century mainstream literature drifted into romanticism and Freudian introspection. Literary criticism became increasingly more "refined" as it abandoned vulgar realism for more profound realms of exploration–the gloomy interiors of the white middle-class soul. Needless to say there were no Blacks to be found in that wasteland of weary individualism; no disturbing ideas to rouse the faithful from their esoteric brooding over America's lost innocence. Under the goading of a literary criticism crusading for old values, restored virtue, and lily-white bliss, the real world gave way to unoffending fantasies. Style replaced seriousness, form reigned supreme while content became suspect. In the mythical world of white middle-class snobbery God became an upper-class Episcopalian.

Certain consequences were inevitable. Reality would become even more estranged from the themes of fiction and life would be depicted devoid of any idea that even suggested social criticism. Man's lot became strictly a personal ordeal. In due course, the world depicted in modern American fiction bore little resemblance to anything familiar. There would be little reference to the hard world of poverty, exploitation, social neglect; little reference to the corrupting greed of a powerful monied class; little reference to their subverting Constitutional ideals with a capitalist ethos; little reference to the unusually punitive oppression of Blacks in the South and across the nation. Such sociological aberrations had no place in American fiction if it were to play a proper role in our developing imperial culture. The literary establishment recognized its role in the scheme of things.

I am not suggesting a conspiracy. Indeed, for the most

part it was probably collusion based more on misguided patriotism and shared chauvinist notions about America's *manifest destiny* than any clandestine boardroom collaboration. The results, however, have been the same. For instance, under the sway of genteel criticism, mainstream literature has helped to foster the myth that the boundaries of civilization ended at the borders of Europe and America. What lay beyond were gradations of savagery as practiced by "natives," "Indians," "Asiatics." On the other hand, one could search mainstream literature from the turn of the century through the fifties and find scarcely any reference to the *existence* of Black people on the American landscape.

The exception of course was the Southern white writer whose portrayal of Blacks in fiction betrayed the inhumanity at the center of his art. Even Faulkner's ability was distorted by the pervasive racism of his redneck traditionalism. But as expected, far from challenging his fictive assumptions about the "nature" of the Black man's character, genteel criticism praised his *Dilseys* as though they were among the finest bricks in the edifice of his talent. Minor writers were even less bridled in expressing their racial pathology. The African captive whom freedom-loving Pilgrim settlers promptly reduced to a slave was depicted in Southern literature as he was treated in real life, as a mortal too deficient in human qualities to deserve moral consideration. Thus mainstream literature legitimized the inhumanity of portraying man as a *nigger*! William Styron's *The Confessions of Nat Turner* provides a singular example of how racism has poisoned the mainstream of American literature and criticism. A novel which sought to discredit a remarkable slave's organized revolt against slavery was hailed as a masterpiece. Blessed with a full complement of *the peculiarities in the Negro character,* Styron's Nat Turner despises his fellow slaves, lives a celibate life but indulges in wild fantasies of having a *white* woman, while having homosexual tendencies into the bargain. To make sure he put this legendary nigger in his proper historical place, Styron dragged in Freudian psychology to validate his racism.

One marvels at the arrogance of the literary establishment, at its cynical disregard for truth and fairness, at its morbid devotion to myths of lily-white virtue. But by his social origins the Black writer threatens the tranquility of such puerile fantasizing. Consequently his work is rejected because he dredges up too many skeletons from the riverbed of the American tradition; too many barbarities from the undertow of transcendental purity. For whose words more eloquently detailed the "grand aggregation of human horrors" of American slavery than those of Frederick Douglass? Whose writings more exhaustively examined the contradictions in our social system than those of Dr. W.E.B. Du Bois? Moreover, could the social criticism implicit in the writings of Paul Laurence Dunbar, James Weldon Johnson, Claude McKay, *et al* have been depicted by white authors—writers ignorant of the ways of Black folk on the one hand and unwilling to condemn the bigotry of American society on the other? In fidelity to historical truth do novels like Styron's *Nat Turner* begin to compare with Margaret Walker's powerful antebellum/Civil War novel, *Jubilee,* as serious literature?

By isolating black writing from the body of mainstream literature, the literary establishment implies that writing depicting aspects of American life from a black perspective is not authentic American literature; that Langston Hughes was less an American poet than Robert Frost; that Chester Himes writes about "Negro" life not about America; that stories written exclusively about Black people are not "universal" enough to deserve critical attention. Such presumptions are as preposterous as they are arrogant. They are made nevertheless because apparently genteel criticism still envisions a literature immured in Old South values and Puritan idolatries rather than one rooted in the soil of social reality. Instead of a humanist literature it has nurtured a kind of *belles-lettres* of white middle-class conceit. While this exclusion has caused the Black writer much hardship, perhaps it has been a blessing in disguise, exempting him from the literary establishment's mean-spirited illiberalism;

freeing him from its corrupting mythologies. Thus the Black writer is left free to develop creative standards worthy of his ideals, standards that will strengthen his commitment to a humanist literature. His art will then become imbued with a liberating freshness and endowed with that spiritual richness gathered during the long winter of the American black experience—portraying its sorrows, defeats, and triumphs in all their manifold complexities. A growing clarity of vision informs him that "a new day is aborning."

History is fast overtaking the despoilers of human freedom. The Black writer knows that those gathered in gloomy council in the bloodstained court of imperialism are doomed, that their social order has become an anachronism of the twentieth century—that the *winds of change* won't abate until that system has been divested of its oppressive power. But knowing this is not enough. The Black writer must become a participant in this change by using his creative powers to help advance the cause of human freedom. In the process he will create a new aesthetic out of what John O. Killens once called the highest form of morality—man's struggle for liberation.

Understandably, such is not the aspiration of the literary establishment and this explains much of its fear of and antipathy for the serious Black writer. But today the Black writer's destiny is in his own hands. His recognition as an American writer no longer awaits the literary establishment's stamp of approval but depends upon whether his work is wedded to the realities of our times, on whether he approaches his work with sufficient courage, dedication, knowledge, talent to gain the attention and respect of Black and Third World audiences. The lesson the literary establishment will finally learn is that the black experience is a vital part of the American experience.

Criteria in Selection of Black Literature for Children

Jacqueline Lee Young

I am the smoke king,
I am black.

I am darkening with song
I am harkening to wrong!
I will be black as blackness can,
The blacker the mantle the mightier the man,
My purpling midnights no day dawn may ban.

W.E.B. Du Bois, 1899

One of the acute problems between Black and white Americans is that society in the United States continually tells these groups that they are different. Not only does it say they are different, but, also that the Black group is inferior to the white group. This message has been communicated in many ways via different social media. This is not a recent development but one that began with the introduction of Black people to America. The nature of this social communication has had a detrimental impact on the individual black self-image and the collective identity of Black people. Much insight is not required to understand what being told for generations that one is inferior will do to that group's own self-esteem and self-evaluation.

The concept of "white over black" has had a significant influence on the shaping and the development of American history. Over three hundred years ago when Blacks first appeared on American soil, they began their "long journey" of reacting to this concept as a means of psychological and physical survival. Several historians, in giving detailed accounts of the black experience of slave passage to America, the institution of slavery, and the adjustment to the "post-slavery" period, have supplied strong testimony to the physical hardships endured by Black people. Lerone Bennett, a Black historian, in describing the passage of Africans to America, has written:

"The newly-purchased slaves, properly branded and chained were rowed out to the slave ships for the dreaded Middle Passage across the Atlantic. They were packed like books on shelves into holds which in some instances were no higher than eighteen inches. . . . Here for six to ten weeks of voyage, the slaves lived like animals. Under the best conditions, the trip was intolerable. When epidemics of dysentery or small pox swept the ships, the trip was beyond endurance. . . . The slaves not infrequently would go mad before dying or suffocating. In their frenzy some killed others in hope of procuring more room to breathe. Men strangled those next to them, and women drove nails into each other's brains.

"It was not unusual to find a dead and a living man chained together. So many dead people were thrown overboard on slavers, that it was said that sharks would pick up a ship off the coast of Africa and follow it to America."[1]*

It is important to remember that when Black people came to this country, their customs, attitudes and desires were shaped for a different place and different life. Being brought to a country, a culture, and a society that are the complete antithesis of one's way of life has been recognized as one of the cruelest aspects of this particular enslavement.[2]

During the period of slavery, Black people responded to their environment with a view of how best to survive. The relationship of master to slave was of extreme importance to

* See notes at end of article.

the slave. There existed no communication between master and slave on any human level, instead the relationship one would have with a piece of property. If you twist the knob on your radio you expect it to play.

It was this condition of inhumanity that characterized the African slave's lot in this country.[3] Survival concerned itself with the need for food, clothing, shelter, and humane treatment. Again Bennett stresses the fact that the treatment of slaves was harsh and brutal:

". . . The food, which was issued once a week was generally coarse and lacking in variety. Each adult was given a peck of corn and three or four pounds of bacon or salt pork. Fractional amounts, usually one-half, were allotted to each child in the family. Most slaves supplemented this meager fare by trapping coons and opossums in the fields or by stealing corn from the master's corn cribs and chickens from his chicken coops. . . .

"Most slaves lived in family type log cabins, but some lived in large barracks literally alive with slaves, of all ages, conditions and size. . . . The majority of the living quarters were dark, dank holes built flat on the ground. . . .

"The usual punishment was thirty-nine lashes with a cowskin whip. It was not unusual, however, for slaves to receive one hundred or more lashes in one day. Few slaves, no matter how obedient or humble, reached old age without receiving at least one lashing. Masters who were psychotic, sadistic or otherwise mentally unbalanced devised ingenious methods of punishment. And 'kind' masters whipped the skin off slaves' backs and washed them down with brine."[4]

It is not the intent of this article to document injustices characterized by inhumane treatment and persecution of Black people. But it is necessary to be aware of its existence and understand its relationship to the psychological development of Black people. Just as the question of physical survival has haunted Blacks, the more subtle question of psychological survival has also been important to the black self-image.

In answering the questions of "Who am I?" and "What am I?" Black people in general have been deprived of a history and culture from which to choose. Instead white society's answers were accepted in explaining the inferiority of Black people. An inferiority based on the rejection of the history and culture of Black people. Thus, Black people came from nothing and therefore they were entitled to nothing.

To gain a clearer understanding of the relationship of physical survival to the psychological development of the Black individual, it is necessary to have an understanding of the outstanding components of personality.

Jersild has structured the image of self as a composite of thoughts, feelings and awareness of individual existence. The concept of the "who" and "what" of a person is basically conditioned by society's concept of "self."[5] "Self" can never be isolated from the complex interpersonal relations in which the person lives. If the appraisal is mainly derogatory, then the person's self-image will also be mainly derogatory.[6] Since the self-image of Black people has been conditioned primarily by white estimation and judgment of blackness, it seems inevitable that Blacks' estimate of themselves will be negative.

Equally important as the historical maltreatment on the psychological development of Black people, has been environmental influence. Presently three out of every four Blacks live in the city. A million and a half left the South in the years 1950–1960. Of the Blacks who live in the North 95 percent now live in cities.[7] Eleven metropolitan areas have Black communities of between 200,000 and one million: New York, Chicago, Los Angeles, Detroit, Philadelphia, Washington, D.C., St. Louis, Baltimore, Cleveland, Houston, and New Orleans.[8] Now the largest percentage of Blacks (of the total population) is in Washington, D.C.; the largest concentration of Black Americans in an urban ghetto area is in Chicago, and the largest number of Black Americans live in New York City.[9]

Black people came to urban centers with great expectations and hopes for a better life. However, as whites left these areas where Blacks were locating, signs of congestion, deterioration and total depreciation grew more apparent as time passed. In short, ghetto dwellers' expectations fall victim to the dirt, the filth and neglect of their communities.

One of the greatest problems of life in Afro-America is the problem of poor housing and is common to all living in the black community. In Harlem, the Mecca of black America, over 232,792 people live within a radius of $3\frac{1}{2}$ square miles. This is more than 100 people per acre. Ninety percent of Harlem's 87,369 residential buildings are more than thirty-three years old and nearly half of them were built before 1900.[10]

In general, the condition of all but the newest buildings is poor. Eleven percent were classified as dilapidated by 1960 Census. Over 33 percent of the buildings were considered extremely deteriorated. They need more repair than would be provided in the course of regular maintenance.[11] There are more people, in fewer rooms, than anywhere else in the city. Yet, the rents and profits from Harlem are unusually high. Ellen Lurie has documented this by saying, "In the early sixties in decontrolled buildings a single room may cost as much as thirty-five dollars a week."[12]

It has been said by many social scientists that the best single index of a community's general health is its infant mortality rate. For Harlem, this rate in 1968 was 48.8 per 1,000 live births compared to 26.2 for New York City.[13] Poor housing conditions, malnutrition, and inadequate health care are undoubtedly responsible. Typical conditions under which ghetto dwellers live are where flies and maggots breed, where plumbing is stopped up and unrepaired, and where rats bite helpless infants, all conditions not much different from those experienced by early Africans in America.

In viewing the physical environment one can gain insight

into psychological influences on the personality and self-image of Black people. Damage often occurs to the personality in the loss of self-esteem and a negative self-image through self-hatred. One begins to see himself and his culture as inferior; his family as less than adequate; and his race as something to be denied or disguised. As a result, talent and manpower are wasted.

The shaping of self-image is of course not inborn, but learned. Outside the family group, the Black individual acquires additional clues to his self-worth. Interaction with teachers, policemen, and storekeepers, directly and indirectly, has some significance on the Black person's picture of "who" and "what" he is.

Education has also had a significant effect on the shaping of the black self-image. The assignment of school personnel works in a subtle way to explain to the Black child "who" and "what" he is. If the administrators and teachers in his school are white, and the handymen, the cleaners, and the sweepers are mainly Black, then the child will have an indelible negative view of himself. He will begin to believe that skin color is the determinant of status. This will be reinforced because the child will be unable to find many Black individuals in occupations of status and prestige. One begins to gain more insight by the response of a six-year-old Black child when he says, "Not me!" to the statement, "Maybe you'll be a doctor?"

In looking at the curriculum of American schools, one begins to see that pervasive racist attitudes are taught to American children. If one examines the presentation of American history, it can be seen to be taught and interpreted according to white values and standards. In the process, contributions of Black people are ignored and distorted. *The Confessions of Nat Turner* by William Styron is exemplary of this type of historical evaluation and interpretation.

Another aspect of racism in the classroom, is in the area of textbooks. Numerous studies of textbooks have shown them to be totally white-oriented, both in verbal and pictorial content.

Harold Isaacs, in studying the content of history and geography books from 1860 up to 1947, found that in many instances Black people were included, but in an extremely distorted and grotesque manner.[14] Going to great lengths to describe the "five races of man," these texts give one insight into the stark contrasts of the white race and the Black race. Publishers usually pictured, in the role of the white race, a dignified looking gentleman, dressed in his Sunday best, with a stiff moustache, a stiff collar, and a smooth lapel. Usually, he was an "Emersonian" figure of a man, shown seated in his library, with shelves of books behind him, a globe and a telephone close at hand, and a small child at his side obviously imbibing his kindly and patient wisdom. In another text where the preferred stress is on beauty rather than brains, the representative of the white race was the head of a Greek statue with its classic features in frozen profile. Its caption added with "objective grace": The White Race—An Ideal Head.

In contrast, the pictorial and verbal representation of the Black man in these same texts portrayed him at a most primitive level. A comparative figure to the "Emersonian" figure in his study might have been an African Chief in ceremonial attire. Instead, the African appears as a most prehistoric figure of a man—naked, primeval, carrying club and shield. In another example of this style of contrast, one text classifies the states of man as "savage" (all Black or red people), "barbarous" (chiefly brown), "half-civilized" (almost wholly yellow), and "civilized" (almost all belonging to the white race).

Concerning the influence of society and its contribution to the development of negative feelings in Black children, it is of major importance to suggest possible solutions to the existing problem. It is important to say that the recognition, understanding, and acknowledgment of these numerous influences are in themselves a necessary beginning toward possible solutions. One positive way in the direction of eradicating the effects of racism on the personality development of Black children is by creating relevant black literature.

Jacquelyn Sanders in an essay, "The Psychological Significance of Children's Literature," suggests an important function of literature and one that is crucial with regard to the current needs of Black children. She feels that children's literature can be of the greatest value when it is created in relationship to the outstanding characteristics and needs of children. In this respect she says:

"As the child grows, he strives to master both the outer world that is continually expanding and an inner world of emotions that are tumultuous. In both of these realms, there are many experiences to be fathomed from 'why does it rain?' to 'why do we cry?' As the child fathoms them, he gains strength from doing so."[15]

Perceiving the value of literature, authors must begin to write for Black children in ways that will deliberately attempt to eradicate the harmful influences that exist. In this way authors will begin to effect a change in the self-concept of Black children. In order to accomplish this task, it is essential that authors not only understand the historical and environmental forces that affect Black children, they must understand the important psychological needs that arise out of the "black experience." With this in mind, authors will begin to evaluate past literature and to create new literature with a new understanding. Black literature must achieve three essential criteria if it is to be of value to Black children: black literature must completely nullify the deceptive influences that prevent Black children from finding self-esteem; black literature must convey realism; and black literature must be authentic.

References
[1] Lerone Bennett, *Before the Mayflower*, Chicago. Johnson Publishing Company, 1962, pp. 40–41.
[2] LeRoi Jones, *Blues People*, New York, William Morrow and Company, 1963, p. 1.
[3] *Ibid*, p. 3.
[4] Bennett, *op. cit.*, pp. 73–75.

[5] William C. Kvaraceus *et al.*, *Negro Self-Concept*, New York, McGraw-Hill Inc., 1965, p. 11.

[6] *Ibid*, p. 2.

[7] Kenneth Clark, *Dark Ghetto*, New York, Harper and Row, 1965, p. 22.

[8] *Ibid.*, p. 23.

[9] *Ibid.*, p. 25.

[10] *Ibid.*, p. 30.

[11] Harlem Youth Opportunities Unlimited Inc., *Youth in the Ghetto*, New York, Haryou, 1964, p. 103.

[12] Ellen Lurie, "Community Action in East Harlem," *The Urban Condition*, Ed. by Leonard J. Duhl, New York, Basic Books, 1963, p. 282.

[13] Harlem Youth Opportunities Unlimited Inc., *op. cit.*, p. 108.

[14] Harold Isaacs, *The New World of Negro Americans*, pp. 163–168.

[15] Jacquelyn Sanders, "The Psychological Significance of Children's Literature," *A Critical Approach to Children's Literature*, Ed. by Sara I. Fenwick, Chicago, University of Chicago Press, 1967, p. 15.

Exemplifying literature dealing with necessary black-oriented themes, is my short story entitled "Treasures." The story revolves around the relationship of a young boy with an old man, who introduces the youth to Frederick Douglass, one of the outstanding figures in black history.

Treasures

Rondall sat motionless in the rocking chair outside Mr. Merriwether's old store. As he waited for the music to start from the corner record shop, thoughts of many fun-filled summer afternoons spent listening to the rich record rhythms raced through his mind. This day, however, was different. With the sudden chill in the air, the street was quiet and empty. He knew that the unpredicted cold that arrived the night before had sent the people into their cramped homes to prepare for the long, hard winter. To Rondall, something comforting resulted from there being no one on the street. Often sitting in the rocking chair hearing the soulful songs a sense of uneasiness was created in him. He was not sure he wanted his friends to discover his pleasure in the rocking chair. After all, what kind of activity was that for the best stick ball player on the street.

Rondall looked in the direction of the door and saw Mr. Merriwether with bent and uneven movements coming towards him. How afraid he had been of the old man the first time he saw him! That was at the beginning of the summer when the rocker first appeared in front of the store. Rondall thought about the many times that Mr. Merriwether had invited him into the old store. There was no electricity inside and the store was very dark, so he always refused the invitation.

"Ei, boy," Mr. Merriwether said, "mite bit cold out here today. Better come and warm yourself by the heater, boy."

Rondall looked inside the store and saw the heater, neatly tucked under an old chair by the door. He also saw that the flames coming from the heater gave the store a brightness, usually not present. Rondall stood up, bent his fingers back and forth, and walked slowly into the store.

The first thing Rondall sensed about the store was its smell. He smiled because he felt that the smell was just right for this store. He didn't think about this long, because he was so busy looking at all the old things that Mr. Merriwether had in the store. Every inch of the store was packed with old furniture and other objects.

"You see that table there under all them chairs?" Mr. Merriwether asked. "Well, Mrs. Johnson over in the projects been tryin' to get it for near over a year. But we can't get it, since all them chairs is in the way. Funny ain't it, how you can see something, touch it and want it, but can't have it. Oh, well." With that, Mr. Merriwether walked in the dimness to the back of the store and began to work on an old camera.

Rondall thought about what Mr. Merriwether had said. All the while, he walked around the store and looked at all the different things. It was often hard to move because there was little room. There was only a narrow aisle that led from the front door straight through to the back door. The youth worked his way toward the middle of the store, where he noticed something that looked like a motorcycle. As he began to examine it more carefully, Mr. Merriwether called from the back of the store, "See that ol' cycle, boy? Well I've had that ol' thing now goin' on thirty years. I've taken it apart and put it together near a hundred times. Don't know if it runs, but it sure is fun to work with. Boy, I bet you didn't think that these ol' hands could do that. You know what . . . these ol' hands is strong. They real strong."

Rondall looked into the darkness toward Mr. Merriwether as he talked. His eyes then roamed around the store and came to rest on a shiny tan box that was on a shelf near where Mr. Merriwether stood. How odd it seemed to him that everything else in the store was covered with dust except this box. When he was right next to the box, he ran his finger over the surface of it and found he was right. There was not a speck of dust on the box.

Rondall couldn't help wondering, why was this box placed with such care on the shelf? What was in the box? Should he look inside? Would Mr. Merriwether mind? As all these things ran through his mind, Mr. Merriwether turned toward Rondall and said, "So you found the box, boy. Take it off the shelf easy and come with me over by the fire where we can see. But be careful, boy! Be careful not to drop it."

The boy stood on the tips of his toes and gently but firmly slid the box off the shelf. He held it tightly and walked toward the fire. When he sat on the floor next to Mr. Merriwether, he was still asking himself what was in the box.

"Now, boy, take the top off." Rondall did. As he lifted the top of the box, he could see the face of a man in an old silver frame looking straight at him. "Boy, do you know who that is?" Rondall looked at Mr. Merriwether with a puzzled face. He looked down again to examine the picture more carefully this time. The man in the tattered frame had smooth brown skin, soft grey hair and deep serious eyes.

"Boy, do you know who that is?"

Rondall looked into the old storekeeper's serious dark eyes once again, still puzzled.

"What they teach you in them schools, boy? Well, I guess

I'm gonna have to tell you about him. How ol' are you, boy?"

Rondall told him that he had just turned eight last week.

"All right, I'm gonna tell you a story 'bout this man when he was your same age. You ready?"

Rondall breathed in, sat back against the cracked wall and waited.

"Well, this man lived a long time ago," Mr. Merriwether began. "So long ago that when he was young, he was a slave. You know 'bout slaves don't you? Well, when he was just your age he was sent from a big ol' plantation to the city. There he saw children learnin' to read. When his master saw that he too wanted to read, he told this boy that slaves were not permitted to read. Well, he was gonna learn to read no matter what. And you know what? He learned to read. This learnin' helped him to know many, many things 'bout being a slave. Now you listen close because I'm gonna tell you his name. You ready? Frederick Douglass, that's his name."

With that, Mr. Merriwether's head dropped and he said no more. All the time Mr. Merriwether was talking, Rondall had been studying the picture. Now he looked up from the picture to Mr. Merriwether and down at the picture again. He thought that this man Frederick Douglass looked a bit like Mr. Merriwether.

It was getting late. The only sound was the popping of the flames against the air. Mr. Merriwether looked at Rondall and said, "Tell you what. You say that you was eight last week. Boy, take this picture as a present from me. My father gave it to me and his father gave it to him. Now it's time to pass it on." Rondall looked into the old man's face. He didn't know what to do. He wanted the picture; but he felt how much this picture of Frederick Douglass meant to Mr. Merriwether and he wanted the old man to keep the picture. He also knew that he had hurt Mr. Merriwether when he had refused to come into the store. He didn't want to take any chances of hurting him again. Rondall reached out and took the picture. He got up and touched the old man's folded hands as his way of thanking him. Then tucking the box carefully under his arm, he turned and walked out of the store.

Rondall smiled because the music was playing again. There in the darkness, he stood looking down at the rocker. "Thank you, chair, for helping me to meet two great men." With a proud feeling inside, he turned and started home toward the Kingsway Projects.

The Social Roots of Afro-American Music: 1950-1970

Thomas J. Porter

The systematic and organized attempt by Western civilization either to destroy or cool-out all traces of any cultures which challenge the cultural assumptions of the West dates back to the early fourth century, when Constantine I recognized Christianity as the state religion of the Roman Empire. Whereupon the priests and monks immediately set out to destroy all memorials of ancient civilization, in order to preserve the shaky foundation of the Church. This destructiveness reached the height of ugliness in A.D. 391, when a fanatical group of Christians destroyed the cathedral at Serapis, and the library at Alexandria (the greatest library in the ancient world).

This necessity of Western civilization to affirm itself through acts of barbarism (witness the shelling and destruction of the ancient city of Hue in Vietnam, and the threatened destruction of Ankor Wat in Cambodia in the present Indo-China War) has changed over historical time only in the sophistication of its tactics and maneuvers; its barbaric nature has remained intact.

A more recent example of this is stated in a quote by Hank Aaron, the Atlanta Braves' player, "I get letters asking me to retire or do anything, but please don't break Babe Ruth's record." Brother Aaron had better be careful. Perhaps the most brutal example in recent years has been the systematic repression of black music, particularly that music which began in the mid-fifties with Miles Davis, Charlie Mingus, Max Roach, Sonny Rollins, and Jackie McLean and reached its maturity through the music of John Coltrane, Ornette Coleman, Cecil Taylor, and their musical heirs such as Andrew Hill, John Gilmore, Benny Maupin, Albert Tyler, Archie Shepp, Sonny Murray etc. The relationship between the conditions of one's life and consciousness has been well established. LeRoi Jones has summed it up this way:

"The most expressive music of any given period will be an exact reflection of what the Negro himself is. It will be a portrait of the Negro in America at that time. Who he thinks he is, what he thinks America or the world to be, given the circumstances, prejudices and delights of that particular America."[1]*

It is very important to understand that music, like all art regardless of its form, is ideological. That is, it reflects or transmits certain political, class, and national interests. A creative and revolutionary music, however, is more than just reflective, but criticizes the very social substance of the society, and ultimately contributes towards giving direction to the social reconstruction of that society.

There is no abstract black music. There is black music reflecting different political positions of Black people. Ramsey Lewis' music is not the same as Cecil Taylor's. So when we talk about black music, we mean the most advanced, the most socially conscious music which historically has been the music called "jazz."

Because of the critical nature of black music by 1960, it became increasingly dangerous to the keepers of the nightmare, and quite possibly, has led to spiritual and physical deaths (John Coltrane, Albert Ayler, Eric Dolphy, Booker Little, Booker Ervin) of some of its major forces.

Despite the horrors of the McCarthy period (an attempt to stifle all progressive political and social thought in America), the Robesons and Du Boises had maintained the continuity of the struggle, regardless of the price. As a re-

* See notes at end of article.

sult, Blacks emerged seemingly more determined than ever to press forward. This determinedness can, perhaps, best be explained by certain fundamental changes in the material conditions of Blacks. By 1956, one out of every three organized workers in the country was Black (a total of two million Black workers). This meant that Black workers were a crystallized force in the production process of the country, which qualitatively changed their social consciousness and intensified the struggle for rights.

This consciousness took many different forms. Politically, there were the bus boycotts at Baton Rouge in 1953, and Montgomery in 1956–57. There was Brown vs. Board of Education in 1954, and Little Rock in 1958. The sit-ins and the freedom rides intensified the struggle which peaked temporarily at the March on Washington in 1963, finally exploding in the open rebellion at Watts, Newark, Washington, D.C., Detroit, Cincinnati and numerous other cities as a material force in the world-wide liberation struggle. Dr. Martin Luther King, Jr., and Malcolm X emerged as the two major ideological leaders with King the more mature, having hooked up the relationship between the class and national character of our opposition.

Culturally, there was a simultaneous motion. While black music has historically been the most critical and advanced, not only has there, historically, been a dialectical relationship between the various forms of art, but also between the more advanced forms of art and the changing circumstances of Black people. For instance, Charlie Parker did a benefit concert at the request of Paul Robeson for the brothers who were caught in the McCarthy madness: Coltrane did benefits for *Freedomways,* and Black Arts Repertory Theatre. These bits of tangential information are just to disprove the fact that Black artist/musicians are apolitical and that art somehow functions outside the framework of society.

Charlie Parker's *Another Hairdo* ushered out the konk (a backyard process) and all it symbolized. However it was his musical heirs such as Clifford Brown, Miles Davis, Fats Navarro, Horace Silver, Wardell Gray, John Coltrane etc., through their hard driving, aggressive music who captured the mood of the masses in the mid-fifties. No wonder this music became known as "hard bop."

While the Miles Davis Quintet of the mid-fifties, which included John Coltrane, instinctively reflected the crystallization of a Black proletariat, it was Mingus (*Fables For Faubus, Scenes of The City*), Max Roach (*We Insist: Freedom Now, Garvey's Ghost, Mendacity*) and Rollins (*Freedom Suite*) in the late fifties who stated it very clearly. Needless to say, neither Mingus nor Max Roach is recorded with any frequency, or is regularly available in clubs. The album which contains *Fables For Faubus* immediately became unavailable for ten years (it was re-released in 1971). Roach's album, *We Insist: Freedom Now,* is still unavailable. Rollins's *Freedom Suite* has since been retitled twice without the original liner notes written by Rollins.

Musicians began to free themselves from the chains of musical orthodoxy, and the limits of worn-out forms. The changes in the form and substance of the music were very similar to the motion in the political and social spheres. The major innovators were Ornette Coleman, John Coltrane and Cecil Taylor.

Ornette Coleman's music, almost as if he were setting the pace for the cadences counted off by the marchers, the sit-ins, and freedom riders, added a new rhythmic concept which was complex in its simplicity, not unlike the early New Orleans jazz music in its emphasis on freedom and group improvisation. Coltrane's contributions are many, but his major one was in his further development of the harmonic nature of the music. Coltrane's wide-open, go-for-broke solos, played dialectically against a chordal substance, were very similar to the movement's reliance on the religious substance of our historical tradition passed down from the Nat Turners, David Walkers, to Dr. King and Malcolm. Coltrane's uniting of certain elements of music, heretofore considered dissonant, was very reflective of the emergence of a group cohesiveness of the masses. Cecil Taylor was primarily interested with "ordering the music" as he called it. He was concerned with getting beyond tunes to the construction and organization of new sounds. A. B. Spellman best sums up Taylor's contribution in the following statement:

> "There is only one musician who has by general agreement, even among those who disliked his music, been able to incorporate all that he wants to take from classical and modern western composition into his own distinctly, individual kind of blues, without in the least compromising those blues, and that is Cecil Taylor, a kind of Bartók in reverse."[2]

Black music through Coltrane, Taylor, Coleman, and the young musicians who followed them such as Archie Shepp, Andrew Hill, Bobby Hutcherson, Benny Maupin, Wayne Shorter, Joe Henderson, Grachan Moncur III, Joe Chamber, Tony Williams, Richard Davis, Cecil McBee, Freddie Hubbard, the late Booker Little, and Eric Dolphy became the Achilles heel, the weak link (and dangerous) in Western culture. The music, like the people, was immersed in Western culture, yet digested the forms without becoming overwhelmed by them. Thus by 1964, Afro-American music, in its fully developed form, had moved beyond critical realism (criticism of the forms), the high point of Western music, to a music which was both critical and analytical of the social substance of the society. By 1964, it became increasingly evident that efforts were being made to formalize or cool-out *both the music and the movement which had produced it.*

These efforts took many forms including political assassinations. Within four years, both King and Malcolm were dead (to say nothing of the two Kennedys). Coltrane, Eric Dolphy, Booker Little, and Otis Redding were also dead by 1968. A new motion in the form of nationalism was superimposed on the Movement in the mid-sixties. This reactionary form of nationalism politically disguised itself as the undefinable notion of "Black Power" which has since emerged as "Black capitalism," occultism, and other mysticisms.

One, therefore, should not be surprised that Stokely Carmichael (the sloganeer of "Black Power") when asked on nationwide television if there were a white person whom he admired replied, "Yes, Hitler"; or that black paramilitary organizations are openly subsidized by the government, the same government of the Pentagon papers.

Culturally, this trend took the form of occultism and mysticism pushed mainly by certain elements which attempted to romanticize the hustler, pimp, and manchild as the substance of our experience. These liberals (Black and white) cop-out musically and politically. Whether it be poetry or music, they merely formalize art for the purpose of monetary gain, always removing the revolutionary essence first. A recent example of this is Frank Kofsky's book *Black Nationalism and the Revolution in Music*, wherein he attempts to manipulate the images of John Coltrane and Malcolm X to support certain erroneous musical and political theses he holds. Kofsky attempts to establish "Black nationalism" as the material basis guiding the music. Neither Coltrane nor Malcolm would support these simple, reactionary notions; both were wider in scope and vision, both understood very clearly the nature of this society which obviously explains their untimely deaths. National consciousness has always been inherent in black music but the music has always embodied both the *class* and *national* characteristics in its criticism of the society. Or, as Archie Shepp says, as a musician performs his art, he "transmits a class experience." It has been correctly stated that "there is nothing more international than colonial products, there is nothing more parochial than colonial labor."[3] It was the Black musicians who went around the world and broke this limited perspective. The music of the Negro people is acclaimed internationally as being very representative among the best in all music. Even Kofsky realizes this when he talks about the use of black music as a weapon in the cold war. He is perhaps too much of a racist, and is carrying too much historical baggage to accept the reasons behind the State Department's use of the music. The answer is quite simple: progressive people the world over are not as interested in so-called Western music as in Afro-American music.

Kofsky misses these points. Black music is not seeking his acceptance, it musically states its superiority to Western music, not out of arrogance, but out of struggle. Coltrane's answers in the following interview negate Kofsky's assumptions:

Kofsky: Some musicians have said that there's a relationship between some of Malcolm's ideas and the music, especially the new music. Do you think there's anything in that?

Coltrane: Well, I think that music, being an expression of the human heart, or of the human being itself, does express just what *is* happening. I feel it expresses the whole thing—the whole of human experience at the particular time that it is being expressed.

Kofsky: What do you think about the phrase, *the new black music,* as a description of some of the newer styles in jazz?

Coltrane: Phrases, I don't know. They don't mean much to me, because usually I don't make phrases, so I don't react too much. It makes no difference to me one way or the other what it's called.

Kofsky: If you did make the phrases, could you think of one?

Coltrane: I don't think there's a phrase for it, that I could make.

Kofsky: The people who use *that* phrase argue that jazz is particularly closely related to the black community and it's an expression of what's happening there. That's why I asked you about your reaction to Malcolm X.

Coltrane: Well, I think it's up to the individual musician, call it what you may, for any reason you may. Myself I recognize the artist. I recognize an individual when I see his contribution; and when I know a man's sound, well, to me that's him, that's this man. That's the way I look at it. Labels, I don't bother with.

Kofsky: But it does seem to be a fact that most of the *changes* in the music–the innovations–have come from Black musicians.

Coltrane: Yes, well this is how it is.

Kofsky: Have you ever noticed–since you've played all over the United States and in all kinds of circumstances–have you ever noticed that the reaction of an audience varies or changes if it's a Black audience or a white audience or a mixed audience? Have you ever noticed that the racial composition of the audience seems to determine how the people respond?

Coltrane: Well, sometimes, yes, and sometimes, no.

Kofsky: Any examples?

Coltrane: Sometimes it might appear to be one; you might say . . . it's hard to say, man. Sometimes people like or don't like it, no matter what color they are.[4]

Despite all efforts by Kofsky to conceal the fact, his intentions are very clear: to freeze the music at a point in time, and politically and culturally manipulate it for his own counterrevolutionary objectives.

Another ideological form which is used to cool-out the music is the current blues thrust. I am referring to current efforts to affirm the blues of the thirties and forties, completely out of historical context, and establish them as the most progressive of all black music today. Peasant culture is great culture, but must be viewed in an historical context.

One of the goals of the psychology of colonialism is to keep oppressed people culturally frozen in time, preferably in a period where the political and social relationships are to the advantage of the oppressor. The "blues" content of our music *will always be there* whether it is in Cecil Taylor's *Unit Structure* or the Collective Black Artist's rendition of *C. C. Rider*; albeit at a higher level in accordance with the new conditions.

Perhaps the most sophisticated mechanism used is to

separate the music psychologically and physically from the masses, the consciousness from the circumstances. Politically, there is the case of Muhammad Ali, whose title was taken from him, at a time when a Black heavyweight champion of the world who refused to be inducted would have serious consequences for the American army, since large numbers of young Blacks are needed in that army. However, Ali was allowed to fight years later and was exonerated by the Supreme Court of draft evasion charges. Another example is the publishing of materials which are progressive in a certain historical context, such as *The Wretched of the Earth* by Fanon, when it had already been superseded by a different political motion.

Culturally this frozen-in-time syndrome is done in several ways. Records such as Mingus's *Fables For Faubus* and Roach's *We Insist: Freedom Now* are held off the market for as long as ten years or released for a short period, only to suddenly become unavailable for all time. We do not yet have all the recordings of Coltrane, Dolphy, Billy Holiday, or Charlie Parker. Clubs are usually located out of the Black community, and are usually priced out of the reach of the average working person.

Socially conscious musicians such as Shepp, Cecil Taylor, Mingus, Max Roach, and the Collective Black Artist, are seldom recorded or featured in clubs or on the festival circuit.

This paper is by no means a history of black music, but is an attempt to explode certain myths, point out certain dangers, and suggest certain solutions. Simple solutions or narrow-minded subjective analysis not related to concrete reality will only deepen the crisis. Despite its condemnation of Western civilization, most art—Black or white—in this country is still rooted in the West. That which purports to relate to the East seems to be stuck in A.D. 39 or B.C., while the Eastern World (Asia, Latin America and Africa) is rapidly embracing the scientific world view, politically and culturally. Those advocates of Negro or Black exceptionalism are protecting their petty, middle-class positions which is why they get so much play.

The Jazz and Peoples' Movement and the Collective Black Artist represent some of the more progressive developments musically, but there are still pockets of occultism, mysticism and reactionary nationalism which are fetters and need to be eliminated. Black music is already international; attempts to nationalize it represent a step backward.

What is desperately needed is a scientific concept of the function of art in society.

References
[1] LeRoi Jones, *Blues People*. William Morrow & Co. Inc., New York, 1963.
[2] A. B. Spellman, *Four Lives in the Be-Bop Business*, Pantheon Books, New York, 1966.
[3] Robert Rhodes, Unpublished manuscript on colonialism.
[4] Frank Kofsky, *Black Nationalism and the Revolution in Music*. Pathfinder Press, New York, 1970.

"The Great White Hope"

Carlton Moss

The Great White Hope is a play on the life and times of Jack Johnson, the first Black heavyweight champion of the world. The title comes from a catch phrase used by a press agent to sell the bout as a fight to demonstrate the superiority of the white race over the Black race.

The author of *The Great White Hope* is Howard Sackler, a white man. This in itself shouldn't mean anything, except that in the United States white men developed the practice of white superiority and white men still have the power to pass it on to their children. Nevertheless, many white people have given their talent, skills and their lives in the fight against racism.

The question this article poses is: "Does *The Great White Hope* expose the dehumanizing character of racism and those responsible for it?" or "Does it perpetuate racism by suggesting that Black people are simple-minded, superstitious, ashamed of being Black, cruel, insensitive, irresponsible, immoral and obsessed with white skin?"

Before we examine the character, plot and scenes in *The Great White Hope* let us first review the historical material upon which the play is based.

Although Jack Johnson was the first Black heavyweight champion he was not the first Black man to achieve prominence in the boxing ring. The original Black boxers in the United States were slaves whose owners backed them with bets. Perhaps the most successful was Tom Molineaux whose father had been a boxing slave before him.

Tom bought his freedom with the money he earned in the ring. He showed how prize fighting could be the means by which a Black man might make a living. Many Blacks tried it and some earned money and fame, but none approached the success of Johnson when he was at the top of his profession. John Lardner, a sports writer, said of him, "Johnson was a haughty, articulate, and shrewd man. He determined to express his nature openly and to assert all his rights in the face of prejudice. He made no concessions at all. But he was a stubborn and pedagogic man at heart, rather than a dangerous and dissolute one."

James Weldon Johnson (Black poet, lawyer, diplomat and one-time executive secretary of NAACP) writing in his biography of Johnson said:

> "I was of course impressed by his huge but perfect form, his terrible strength and the supreme care and grace of his every muscular movement. However, watching his face, sad until he smiled, listening to his soft Southern speech and laughter, and hearing him talk so wistfully about his big chance yet to come, I found it difficult to think of him as a prize fighter. I had not yet seen a prize fight but I conceived of the game as a brutal force as well as skill and quick intelligence and I could hardly figure a gentle Jack Johnson in the role. Frederick Douglass had a picture of Peter Jackson (a black prize fighter) in his study and he used to point to it and say, 'Peter is doing a great deal with his fists to solve the Negro question.' I think that Jack, even after the reckoning of his big and little failings has been made, may be said to have done his share."

Jack Johnson was born in Galveston, Texas, on March 31, 1878. Rutherford B. Hayes was in the White House and all was well. The Federal troops had been removed and the defeated Confederates were free to have their "vigilante groups" put the "niggers" back in their place.

Johnson's father was a school janitor. His mother, fondly called "Tiny," was well thought of in the neighborhood on the Northside where the family lived.

Jack left school at the fifth grade to go to work. Though his formal education was limited, his handwriting was legible and he could read with ease. In time he became an avid reader. Once he remarked he was particularly partial to Herbert Spencer, the philosopher.

Johnson's first fight (self-defense) was with a bully on the docks where he worked. Those who saw the fight marveled at the swiftness of Jack's counterattack. When his parents reproached him, all he would say was, "Tough times make tough people."

Prior to Johnson's time, fight promoters would not match Black and white heavyweights in a title bout. But Jack, courageous and articulate, persuaded a promoter to match him with the then heavyweight champion, Tommy Burns, of Australia. The bout was held in Australia on December 26, 1908. Jack Johnson won. Immediately the cry went up in America: "Somebody has got to beat that big nigger." After a futile search for a possible white contender the sportsmen goaded Jim Jeffries, an undefeated former champion, to come out of retirement and meet Johnson. At last a "white hope" was found and the daily press took over. Every morning readers were told this is the fight of the century – the security of "white civilization" depends upon the Negro's defeat.

On July 4, 1910, 20,000 whites and a handful of Blacks jammed an outdoor arena in Reno, Nevada. When news of Johnson's victory hit the wire the Blacks throughout the nation rejoiced, but the rejoicing was shortlived as Blacks were attacked by white mobs in Pennsylvania, Maryland, Ohio, Mississippi, Virginia, Missouri, Georgia, Arkansas and Colorado. All told, two white persons and nine Negroes were killed by mob violence. Hundreds were injured. To compound the resentment among whites over Johnson's victory news became widespread that Johnson entertained white women–something he made no attempt to hide. In fact, shortly after his victory he married a "respectable" white girl from Minneapolis. The girl's mother followed within a short time and charged Johnson with abduction. The girl was arrested but later released for lack of evidence. However, the die was cast. Shortly thereafter Johnson was harassed with a series of violations against his night club and finally arrested and brought before a Grand Jury on a charge of violating the Mann Act (a law that forbade interstate transportation of women for immoral purposes). The witness against him was a prostitute that he had once befriended. She, the prostitute (daughter of a policeman), followed the course of action that is part of any career prostitute's repertoire. After the recital of offenses Johnson was found guilty and sentenced to prison for one year, plus $1,000 fine. Rather than serve sentence he jumped bail and fled to Europe.

After a long stay in Europe, broke and homesick, Johnson made an arrangement whereby if he returned to the United States, lost a fight to a "white hope," he would be given a sizeable amount of cash and his sentence reduced. It is suggested that the government was behind the "deal" because it was important for them (the Blacks) who were beginning to crowd the Northern cities, to know that they couldn't do what Jack Johnson had done and get away with it.

Johnson returned, lost to Jess Willard on April 15, 1915, and served six months of this one-year sentence, with unusual prison privileges, including his own cook.

This, briefly, is what *actually* happened. Now, let us see what is happening on the New York stage.

The time is 1909. We see the front of a picture book farmhouse and a group of white men standing around obviously awaiting an important statement from their host, Fred Brady. Brady, a retired champion, is an impressive-looking man. But now the expression on his face seems to be saying, "Gee, fellows, don't do this to me," as he speaks these words:

"Get Burke, or Kid Foster, Big Bill Brain. I ain't gonna fight no 'dinge' " (a derogatory term for black).

His friends plead with him but he is reluctant. Finally they tell him he is their "white hope" and it is his duty.

"How you gonna like it when the whole damn country says Brady let us down; he wouldn't stick his fists out to teach a loudmouth nigger; stayed at home and let him be champion of the world."

That does it. Brady agrees to come out of retirement and teach the "nigger" a lesson.

To heighten the excitement a newspaper man who had seen the "nigger" (Jack) fight warns Brady not to take him on. But racist loyalty is thicker than reason. Only Jack's manager, Goldie, has to be dealt with. Goldie comes for as much as he can get but settles for what they offer him. As the deal is closed Fred (the "white hope") takes Goldie aside and with a voice filled with self-doubt says,

"Don't let your boy take that nigger stuff to heart. Explain how it's gonna pack them in. That's all."

Goldie assures him that everything will be all right.

Now we move to a small gym where we find Jack shadowboxing. Present are his Black trainer, Tick, and Eleanor, a white girl. Jack is stripped to the waist, and presents the picture of a muscular he-man with his tight-fitting trunks. His head is bald and his body glistens with sweat. His voice is big and hollow. (Jack Johnson had a soft voice with a pleasant accent, reflecting the area of the country in which he grew up. But for the sake of the play the director is entitled to use dramatic license, so far as the voice is concerned.) But the stage-Jack speech is something else. It is the damnedest dialect you ever heard. It's all the voices you've heard of white comics and minstrel end men, trying to talk the way they think Blacks talk. It's a mixture of fictional dialect and modern day musicians' jargon.

The "respectable" white lady standing nearby is Jack's girl friend. She has her eyes glued on him as his muscular arms bat the punching bag back and forth. Jack is all business until, for the third time, his trainer uses the word "beauty" in referring to one of his punches. Jack, as if inspired, turns to his guest and says,

"Honey, [he calls her 'honey'] you juss know you tired a sittin here. Whyn't you go buy yourself a 'pretty' or somein!"

"No," [she protests with all the genteelness of her good breeding] "let me stay, unless you mind me here, Jack." (She means she's afraid there might be trouble if some of the fight men come around. He may be embarrassed having her on the scene.)

Jack replies with all the authority of a he-man, "Yo mah lady luck. I don' mine you nowhere."

Like an echo, Tick, the trainer, adds, "Oh, long as you lookin' at him he don' mine."

Jack's heart softens and he says, "Ain't this too much rough house for you honey?"

The relationship between them is established for us. She loves him because . . . and he loves her because . . . Well, that will all come out later.

Suddenly Goldie pops in with news of the championship fight to be held on July 4 at Reno, Nevada. Jack roars with laughter. The idea of having it on the Fourth of July "juss tickles mah funny bone, dassall." Goldie suddenly notices Eleanor. He is alarmed, but immediately sees that she is a lady and not another one of Jack's pickups. He politely asks her to leave. Jack will have none of it. Eleanor senses the situation and volunteers to go, but Jack puts his big foot down. Goldie, bent on protecting his investment reads Jack the riot act, warning him that this can lead to serious trouble. He reminds him they hate him for being a good fighter. They're going to hate him more if they know this is going on. Jack is furious.

"Whut Ah s'pose to do! Stash her in a iddy, biddy hole somewhere in Niggertown?"

It sounded like Jack was saying, "How dare you suggest that I take my precious white flower to Niggertown." Whatever the words, I thought the action was childish, defiant. The real Jack Johnson would very sternly have said, "This lady is my company. If it is all right with her I don't see what business it is of yours." (It's funny, people who write plays about companionship of any kind between white women and Black men always make it sound like the white woman had no choice in the matter. She was either voodooed, drugged, out of her mind, or compelled by some strange– who knows what?)

You see the real Jack Johnson was never defensive about

his association with anyone. Further, he believed that money talked. He could see that people with money never paid attention to conventions. He put it this way, "The thing [meaning society] is run by money. My money is as good as theirs." The stage-Jack falls apart when the press descends on him and starts crying for news stories to promote the fight. Jack defensively introduces Eleanor, his white lady friend, as his secretary. Pressing for a statement, the newsmen ask Jack if he is the "black hope." Not only is he not, he says, but he gratuitously adds, "I expect some Negroes are fearful of my winning." The newsmen press on. They can make something out of this. They want to know how he feels about his people; does he identify with them. Jack makes it clear that he doesn't. He spells it out this way: "I ain't running for Congress. I ain't fighting for no race. I ain't redeeming nobody. My Mama told me that Mr. Lincoln done that. Ain't that why you all shot him?" Then he roars with laughter. I've a hunch Tiny, the *real* Jack's mother, told him more than that Mr. Lincoln freed the slaves. I'm sure Jack Johnson learned as a child that thousands of Negroes fought to free themselves. He may even have seen many of the veterans of the Civil War. He would have learned that Mr. Lincoln freed the slaves because he wanted to win the war.

But Jack's laughter is interrupted by Clara's entrance. Clara is Jack's ex-girl friend. She is Black, in sharp contrast to the gentle, soft-spoken white girl, Eleanor. Clara is loud, vulgar, and violent. She both threatens and warns Eleanor, "Hear me grey meat. Get it while you can."

Jack assures Eleanor things will be all right after all. "I'm from the jungle like you, baby," he says to Clara as he orders her out.

Throughout this scene Eleanor becomes increasingly fearful of what she is getting herself into. Goldie is only concerned with what effect this may have on the box office. He pleads with the press not to print anything about the confrontation between Clara, Jack and especially Eleanor. His attitude toward Jack seems to be that of a horse owner to a horse. If you challenged him in a restaurant he would probably tell you, "I make a living off this guy so I have to put up with him. I can generally manage him except when he starts chasing white women." Somewhere in the scene Goldie says as much to Jack when he says,

"They don't like to see you win. They don't like to see you smiling at them. They don't like your bragging. They hate your guts. But they'll put up with you because you're a helluva good boxer. But dammit, they're not going to stand for your chasing white women."

The play doesn't tell us much about Jack as a person. He shouts, stomps his feet, waves his arms, but we never know what's inside him. He just seems to be there to say things to build up a case against himself. For example, a group of Blacks come to wish him good luck in the coming fight. He is unfriendly and lectures them about "Blacks can be crabs in a barrel" but they're with him just the same. During the fight they stand outside the arena singing a paraphrase of the song "You Got to Come in Through the Door."

Following the fight, a spokesman for the loser's side gives the audience the "white line." He tells them that Jack's victory is worse than having a Negro the best engineer, the best opera singer, or peanut genius. A Black heavyweight champion throws a shadow across the world. What do we do? "We beat the bushes for another 'white hope'—boost them up until one stays." He, too, is loud and vulgar, but underneath his shouting there is a negative message, the kind of message that feeds racism. Isn't this the situation? In the United States white people decide how far and how fast Blacks can move forward. The center of the play is the action of a Black man who challenges this. He outsmarts them by forcing a chance to compete for the heavyweight championship, and wins. To compound his victory he breaks one of their most "sacred" rules. He marries a white woman. To follow the racist thinking to its logical conclusion such a Black man should be made an example of and publicly punished for his "misbehavior."

(Historically, shortly after Jack Johnson married a white

woman virtually identical bills against marriage between Blacks and whites were introduced in Wisconsin, Iowa, Kansas, Minnesota, New Jersey, Michigan and New York. Many states already had such laws. Similar bills were introduced in Congress with penalties varying from imprisonment to forced castration.)

Following the victory we move to the Café de Champion. Here, some Blacks, the people he was accusing of being crabs in a barrel, are whooping it up as his guests, and he is loving it. The air filled with hero worship. Soon the holiday spirit is broken by a parade of temperance activists. As they leave, the heartbroken parents of Eleanor come to take their daughter home. The daughter refuses to see them. They leave, swearing to return with legal support to take her from Jack. They go to the District Attorney's office.

The District Attorney is a very nice man. He is one of those young men you know is going to make it. Senator Dirksen must have looked like this attorney when he was young. In true "democratic" fashion he has assembled a citizens committee, including one "distinguished Negro" to discuss what should be done about Johnson's outrageous behavior. As it turns out he has called the meeting to find a way to stop Jack from "chasing white women." All are in agreement that some action must be taken. The "distinguished Negro" is very vocal in pledging his support for a measure condemning Jack's behavior. After they "democratically" vote for this action the District Attorney goes to work. First he calls in Eleanor (voluntarily on her part) for an interview. In the beginning the conversation is polite and genial. Then, poor Eleanor makes the mistake of telling him she is a divorcee. Well, you know, in 1910 a lady just didn't get a divorce no matter what the man did to her. To make it worse, Eleanor went all the way to Australia, by herself, to get this divorce.

"My, my," says the District Attorney. "Where did you meet Jack?"

Eleanor confesses that she met him on the boat coming home, that it was her doing, he had nothing to do with it.

She saw him and just couldn't resist responding to his physical appearance. Finally she asked the captain to make an introduction. (Now, that's that compelling thing I was talking about.) This is the way the conversation went.

Yes, she had had dinner in his cabin – yes, several times. Why? Because she felt uncomfortable when she discovered that other passengers would stare at her when she was with him. Did the staring bother Jack? No, nothing bothers him. Why do you like him? Oh, he's so kind and sensitive. (This, after we have seen him throw Clara out and threaten to knock her block off if she came around again.)

Like a spider weaving a web, the D. A. getting closer to the center. With a voice dripping with consideration he asks, "Does he like you?"

"Yes, I don't know why. I'm no beauty. He could have any number of beautiful women." She cries. The D. A. is very tender, but at the same time twisting the knife. He says, "Why do you cry? You have this wonderful man to love you." Through her tears she says, "I'll never give him up."

The D. A., "Of course not. But why be ashamed?"

Eleanor, realizing he's trying to break her down, switches into a fighting mood. "I'm not ashamed. I swear I'm not. I didn't know what it was until I slept with him."

That admission is what the D. A. was working for. Now he begins to crucify her. He smiles as he says, "You would stay with him, even if it seemed unnatural to . . ." She cuts him off with, "Why are you smiling?" He says nothing. She continues, "You slimy, two-bit no-dick [penis] mother-grabber." (The author's direction is for Eleanor to say this with a Negro inflection. I suppose it is his way of saying she is only a white woman in appearance, or better yet, she's Clara in a white skin.)

After she leaves, the D. A. drops his mask and shakes his fist as he says, "I'll have that bastard watched day and night."

Meanwhile, Jack and "Honey" (Eleanor) take off for a weekend at a lakeside cottage. We discover them in bed.

(I don't know whether this is a step forward or not. When Paul Robeson, playing in *All God's Chillun*, a play about intermarriage, produced thirty years ago, had a scene showing him marrying the white girl, the authorities would not allow the scene to be played. It was read by the stage manager. In the same play, the authorities also objected to a scene in which some children were playing together and the point was being made that prejudice is something that is put into you—that it doesn't come naturally.)

In this bedroom scene, the two are in bed all right. But they don't act too much like a man and woman. Their conversation centers around discovery that he can't get sunburned and her desire to get as dark as she can so she can pass for colored. Then all her problems will be solved. He chides her that it won't work because everybody knows he's off colored women.

Here you have the racist theory played out. The Black man wants her because she is white. She wants him without being white. In other words, she wants to move over to that world where people are "different from white people." One difference, according to her, is that white men are without normal male sex organs.

Of course the love nest is raided and Jack is carted off to jail. However, as a courtesy to him, the "considerate policemen" do not arrest her. Out on bail, Jack decides to skip the country.

As the play moves on, it seems to move toward setting Jack up to be punished for his transgressions. His characterization reveals a series of incidents which make it difficult for the audience to have genuine sympathy for him. You get the feeling that the sympathy is for Negroes, as a group, but not for the individuals and their situation on the stage.

The first stop in Europe is in London. But soon Jack is in trouble. He is hailed into court by his landlady who says she was reluctant to rent to him, but seeing a white lady with him, she figured maybe *she* could keep things under control. She couldn't. Jack was accused of vulgar language, violent temper, and making himself completely undesirable.

In France, his brutality against a challenger in the boxing ring brought thunderous boos as he left the arena. In Paris, Eleanor begins to show signs that indicate the District Attorney was right when he told her "it was unnatural" for the two of them to be together, that they were "different." She's revolted by the ring brutality, the bickerings in the streets, the clashes with the authorities and Jack sometimes has intemperate outbursts against her.

In Budapest, he works in a cabaret; he and Eleanor play Uncle Tom and Little Eva. In their act a fantasy takes place. Jack dreams of being with her forever and she, weary, confused, and sick at heart, alludes to going away to a far, faraway place and never coming back.

Finally, broke and homesick, hostile to his "Honey," they head home. Not all the way. They stop in Mexico, hoping to draw attention to his being on the border and arousing enough interest to be allowed to come back in without paying his penalty.

In between all of these scenes, a Black character, called Scipio, appears and talks directly to the audience. (Of course, he's speaking to the Negroes.) He mumbles something about Blacks ought to stop wanting to be white, they ought to stop chasing white poontang (sex); they ought to stop wishing to be rich like white folks. Then, the girl's mother makes a passionate plea to the audience, begging them to understand that though they don't know it, what is happening to her daughter could happen to them and theirs. Then they would realize what a terrible thing this is. In between these lines there is some rhetoric about man's inhumanity to man, and how men ought to be brothers, but the heart of it is "never the twain shall meet."

Clara (Jack's former colored girl friend) also appears to deliver a monologue. The script reads: "As she speaks she clutches a flimsy stained night gown to her."* In part she says, "that Jack be dragged down for every black ass woman

* She speaks following a scene in which we have seen Jack at his lowest ebb.

he has turned on." The script continues: "She holds out the garment at full length, a night gown stiff with blood and excrement."

In Mexico, Jack finds that he can return but on the white man's terms. He must give up his crown and serve his time. He cannot under any circumstances return because it would give the other Blacks the idea that what he has done is permissible. Eleanor pleads with him. She explains that she can't take much more of it. In her hysteria she cries out that she now understands what makes a "nigger." Jack berates her and tells her, "Now you're satisfied. I guess that's what you always wanted to be." Then he tells her to "get out. Go find yourself another 'nigger.' " (Now the punishment is meted out to Eleanor, because she, too, must be punished, for her transgression.)

Suddenly, she begins to realize that she is caught in something that she can't get out of. She pleads with Jack to let her love him, once more. She's sure this will make things all right. To her surprise, for the first time in their "romance" he tells her "no"—to "get out"— he's through. There is only one course for her to take. They find her body in the lake.

In remorse, Jack agrees to return to the United States, and on the white man's terms. He loses the title to a "white hope."

The question we posed in the beginning of this article has been answered. *The Great White Hope* obviously perpetuates racism. Many people have seen the play and been stirred by a scene here and a line there. May we suggest that they read the script, for without the colorful, theatrical presentation, the dynamic personality of the leading actor, the weird, off-stage sounds, and the unintelligible dialect, the message comes through. It leans toward that division of two nations in one, as reported by the United States Riot Commission Report, 1968.

If we are to take seriously the report's warning which says:

"What white Americans have never fully understood—but what the Negro can never forget—is that white society is deeply implicated in the ghetto. White institutions created it, white institutions maintain it, and white society condones it," then we must expose racism and those responsible for it. We must learn to reject the tranquilizer who gives us a distorted version of what racism does to the victim, and fiendishly works to make us think he's telling it "like it is."

The Great White Hope has defiled the tradition of Harriet Beecher Stowe's drama against slavery and Steel MacKaye's anti-Ku Klux Klan play of the 1870's.

The theatre in the United States is in the hands of those who profit by providing entertainment for the "carriage trade." "Black entertainment" takes its cue from the pattern set by the slave owners. Since then it has been accepted that Blacks are "natural" singers and dancers and can be "funny as all get out" when laughing at themselves. In the drama, or melodrama, dramatists have been encouraged to write plays that persuade middle-class whites to support the status quo. This too, takes its cue from the plantation owners who determined that Black people are "different," "childlike," "irresponsible" and "subhuman," therefore must for their own good and for the safety of the white population be controlled.

But the course of the world is rapidly changing and the Black people, consistent with their historical past, are generating the force that will provide the unity necessary for the progress of the nation. As this move matures it will reflect its strength and power in all areas of our life. At that time Black men will appear in books and plays as they are— men and women who have the wisdom, courage and determination to struggle to change their environment and that they have the desires, feelings, and ambitions of all human beings.

Some day, someone will write a play in which it will be said that Jack Johnson, "despite his big and little failings, did his share." The present play has no resemblance to any person, living or dead.

Theodore Ward
Black American
Playwright

James V. Hatch

The purpose of this essay is not to ask how benign neglect could happen for we know how black genius is expurgated from history; the purpose is to call attention to the achievements, the talent, and to the dues paid by one of our finest living playwrights.

Theodore Ward has been watching America come apart for seventy-two years. For thirty-eight years, out of his vision of a disintegrating nation, he has crafted the shattered pieces into works of art for the theatre. When his play, *Big White Fog* was produced in Harlem in 1940, Ralph Ellison wrote, "Seldom in literature or on stage has the inner dignity of an oppressed people struggling to affirm its nationhood risen so indestructibly, so magnificently as in the Negro family portrayed in *Big White Fog*."

Mr. Ward's play, *Our Lan'*, produced on Broadway in 1947, is nearly the only black play to reach the *"Great White Way"* that is concerned with an authentic black history.

From his eighteen completed plays about the Black presence in America, some have been produced by black colleges and community groups; however, a number of his scripts have not been produced at all. Only two have been published in their entirety. The playwright is not listed in *Who's Who in the American Theatre*, and except for Loften Mitchell's history, *Black Drama: The Story of the American*

The material for this article was taken from letters and from a four-hour recorded interview in the Hatch/Billops Oral Black History Collection.

Negro in the Theater, and Doris Abramson's *Negro Playwrights in the American Theatre, 1925–1959*, little is available to a reader who might be wondering how a playwright could receive the Theatre Guild Award, a John Simon Guggenheim Fellowship, grants from the National Theatre Conference, a Broadway production, and still be absent from American theatre history.

Mr. Ward was born September 15, 1902, in Thibodeaux, Louisiana, where he attended grammar school. His father, John E. Ward, Sr., was a schoolteacher, who supplemented his income by selling books and patent medicines on the surrounding plantations. Following the death of his mother, young Ward ran away from home. His wanderings through his teenage years took him from New York and Chicago to the Pacific Coast; he supported himself as a bellboy, a boat boy, a barber, etc., until he landed in Salt Lake City, where a white newspaperman, Gail Martin, discovered his talent as a writer.

While studying in the writing workshop at the University of Utah, he won the Zona Gale Scholarship to the University of Wisconsin; here for two years he studied and wrote. In 1937 he wrote his first one-act play, *Sick and Tiahd*, a drama about a Black Mississippi Delta farmer who, during an altercation over the amount of indebtedness, strikes his white creditor. The play won second prize at the city-wide contest for the Chicago Repertory Company.

In 1938 Mr. Ward's first major play, *Big White Fog*, was produced by the Federal Theatre Project of Illinois at the Great Northern Theatre in Chicago, and later by the Negro Playwrights Company of Harlem at the Lincoln Theatre in 1940. About this production which starred Canada Lee, the poet Langston Hughes wrote: "It [*Big White Fog*] is the greatest, most encompassing play on Negro life that has ever been written. If it isn't liked by people, it is because they are not ready for it, not because it isn't a great play."

While a perceptive few like Langston Hughes and Ralph Ellison saw the play as one of the great American dramas, others were put off by what they thought were its leftist politics; still others were annoyed by its central character: a Black idealist who supports Marcus Garvey and his Universal Negro Improvement Association. Mr. Ward summarizes the idea of the play himself:

"A family of Blacks which joined the great Hegira from the South seeking freedom and happiness in the North, discover white racism there as a natural force, as a Big White Fog, denying their democratic aspirations.

"Despite the gloomy prospects, one of the family adheres to the pleasure principle of hedonism; still another to the hope for social change through revolution; and still another, who despairing for American democracy, fixes his star on national independence in Africa. . . ."

In 1938 *Big White Fog* embodied the major life options open to Black Americans today: nationalism, Communism, and "party-time." The play is also a "first" in that it is the seminal play of Black family life in Chicago; others to come were *Native Son* in 1940 and *A Raisin in the Sun* in 1959. For the modern theatre-goer who has seen *The River Niger*, it is a stunning experience to see how seriously many of the same issues in Joseph Walker's drama were written about thirty-five years ago.

By 1940 Mr. Ward had written a second masterpiece. *Our Lan'*, originally produced at the Grand Theatre of the Henry Street Settlement House in New York, was taken uptown to Broadway in 1947 by Eddie Dowling and Louis Singer. Over this play, too, there was controversy. The playwright's description of the situation gives the clue:

"*Our Lan'* is a play of the Reconstruction in the South, dealing authentically with the settlement of Black freedmen on an island off the coast of Georgia by General Sherman with the promise that the Federal Government would confirm their title to Forty Acres and a Mule. However, they were eventually exterminated by Federal troops when the freedmen refused to vacate the island under the policy of the Johnson Administration, which restored the property to its former white owners despite their rebellion against the flag of the United States."

Our Lan' has been published twice, first by Kenneth Rowe in 1960 and again by Darwin Turner in 1971. It has been reviewed twice: by the Center for the Performing Arts, Chicigo, in 1967; and by Washington University of St. Louis in 1974.

This same year also welcomed the belated premier of *The Daubers,* a script which had been completed in 1953; a play which, when it was shown to producers in the 1950's, brought grimaces and vigorous shakes of the head. *The Daubers* dealt with an epidemic of heroin that Mr. Ward predicted would sweep not only America's poor, but her middle class. No producer or director who saw the script in the 1950's or even 1960's recognized that Mr. Ward had not only written a human drama and a carefully crafted script, but a prophesy. This spring *The Daubers* was produced by the X-Bag, an Experimental Black Actors Guild in Chicago. It ran to full weekend houses for two months. Here is the playwright's description of the action:

> "A historically authentic tragedy of the affluent Blacks, who insist that the Judeo-Christian ethic offers a sure road to social equality and advancement. It depicts the fallacy of the code in relation to the pressures of American life, under which the children of the best homes tend to reject the values projected by their parents, while the latter, themselves, are inadvertently corrupted by the system of political and moral depravity infesting the national life."

There is no space here to deal with Mr. Ward's other plays in detail, but it is enlightening to mention the titles and subjects of a few. *John de Conqueror,* a folk opera of a colony of Maroons (former slaves from Jamaica), existing on the shores of the Gulf of Mexico near Biloxi, Mississippi; *John Brown,* a play dealing with the inner conflict between the hero and his family; *Even the Dead Arise*, a fantasy uprising of the Black heroic dead in Hell; *Throwback*, a drama of a Black man who kills a white man who has abused his wife and made her pregnant; *Whole Hog or Nothing*, a play of the struggle of Black servicemen in the South Pacific; and *The Creole*, a dramatization of a story by Frederick Douglass on the capture of the slave ship and the black revolt aboard.

Even without examining his other plays, one thing emerges—Mr. Ward writes about Black people's history, personal and national, in heroic terms. Given the American theatre's 200-year blackout of Afro-American history, it is possible to see why an Afro-American who has been recognized as a fine artist and playwright might suffer years of neglect. But why he continues to be ignored is more puzzling.

Is it that the young lions among Black theatre producers have not heard of him? Or do they not have time for the past? Or must a man's spirit leave this earth before an artist's recognition can come? White producers may not touch Theodore Ward for years to come—unless they discover that paying Black audiences will come. And they will!

If genius is to receive its just deserts on this planet, and maybe a little money too, let black theatres now do the plays of one of their all-time great writers—Theodore Ward.

Survey of Afro-American Playwrights

Jim Williams

The depression in the thirties was so pervasive that it left few people and fewer institutions undisturbed. The economic crisis gave birth to the vast Federal Theatre and new dramatic forms such as the Living Newspaper; the Group Theatre with its Stanislavski-inspired approach to realistic acting and opposition to the phony mannerism and conventions that had encrusted commercial theatre; Clifford Odets and a spate of plays "of revolt" also came into being. Even more paradoxically, the Federal Theatre and the Federal Writers Project provided a heretofore unheard of opportunity for some Black artists to earn a living wage while practicing the acting and writing crafts. Also Hall Johnson and Langston Hughes made significant contributions during this period with *Run, Little Chillun, Mulatto* and *Don't You Want to Be Free?*

Additionally the Rose McClendon Players, a Black theatre group, was born at this time. Thus the reaction of Black and white theatre people to the economic crisis during the thirties was vigorous, creative, militant and experimental.

A similar ferment is taking place today in the world of theatre. This time, however, the catalyst has little to do with outright poverty but more to do with pockets of poverty in the midst of plenty. Also the poverty of ideas and ideals and the growing recognition and dissatisfaction of youth with the war and the concomitant omnipresent hypocrisy and ubiquitous "bull-shit" pervading American life are critical.

The sight of the non-violent struggles of Blacks and their allies unsuccessfully trying to bring to their lives the hundreds of years of promises of democracy and equal opportunity has been shattering. All Blacks have been bitterly affected as well as many whites, again especially the white youth, many who have never known hunger or deprivation. Add to this the gruesome sight of American imperialist might being arrayed against the small, tough, proud Vietnamese via the draft accompanied by overwhelming superior fire power and vast technology and you begin to have a growing spiritual crisis among rather large sections of the population. Thus in the sixties, unable to justify the continued denial of full democracy to Blacks or to justify the Vietnam war which is being peddled as protecting the freedom and democracy of South Vietnamese, Blacks and youth are in full cry against the bogus, oppressive institutions of American society.

Once again, a paradox becomes apparent with what seems a dramatic increase in the numbers of Black writers and the growth of a market and audience of Blacks and whites interested in consuming almost everything presented and published about or by Blacks. Hence Ernest Kaiser who writes the "Recent Books" reviews appearing in most issues of this publication is hard put to keep up with the flood tide of publications.

Nonetheless four valuable volumes have fortunately come my way on the theatre with which we shall attempt to deal at some length.

1. *Anthology of the American Negro in the Theatre: A Critical Approach.* Compiled and edited by Lindsay Patterson.

2. *New Black Playwrights: An Anthology.* Edited by William Couch.

3. *Negro Playwrights in the American Theatre: 1925–1959.* By Doris Abramson.

4. *To Be Young, Gifted and Black.* By Lorraine Hansberry. Adapted by Robert Nemiroff.

All four of these volumes are valuable contributions to the thin but growing library of books relevant to black theatre. The first, which shall henceforth be called simply *Historical Anthology* for the purpose of brevity, shows signs of the rush to publish or making it to market. For example, the title information on the back of the book has with very little handling already become almost indecipherable. One also gets the feeling of considerable repetition in *Historical Anthology,* especially in articles devoted to theatre history. Therefore one feels that with more time Lindsay Patterson could have been more selective. There are several pieces that could have been dropped while including others, perhaps more obscure but broader gauged or more penetrating.

The print of the *Historical Anthology* is large as is the book, which is divided into two columns making for easy reading. Mr. Patterson has broken his book into several convenient broad headings such as Section I, "In the Beginning," composed of seven articles by experienced and talented Black writers who give us accounts of the earliest days of black theatre. Here are some of the remarks which may give an idea of the historical progress as well as of the continued concerns of black theatre.

The late Allan Morrison had this to say in the lead article written in 1963, entitled "One Hundred Years of Negro Entertainment":

> "The last 100 years has seen great improvements in the condition and status of the Negro entertainer. Starting as a figure of ridicule, a comic type and an object of the white man's amusement, he has slowly moved to a position of dignity and even protest and struggle. Serving his apprenticeship in minstrel companies, he acquired professional polish in musical comedies and finally emerged as a creative performer of more than one dimension. Out of the ranks of Negro entertainers came musicians, composers, comedians and creators of songs and dances."

Allan Morrison also reminds us of the very recent disappearance of Jim Crow seating practices as the American Guild of Variety Artists urged its 15,000 members to refuse to appear in Jim Crow places.

Gerald Bradley in "Goodbye, Mister Bones," written in 1964, tells of the early appearance of the shuffling darkie on the American stage. He says Ralpho, a character in Robert Manford's *The Candidates*, appeared in 1798 and has been around on stage and in print ever since. Bradley also says:

"... The Negro playwright, seeing his characters from the inside, so to speak, can better avoid the stereotype and create Negro characters that have particularity as Negroes and complexity as human beings. If the Negro playwright has the dramatic skill to create three-dimensional characters, these creations will begin to point to Everyman—universal, generalized mankind; and their portraiture, gaining authenticity from the playwright's intimate knowledge of the colored man, can transcend color and point to the whole of humanity. It can do so because this knowledge enables him always to see the Negro as a human being."

Alain Locke, writing in 1927, sounds as contemporaneous as though he had written in 1967. He had this to say in "The Negro and the American Stage":

"... Negro dramatic art must not only be liberated from external handicap and disparagement, but from its internal and often self-imposed limitations. It must more and more have the courage to be original, to break with established dramatic convention of all sorts. It must have the courage to develop its own idiom, to pour itself into new molds; in short, to be creatively experimental....

"More and more the art of the Negro actor will seek its materials in the rich native soil of Negro life, and not in the threadbare tradition of the Caucasian stage. In the discipline of art playing upon his own material, the Negro has much to gain. Art must serve Negro life as well as Negro talent serve art. And no art is more capable of this service than drama. *Indeed the surest sign of a folk renascence seems to be a dramatic flowering. Somehow the release of such self-expression always accompanies or heralds cultural and social maturity.*"

In the article "The Drama of Negro Life," written in 1925 by Montgomery Gregory, a now familiar theme was struck.

"Our ideal is a national Negro Theater where the Negro playwright, musician, actor, dancer, and artist in concert shall fashion a drama that will merit the respect and admiration of America. Such an institution must come from the Negro himself, as he alone can truly express the soul of his people."

And in seeming contradiction: "The hope of Negro drama is the establishment of numerous small groups of Negro players throughout the country who shall simply and devotedly interpret the life that is familiar to them for the sheer joy of artistic expression."

Section II deals with The Negro as Playwright. Raoul Abdul in "The Negro Playwright on Broadway" briefly evaluates and mentions many Black dramatists from the first known *Escape* by William Wells Brown, 1858, through what he terms "the true beginning of serious Negro theatre [which] can be precisely dated April 5, 1917, when three one-act plays by Ridgely Torrence—*The Rider of Dreams, Simon the Cyrenian* and *Granny Maumee*—were presented by Mrs. Emilie Hapgood with an all-Negro cast. ..." to Lorraine Hansberry's *The Sign in Sidney Brustein's Window*, October 15, 1964, and Baldwin's *Blues for Mister Charlie*, April 23, 1964.

Abdul ends with the following:

"Some of the young Negro playwrights of today, acutely conscious of being Negro, may choose to by-pass Broadway. For them, off-Broadway offers opportunities but a more challenging alternative would be the establishment of a professional working theatre in the Negro community."

"The Negro Dramatist's Image of the Universe, 1920–1960" by Darwin T. Turner goes into more depth than

Abdul. Turner's article is restricted to comparisons of the characteristic images of dramatists of the twenties, thirties and fifties. During the pursuit of this goal Turner deals with some dramas and writers mentioned by authors appearing earlier in the anthology, but he also comes up with additional plays. *The Passing Grade* by William Robinson, 1959, Georgia D. Johnson's *Plumes* and Pawley's *Jedgement Day,* are not mentioned throughout the *Historical Anthology* except by Turner. Turner concludes with the following:

"The changes in the Negro dramatist's image of his hero, his attitude toward education, his attitude toward the North, and his image of his society and its problems parallel those which can be observed in other media utilized by Negro literary artists: from idealization of Negroes to efface the caricatures created by white authors, to strident, self-conscious defense of the vices of Negroes, to objective appraisal. Unlike the Negro novelist, the dramatist cannot escape easily into a world of racelessness. . . . For that reason, perhaps, the Negro dramatists, more than the novelists, have continued to emphasize problems unique to the Negro race. . . . The Negro dramatists of the present and of the future are no longer compelled to regard themselves as spokesmen for a race which needs educated and talented writers to plead its cause. Now they can regard themselves as artists, writing about the Negro race only because that is the group with which they are the most familiar."

Alice Childress in "A Woman Playwright Speaks Her Mind" deals with the extra special problem of the Black woman in the theatre. The question of the woman in the theatre and more particularly the Black woman has been so neglected that much writing and discussion are urgently needed to begin to put it into some social and artistic perspective.

In "American Theater: For Whites Only?" (1966) by Douglas Turner Ward, he says the following:

"But for a Negro playwright committed to examining the contours, contexts and depths of his experience from an unfettered, imaginative Negro angle of vision, the screaming need is for a sufficient audience of other *Negroes,* better informed through commonly shared experience to readily understand, debate, confirm, or reject the truth or falsity of his creative explorations. Not necessarily an all-black audience to the exclusion of whites but, for the playwright, certainly his primary audience, the first persons of his address, potentially the most advanced, the most responsive or most critical. Only through their initial and continuous participation can his intent and purpose be best perceived by others."

I find myself in complete agreement with this statement as it echoes an article of mine entitled "The Need for a Harlem Theatre," published in 1963 and appearing in this *Anthology.*

James Baldwin in his article written in 1961 says:

"It is a sad fact that I have rarely seen a Negro actor really well used on the American stage or screen or on television. I am not trying to start an artificial controversy when I say this, for in fact most American performers seem to find themselves trapped very soon in an 'iron maiden' of mannerisms."

Ruby Dee in "The Tattered Queens" (1966), an article about the Black actress, says:

"The reality is that we are but 10 percent of a population which is geared to segregate and to discriminate–improving, I believe, but desperately in need of artistic effort to help change the image of the Negro and so effect social change more quickly. As art not only reflects life but also influences it, we must dedicate ourselves to the improvement of life and its truths–about women, about Negroes."

Woodie King, Jr., in "Problems Facing Negro Actors" (1966) declares that:

> "The only place [for a Black actor] to obtain acting experience is the drama school. ... Now, after a long and arduous journey, the young Negro aspirant becomes a professional actor. Some use the achievements of the past to guide their future. ... Now it is fine to be of the present; no one would knock this; but when a performer knows absolutely nothing of the history of his profession, how can he possibly understand the present? The most proficient actors in the business—James Earl Jones, Robert Hooks, Al Freeman, Jr., Diana Sands, Cliff Frazier, Brock Peters, Ivan Dixon, Abby Lincoln, Gloria Foster, Clarence Williams III, Roscoe Lee Browne—know the past, present, and have ideas of future problems they will encounter."

Section VII is composed of four articles stating the great need for black theatres: "The Negro Theatre and the Harlem Community" by Loften Mitchell and "The Need for a Harlem Theatre" by myself, both appeared in the same issue of *Freedomways* magazine in 1963. They followed an article by Ossie Davis entitled "Purlie Told Me!" which appeared in a previous issue. In 1965 Langston Hughes wrote an article called "The Need for an Afro-American Theatre" which also appears in this section of *Historical Anthology.*

The *Anthology* terminates with Adrienne Kennedy's *Funnyhouse of a Negro,* a one-act play. This play was presented at the Cricket Theatre in the Greenwich Village section of New York in 1964. *Funnyhouse* was obviously not meant to communicate with a Negro audience. Written in the dense, subjective, idiosyncratic, pessimistic, murky manner of the obscurantist absurd school, it seems to be saying something about Miss Kennedy's hang-ups over being a Black.

At this juncture in the struggle of Blacks to bring some clarity to our collective lives in order the better to create the conditions for full freedom and manhood, we can dispense with this type of pathetic imitation of sterile, white absurdities.

Preceding *Funnyhouse* are pieces on "History and Theatre," on LeRoi Jones, Dance, Films, and Radio and Television. *Anthology of the American Negro in the Theatre* also contains a fine bibliography and a thorough index. Many of the photographs and theatre programs are collectors' items and record graphically what can only be described as a glorious record of indigenous Black American artists.

I have quoted liberally from Lindsay Patterson's contributors to the *Anthology* in hopes that every reader may be inspired either to buy the volume or at least go to the library and study this fine record. For those who don't do either but who may wade through this review—I hope you will have gotten a better idea of the extent of the struggle of Black theatre artists as they developed to the present. Today we still work to acquire technical training and craft mastery the better to say what must be said and presented about black life, the better to fight for more freedom in order the better to fight for more and more.

Another anthology, *New Black Playwrights* edited with an introduction by William Còuch, Jr., is a collection of six plays by five Black playwrights: *Happy Ending* and *Day of Absence* by Douglas Turner Ward, *A Rat's Mass* by Adrienne Kennedy, Lonne Elder's *Ceremonies in Dark Old Men*, *Goin' a Buffalo* by Ed Bullins, and *Family Meeting* by William Wellington Mackey. The book jacket says:

"The plays brought together here represent a variety of styles, approaches, ideas, and attitudes. They have one thing in common: the attempt to show how, as one of the playwrights puts it, 'people bear up under the hazardous and interminable crime of being a Negro.' Several are in the tradition of the revolutionary theater. Although they will not make 'pleasant' reading for most whites, they offer a good sampling of the concerns of modern black consciousness."

One reservation I have about this statement is the abuse of the word "revolutionary" which has become so overworked as to now mean at best militant or perhaps black, and sometimes so diluted as to mean simply different.

Doug Turner Ward's two one-act plays, *Day of Absence* and *Happy Ending* which garnered for Ward the Vernon Rice Drama Award and an Obie for his acting, are referred to as masterpieces of satire. It is this writer's opinion that they are neither masterpieces nor satire. They are, however, clever burlesques written by a multi-talented writer. Ward took two jokes and by the sheer artistry of language extended them into two funny one-act caricatures of the caricaturists.

In his introduction Couch sketched in a brief but succinct general historical background on black theatre from which these six plays may be viewed. As can be seen from the following paragraph Couch, who is a Black professor of English at North Carolina College in Durham, is involved with more than data gathering and getting published.

"As for black playwrights, it is possible that George Jean Nathan, in acclaiming Negroes as 'born actors' and praising Paul Robeson for his ability to act without any training, inadvertently put his finger on the source of the problem. Actors perhaps, may be 'born,' but the experience and craftsmanship necessary for successful playwriting is more likely to come through close contact with the stage. Denied access to the full ambience of the theater, yet driven by an understandable urgency to make public their protests, Negro playwrights too often have suffered from the twin disasters of racial discrimination and hastily done work. Moreover, the relative preeminence of the black actor over the black playwright is in some degree the result of the public's tendency to regard actors as entertainers, a role traditionally 'acceptable' for Negroes. . . . Poets and novelists work in solitude, their task being accomplished when they have had their say; but in the world of the theater, which demands relationships and interaction, the national ritual of race predominates."

To anyone who has tried to write plays, the gross distinction between one-act and three-act plays is enormous. A small slice of life can sustain a one-acter while a three-act play requires a qualitatively more significant human conflict or set of problems. Needless to say a greater mastery of craft is also necessary to fill the larger canvas which the three-act play represents.

Another consideration is where were the plays in question presented and has the theatre in any way influenced the play? Was it on or off Broadway? Was the theatre large or small? Was the audience Black or white or mixed? For whom was the work originally intended, Blacks or whites? And importantly, how do the plays stack up as literature since now that they have received publication they may be read by far more people than will ever see them produced. All these questions are important because they affect what the author is trying to say as well as how he says it. Additionally, of course, is an evaluation of the individual skill and mastery of technique and how it may have helped or hindered the writer's intentions.

Ed Bullins' *Goin' a Buffalo* and Lonne Elder's *Ceremonies in Dark Old Men* are both three-act plays. The remaining four are one-act. Ward's *Day of Absence* and *Happy Ending* as well as *Ceremonies* were presented by the Negro Ensemble Company. Both authors are on the N.E.C. staff; Ward is one of the three founders and Elder is director of the Playwrights Workshop. Both men had completed their plays prior to the birth of the N.E.C. so that they could not have had the St. Marks Playhouse in mind when the plays were written. However, had there been no N.E.C. it is doubtful that either author would have had the benefit of seeing his works as fully produced nor would I have been privileged to see them performed. Unlike the New Lafayette Theatre which is presently housed in an old movie house on Seventh Avenue in the center of Harlem, the St. Marks Playhouse, N.E.C.'s theatre, is located on the second floor of a building on the lower East Side.

Nonetheless the ethnic composition of N.E.C. audiences

ranges from 25 percent to 50 percent black. With so many Blacks coming to the East Side one can be sure the plays had more than good publicity directed toward Blacks. I would think that the Ward and Elder plays were written with a Black audience in mind. Though much of the humor and some of the tragic dimensions of the plays will inevitably be lost on whites, the Blacks get a good look at themselves and the whites are privileged to participate in some truthful aspects of black life. Augmenting this, honest black attitudes towards whites were laid bare by both dramatists, humorously by Ward and tragically by Elder.

It is clear that *Day of Absence, Happy Ending* and *Ceremonies* were all written to be acted on the stage before a Black audience. The Ward duo stand more as literature than does *Ceremonies*. They do not so much because Ward is necessarily more preoccupied with words or the fine, cerebral, unemotional, intellectual approach to drama, as that the clear-cut confrontations and conflicts of large themes —necessary for plays—are missing and therefore Ward could sustain interest only by heavy reliance on the written word.

In *Day of Absence,* a burlesque of the problems visited on a southern white community when their "Nigras" disappear for one day, great fun was poked at the white folks played as caricatures by Black actors in white face. The white caricatures that emerged seemed much truer to life than the usual black mockeries by whites simply because the white one-dimensional view of Blacks is deeply imbedded and far more universally accepted as valid.

Ceremonies discloses conflicts in a poor Black family as they strive to acquire some of the good things of life without going to work for the (white) man on some of his marginal dignity-destroying jobs. The turmoil between the generations, sexes and siblings, as they strive to primitively acquire money by setting up a Mafia-type bootlegging operation, is enough to sustain tension and interest. Elder's writing frequently adds another dimension as it soars to poetic heights. Hence both writers make for good reading. Blacks will enjoy reading the plays also for the true notes sounded throughout about their lives. I don't think the plays as reading will be relished as much by whites, as the direct uncomfortable facing of warm black bodies on the stage as well as sitting together with a Black audience, helping to cue them in on our humor, is necessary to them for a truer appreciation of the intent of Black dramatists.

This brings us to the other three-act play presented in *New Black Playwrights: Goin' a Buffalo* by Ed Bullins. This play, written about the mean, treacherous lives endured by Black hustlers, junkies, whores and pimps, I unfortunately have not seen performed. *Goin' a Buffalo*, as I see it, is the best technically written play of the collection. Most Blacks who read the play shorn of middle-class blinders will recognize some of the harsh three-dimensional characters created by Bullins. The shrewd, selfish, unscrupulous ruthlessness of the individualist Bullins people would have made some of them wealthy industrialists or great capitalist financiers had they been white and given the opportunity to become "legitimate" businessmen.

Bullins is clearly not concerned here with compensating for the caricatures and stereotypes of Blacks by white authors. He also most decidedly has a Black audience in mind as he deliberately lays bare the lives of Black men enclosed in that underworld existing scarcely below the surface of every Black urban community. His language discloses a sharp, true ear for authentic dialogue and familiar (black) argot. The tension and conflicts steadily mount in the play as Art the protagonist waits for his main chance. Art coldly sets up and betrays the men who befriended him. How he does it I will leave for you the readers to discover as that and the way Bullins tells it are the play.

Neither Bullins nor his characters are pretty nor are they sentimental. One fervently wishes, however, that somewhere in the world of the *Goin' a Buffalo* hustlers one person was neither victim nor victimizer; that one person might have vision of a more humane possibility than just *Goin' a Buffalo* where the rustlin' grass is greener. " 'Cause like things is tough all over but it ain't really that bad, baby."

6

Nevertheless Ed Bullins may very well be "one of America's great black hopes in the theatre," to paraphrase Charles Marowitz in an article datelined London appearing in *The New York Times,* April 13, 1969, under the rubric "Theatre in London." Marowitz writing of Bullins also asks the question, "How can you tell a man he has written a very good diagnosis of your criminality (whites) and keep a straight face. Ah, therein lies the rub."

Adrienne Kennedy's *A Rat's Mass* I have fortunately not seen. She clearly did not have a Black audience in mind in this *play*??? I'm damned if I can understand Miss Kennedy's need to write this opaque drivel—unless of course she is driven to please her friends, get published and/or acquire a "reputation." Why a Black woman playwright, who we suspect possesses a poetic talent, must join in the decadent intellectuals' flight from the great moribund capitalist real world into the tiny irrational bag of esoteric images and private fantasy is a mystery to me. If Miss Kennedy were only to strive to add color and clarity to the deep mirror of black life being created by our current crop of Black artists, she might not be in such neurotic despair and confusion over her personal problems with her blackness. When I have time I'll try to find out what she's saying in order to determine with absolute certainty whether she will remain "part of the problem or become a part of the solution."

Perhaps Miss Kennedy's association with Edward Albee's Playwrights Workshop accounts for her strange creative preoccupation with the surreal. At this time of ever-soaring pride and a growing sense of essential worth among Black people, as we organize and attack symbol after symbol and citadel after citadel of American capitalism, we of course need the help of all Black artists in order to win a better world. It is the right of Miss Kennedy to choose any artistic path she desires but it is also the duty of Black critics to begin to evaluate her according to their lights. At the moment one wonders what would happen if she wrote a theatre piece with a Black audience in mind.

Lastly William Wellington Mackey in his *Family Meeting*

taking dead aim at the most parasitic and pathetic of middle classes–the Black bourgeoisie–flogs that half dead horse with a cartoon cane. Mackey's dramatic talent deserves a more worthy opponent.

The third volume in this series is undoubtedly the most requisite. *Negro Playwrights in the American Theatre, 1925–1959* written by Doris Abramson is a gem. This book by Miss Abramson, begun as her doctor's dissertation, is a model of discriminating scholarship and sustained, tenacious hard work.

The sympathy and warmth that Miss Abramson, who is white, has for her subject help to raise *Negro Playwrights* far above the level of the usual works by white scholars on black subjects.

The book carries out the author's formidable intentions, as stated in the preface–to consider where the twenty plays in her critical orbit were produced, as well as the period and the socio-economics prevailing at the time they were written. She also deals with the oft-neglected artistic questions and considerations of each playwright and play.

And she did as she said analyze individual plays

"for their reflection of Negro problems. Each analysis begins with a biographical comment on the playwright and ends with critical appraisal of the play as literature and as a theatre piece. Conclusions at the end of each chapter provide further opportunity to show (1) relationships between periods and between plays, (2) developing dramaturgy, and (3) continuing concern on the part of Negro playwrights for current and persistent problems."

We can say categorically *Negro Playwrights* shows no signs of the rush to publish. Indeed, it seems that Abramson has taken many years of painstaking research to complete this excellent volume about the works of seventeen Black playwrights.

The character of her book has been further informed by

interviews and/or letters with Ted Ward, Langston Hughes, Bill Branch, Ossie Davis, Paul Green, Alice Childress, Amy Goodwin and others. Further depth has been added by her studies of the following more obscure sources: Fannin S. Belcher, Jr., *The Place of the Negro in the Evolution of the American Theatre, 1767 to 1940* (unpublished Ph.D. dissertation, Yale University, 1945), Hilda Josephine Lawson, *The Negro in American Drama* (unpublished Ph.D. dissertation, Dept. of English, University of Illinois, 1939) and Frederick O'Neal, "The American Negro Theatre–Ten Year Effort, Notes for Theatre Arts Seminar of Southern Illinois University," October 27, 1962. Transcript in possession of Frederick O'Neal.

Perhaps we can best illuminate the value of this volume by dealing with its most important single contribution, the rescue from criminal neglect of the play *Our Lan'* by Theodore Ward. *Our Lan'* in my estimation is the best play ever written by any American, white or Black.

Unfortunately, I did not see the Off-Broadway production of *Our Lan'* which critics claimed was more powerful in its simplicity than the Broadway show which followed shortly. Nevertheless, the experience, for that is the least that can be said of living through *Our Lan'*, shall ever remain among the most moving and unforgettable in my life. It was not simply a dazzling theatrical presentation which one applauds and cries bravo till the last curtain descends. Nor was it a show after which one seeks the stars to congratulate them and shakes their hands for brilliant performances and then promptly forgets the whole thing. *Our Lan'* was the kind of play that grabbed one's guts and held one's heart in the firm but warm embrace of its particular but nonetheless universal, inexorable dramatic unfolding.

Has there been before or since a more indigenous American question than land and African slavery? Indeed the unredeemed promise of land reform (40 acres and a mule for the freed slaves) which was inherent in the second American Revolution (The Civil War) remains to haunt us twenty-four hours every day since. Depriving the freedmen

84

(Black) of an economic base upon which to build their lives is as directly responsible for the assassinations of President Kennedy, Robert Kennedy, Malcolm X and Martin Luther King as slavery in general was for Lincoln's murder.

Could there be such deep conflicts over "black capitalism," assimilation, integration, segregation, separation etc., as engage us today had the land question been settled after the Civil War? Could atomic bombs have been dropped on the yellow-skinned Japanese when the war was already won by us or could we now be engaged in the Vietnam war had the Joshuah Tains of *Our Lan'* been given the land they helped win in the war with the Southern rebels? I doubt it. So, *Our Lan'*'s theme is woven in the colored texture of American history. The play is as contemporary today as it was in 1947 or would have been in 1863. Even today, I cannot think of the play, *Our Lan'*, without inner crying over the palpable cruelty and betrayal of the Black freedmen it so skillfully laid bare.

Not only is the same rapaciousness evident in the continued maltreatment of Blacks but the insatiable greed of business, commercial interests and their state institutions continues to push the original American—the American Indians—off land and into genocide. America, what price profit?

But let's hear what Miss Abramson says about *Our Lan'* and its author, Theodore Ward.

"To read *Our Lan'* is to realize that here is a nearly perfect play. There may be, as Kenneth Rowe points out, a few trite sentences from 'non-folk characters,' and too little is done with Miss Libeth [the New England schoolteacher] after her first entrance; but even a reading of the play supports general critical opinion (based on theatrical productions) that *Our Lan'* is remarkable. It may be the finest play ever written by an American Negro. That it was written by the same man who wrote *Big White Fog* at the turn of the decade is greatly to his credit as an artist. Theodore Ward – through research, study, and experience in the theatre – learned how to write an effective play. ... He wrote a play that is well informed by historical evidence and yet not overwhelmed by historical detail. He wrote about Negroes so truthfully that they gained universality; he made his hero, Joshuah Tain, noble–without sacrificing his humanity."

Also in discussing the usual tendency to present Black characters as symbols lacking human dimension, Abramson quotes Alfred Kazin speaking to and about Black artists, "It all goes back to one house, one street, one uncle or grandmother, or whatever," and she says Theodore Ward had the good sense to go back to one ex-slave, one leader who by his actions helps us to understand Afro-Americans.

Here our author reveals in the last statement the limitations of even the best intentioned of whites. Unfortunately, it is not only we Blacks whom whites must understand but far more importantly it is whites who must understand themselves. Theodore Ward in *Our Lan'*, by its dramaturgically artistic presentation of a heroically critical period in American history through the actions of a theoretically sound hero, Joshuah Tain supported by real three-dimensional stage characters, gives whites (90 percent of the population of This Lan') a rare opportunity for insight which should be cherished. Indeed the prime reason that *Our Lan'* had such a pathetically short run and has not been revived since 1948 is precisely because it mirrored all too clearly the depravity and degeneration of American whites north and south. We are grateful for Doris Abramson's *Negro Playwrights*, if for no other reason than her "rediscovery" of Ted Ward's *Our Lan'* which must soon be produced once again on our stages from Broadway to "off," from local to university theatres.

I believe today's white audience is not only better able to accept the picture of themselves seen in the eyes of Joshuah Tain but it is essential that they do. In addition militant Blacks who today are incensed over Styron's *Nat Turner* will be strengthened in their determination to change the institutions that limit them, by the examples of Ward's Joshuah Tain.

One interesting and I don't think accidental aspect of *Our Lan'* is that its strongest character, Joshuah Tain, is a blacksmith thus heralding the triumph of the industrial revolution which today has transformed even farming from its reliance on people and animals, to a mass productive, machine-dominated enterprise.

But our author goes even far beyond the foregoing as she surveys the whole gamut of black drama from the earliest works by William Wells Brown, Joseph S. Cotter and Garland Anderson to Lorraine Hansberry. Analysis of Wallace Thurman's *Harlem,* Langston Hughes' *Mulatto,* Hall Johnson's *Run, Little Chillun* written in the twenties and thirties stand out. She gives justified consideration to the fifties and the skillful playwrights Alice Childress, Bill Branch and Louis Peterson. In my opinion, Loften Mitchell's *A Land Beyond the River* comes closest in the historical importance of its material to the landmark *Our Lan'. Land Beyond the River* dramatized the contemporary experiences of Rev. Joseph A. De Laine of South Carolina who, in fighting for school buses for Black children in his county, started a case that helped eventually to bring the Supreme Court to the decision to declare segregation in schools unconstitutional. Today rear guard southern reactionaries are still resisting and many northern schools are in fact still segregated.

This play also deserves to be revived and should be played in local theatres across the country. While the non-violent position of the Rev. Joe De Laine, in the play, is not at the moment in favor, nevertheless *Land Beyond the River* has much to say to today's audiences, both Black and white, about our recent history. Unlike Ward, however, Mitchell did not quite find the best form for the content of his play. Its dramatic action, as Abramson says, is frequently stopped by long didactic speeches. I played in the Newark production of *Land Beyond the River* and felt, despite its limitations, that audiences got a great deal from the lofty message of the play. Also in playing the roles, actors frequently gave

87

dramatic realism and humor to many lines that were not inherent in the script.

The last decade dealt with the fifties, ends with Louis Peterson's *Take a Giant Step* and Lorraine Hansberry's *A Raisin in the Sun*. *Take a Giant Step* is about an adolescent Black youth's efforts to grow into maturity while living in an all-white neighborhood. I felt a close kinship with this play as it was similar to my own lonely and frustrating experiences as a Black youth in an "all-white" neighborhood.

Again, here is a play that has pertinence today and provides some insights necessary to understand more fully the students' fight for Black Studies, black dormitories and black caucuses.

In truth, with the present paucity of new plays on Broadway and the consequent penchant for revivals, a list of good black plays could easily be assembled with considerable timeliness for today's Black and white audiences.

The last of the plays evaluated and analyzed by Doris Abramson is *Raisin in the Sun* by Lorraine Hansberry. What can one say about *Raisin in the Sun* except that it and its author enjoyed a justified success. If you missed its long Broadway run you might see it in the movie and if you missed that you might catch it on television and if you missed that you might see parts of it in *To Be Young, Gifted and Black* dramatized by Robert Nemiroff, and if you even missed that you may now read it, and other Hansberry published and unpublished writings as well as some biographical material in the book, *To Be Young, Gifted and Black* edited by Nemiroff.

Black Playwrights says of Lorraine, our best-known playwright:

"One of the saddest aspects of her career is that she died still serving her apprenticeship as a playwright, having written *A Raisin in the Sun*, a naturalistic play *non plus ultra,* and *The Sign in Sidney Brustein's Window* (1964), a brave step toward the future in spite of a social commitment reminiscent of the thirties. Unfortunately, she did not live to achieve a synthesis of these two strands of her promising talent, the domestic and the didactic. ... No single play considered in this study is dramaturgically sounder than *A Raisin in the Sun.* Whether or not it is soap opera, it is a well made play. The characters are clearly defined, the plot moves forward with adequate motivation, the dialogue is both entertaining and revealing."

And finally:

"So in a real sense, *A Raisin in the Sun* is both a synthesis of the major problems and attitudes seen in Negro drama since its inception and a proof of the dramaturgical and literary advances made by American Negro playwrights –a summary, a proof, and the end of an era. ...."

In her epilogue, Doris Abramson mentions some of our more recent writers and their works: LeRoi Jones' *Dutchman, The Toilet, The Slave;* Ossie Davis' *Purlie Victorious;* James Baldwin's *Amen Corner, Blues for Mr. Charlie;* Ed Bullins' *In the Wine Time, The Electronic Nigger* and others; Robert Milner's *Who's Got His Own* and the black absurdists' school (isn't this the height of absurdity?) Adrienne Kennedy's *The Funnyhouse of a Negro;* and Archie Shepp's *June Bug Graduates Tonight.*

A quote from Abramson's epilogue:

"Quiescent during the war years, the American theatre in the late forties produced two major talents, Tennessee Williams and Arthur Miller, who between them synthesized the psychological emphasis of the twenties and the social emphasis of the thirties. Again Negro drama seemed a decade behind the times. Theodore Ward's *Big White Fog,* produced in New York in 1940, was really a Federal Theatre play of the late thirties and comparable to Clifford Odets' early plays. Ward's later historical play, *Our Lan'* (1947), resembles historical plays by white playwrights—Sidney Kingsley's *The Patriots* (1942), Robert Sherwood's *Abe Lincoln in Illinois* (1938). The other outstanding Negro playwright of the forties, Richard Wright, did root his *Native Son* (1941) in both society and individual psychology, but it fails to achieve either the degree of symbolic sophistication or the dramatic strength of *Death of a Salesman* or *A Streetcar Named Desire.*"

I submit that Tennessee Williams and Arthur Miller are two major talents but neither of them has synthesized the sociological and psychological aspects of American life. Sophisticated they are, dramatic skill they possess, but neither has been courageous enough to overcome the pall of fear of being blacklisted which reached its peak in the Joe McCarthy era nor the fear of failure inherent in the knowledge that entertainment and titillation are in the main the open sesame to purse strings, to production and praise in American Theatre.

Tennessee Williams writes about a South in which Blacks appear, if at all, merely as a backdrop for the bizarre degeneracy of his white characters' twisted psyches. Everyone knows that "niggers" are at least as much a preoccupation of every Southerner as are Queens housewives. So where is the social synthesis?

That Ward's *Our Lan'* resembles *The Patriots* and *Abe Lincoln in Illinois* is certainly not significant since all three are historically based.

Arthur Miller's latest sociological contributions to dramaturgy have consisted of how to sell second-hand furniture and the question of responsibility for parents or self—*The Price* and the purgative Marilyn Monroe episode—*After the Fall.* I ask you where is the socio-psycho synthesis here? On the contrary, both Miller and Williams hold their audiences' interest with content of peripheral psychological and marginal sociological interest and depth but more than passing mastery of dramaturgy. In reality, a statement made by Abramson referring to recent Black playwrights applies perfectly to Miller and Williams, ". . . they have made drama-turgical advances, but they have failed as true social commentators in a decade that badly needs such commenta-tors."

I have always felt that Williams' protagonist in *Orpheus Descending* played by Marlon Brando in the movie adapta-tion entitled *The Fugitive Kind,* should have been a mulatto Black who was easily mistaken for a white. Here is a theme in which Williams could try his skill at synthesizing the sociological and psychological.

For the truth of the matter is that the American people have never been prepared to look at themselves through drama because of the cash nexus schizophrenia encouraged by slavery, the color line and the attendant pursuit of capi-talist profit and imperialist domination. It is only in opposi-tion to the foregoing and the exposure of its cultural super-structure that a realistic theatre synthesizing the social and psychological can come about. Then and only then can an experimental search for new content and new forms be more than an escape from reality and freedom.

If freedom is the recognition of necessity, then the decade of the seventies must give birth to a cultural flowering in which Black dramatists will make outstanding contributions. Only Black artists can create one-half of the bifocal lens so necessary for America to see itself in order to help change itself into a force for humanity and life instead of inhuman-ity and death.

With the publication of the last book with which we deal in this review, *To Be Young, Gifted and Black,* there seems little more to be said about Lorraine Hansberry, cut off from us too soon.

James Baldwin in his introduction "Sweet Lorraine" mentioning the historical importance of *A Raisin in the Sun* says:

"What is relevant here is that I had never in my life seen so many black people in the theater. And the reason was that never before, in the entire history of the American Theater, had so much of the truth of black people's lives been seen on the stage. Black people ignored the theater because the theater had always ignored them."

I'm sure at least most of that statement is true—the unprecedented number of Blacks attending the *Raisin* theatre, but if you have read the beginning of the series you will know that I believe that more truth was revealed by *Our Lan'*, a play by Ted Ward produced a decade earlier.

In one of my three close-up encounters with Lorraine, we discussed the difficulty at that time for a Black to be a man and remain alive. By way of agreement, she mentioned a cross-country trip she and her husband Robert Nemiroff took. They had stopped in all kinds of hotels without the slightest unpleasant incident, though Nemiroff happens to be white. Lorraine wondered rhetorically, what would have happened had she been white and Robert Black. We agreed at that time, the middle fifties, that someone would have "put a hurtin' " on a Black Bobby. She added that the play she was currently working on was precisely about the struggle of a young, Black man for manhood and maturity in a white world and a Black family conditioned by that world to deny him.

Though I was not privileged to read the unpublished script, I had the feeling that the part of the son, Willie Younger, was weakened and the part of the sentimental religious Black mother was strengthened in order to satisfy the sensitive psyches of the white audience expected to repay the bold Broadway producers.

Well, Lorraine is gone now.

I'd like to quote one line from *To Be Young, Gifted and Black* because it is as I remember her—in her voice, "Eventually it comes to you: the thing that makes you exceptional, if you are at all, is inevitably that which must also make you lonely."

To attempt to sum up, it appears as though more questions have been raised by the four foregoing books than have been answered. What can whites get from well written, vital plays by Blacks? What can Blacks derive from the same plays? Should plays written by Blacks be directed at all to whites? Aimed at Broadway or "off"? What forms are best for black material? Naturalistic, realistic, poetic or existential? What's the relationship of form and content? What is the importance of actors and directors? Producers? Complete articles could be written and I hope shall be about any one or a combination of the preceding.

As I reread these reviews, I'm sure I have not done justice to any of the four books. If you read them, you will discover many bright corners of light on the black theatre.

Bibliography

ANTHOLOGY OF THE AMERICAN NEGRO IN THE THEATRE: A CRITICAL APPROACH. Compiled and edited with an introduction by Lindsay Patterson. A volume of International Library of Negro Life and History. Association for the Study of Negro Life and History, 1538 Ninth St., N.W., Washington, D.C.

NEGRO PLAYWRIGHTS IN THE AMERICAN THEATRE: 1925–1959. By Doris Abramson. Columbia University Press, New York. xii + 335 pages. $12.50 (cloth); $2.95 (paper).

NEW BLACK PLAYWRIGHTS: AN ANTHOLOGY. Edited by William Couch, Jr., Louisiana State University Press, Baton Rouge. xviii + 258 pages. $4.95.

TO BE YOUNG, GIFTED AND BLACK. By Lorraine Hansberry; adapted by Robert Nemiroff. Pentrice-Hall, Englewood Cliffs, N.J. xxii + 266 pages. $8.95.

Look Homeward Baby

Ollie Harrington

A large number of the brothers stayed on in Europe after the war's end in 1945. I think the main reason was that they couldn't ever again accept being cooped up in ghettos. The ghetto isn't only meant to restrict the movement and growth of bodies. It's also been deliberately organized to stultify and even to deform black minds. When Sam's draft boards began mailing out those "greetings" to the brothers they also unwittingly enclosed the jailhouse keys. These escapees from the land of "freedom and justice for all" were particularly welcomed by the French people, who seem never to have forgotten that during World War I the American command- er General Pershing refused to have anything to do with allowing Black Americans to shoot and bayonet white Ger- mans. But the French were up-tight and fighting for their lives. General Foch very gratefully accepted the four Black American infantry regiments. These proved to be so effec- tive that all of them received the highest French wartime decorations.

Paris of course was the main attraction. But there is something about picking up stakes and moving on that never really seems to work out. The restlessness which compels so many humans to go see what's on the other side of the hill, or river, is self-defeating. There are so many hills and so many rivers. And in the end one sits on some cold stone under an improbable tree and sings the blues. Naturally a Paris boulevard is just about the last place to ever think of singing the blues and so the Black exile does the next best thing. He takes the Metro to the foothills of Montmartre where he will find Leroy Haynes, himself an exile, who will fix any brother or sister with generous helpings of chitlins

This is the second part of "Look Homeward Baby."

with collard greens, red beans and rice, and even corn bread! Haynes with his restaurant has struggled valiantly with this problem of nostalgia and in the process has come up with an assortment of chili-based condiments. The most famous of these are called Big Brother and Little Sister. For those who prefer a "mild" condiment Haynes recommends Little Sister. What he evidently means is that a drop or two of Little Sister on the hawg maws need not necessarily remind the diner of the film *Is Paris Burning?* But Haynes honestly makes no such claims for Big Brother which he frankly states "is for folks who really dig hot stuff." I have overheard groups of Black surgeons, who'd taxied up to Haynes' between planes from Orly, observe that even a layman must notice that *one drop* of Big Brother caused a rather alarming protruding of the eyeballs accompanied by a quickening of the respiration which should not be confused with the process of breathing. Obviously what Haynes had in mind when he concocted these diabolical sauces was a surcease of nostalgia. But in fact it is more like curing heartburn by smashing one's big toe with a sledge hammer.

These observations are not meant to imply that Black expatriates, especially painters and sculptors, are unhappy in Europe, especially in France. The art community in Paris, for example, is a completely open one. The only criterion is, are you a good artist? Or at least are you working like hell to become one? Such a criterion induces an atmosphere of camaraderie, a sharing of ideas, techniques, and often soup, all of which seem indispensable in the making of an artist. I never even remotely experienced anything like that at "home" except perhaps in Harlem among a group of really beautiful human beings and artists like the late Augusta Savage, or like Aaron Douglas, Ernie Crichlow, Elton Fax, Romare Bearden and Bob Pious. There is another quality which made Paris a truly civilized place and that was the fact that it was no disgrace to be poor and unsuccessful, with all of the abominable things that word implies in the rat-race society of the "silent majority." At least that was Paris when I arrived in 1951. There's no doubt but that without this liberté, égalité and fraternité there could not have been a Monet, Modigliani, Picasso, or Giacometti. And there certainly could not have been a Henry Tanner, that great Black master whose paintings hang alongside the greats of France in the Louvre, although he is virtually unknown in his native Philadelphia. If this sounds like Paradise forgive me. It isn't, there are pitfalls. But later. . . .

I sort of stumbled on the Café Monaco not long after I got to Paris. I'd been wandering through a maze of incredibly narrow streets in the Latin Quarter which couldn't have changed since the time of Rabelais. From the outside there was nothing even remotely seductive about it. As a matter of fact it seemed seedy. But in the murky interior I noticed a tall Black brother sitting with his back against the far wall. Although it was obvious that the sun had never shone in that street since it stopped being a cowrun down to the nearby Seine, the contemplative brother was wearing seemingly opaque sunglasses. What really grabbed me though was the rest of his togs. The main focus was at the top, a black leather cap. Then followed a black turtle-neck sweater, black suit under a black overcoat–although it was July–black shoes and socks. I walked in, found myself a small table and ordered a beer. The brother never turned his head and if he ever batted an eye behind those glasses you wouldn't know it without an x-ray machine. After about an hour, and still never turning his head in my direction, the brother whispered, "Where you from, Mon?" That was my introduction to Monsieur Slim Sunday. He was–or had once been–Nigerian. No, he never wore anything but black and he emphasized the fact that his underwear which he dyed himself, was also black! He never sat with his back to anybody's door or window. "I got no trust, Mon," he explained.

The Monaco was a typical French working-class café which noisily raised its sheet-metal shutters at seven when the local clientele, butchers, bakers, hairdressers and little craftsmen, would begin drifting in looking for their *café au lait,* laced with cognac. They would look in again four or five times during the day for some additional fuel–usually *vin blanc* or *rouge*–until knocking-off time.

About nine every morning a radiantly angelic and obviously American girl would skip in and take her favorite seat, smiling at the morning like one of Raphael's virgins. There were always ten or twelve little saucers stacked up in front of her on the marble-topped table and I figured she played some kind of expatriate game until I asked one of the brothers. "Well, that's the only way the waiter can keep the count," was the way he explained it to me. I had to ask what kind of a count the waiter was keeping. He stared at me, "You don't know? Where you been, Baby? Well, that's little Julie and she been stoned for near 'bout two years. Every one of them saucers represent one rum!" Later I learned that little Julie's father was, in the words of another brother, "real big shit at one of them Ivy League colleges when he ain't down in Washington helpin' the President to fuck up foreign policy." Julie sat there with her stack of saucers for another year or so and then one morning she wasn't there. Gone back to New England, they said. About six months later we heard that little Julie had hanged herself. "The trouble wid Julie," explained Ula, the Danish girl whose specialty was gin with beer chasers, "wass she wass a decent kid. She couldn' stand dat shiddouse hypocrits wass sellin' in dat fugginn American collitch. So she stayed stoned!" I guess little Julie forgot to stay stoned.

The Monaco was something the likes of which had never been seen in the "land of the free." The word to describe it was "harmony." There were the regular French patrons and there were *les amis*. Of these, half were American, about twenty of these were brothers. The rest were English, Canadian, Swedish, a few Danes, one Czech, one Nigerian, two Senegalese and one Indian "untouchable." "All these beautiful s.o.b.'s are here trying to become human beings," explained the ex-cowboy who sat in the window seat all day making quick sketches of everyone who came in. There was a jukebox but it seemed that the only thing anyone ever wanted to hear was "Pops" (Armstrong) singing:

I see friends shakin' hands
Sayin' how do you do
What they're really sayin'
Is I love you.

There were quite a number of U.S. bases spread about
the French countryside in those days which were not the
spiritually uplifting places their commanders claimed them
to be in their reports to the Pentagon. The more decent GIs
couldn't wait to get the hell out on weekends and quite a
few dug what was happening in the Monaco. The base security sections were considerably less than pleased with the
idea of exposing clean-cut and freedom-loving American
youths to the Left Bank with its "French immorality" or
"treasonable niggers." This probably accounted for the two
or three flamboyantly inconspicuous "journalists" who joined
the Monaco family.

Another kind of bloodhound eventually showed up, sniff-
ing around the tables and grinning lasciviously. An outlay
of a few pre-inflationary dollars to cover the price of *vin
rouge* and beers for some of the café's thirsting brothers
unearthed enough life stories—invented on the spot—for him
to fill out a prefabricated masterpiece called *The Black
Expatriate,* which eventually surfaced in a well-known news
magazine. One could say that in spite of its clumsily concealed liberal racist paranoia, the cover story was "a step forward." But only because Black Americans hadn't yet been
discovered in the United States as people. Yet it would be
safe to assume that the main inspiration for its appearance
was a dearth of news. Pickings in the heap of human chaos
which usually inspires what William Randolph Hearst called
"great American journalism" were scrawny. There were no
earthquakes, famines or train wrecks. Billion dollar bank
heists had dried up on the editors and of course airplane
hijacking hadn't yet been invented. The foreign news section
dozed in the same postwar atmosphere which led most otherwise mentally capable world leaders to conclude that the
"natives" of the world had forgotten the promises of free-

dom made in the heat of battle. This serenity, which is the bogeyman in the lives of advertising and circulation vice-presidents, presented the Paris correspondent with a chance to do his thing. Result, *The Black Expatriate.*

It wasn't that the piece was offensive, or at least no more so than the usual Anglo-Saxon, myopic view of things which aren't well-bred enough to go out and drop dead. But it definitely exuded the unmistakable bouquet of Establishment disdain despite its well educated admission that Paris had always lured expatriates. There were even American expatriates like Benjamin Franklin, Edgar Allan Poe, F. Scott Fitzgerald, Hemingway and Henry Miller. But the real message was that any brother who hinted, by taking off, that God's country could contain anything unpalatable was messing around with subversion, if not outright treason!

Eventually the number containing the article found its way to the Monaco, where Dick Wright read it to the glee-fully agitated crowd with more than his usual gusto, punctuating each lamentably ill-informed fact with, "Keeee-ryess, now ain't thatabitch?" Chicago George spasmodically stamping both feet and giggling, fell out. "Expatriate," he shrieked. "Sheeeeee-ittt, them mothahs ain't even 'lowed me to be a patriot so hownafuggg I'm gon' git to be a EX-patriot?"

Some afternoons when I'd finished work I'd stroll over to Montparnasse hoping to find Harris. Brother Harris was unadulterated "country," from praying on his knees every night before hopping into the sack, to making clicking noises when the cussing got to be too colorful for his AME Sunday school background. Harris had never even been to the town *next* to his in Mississippi when the long arm of the U.S. Army, Mess Section, reached in and plucked him out. Harris had cooked powdered eggs and dehydrated spuds from El Alamein to Anzio, where a redneck from the 82nd Airborne, perhaps believing that Black brothers deserved Purple Hearts more than most folks, shot Harris in his right buttock. When the war ended Harris had convinced himself that it was God who'd plucked him out of good ole Mississippi and so damned if he wasn't going to show God his appreciation by staying out! Harris also had a theory. "I never seen no diff'ence 'tween them SS and these airborne," Harris explained in his gentle voice. "They even looks alike an' I have seen 'em buddyin' around together over in the prisoner of war compound. You realize what that mean?" I had to admit that I didn't, knowing Harris was going to tell me anyway. "Well Brother, I'm gon' tell you," said Harris. "It mean that now that this war is over they gon' kiss an' make up. It also mean that when I get back home the best I can do is maybe get me a job out at the white folks country club, an' there *they* be hollerin' 'Harris get me this,' and 'Harris get me that,' an' befo' they go in to play the pinball machines they be wantin' to rub my head fer luck. An' because one of 'em is a nice blue-eyed SS an' the other is a nice blue-eyed airborne, I got to let 'em or else have some trouble with the sheriff. Tha's the American Dream, Brother! An' tha's also why Ma Harris' youngest boy is gon' make tracks." Harris was as good as his word. He got himself demobilized in Paris, heard about the GI Education Bill and signed up to study drawing and painting at the Grande Chaumier. It was Herb Gentry and Larry Potter, two Black expatriate painters, who told me between squalls of laughter, about Harris' first day at the Grande Chaumier. Harris had signed up for the "life class" although he didn't quite know exactly what that meant. He found a seat in the huge studio and did what everyone else was doing. He opened his large drawing pad, steadying it on the chair in front, opened his box of brand-new charcoal pencils and erasers and then looking up, realized that there was a completely nude woman standing on the platform just above him in the first pose of the afternoon. Harris split, leaving all of his equipment and his most prized possession, his beret. He didn't stop galloping until he'd locked the door of his tiny hotel room in the Rue Delambre! "Thought the rednecks had finally trapped him," gasped Gentry, wiping the laughing tears from his eyes. It took a week to convince Harris that the French didn't have any rednecks, and so Harris cautiously went back. Of course everyone knew that

Harris would never become even a third rate painter but he was so beamingly happy that not even the instructors had the heart to tell him.

I usually found Harris around three or four in the afternoon at the Café Select in the Boulevard Montparnasse, where we'd discuss art and what Harris called "deep stuff" until dinner time. One rainy afternoon I poked my head in, looking down toward the corner table where Harris usually roosted with his drawing portfolio on the seat of the wicker chair beside him, his broad forehead puckered over some book of reproductions. As usual, Harris was there, but he didn't jump up and wave enthusiastically as he customarily did. I walked toward his table, shaking the rain from my *impermiable*. Before I reached the table I realized that there were tears streaming down Harris' face. The old waiter, Ramon, stood nearby staring at Harris, his usually genial face twisted in anguish. I questioned Ramon with my eyes but he just lifted his shoulders in that most expressive French gesture which says, *Je ne sais pas.* I sat down opposite Harris who seemed unable to speak. "Jesus Christ, Harris, what's happening?" I asked. Harris roughly wiped one side of his face with his sleeve. After a while he looked up and growled, "This is what the bastards have did to me!" I guess hearing Harris curse for the first time shook me up more than the tears and so I asked who had done what. "All of 'em. Every lousy-assed one of 'em goddamit," he hissed. I ordered a couple of beers and ham sandwiches from Ramon, who seemed reluctant to leave Harris' side. Then Harris told me the story.

He'd been walking along the Boulevard casually looking into the gay shop windows. It hadn't started to rain yet and the streets glowed in that exhilarating luminosity which exists only in Paris. Harris remembered that he'd felt "happier than a Baptist preacher at a banquet of fried catfish and cornbread." He stood in front of a gift shop looking at the seductive objects on display and after several moments he realized that there was a girl standing beside him looking at some green crystal glasses. He could see her face reflected in the clear plate glass but then he caught his breath. The reflection was smiling directly at him. Harris turned in the other direction automatically, thinking that the girl was smiling at someone else. But there was no one else. She was small and very pretty, hugging a steno notebook under one arm. Harris gulped when the girl turned from the window and smiled directly at him before she turned to walk slowly toward the Rue Vavin bus stop with a mesmerized Harris trailing after her. When the 85 bus arrived she stepped up to the platform, still smiling. Harris froze. He simply could not follow her into the bus "like I know she wanted me to." The girl seemed puzzled but stepped down quickly before the doors shut and several bored passengers quipped remarks about people not making up their minds. The girl walked slowly toward the Metro station, turning again to smile encouragement at Harris. Reaching the green *art nouveau* Metro sign she began to descend the stairs and making sure that Harris was still there she handed her ticket to the collector, who punched it and reached over her shoulder for the next, which should have been Harris but Harris was already racing trembling back up the steps to the Boulevard. He'd been sitting for more than an hour in the Select while the sky darkened and the rain slashed down, groaning, "That's what the dirty bastards have did to poor old Harris!"

In the twenty-two years of what some people insist on calling "self-exile" I've lived, or made long visits to many places, from the southern tip of Sicily to the hauntingly beautiful north of Sweden. And in all that time and in all those places I've never felt that I was an exile. Or perhaps one might say that Black people are all exiles unless they're African people living in Africa. I'm fairly well convinced that one is an exile only when one is not allowed to live in reasonable peace and dignity as a human being among other human beings. Where one can give love and respect and receive the same from one's neighbors one is no exile. Where one can even get pissed off with the goddamned neighbors just as the neighbors will get pissed off with us at times—because we're humans and not angels. I remember expressing something similar late one night in a place called the Mars Club in Paris, when Beauford Delaney said, "Brothers, who knows. Maybe the angels get pissed off with one another too. After all, we don't know what goes on on the *other side*." And pianist Art Simmons banged his whiskey glass down and solemnly intoned, "You know something else brother, I *don't want to know!*"

Whenever I rap with myself over this question of exile I remember Harris' theory about the SS and the airborne cats giving him a hard time *if* he'd goofed and returned to Mississippi to flunkey out at the country club. Who would be the exile, the now naturalized SS cat—or Harris? Do I hear you say it's a setup example? Okay. Let's just drop the SS part and select a less abstract example. Let's say Wernher von Braun, now a solidly integrated part of the Establishment (Alabama section). Do you think for one moment that Hitler's monstrously effective V-bomb expert has ever been barred from any Alabama country club, or got busted in the mouth by a sadistic sheriff like *any* Black American who fought on *our* side? Hell no! And do you think that Herr von This and Herr von That don't have thousands of Harrises to serve them hand and foot—and maybe get their heads rubbed for luck in the bargain? Isn't *this* the American Dream? Well who in the hell is the exile? Certainly not von Braun. He's among his own having a ball. And not Harris either. He's still in Paris, selling a drawing now and then, or working out at the Renault automobile plant occasionally, and living among *people* who love him because he's a thoroughly lovable human being.

Still, there are only two kinds of people in Europe where I fully experienced this *complete* human integration. They were Russian people and French people. I admit that I spent only two and a half months in the Soviet Union, as a guest of the Soviet satirical magazine *Krokodil*. In that space of time I traveled from Leningrad to Tashkent sketching, talking, drinking and laughing, and once in an open-decked bus on the twisting road up to Lake Ritza, in the Caucasus, I sang along with the Russian tourists. They were city folk and peasant folk with a sprinkling of vacationing Soviet GIs and their wives or girl friends. Hell, I didn't know the words of their spontaneous songs, but I knew the music and I sensed the immense generous heart beating beneath that music, sometimes gay, sometimes plaintive, always human. And as those people realized that I had joined their singing—and it was a thoroughly unconscious act—I saw tears well up in many eyes and a shimmering light seemed to envelope that bus. We'd reached a dizzying height—and it had nothing to do with mountains.

Twelve of those "exile" years I spent in France and as a result I can only say that I love the French people. Above all I love and deeply admire the French working class, its proudly working class artists, poets and other intellectuals, and when all is said and done, these are *the* French people. *They* are France. But space doesn't permit me to do justice to this subject.

In the summer of 1972, John Pittman one of the editors of the *Daily World* wrote me from New York suggesting that I grab a flight and pay them a visit in September. I'd been very, very happily turning out two political cartoons each week for the *Daily World* and it seemed that the arrangement was mutually rewarding. It's all right to live in Europe drawing and painting for personal satisfaction while turning out illustrations and cartoons for European publications for pork chops, but there is something missing somehow. I'm Black, and my people are engaged in a difficult and heroic struggle for freedom. While this is a world-wide struggle of oppressed people against the injustice and savage brutality which seem to be essential weapons for the maintenance of capitalism, my personal part of that struggle seems inseparably bound to how that struggle is being waged in the United States. Although I believe that "art for art's sake" has its merits, I personally feel that my art must be involved, and the most profound involvement must be with the black liberation struggle. My cartoon character Bootsie has been a part of that struggle for thirty-nine years and I believe, as Langston Hughes did, that satire and humor can often make dents where sawed-off billiard sticks can't. In 1968, when John invited me to become a part of the *Daily World* staff I felt that here was an opportunity to get some licks in. I've often gotten letters from friends asking me how I manage to keep up with what's being put down in the U.S.A. when I've lived for so long in Europe. I can only think of that very corny reply: "You can take the boy out of the country but you can't take the country out of the boy." But things do change in two decades and I felt that it would do me a lot of good to see it. I took the leap in September fortified by Czechoslovakian beer, the best in the world as far as I'm concerned. Furthermore you can have as much as you want on Czech Airlines, which is the one I took. Thus fortified, by the time the pilot announced that we were forty thousand feet above Newfoundland on the last leg to Kennedy, I'd managed to get on top of my conflicting emotions to such a degree that I found myself chuckling to the music going around in my head, which was "Pops'" incomparable growling of *Bill Bailey Won't You Please Come Home!*

Dorothy Robinson, that great soul sister, who is business manager of the *Daily World,* came out to Kennedy to meet me accompanied by her sister. Dorothy and I had never met and so she'd provided herself with a photograph which her sister apparently hadn't seen because when we finally "linked-up" Sis said, "Baby, I had *no idea* you were Black," and throwing both arms around my neck she said, "Welcome home, Sugar!" That did it. I *was* home. I was with *people.* I was also in the midst of a different civilization from the one I'd left just a few hours ago, I began to realize as we zipped along the highway from Kennedy to the Triboro Bridge. This realization grew as I began counting the wrecks scattered along the centerpiece which *sometimes* separates east from west bound traffic. I really couldn't figure out what had been going on since I hadn't had any news of that highway having been accidentally strafed by air force jets. Inevitably my curiosity got the upper hand

and so I asked Dorothy about all that twisted metal. Before she could answer Sis said, "Labor Day weekend, Honey," in a tone which implied that *any* idiot should have been hip to that. After a few miles it dawned on me that *somebody* was getting something out of this endless scene of disaster. At regular intervals along the freeway there were immense billboards proclaiming the sheer impossibility of enjoying life without a Ford, Plymouth, Cadillac, well, you name it. This was nothing less than psychodelic. There we were whizzing past these chewed-up, burnt-out metal cadavers on one side; on their backs, on their sides, completely flattened and impossibly twisted. And on the other side were these billboards saying "Baby, don't let this scene get you down. *All you need* is *this* gleaming 200 m.p.h. monster—and a countdown! *Easy credit terms available.*"

When we turned off the Triboro into 135th Street I knew that somebody *up there* had simply been hardening me up for the main event! That kaleidoscopic graveyard of mangled rubber tires and chrome, scorched lacquer, disemboweled hoods and rib-like door frames left behind us was only shadowboxing. Racing cross-town, turning up Lenox to 145th, turning again up the hill to Broadway with the car windows up was like flying at treetop level through an utterly soundless nightmare. Harlem's harried crowds swirled across streets, streamed along sidewalks, through and around poverty's bomb craters of garbage and senseless debris. Brothers, sisters, children, all Black, scampered or teetered on the brink of constant and unseen disaster while the needle-scarred casualties lurched against plate glass or lay spread-eagled half in, half out of weeping doorways. Looming up on all sides were the mummies of slum buildings embalmed and wrapped in rusted sheet metal, street level openings sealed with planks. Staring up at one of these stone ghetto cadavers into its rows of black-windowed-empty-eye-sockets I felt the goose pimples. It wasn't completely dead. High up in a blackened fifth floor window was a quite motionless figure in a floppy hat and threadbare overcoat. Both of its elbows were propped on the window sill steadying a pair of binoculars trained, as far as I could see, on nothing! A once blue painted sign nailed up against a murky store front plaintively boasting THE WORLD'S MOST FASTEST BARBER quickly disappeared as Dorothy swung the wheel and we slid down the hill toward Riverside Drive and the Hudson. We stopped, double-parked and I stared down through the canyon of brownstones to the river and across to the New Jersey cliffs crenelated with white-gleaming condominium giants where Charlie and Miss Anne sat on their Babylonian terraces gleefully regarding the terrible revenge exacted against those who'd dared to hope. With the binoculars of my mind I imagined them sipping their six martinis and gradually sliding down their reclining chairs to the red tiles slowly turning amber. Charlie's overworked bladder released his stored-up piss to form a Rorschach easily identified as The American Dream. Sure, Charlie had put the "niggers in their place," as he had put the Indians in theirs, and as his paid mercenaries were obediently applying the formula all over Indo-China. At least, that is what he stupidly thought.

A few days later, on my way to visit old friends in Vermont the train slithered into a bleakly lit station. I'd been dozing and when the discreet squealing of the brakes jerked me awake I looked at my wrist watch. It was three a.m. and there were wisps of fog swirling along the vapored windowpanes. Outside in the gloomy light filtering through the windows there was this cat weaving under his load of Old Grand Dad or something. He'd evidently climbed down out of one of the train's rear cars and was stumbling along just outside my window. A blurry white face was turned up to me and I saw the mouth move soundlessly. I shoved the window up a bit and he teetered precariously trying to focus. Then he pointed his finger at me and I heard him ask, "Shhhay buddie—*where are you*?" I couldn't see a station sign or anything and so I told him that I'd be damned if I knew. He blinked fuzzily for a second, put his head down, mumbling, "Goddamned fuckin' dumb nigger," and staggered off into the darkness, presumably back to his own coach.

Now I knew where I was. I was home Baby!

But home wasn't what it used to be. There *had* been some changes made. My old and very dear friends Henry Winston and Jim Jackson, along with John Pittman, had brought up the notion of my helping out in the circulation drive the *Daily World* was putting on. This meant traveling around the country a bit. "It would be a great opportunity for you to get the feel of things again," Winnie suggested which I realized was absolutely true, not only for grabbing hold of what's been happening but there would also be the visual thing which is extremely important to a graphic artist.

A week later I was in Nashville. Now let me tell you about Nashville in 1948, the last time I was there. My job then was public relations director in the national office of the NAACP in New York, a post I'd accepted after much soul-searching. It was terribly difficult giving up art but one day when I'd heard about the South Carolina cops gouging out both eyes of a Black veteran, Isaac Woodward, that ended the debate. Or as my wartime buddies used to say, "That's all she wrote!" But sitting in a beautifully appointed office in West 40th Street watching the pigeons do their thing atop the classical façades of the main New York Public Library tends to develop a lot of fat around the brain. This sad condition was painfully brought to my attention at the Nashville Airport when I scampered into the gleaming Braniff DC6, rushed for a window seat and buckled myself in. A few seconds later an elegantly togged lady who seemed to be smelling something very unpleasant, edged into the outside seat. When the stewardess came down the aisle there was a whispered conversation which terminated when the stewardess turned her white mask toward me with the advice that I'd be acting real smart if I got the hell out of that seat and moved up forward. She didn't add "or else" but it was there beneath the words. I moved. I still had enough of my wits left about me to remember that I was, after all, in this greatest of all democracies, Black and outnumbered. You dig? But it turned out much better than I deserved. The only vacant seat left was up front next to a sister who turned out be so cool, so full of quietly brilliant humor that I almost forgot the honey-suckle-drenched woman who carried the power of the whole U.S. government and its "law" enforcement thugs firmly clutched between her miserably scrawny haunches.

Now here I was, in 1972, twenty-five years later, at the same Nashville Airport. When I heard my flight being called I took the escalator down to the port boarding room where I took a seat near the door. A few minutes later that same goddamned woman came into the room. Of course, when I got myself together I realized that it wasn't she but it sure as hell could have been. Something had happened to Miss Anne in the intervening years. She'd lost that mulishly arrogant canter. Instead of sweeping into the room she trick-led in. The megalomaniac White-Fairy-Queen glare, which best-selling novelists describe as "a *level* stare" wasn't working. Instead she wore a simpering plea of helplessness with which she checked the room. I was the only Black pas-senger in the room and so, naturally, those hypocritically cunning eyes stopped and she moved toward me like the mesmerized lady in *Dracula*. She took the next seat and leaning toward me she said, "Suh, ah sho to goodness hope that nobody in heah is gon' hah-jack our plane this tahm. Do you s'pose they will?" Talk about Bugville. That's where I was at! When I finally got my mouth to close up I wanted to laugh until I cried but when I managed to get myself together I told her, "Well no, Miss Anne, I don't think there's anything to worry about." She smiled even more and hurried to say, "No, I'm Miss Lurleen. . . ." I didn't hear the rest of it because this time the chuckles were breaking through my cool. Seeming somewhat relieved, but not much, Miss Lurleen continued, "Do you reckon anyone in heah is ca'ing a guuuun?" "No," I assured her, "if anybody, you for instance, were carrying a gun in your handbag all these elec-tronic devices around here would start acting like the Fourth of July!" She settled back then and sighed. "Ah do hope you're raht, Sirrrr. It was real nahse talkin' to ya." But I know she was thinking, "If anybody is going to hi-jack this plane it's got to be this Black man. And I really can't rightly put my finger on the 'why.' All I know is that he *should!*"

Then there was Chicago and the composite portrait of this new America began to take on form in my mind. The shapes were surrealist, sick, the colors grating and ominous. But there were passages suggesting movement, even dynamic movement, and buried in these masses were flashes of vibrant, even beautiful light. Walking around the Loop, in the grim shadow of the constantly rumbling elevated tracks above, I went into a rambling bar restaurant, one of those quick-service American inventions which are beginning to pollute the relaxed atmosphere and the digestive habits of many European cities. I had a couple of hours to spare before my appointment with Ish Flory, who was a very busy candidate for the Illinois governorship. The fact that Ish was Black *and* running on the Communist Party ticket would have brought at least one division of the Illinois National Guard swarming into the Chicago ghetto with live ammunition only a few years ago. Only a few nights before I'd listened to an unbelievably courageous Mr. Flory tell a solidly Wasp audience that if they had any sense and real concern for the future of the country they'd realize that they *needed* men like him in office if only for the fact that they were the only ones who couldn't be indicted for very grand larceny. The Wasps actually applauded—and that was before Watergate!

I walked through the self-service restaurant to the bar and hoisted myself onto a stool where I could watch the World Series in color on the TV set suspended up above the rows of bottled liquid libations, and where I could drink in the movements, also in color, of one of the most beautiful barmaids I'd ever seen on either side of the ocean. She was a sister and the characters at the bar called her Mink, but with the careful air of men handling live ammunition. Mink was as cool as she was striking and she placed the straights and highballs before the mixed clientele with courtesy mixed with an indefinable aura which cautioned the cats, sober or drunk, against asking for anything that wasn't on the alcohol list. A few minutes later, while Sal Bando was busting up the ball game with one over the fence in the tenth inning, a couple of redneck hardhats came in and grabbed two stools in the midst of the hysteria which had taken over. They ordered a couple of beers, which Mink served up dead-pan but courteously, and began like everyone else to second guess the losing manager's choice of putting in a right-hand pitcher to a left-hand batter. The joint calmed down and the hardhats ordered another round.

When Mink stood before them, deftly flicking the spatula to skim off the overflowing foam, one of the hardhats asked if he could pin something on the front of her blouse. The other clients tensed but the hardhats, undoubtedly on another frequency, continued their subtly lascivious program. I heard Mink ask, "What is it?" One of the hardhats had a little plastic American flag, the kind which clips into the lapels. In a soft undertone Mink said, "Look Baby, I *don't want it!*" The hardhats tensed. "You sayin' you won't wear *your* flag?" Tiny and tense, but cool, Mink's low voice cut through the silence like a straight razor. "Mister," she said, "that flag used to be decent but y'all went an' shit on it so much that I *do not want no part of it!*" The hardhats were incredulous. "You mean . . ." one of them stuttered. "Yes. I mean you go an' clean it up. Then I'll think about it." The other hardhat said, "Love it or leave it." Mink's eyes cracked lightning, "Look Muuurrrfuggger," she hissed, "I ain't lookin' for trouble, see? That's why Saturday is my last day here. Ya wanta know why? 'Cause the other day I had to lay one up side the head of the lousy peckerwood that runs this crappy joint. Dig?" The thoroughly confused hard-hats jerked back from the bar and one of them said whining-ly, "But the American flag. . . ." "You heard me," said Mink. "It's because of phoney shits like you hardhats that every time I sees a picket line I get on it. And I don't care *what* the fuck they picketin' about!" The hardhats sat staring at their half-emptied beer glasses and then when they felt that no one was looking at them they slunk out shaking their heads sadly. A half hour later when I met Ish I asked him if he needed someone for a picket line. Then I told him about Mink and the hardhats. Ish listened with that enigmatical grin of his, his laughing eyes half shut as if he were tasting a rare wine. "Ollie," he mused, "these sisters are something else. There are sisters like the one you're telling me about all over this land and when the *man* looks into their eyes he *knows* they ain't playing."

Traveling through the betrayed American cities, I became aware of a profound trembling of the earth in every ghetto. Young Black people with amazingly straight backs, knowing, or better still, *convinced* that Black *is* beautiful too are now enabled to release the blindingly creative energies which have always been bound in chains by a criminally bigoted system. A revolution is taking place in the ghettos if one has the eyes to look behind the frightening façade. And revolutions require expression. Black kids painting huge murals on discouragingly neglected slum buildings are expressing that revolution. Sidestreet theatres, poetry readings, and neighborhood museums are part of that expression. They're all expressing ideas with which Black people can identify. A Black Renaissance has already been born. ...

Cheikh Anta Diop and the New Light on African History

John Henrik Clarke

Cheikh Anta Diop, one of the most able of present day scholars writing about Africa, is also one of the greatest living Black historians. His first major work, *Nations Negres et Culture* (1955) is still disturbing the white historians who have made quick reputations as authorities on African history and culture. In this book Dr. Diop shows the inter-relationships between African nations, north and south, and proves, because in this case proof is needed again and again, that ancient Egypt was a distinct African nation and was not historically or culturally a part of Asia or Europe. More myths about Africa are put to rest in another one of his books, *The Cultural Unity of Negro Africa* (1959). The publication of his first book in the United States, *The African Origin of Civilization: Myth or Reality*, is a cause for celebration. This book and others of recent years, all by Black writers, have called for a total reconsideration of the role that African people have played in history and their impact on the development of early societies and institutions.

Cheikh Anta Diop[1]* was born in the town of Diourbel, in Senegal, on the West Coast of Africa in 1923. His birthplace has a long tradition of producing Muslim scholars and oral

THE AFRICAN ORIGIN OF CIVILIZATION: MYTH OR REALITY. By Cheikh Anta Diop. Edited and translated by Mercer Cook. Lawrence Hill and Company, New York. 316 pages. $12.95 (cloth); $5.95 (paper).

* See notes at end of article.

historians. This is where his inspiration and interest in history, the humanities and social sciences from an African point of view began. After the publication of his first book, *Nations Negres et Culture,* that had been rejected as a Ph. D. thesis at the Sorbonne in Paris, he became one of the most controversial of present day African historians. *Nations Negres et Culture* is both a reassessment of the African past and a challenge to Western scholarship on Africa. He refutes the myth of Egypt as a white nation and shows its southern African origins. It is his intention to prove that, through Egyptian civilization, Africa had made the oldest and one of the most significant contributions to world culture. This is not a new argument that started with Cheikh Anta Diop's generation of Africans. The Ghanaian historian, Joseph B. Danquah, in his introduction to the book, *United West Africa at The Bar of The Family of Nations,* by Ladipo Solanke, published in 1927, four years after Cheikh Anta Diop was born, said exactly the same thing. His statement reads:

"By the time Alexander the Great was sweeping the civilized world with conquest after conquest from Chaeronia to Gaza, from Babylon to Cabul; by the time the first Aryan conquerors were learning the rudiments of war and government at the feet of the philosopher Aristotle; and by the time Athens was laying down the foundations of European civilization, the earliest and greatest Ethiopian culture had already flourished and dominated the civilized world for over four centuries and a half. Imperial Ethiopia had conquered Egypt and founded the XXVth Dynasty, and for a century and a half the central seat of civilization in the known world was held by the ancestors of the modern Negro, maintaining and defending it against the Assyrian and Persian Empires of the East. Thus, at the time when Ethiopia was leading the civilized world in culture and conquest, East was East, but West was not, and the first European (Grecian) Olympiad was yet to be held. Rome was nowhere to be seen on the map, and sixteen centuries were to pass before Charlemagne would rule in Europe and Egbert became first King of England. Even then, history was to drag on for another seven hundred weary years, before Roman Catholic Europe could see fit to end the Great Schism, soon to be followed by the disturbing news of the discovery of America and the fateful rebirth of the youngest of world civilizations."[2]

Here Dr. Danquah is showing that African history is the foundation of world history. In the present book by Cheikh Anta Diop, and in most of his other works, his objective is the same. In his first major work on history, Dr. Diop has said:

"The general problem confronting African history is this: how to recognize effectively, through meaningful research, all of the fragments of the past into a single ancient epoch, a common origin which will reestablish African continuity. ... If the ancients were not victims of a mirage, it should be easy enough to draw upon another series of arguments and proofs for the union of the history of Ethiopian and Egyptian societies with the rest of Africa. Thus combined, these histories would lead to a properly patterned past in which it would be seen that (ancient) Ghana rose in the interior (West Africa) of the continent at the moment of Egyptian decline, just as the Western European empires were born with the decline of Rome."

While using Africa as the vantage point and the basis for his thesis, Dr. Diop does not neglect the broader dimensions of history. He shows that history cannot be restricted by the limits of ethnic group, nation, or culture. Roman history is Greek as well as Roman, and both the Greek and the Roman histories are Egyptian because the entire Mediterranean was civilized Egypt; and Egypt in turn borrowed from other parts of Africa, especially Ethiopia.

Africa came into the Mediterranean world mainly through Greece, which had been under African influence. The first Greek invasion of Africa was peaceful and scholarly. This invasion brought in Herodotus. Egypt had lost its independence over a century before his visit. This was the beginning of the period of foreign domination over Egypt that would last, in different forms, for two thousand years.

The African Origin of Civilization: Myth or Reality is a one-volume translation of the major sections of the first and last of the books by Cheikh Anta Diop, i.e. *Nations Negres et Culture* and *Antériorité des Civilisations Negres.* These two works have challenged and changed the direction of attitudes about the place of African people in history in scholarly circles around the world. It was largely due to these works that Cheikh Anta Diop, with W.E.B. Du Bois, was honored as "the writer who had exerted the greatest influence on African people in the 20th century" at the World Festival of Arts held in Dakar, Senegal, in 1966.

The main thesis of the present work is a redefinition of the place of Egypt in African history in particular and in world history in general. Dr. Diop calls attention to the historical, archeological and anthropological evidence that supports his thesis. The civilization of Egypt, he maintains, is African in origin and in early development.

In his book Dr. Diop says: "The history of Africa will remain suspended in air and cannot be written correctly until African historians connect it with the history of Egypt."

He further states: "The African historian who evades the problem of Egypt is neither modest or objective, nor unruffled, he is ignorant, cowardly, and neurotic."

Dr. Diop approaches the history of Africa frontally, head-on with explanations, but no apologies. In locating Egypt on the map of human geography he asks and answers the question: Who were the Egyptians of the ancient world?

The Ethiopians say that the Egyptians were one of their colonies which was brought into Egypt by the deity Osiris. The Greek writer Herodotus repeatedly referred to the

Egyptians as being dark-skinned people with woolly hair. "They," he says, "have the same tint of skin which approaches that of the Ethiopians." The opinion of the ancient writers on the Egyptians is more or less summed up by Gaston Maspero (1846-1916) when he says, "By the almost unanimous testimony of ancient historians, they [the Egyptians] belong to an African race which first settled in Ethiopia on the Middle Nile: following the course of the river they gradually reached the sea."

"The Greek writer, Herodotus, may be mistaken," Cheikh Anta Diop tells us, "when he reports the customs of a people. But one must grant that he was at least capable of recognizing the skin color of the inhabitants of countries he visited." His descriptions of the Egyptians were the descriptions of a Black people. At this point the reader needs to be reminded of the fact that at the time of Herodotus' visit to Egypt and other parts of Africa (between 480 and 425 B.C.) Egypt's Golden Age was over. Egypt had suffered from several invasions, mainly the Kushite invasions, coming from within Africa, and starting in 751 B.C., and the Assyrians' invasions from Western Asia (called the Middle East), starting in 671 B.C. If Egypt, after years of invasions by other people and nations, was a distinct Black African nation at the time of Herodotus, shouldn't we at least assume that it was more so before these invasions occurred?

If Egypt is a dilemma in Western historiography, it is a created dilemma. The Western historians, in most cases, have rested the foundation of what is called "Western Civilization" on the false assumptions, or claim, that the ancient Egyptians were white people. To do this they had to ignore great masterpieces on Egyptian history written by other white historians who did not support this point of view, such as Gerald Massey's great classic, *Ancient Egypt, The Light of the World* (1907) and his other works, *A Book of the Beginnings* and *The Natural Genesis*. Other neglected works by white writers are *Politics, Intercourse, and Trade of the Carthaginians, Ethiopians, Egyptians,* by A. H. L.

Heeren (1833), and *Ruins of Empires,* by Count Volney (1787).

In the first chapter of his book, Dr. Diop refers to the Southern African origins of the people later known as Egyptians. Here he is on sound ground with a lot of support coming from another group of neglected white writers. In his book *Egypt,* Sir E. A. Wallis Budge says: "The prehistoric native of Egypt, both in the old and in the new Stone Ages, was African and there is every reason for saying that the earliest settlers came from the South." He further states: "There are many things in the manners and customs and religions of the historic Egyptians that suggest that the original home of their prehistoric ancestors was in a country in the neighborhood of Uganda and Punt." (Some historians believe that the biblical land of Punt was in the area known on modern maps as Somalia.)

European interest in "Ethiopia and the Origin of Civilization" dates from the early part of the nineteenth century and is best reflected in a little known, though important, paper in Karl Richard Lepsius' *Incomparable Survey of the Monumental Ruins in the Ethiopian Nile Valley in 1843–1844.* The records found by Lepsius tend to show how Ethiopia was once able to sustain an ancient population that was numerous and powerful enough not only to challenge but, on a number of occasions, to conquer completely the populous land of Egypt. Further, these records show that the antiquity of Ethiopian civilization had a direct link with civilization of ancient Egypt.

Many of the leading antiquarians of the time, based largely on the strength of what the classical authors, particularly Diodorus Siculus and Stephanus of Byzantium, had to say on the matter, were exponents of the view that the ancient Ethiopians, or at any rate, the Black people of remote antiquity were the earliest of all civilized peoples and that the first civilized inhabitants of ancient Egypt were members of what is referred to as the Black race who entered the country as emigrants from Ethiopia. A number of Europe's leading writers on the civilizations of remote antiquity have written brilliant defenses of this point of view. Some of these writers are Bruce, Count Volney, Fabre, d'Olivet, and Heeren. In spite of the fact that these writers defended this thesis with all the learning at their command and documented their defense, most of the present-day writers of African history continue to ignore their findings.

In 1825 German backwardness in this respect came definitely to an end. In that year, Arnold Hermann Heeren (1760–1842), Professor of History and Politics at the University of Göttingen and one of the ablest of the early exponents of the economic interpretation of history, published, in the fourth and revised edition of his great work, *Ideen Über Die Politik, Den Verkehr Und Den Handel Der Vornehmsten Völker Der Alten Welt*, a lengthy essay on the history, culture, and commerce of the ancient Ethiopians, which had profound influence on contemporary writers in the conclusion that it was among these ancient Black people of Africa and Asia that international trade was first developed. He thinks that as a by-product of these international contacts there was an exchange of ideas and cultural practices that laid the foundations of the earliest civilizations of the ancient world.

The French writer Count C. F. Volney, in his important work, *The Ruins of Empires*, extends this point of view by saying that the Egyptians were the first people to "attain the physical and moral sciences necessary to civilized life." In referring to the basis of this achievement he states further:

"It was, then, on the borders of the Upper Nile, among a Black race of men, that was organized the complicated system of worship of the stars, considered in relation to the productions of the earth and the labors of agriculture; and this first worship, characterized by their adoration under their own forms and national attributes, was a simple proceeding of the human mind."[3]

Over a generation ago African-American historians such as Carter G. Woodson, W.E.B. Du Bois, Willis N. Huggins,

J. A. Rogers, and Charles C. Seifort read the works of these radical writer-historians and began to expand on their findings. This tradition continued and is reflected in the works of present-day Black historians such as John G. Jackson's *Introduction to African Civilizations* (1970), Yosef ben-Jochannan's *Black Man of the Nile* (1972), and Chancellor Williams' *The Destruction of Black Civilization; Great Issues of a Race From 4500 B.C. to A.D. 2000* (1971).

Until the publication of James G. Spady's article, "Negritude, Pan-Benegritude and the Diopian Philosophy of African History," in *A Current Bibliography on African Affairs* (volume 5, number 1, January, 1972) and the recent interview by Harun Kofi Wangara, published in *Black World* magazine (February, 1974), Dr. Cheikh Anta Diop was known to only a small group of Black writers and teachers in the United States. For over seven years his books were offered to American publishers with no show of interest. Now two of his books will be published in the United States within one year. The Third World Press in Chicago is preparing to publish his book, *The Cultural Unity of Negro Africa*. All of his books were originally published by *Presence Africaine*, the Paris-based publication arm of the International Society of African Culture.

Egyptology developed in concurrence with the development of the slave trade and the colonial system. It was during this period that Egypt was literally taken out of Africa, academically, and made an extension of Europe. In many ways Egypt is the key to ancient African history. African history is out of kilter until ancient Egypt is looked upon as a distinct African nation. The Nile River played a major role in the relationship of Egypt to the nations in Southeast Africa. During the early history of Africa, the Nile was a great cultural highway on which elements of civilization came into and out of inner Africa. Egypt's relationship with the people in the South was both good and bad, depending on the period and the dynasty in power.

In his chapter called, "What Were the Egyptians?," Dr. Diop explains the rise and fall of Egypt's Golden Age and the beginnings of the invasions, first from Western Asia, that turned this nation's first age of greatness into a nightmare. This was the period of the Hyksos, or Shepherd Kings. During this time seventy Jews, grouped in twelve patriarchal families, nomads without industry or culture, entered Egypt. These Jews left Egypt four hundred years later 600,000 strong, after acquiring from African people all of the elements of their future religion, tradition, and culture, including monotheism. Whosoever the Jews were when they entered Africa, when they left, four hundred years later, they were ethnically, culturally, and religiously an African people. In this part of his book, Cheikh Anta Diop leaves no room for argument.

In the chapter called, "Birth of the Negro Myth," Dr. Diop shows how African people, whose civilizations were old before Europe was born, were systematically read out of the respectful commentary of human history. This examination is continued in the chapter called, "Modern Falsification of History." Here, Cheikh Anta Diop deals with how Western historians, for the last five hundred years, wrote or rewrote history glorifying the people of European extraction and distorted the history of the rest of the world.

Those who read this book seriously are in for a shock and a rewarding experience in learning. This is a major work by a major Black historian. At last, the renaissance of African historiography from an African point of view has begun, and none too soon. I will say again, the publication of Cheikh Anta Diop's book *The African Origin of Civilization: Myth or Reality* is a cause for celebration.

References

[1] *The Ideology of Blackness.* Edited by Raymond F. Betts. D.C. Heath and Company, Lexington, Massachusetts, 1971. pp. 127–133.

[2] *United West Africa (Or Africa) at the Bar of the Family of Nations.* By Ladipo Solanke. First published 1927, reprinted 1969 by African Publication Society, London, England.

[3] *The Ruins; or Meditation on the Revolutions of Empires: and the Law of Nature.* By C. F. Volney. Peter Eckler, New York, 1890.

II. Racism's New Face

Science and Racism

Dorothy Burnham

Some of the gravest problems that minority people of the United States face today have their origins in the misuse of science and technology. Frequently the individual scientist has little control over the uses made of his research and studies. However, there are many who know what is going on in the scientific arena, which can bear only harmful consequences to mankind, and yet they say and do nothing to end the danger and the injury.

The life scientist is concerned with the form and function of living organisms and the dynamics of the inter-relationships at every level. The molecules of the gene have a characteristic chemical structure. The expression of the gene trait depends not only upon its particular structure but also on its reactivity with other gene molecules and with the rest of the environment. This is not the lowest level of interaction and there are multitudinous other levels of interrelationships within and among cells, tissues, organs. This interdependence may be demonstrated at every level up to and including man who interacts with others of his species as well as with the physical and cultural environment.

The scientist, like other creative scholars, is dependent on his precursors and upon his or her fellow workers for the development of thoughts, ideas, conceptions. The scientist's most original ideas are shaped by the culture, and the political and social milieu in which he or she operates. Just as the actions of genes are expressed in a given environment and repressed in a different environment, so it is that some ideas bloom and flourish in a given climate and other ideas are repressed.

The ideology of racism and the oppression of Afro-Americans has been and continues to be a dominant theme in

American life. The American scientist is not isolated from this ideology. It is a part of his or her culture and becomes a part of his or her subconscious and a bias of life and work. There are scientific workers who have brought these subconscious ideas to a conscious level and actively reject racism, working at every level to prevent the poison of racism from contaminating their scientific work and contributions. And there are those who consciously serve the ruling class, by openly and flagrantly devoting their careers to the service of racism and class bias.

In the past few years there has been an acceleration of scientific research which has been directed against the human interests of the poor, the oppressed and minority groups. One notes with alarm the rapidity with which this research has been popularized in all the media and passed on to feed the fires of racism and class prejudices.

Dr. Inez Smith Reid in an address before the American Association for the Advancement of Science in January of this year warned:

"If thousands should cry out in the next five years: 'Let the darker peoples of the world starve unto death, or be sterilized into extinction; they are dumb, unhealthy, poor, an unnecessary burden!' that should not be surprising for the seeds of those cries have been crushed into fertile soil and only await the spring of their blossom."

It is with these warnings in mind that we must look at the developments and research in the field of genetics, behavior modification, psycho-surgery and drugs for the so-called aggressive peoples.

It seems as though it is only a few short years since Dr. Arthur Jensen made the scene, propounding his thesis of the genetic inferiority of Afro-Americans in regard to the IQ tests. A veritable mountain of evidence has piled up since that time exposing the weakness of his evidence and the falsity of his conclusion, all of which is convincing enough to relegate his work to the same domain as the flat earth theory. Jensen has, however, persisted in promoting his ideas and has found many friends among those who believe in the natural inferiority of Afro-Americans. William Shockley has, indeed, made the promulgation of the genetic inferiority of Afro-Americans the crusade of his life. Falsely linking the advocacy of racism to the issue of freedom of speech, he appears on radio, television and on campuses throughout the land. And he has carried the theory one dangerous giant step forward advocating the sterilization of the "low IQ unfit."

Among the most significant developments in the past fifty years in the science of biology has been the determination of the biochemical basis of heredity. The isolation of genetic material from the cell and the elucidation of its chemical components lead to the possibility of changing the inherited characteristics of the living organism in the laboratory. This is called genetic engineering. The possible benefits of this research are far-reaching. Yet, geneticists and other scientists have raised serious questions about the ethics and possible outcome of such experimentation. In July of 1974 a group of leading molecular biologists, with the backing of the National Academy of Scientists, published a letter in three leading science journals (Science, Nature, NAS Proceedings) calling for a temporary halt in certain types of genetic research.

Experimental work on the altered genes from bacterial and viral sources is underway and indications are that a number of laboratories are engaged in genetic research of this type. It would be inconceivable that the military would not be exploring the possibilities for the use of this research in biological warfare.

At a conference held to discuss the social impact of modern biology, Prof. G. Pontecorvo of the University of London cautioned:

"We are just deluding ourselves if we think that human genetic engineering is so in the realm of science fiction that we don't need to start thinking about it. My worry is that the advances will be extremely slow and minor to begin with; for instance, I would estimate that within four to five years it will be possible to cure to a very minor, limited extent by genetic engineering, certain genetic deficiencies; nobody will object to that and so we will go on to the next step, and the next step, and so on. And if we don't start discussing these matters now, we shall get to the state, as we did with the atom bomb, when nobody knows what is going on."

Warnings such as those of Professors Reid and Pontecorvo may seem exaggerated. But a look at what has been done in the name of science in the past generation shows otherwise. Dr. Arlene P. Bennett* listed and documented the outrages perpetuated by the eugenicists in the period 1890–1930. In the paper she pointed out that twenty-six states still have Eugenic Sterilization Laws. In 1972 alone at least 16,000 women and 8,000 men were sterilized by federal government programs. In Puerto Rico, it has been claimed that 35 percent of the women of childbearing age have been sterilized. These sterilizations were carried out with the tacit or explicit consent of medical people for reasons ranging from alleged violence to getting the poor off welfare rolls.

"Uncle Sam is now the major provider of birth control services in this country, and his contribution is unmistakably on the poor ... more and more both poor and middle class women and especially third world women are finding that birth control services are accessible and free while other health services for themselves and their children are not. ... " (*Health/PAC Bulletin,* No. 40, April 1972.)

* See p. 130

Behavior Modification

In the name of scientific research an assault is waged on the children of the poor and minority groups. Most shameful are the behavior modification programs being carried out in the schools and institutions of the country. The combination of research and technological scientists engaged in the work includes psychiatrists, psychologists, pharmacologists and physicians.

The child most likely to be targeted for behavior modification treatment is labeled hyperkinetic. And what is the range of symptoms of the hyperkinetic child? The list includes restlessness, not completing assignments, moving from one activity to another, short attention span. The American Academy of Pediatrics objected to the treatment proposed for hyperkinetic children and criticized the glib diagnosis of hyperkinesis in the absence of standardized requirements for precise diagnosis. Yet the inaccurate diagnosis and the cruel treatment continue.

Frequently it is the harassed teacher with an overflowing classroom who is called upon to make the observations on which the diagnosis is based.

The treatment for this poorly defined disease victimizes the child who is already singled out for special treatment by reason of his poverty or his minority status. The children are treated with amphetamines and related drugs, to the profit of the drug companies and the disaster of the child. The drug has the desired effect, not for the child, his family or society, but for the ruling class whose greatest desire is to have a passive population which can be passively exploited. The treated child becomes a passive child who grows into a passive adult. In addition to the psychological effects, the physical effects on the child include poor growth, poor appetite, weight loss, abdominal pain, insomnia and possible drug addiction.

A scientist who makes clear his commitment to ruling class goals is Dr. Arnold Hutschnecker, a psychiatrist and consultant to the National Commission on the Causes and

Prevention of Violence. He advocates, as one way to curb ghetto uprisings, the psychological testing of all children between the ages of six and eight. The recommendation then is that if the tests show a propensity towards violence or other abnormal behavior, the child would be committed to a rehabilitation camp. As in the case of the hyperkinetic child, the men and institutions involved in making the diagnoses have in mind the early recognition and suppression of children who express their just hostility to a system designed to keep them poor and servile.

Especially vulnerable to scientific experimentation are confined populations: prisoners, the mentally ill and the poor in institutions. New drugs, questionable treatments and surgery have victimized these inmates who have been made immune to claims of humanity by institutionalized racism and who have been used as guinea pigs by men and women of science.

As with the children, prisoners are selected for behavior modification programs. The majority of prisoners used in these types of experimentation are members of minority groups—Afro-Americans, Chicano-Americans, Native Americans and Puerto Ricans. Those most likely to be selected are the politically active prisoners, those who struggle for prisoner rights within the walls. The goal in the use of drugs is the reduction of the prisoner to a passive, manageable individual. The side effects of some of these drugs are horrible to contemplate. The "patients" have suffered loss of memory, loss of powers to concentrate, loss of the power of abstract thinking, loss of emotional reactions.

Psycho-surgery

Not content with this type of destruction of the mind, a number of scientists are opting for psycho-surgery to treat "violent" and "violence prone" individuals. As with hyperkinesis, the definition of violent and violence prone is made to fit those selected for treatment. Even Dr. Vernon Mark and Dr. Frank Ervin, authors of the book on psycho-surgery, *Violence and the Brain,* have trouble with the meaning. They admit: "The definition of 'unacceptable violence' is of course a major stumbling block." They then come up with the following: "We should define 'acceptable violence' as the controlled minimum necessary action to prevent physical injury or *wanton destruction of property* . . . and all violent acts that did not fit this category would be 'unacceptable.' "

Note that the authors who write the above definition (?) of "unacceptable violence" have spent some hundred pages or so describing psycho-surgical treatment for those individuals unlucky enough to fall into the net of that definition.

Psycho-surgery as a weapon in the arsenal of control is certainly one of the most sinister devised by mankind. Early brain surgery for the treatment of persons judged mentally ill included lobotomy and lobectomy, both aimed at destruction of frontal lobes. This destruction was performed on thousands of men and women trapped by the system. This type of operation is now thought to be too crude an assault. What has been substituted is destruction of smaller parts of the brain by stereotactic surgery. Electrodes are implanted in the brain of the patient for the destruction of specially selected regions of the brain or for the monitoring of brain wave activity.

In psycho-surgery the higher functions of the brain are irreversibly damaged. There is a marked loss of ability for introspective thinking, a loss of creativity, a loss of memory. But the outstanding and desired result is the passivity of the victim.

When one considers the complexity of the brain and the comparatively limited knowledge which neurologists have of the relationship of the brain structure to emotional response and intellectual functioning, these operations are comparable to a motorcycle mechanic repairing a spaceship with a monkey wrench. Of course no one would consider letting the mechanic near the spaceship because of the millions of dollars involved. But humans and their brains are considered expendable.

Perversion of Science

It is to the credit of the scientific community that the majority of scientists have rejected these inhumane and anti-scientific projects and will have nothing to do with them. Many have spoken out against their colleagues and others have challenged the basic anti-working class and racist bias of the research and experimentation.

Yet these disgraceful studies and work continue and grow in the name of science. What is briefly summarized in this paper reveals only a small part of the work being carried on in the laboratories and institutions. It is clearly evident that the work has the support and encouragement of the government because it serves ruling class interests.

In this period of deepening economic crisis, racist ideology burgeons and spreads into every area of life. The racist scientist who becomes a willing spokesman for racist ideas finds that his words are accepted and even respected, even when he speaks outside the area of his expertise. The white worker parading in the streets of Boston against school integration carries a banner promoting the ideas of the racist scientist and is thus diverted from his own necessary struggles against inflation and unemployment and exploitation.

It is not only in the area of ideology that the scientist is used. At worst, the works of science are converted and perverted into instruments of genocide. It is almost twenty-five years since the petition of the Civil Rights Congress to the United Nations, *We Charge Genocide*. The following words of William L. Patterson introducing the petition need to be heeded today:

"Out of the inhuman Black ghettos of American cities, out of the cotton plantations of the South, comes this record of mass slayings on the basis of race, of lives deliberately warped and distorted by the willful creation of conditions making for premature death, poverty and disease. It is a record that calls aloud for condemnation, for an end to these terrible injustices that constitute a daily and ever increasing violation of the United Nations Convention on the Prevention and Punishment of the Crime of Genocide."

Unfortunately from the records of the science journals one can add, in no small measure, to the list of crimes against the Afro-American people. Those who are responsible must be exposed and stopped.

Eugenics as a Vital Part of Institutionalized Racism

Arlene P. Bennett, M.D.

A tremendous amount of time and energy has gone into rhetoric and studies on the psychodynamics of racism against Blacks. Unless we explore the history of institutionalized racism in America from the 1890's through the 1930's, our ideas and strategies for dealing with racial hostilities are going to remain isolated, irrelevant and ineffective. There are very important correlations between the way that the Nordics (northern Europeans or "native" Americans) treated the non-Nordic immigrants (central, eastern and southern Europeans, Jews and Catholics) and the way that the Nordic and non-Nordic Americans are treating the Blacks and other minorities of color today. The Nordics who also referred to themselves as white Anglo-Saxon Protestants were the establishment's teachers, religious leaders, doctors, lawyers, legislators, scientists, sociologists, psychologists, scholars, journalists and other individuals who could contribute to the so-called "proof" of the biological inferiority of the immigrants. This community made up the eugenic circle of the 1900's. Eugenics is defined as the science which attempts to improve the human race by discouraging or preventing reproduction among the genetically or biologically unfit or inferior citizens. What is meant by "race" and "genetically unfit"; and who decides? It is usually decided by the group in power.

The information which comes out of this embarrassing period of American history is much the same as the racial history which is being made today. This history has the power to show all people how the tissue paper ego of "race" gets propped up by each generation's believers in racial or genetic superiority. It tends to make the proponents and their pronouncements of white superiority and black inferiority seem rather silly even though each generation cloaks its racism in the "scientifically acceptable" jargon of its day. Thus the Jensens, Shockleys, Herrnsteins, Moynihans and Armors and fans turn out to be nothing more than modern day Thorndikes, Termens, Davenports, Laughlins, Rosses, Wiggams and Madison Grants. Ludmerer summarized the myths when he made this statement in his recent book entitled, *Genetics and American Society:*

"To eugenicists the high incidence of disease, illiteracy, poverty, and crime in immigrant neighborhoods constituted sufficient testimony to the newcomer's innate inferiority. ... They maintained that heredity is far more important than environment, an assumption which justified their claim that immigrants' 'undesirable' features could in no way be corrected or improved."[1]*

The Immigration Restriction Act of 1924

The use of popularized genetics as a vehicle for formulating racist-oriented legislation was epitomized by the Immigration Restriction Act of 1924. This law was aimed squarely at the immigrants who were not only non-Nordic but also poor and without social status. The Act limited their incoming numbers to two percent of the 1890 census which just happened to coincide with that time in American history when their numbers were negligible compared to those of British, Scandinavian and German ancestry. The passing of this law had been preceded by a ground swell of books, articles, lectures and ethnic societies including superpatriotic and religious ones which supported the restriction and provided "professional evidence" of the undesirability of admitting these "biologically inferior" stocks. Some of the

* See notes at end of article.

names of the organizations paint a vivid picture of the mentality of the times–American Breeders' Association, American Defense Society, Immigration Restriction League. Some of the statements made by members of Congress during that period point up the acceptability of racism as a basis for legislation. Representative Robert Allen of West Virginia explained: "The primary reason for restriction of the alien stream, however, is the necessity for purifying and keeping pure the blood of America."[2]

Representative John N. Vaile of Colorado summed up the mentality of the day when he said:

"Let me emphasize here that the 'restrictionists' of Congress do not claim that the 'Nordic' race, or even the Anglo-Saxon race, is the best race in the world. Let us concede, in all fairness, that the Czech is a more sturdy laborer, with a very low percentage of crime and insanity, that the Jew is the best business man in the world, and that the Italian has a spiritual grasp and an artistic sense which have greatly enriched the world and which have, indeed, enriched us all. ... What we do claim is that the northern European, and particularly Anglo-Saxons, made this country. Oh, yes, the others helped. But that is the full statement of the case. They came to this country because it was already made as an Anglo-Saxon commonwealth. They added to it, they often enriched it, but they did not make it, and they have not yet greatly changed it. We are determined that they shall not. It is a good country. It suits us. And what we assert is that we are not going to surrender it to somebody else or allow other people, no matter what their merits, to make it something different. If there is any changing to be done, we will do it ourselves."[3]

How did the Administration in power view this? A representative stated before Congress that it was ". . . one of the greatest achievements of the domestic policies of the Republican Administration. . . ."[4]

These and many other similar statements can be found in the House Congressional Records for April 1924. The Immigration Restriction Act (1924) was modified by the Cellar Act of 1965 but, for the most part, remains in force today.

The Eugenic Sterilization Laws in America

The Eugenic Sterilization Laws which had been passed in thirty states in America by 1931 were another example of popularized genetics directing state-enacted legislation. Some over-enthusiastic eugenicists had secretly performed sterilization procedures as early as the 1890's. Dr. F. Hoyt Pilcher castrated forty-four boys and sterilized fourteen girls at the Kansas State Institution for the Feeble-minded (1897). Dr. Harry C. Sharpe, who devised the vasectomy operation, sterilized between 600 and 700 boys at an Indiana Reformatory—well before the passage of the Indiana Sterilization Law of 1907. Most if not all those sterilized were white, non-Nordic and poor. Minorities of color were not only denied admission because of segregation policies but also constituted a very small percentage of the "inner city" population at whom these eugenic measures were directed. The candidates for sterilization included the mentally ill, mentally retarded (feeble-minded), epileptic, those infected with TB or VD, prostitutes, criminals and paupers—all conditions believed to be inherited at that time.

Today twenty-six states still have Eugenic Sterilization Laws. A study of states without sterilization laws revealed that several institution officials admitted performing sterilizations both with and without parental consent. There has been a recent shift from the eugenic emphasis of old to a new emphasis on sterilization as a means of reducing welfare recipients; making it a requirement for parole, for those classified as mentally retarded and socially inadequate, and people associated with drugs.[5]

The most recent legislation inspired by popularized genetics aimed at a particular segment of the American population has been the passage of Sickle Cell testing and counseling laws, both voluntary and compulsory, for Blacks. The politicizing and over-reacting associated with this particular genetic disorder has affected industry, insurance companies and the public and many other agencies in a manner unequaled by any of the other 1,880 genetic diseases known.

The Strict Constructionist

Most people can remember the recent struggles between President Nixon and the legislative bodies over his choice of Haynesworth and Carswell as the Administration's ideals of strict constructionists for Supreme Court vacancies. A strict constructionist is an individual who claims to interpret the Constitution along its most narrow terms—the very nature of which enhances the position of the privileged classes. He emphasizes the letter of the Constitution rather than the spirit. The spirit would usually afford a broader interpretation based on "The Federalist Papers," notes, minutes of the Constitutional Convention and writings of famous statesmen. Strict constructionists have been found for the unoccupied seats on the Supreme Court during the late 1960's and early 1970's. It has resulted in general reversal of policies assigned to deal with unequal treatment of Blacks and other minorities who must depend on the courts for most social justice. The strict constructionists who governed during the anti-immigrant administrations of the 1920's quoted George Washington who said:

> "Against the insidious wiles of foreign influence, I conjure you to believe me, fellow citizens, that jealousy of a free people ought to be constantly awake, since history and experience prove that foreign influence is one of the most baneful foes of republican government."[6]

Benjamin Franklin was frequently cited as expressing his

feelings about immigrants in this manner: "Those who come hither are generally the most stupid of their nation."[7] He made this statement on May 9, 1753.

Today, as in the 1920's many people fearing social and economic displacement are again questioning the meaning of the phrase "all men are created equal." During the 1920's, a period of all-out anti-immigrant feeling, it meant that the Englishmen who came to America were just as good as the Englishmen who stayed in England. Now, in the 1970's, a period of anti-black sentiment, it means that the non-Nordics are as good as the Nordics and have collectively earned the title of "Anglo-Americans."

Superpatriotism and Religion

Superpatriotism with religious fervor is often used to legitimatize almost everything from Vietnams to Watergates. This was also the case back in the early 1900's when it was used to legitimatize and dignify America's first exercise in institutionalized racism against the immigrants. Nordic or Anglo-Saxon superiority was supported not only by many patriotic and heritage clubs but also religious groups. The clergy preached the need for encouraging a higher birth rate among the "genetically gifted," meaning the northern Europeans.

The "Communist or red scare" has always served the superpatriot. He explains away all of his critics and opponents as Communists or subversives. Any attempt by the immigrants to challenge the establishment of the day was construed to be a "Communist plot." Anti-Communism, anti-Semitism and anti-Catholicism provided a hard core following for the Immigration Restriction Act of 1921 which was to receive final passage in a form acceptable to more representatives of the establishment in the 1924 Act. History repeated itself, as can be seen in this relevant piece of history. On May 6, 1973, R. W. Apple, Jr., White House correspondent for *The New York Times,* wrote of President

Nixon's former Chief of Staff Harry R. Haldeman: "His grandfather had been one of the originators of the Better American Foundation, an early anti-communist organization, and Haldeman shared his views." On examining a few old articles about this organization, I found that a Mr. Harry M. Haldeman had founded the Better America Federation in Los Angeles, California, around 1910. From the description of various activities which took place, the organization would fit the "anti-immigrant, pro-eugenic" syndrome of the 1900's complete with anti-Communist, anti-labor, anti-welfare, anti-Catholic, pro-privilege class and pro-management sentiments. According to one article its superpatriotic fervor inspired an active espionage service. George P. West had this to say in 1921 about the Better America Federation:

"Senator Inman of Sacramento led the State Administration fight for the King bill to increase the taxes of corporations. In a final appeal on the floor of the Senate he bitterly denounced the Better America Federation and Mr. Haldeman by name, charging that they planned the capture of the next legislature and the election of a Governor in order to 'reopen the doors of the Capitol to specific privilege. They simply want big business to be free to engage in unregulated and unbridled exploitation of the people. The greedy advantage of the few, as against the many, is their religion.' "[8]

He goes on to say: "Atrocious bullies can no longer carry things with a high hand by wrapping themselves in the flag they have disgraced."[9] A recent example in Newark brings this to the present day. The white citizens of the North Ward were led by Assemblyman Imperiale in picketing the Kawaida Towers construction site, a black enterprise. The whites carried American flags and sang "God Bless America." Perhaps the time has come to challenge the superpatriot in the terms that he understands in order to beat him at his own game. When one thinks of the length of time and amount of service that Blacks have given in America, they had just as much right to carry the American flag and sing "God Bless America."

Ethnic Voting Blocs

During the 1970's, members of the present Republican Administration spelled out in several articles just how they would build a new majority based on the ethnic vote of Italians, Greeks, Poles and Jews and other non-Nordic whites. The irony of history is that they were rebuilding the very voting blocs that their Nordic grandparents had tried to destroy. Edward R. Lewis in his essay entitled "European Prejudices and American Politics" complained:

"Such numbers, living largely in racial colonies, long retain ancestral prejudices. They vote, to a large extent, as racial units. For seventy-five years we have had a German and an Irish vote, and now in addition, we have a Greek vote, an Italian vote, and a Polish vote. The county offices and the judgeships in these large cities have been deliberately parceled out among the various racial groups."[10]

He wrote this essay in the early 1900's and made a further statement which pretty much sums up the plight of the native minorities of color:

"We appear today to be more concerned with the alien prejudices of our voters than with America's needs. One man, claiming to represent an alien group, gets more attention than a hundred native born and native thinking Americans."[11]

No discussion of ethnic voting would be complete without some attention to the private versus public school issue and the "Law and Order" craze.

In the early 1900's America was divided into two separate societies—one northern European and one non-northern European (immigrants, Jews and Catholics) much the same as it is divided today into white and non-white societies now that the Black is presenting an economic threat in the 1970's. The northern Europeans fled to the suburbs; they built private schools for their children; they withdrew to private clubs; and they formed anti-Communist, anti-immigrant, anti-labor, anti-Catholic, anti-welfare reform, superpatriotic and eugenic leagues. The parochial schools have only recently become the focus of much attention and government financial and moral support as the establishment has gained a larger non-Nordic representation. In the early 1900's the general attitude was clearly expressed by Madison Grant: "They came into conflict with the native Americans by trying to introduce their church institutions and parochial schools, which were and are regarded as hostile to the public school system of the United States."[12]

Today in America it is not uncommon to have public school boards composed of several people whose children have or are attending private and parochial schools and/or who hold sometimes significantly prominent positions in national organizations dedicated to the growth and expansion of parochial schools. And yet citizens expect these people to be sensitive to the 1970 problems in the public schools. It is interesting that with the present talk of voucher systems, parochial aid and resistance to busing, we now see articles and editorials questioning whether quality education and even public school education are rights guaranteed by the Constitution. This calculated destruction of public schools coupled with Revenue Sharing comes at a time when the Blacks and other minorities of color are becoming an economic threat.

The native-born Americans who were the "Law and Order" advocates of the 1900's felt that the immigrants caused a "rising tide of crime." Congressman Lilly in defense of the Restriction Act stated: "If you will scan the court records, you will find that more than 50 percent of the persons convicted of high crimes and misdemeanors are of foreign birth."[13] Just as the riots of 1967 caused increased preoccupation with law and order tactics, even renewed interest in psycho-surgery, Albert E. Wiggam in 1924 felt that alien restriction, sterilization laws and other stringent methods would be needed to control the immigrants whom he saw as the "crime ridden or prone" population of that period in history. He said:

"It [immigrant blood or heredity] has cost America a large share of its labor troubles, its political chaos, many of its frightful riots and bombings—the doings and undoings of its undesirable citizens. Investigation proves that an enormous portion of its undesirable citizens are descended from undesirable blood overseas. America's immigration problem is mainly a problem of blood."[14]

Heredity and Environment

Conservative attitudes on social and public policy depend quite heavily on "heredity" for justification. The political power seeks out individuals who claim to have scientific evidence that attempts to provide equal opportunity will be wasted on a given target population since they are believed to be biologically inferior and thus unequal to the establishment in genetic terms. Jensen's pronouncements in 1969 helped pave the way for the indiscriminate destruction and dismantling of the Office of Economic Opportunity programs and were direct attacks on compensatory education, such as Title I, Get Set and Headstart. He claimed that Blacks scored lower than whites even when matched for socio-economic background. His explanation for this difference was that it was due to genetic deficiencies rather than environmental differences. Like the racist reports of the early 1900's, his 123-page review of the literature was read into the House Congressional Record in 1970. In 1924 a representative was talking about the genetic deficiencies of the non-Nordic white immigrants when he made his pronouncement in the House Congressional Record: "We are slowly awakening to the consciousness that education and environment do not fundamentally alter racial values."[15]

This statement had originally been made by Dr. Henry Fairfield Osborn, a paleontologist at the Museum of Natural History in 1924. These same beliefs held back then by people from all disciplines are widespread among the different disciplines today—from educators to physicists to legislators. Just as one had to be Nordic to be an expert on "non-Nordic inferiority," today, 1970, one must be white to be an expert on "nonwhite inferiority." All heredity advocates (the proponents of racial superiority) usually stress their non-partisan interest in letting the "scientific chips fall where they may." It is more than a coincidence that D. J. Armor, a teacher at Harvard, in discussing the "intellectual inferiority" of Blacks in 1972 said:

"Since I am a scientist I feel that it is wrong to keep the findings from the community—that goes against the ethics of being a scientist; we must not suppress data just because they have negative consequences."[16]

In 1924 when Harry R. Laughlin was discussing the "intellectual inferiority" of non-Nordic whites, he said:

"If, because of these reports, those who favor a restriction of numbers and a rigid selection of immigrants have found more ammunition than those who favor open immigration, that is a sequence for which the investigator is not responsible."[17]

Thus just as the Nordic professionals "documented" immigrant or non-Nordic incapacity for learning in the 1900's, the white professionals of 1973 are attempting to "document" nonwhite or black incapacity for learning. The character deficiencies, for instance, of the Irish Catholics in the 1920's "documented" by people like Madison Grant and Edward A. Ross, a sociologist, were biased, weighty and burdensome to Moynihan's grandparents. In modern times, Professor Moynihan's pronouncements and "modest proposals" for Black Americans have caused an equal amount of political and racist mischief.

Intelligence or IQ Testing

In most cases the heredity versus environment argument begins and ends on the subject of IQ testing. Most people have been led to believe that the IQ test is a measure of innate potential for learning. They also believe that IQ tests measure intelligence while achievement tests measure what has been learned. The fact is this: If any psychologist were asked to lay down his or her life as proof that innate intelligence could be accurately measured there would be no volunteers. What then are they measuring? They are measuring the likelihood or predictability of academic success in an Anglo-dominated country and public school system; the degree of exposure and assimilation into the dominant culture and value system; the likelihood that a given child will or will not survive in a school system which has yet to respect his cultural background. Thus, the further away from the life style of the Anglicized child, the greater the difference in scoring. A mature investigator who is knowledgeable in cultural and language differences would find the so-called differences—IQ or other tests—between individuals of different races of about the same magnitude as those found between individuals of the same race.

In the early 1900's Edward L. Thorndike of Columbia observed that "equal educational opportunity" only served to put the faster group even further ahead.[18] During the same period, Lewis M. Termen, a professor at Leland Stanford, gave IQ tests to California schoolchildren and found that superior intelligence was "five times as common among children of superior social status as among children of inferior social status."[19]

These and other men found similar correlations between professional status of parents, level of skilled labor and area of residence. Correlations of these types would be expected but racism added another dimension. Since immigrants were poor, without social status and un-Americanized at that point in history, the testers read "innate intellectual inferiority" into their results. At this point in history the non-Nordic immigrants' children have been Anglicized and now the same disparities in tests previously found for the immigrants are found for the minorities of color.

The serious consequences of the intelligence testing game have not changed. In 1973 about 70 to 75 percent of Black and Hispanic children placed in classes for the mentally retarded are by medical and legal definitions not mentally retarded. This is a national phenomenon. Most states have specific laws and regulations which legalize this administrative misuse of a medically and legally defined condition—Educable Mental Retardation. These children so labeled by the schools are known in professional circles as the "Six Hour Retardates." Both Black and white professionals are aware of this misadventure. However, the major challenges so far have had to be initiated by parents who had enough guts to go to court. Thus IQ testing has been stopped in California. Both New York and Massachusetts have set up new procedures for evaluating learning problems. There is really no reason that individuals and small groups of Black and Hispanic parents should have to fight this form of child abuse in each local school district around the country. This issue could give Black professionals the opportunity to demonstrate some social responsibility on a national level.

Perhaps everyone involved in the classification of children as "borderline mentally retarded" or "Educable" needs to be made aware of the rationale of the modern day anti-Black eugenicists like Jensen and Shockley when they warn about a "dysgenic threat" and the need to utilize Eugenic Sterilization for people with low IQs. Their feeling is that most of these individuals are Black.[20] Moya Woodside, a psychiatric social worker from England, expressed it rather well:

"It is rather those dull and stupid individuals, of border-line intelligence, yet not sufficiently abnormal to require community care, who constitute the greatest menace to the preservation of sound and healthy human stock. Dullness is antecedent to defect; dull or defective children are more likely to be born to parents of this caliber than to parents of normal intelligence; the fertility of the least intelligent families is much higher than that of those at the other end of the scale. Like tends to mate with like, and all observations, psychiatric or sociological, confirm the tendency toward similarity of intelligence of marriage partners. Hence, although normal genes are dominant over those for feeble-mindedness, it is improbable that a normal person would choose to marry a defective or markedly dull individual, and such partner as they find is likely also to be of relatively low intelligence. Inbreeding of this sort tends to perpetuate not only mental dullness but a variety of other handicaps—epilepsy, insanity, physical defect—which have been noted as characteristic of subnormal groups."[21]

More about Dysgenic Threats

A dysgenic threat may be defined as the accumulation of bad or undesirable genes in a given population. According to the eugenic mind, a dysgenic threat occurs if the "biologically unfit" are allowed to reproduce or if programs such as welfare, medical services or community improvements are made available to the "unfit."

The Social Darwinistic thinking of the eugenicists in the 1900's was to believe that any government efforts to legislate social or welfare reforms were an infringement of the individual's right to be poor and an infringement of the taxpayer's right to keep his earnings. In supporting the "unfit" these welfare programs would interfere with natural selection or the survival of the fittest. The general consensus of those who had money was that if a poor man was genetically fit, he would rise out of his poverty. Self-help and competition were the key to success. Madison Grant was complaining about the immigrants when he said:

"Where altruism, philanthropy or sentimentalism intervene with the noblest purpose and forbid nature to penalize the unfortunate victims of reckless breeding, the multiplication of inferior types is encouraged and fostered."[22]

It is interesting to note that the American establishment of the 1920's complained loudly about giving welfare (called dole or bonus legislation) for the immigrants. William Starr Myers summed up the establishment attitude when he wrote:

"Instead of following a sound American idea and ideal, that of helping people to help themselves, and thus preserving equality of opportunity, we have presented the plan of helping people in spite of themselves, a paternalistic idea brought here from the decadent feudalism of Continental Europe."[23]

Thus any programs covering a broad range of comprehensive services like those under OEO would to the eugenic mind pose a dysgenic threat. This was the case in 1900 and it seems to be the case now in 1970—only the color of the minority has changed.

Birth control was seen as a double-edged sword. It was meant for the immigrants but the eugenicists were well represented by Wiggam when he said that there was "immense danger that our birth controllers will influence limitation of families in the one class that ought not to limit its birth rate to any great extent."[24] Eugenicists who believe in white race superiority today must be quite nervous. The greatest impact of "the pill" was felt by white adoption agencies that had previously conducted a lucrative business of placing white infants for adoption. (Adoption fees have, in the past, contributed significantly to these agencies' income.) Some agencies over the past few years have been forced to close because of "the pill." And now the liberalized abortion laws, which are used more extensively by whites, have almost eliminated white babies available for adoption. It is quite possible that a significant amount of opposition to the recent Supreme Court decision on abortions is seen as detrimental both to the adoption agencies and white population growth. These reasons have probably not come to the attention of the public because they are less attractive than the religious or morality argument which have a very vocal following.

The Present and Past State of Human Experimentation

According to Dr. Donald T. Chalkley of the National Institute of Health, controversy over unethical human research in the U.S. rages

> "around less than a dozen projects. ... Four of these activities involved Blacks, four of them involved children, two of them involved Mexican-Americans, one of them was restricted to Jews, and one involved mentally retarded children."[25]

Most of these experiments were initiated in the 1950's. There is even greater cause for alarm to find that in these times Dr. Bernard Barber of Barnard College has found that "as many as 28 percent of our respondents would approve such a high-risk study where no proportionate therapeutic benefits to the subjects are provided."[26] Who were the respondents? 293 research institutions; 331 active researchers at a University-Research Hospital Center and 256 researchers at a Community-Teaching Hospital. Who is the most likely target population or captive audience? The inner city Blacks and Hispanics who fill the hospital wards, make up the majority of prisoners, and fill the city public schools.

The possibility of other Tuskegee-type experiments is not as remote as it seems.

The Tuskegee experiment which permitted the use of Black males as subjects for a syphilis study (some were treated while others went untreated so that the various stages of syphilis could be observed) occurred at an interesting time in American eugenic history. The Depression of the 1930's helped to end the notion of Nordic superiority which had been based primarily on wealth and social status. Another event eventually upset the American people. Several American eugenicists admired Hitler's eugenic programs (250,000 sterilizations in six years) and swore that his activities were not racially oriented. But the mass exterminations between 1939 and 1941 caused many Americans to retreat in horror from their preoccupation with eugenics. It is regrettable that this sudden surge of humanism and compassion did not extend to the non-white people. Thus, the Public Health Service experiment, better known as the Tuskegee Study, was started around 1933 and terminated only last year in 1972. We know that this new respect for man did not include the non-white man—not in America, not in Hiroshima, not in Vietnam and not in South Africa.

As reviewed in the February 1973 issue of *Ebony,* the use and suggested use of psycho-surgery as a solution for the "prevention of violence" grew because of the riots of the 1960's and because of generous funding from the Justice Department's Law Enforcement Assistance Administration. The purpose of the funding was to screen "habitually violent" male prisoners for "brain damage."[27] Unless there are close scrutiny and constant surveillance, psycho-surgery could become a modern and more acceptable form of extermination—neurological euthanasia. We see in these cases of human experimentation and manipulation a continuation of the history of abuse of and disrespect for the powerless— whoever they are—during a given period of history. In the 1970's Dr. Orlando J. Andy of the University of Mississippi Medical School has been criticized for performing thirty to forty "unjustifiable" brain operations on institutionalized individuals–mostly children. Dr. Willard Gaylin of the Hastings Institute has termed Dr. Andy's methods of diagnosis, selection of patient and follow-up as "casual to the point of irresponsibility" and has emphasized Andy's "limited sensitivity to the ethical issues."[28]

Thus in this climate of past and present ongoing politicized genetic exercises and beliefs in racial inferiority, the political Sickle Cell crisis was born in 1971. While it is felt that many Americans–both Black and white–believe that all Blacks should be screened for Sickle Cell Trait–by law, school-based programs or any other method–most Americans do not believe that all Jews should be screened for Tay Sachs; that all Italians and Greeks should be screened for Cooley's Anemia; that all northern Europeans should be screened for PKU (Phenylketonuria), Cystic Fibrosis and Muscular Dystrophy; or that all pregnant women forty years old or above should be required to undergo amniocentesis to detect mongoloidism. The interesting fact of history is that few people would have seen anything wrong or potentially abusive if Tay Sachs or Cooley's Anemia had been so politicized and popularized in the early 1900's when institutionalized racism was directed at the immigrants from central, eastern and southern Europe.

Conclusion

A relatively unpublicized period of American history from the 1890's through the 1930's reveals that Blacks are not the first American citizens to have experienced blatant forms of racism at the hands of their fellow Americans. The white Anglo-Saxon Protestants or Nordics feared competition and economic displacement by the non-Nordic immigrants. They used every means to prove that the immigrants were genetically inferior and passed repressive legislation based on this as justification. Now because they present an economic threat, the Blacks and other minorities of color are expected to suffer through the same pages of history at the pleasure of the children of the old Nordics and the Anglicized children of the old immigrants. This is white American history that every Black should know. And it is just as important that every Black let white Americans know that he knows it.

"Those who cannot remember the past are condemned to repeat it."

George Santayana
(1863-1952)

References

[1] Kenneth M. Ludmerer, *Genetics and American Society* (Baltimore, Johns Hopkins University Press, 1972), p. 101

[2] Congressional Record–House (April 5, 1924), p. 5693

[3] *Ibid.* (April 8, 1924), p. 5922

[4] *Ibid.* (April 5, 1924), p. 5640

[5] E. Z. Ferster, "Eliminating the Unfit–Is Sterilization the Answer?" *Ohio State Law Journal*, 27: 591-633 (1966)

[6] *The Writings of George Washington,* collected and edited by W. C. Ford, Letter-Press Edition, 1889, Vol. XII, p. 315 cited in *The Alien in Our Midst,* ed. Madison Grant and Chas. S. Davison (New York: Galton Pub. Co. Inc., 1930), p. 238

[7] *The Complete Works of Benjamin Franklin,* compiled and edited by J. Bigelow, Letter-Press Edition, 1887, Vol. II, p. 291 and *Ibid.,* p. 112

[8] G.P. West, *The Nation,* pp. 112, 869 (1921)

[9] *Ibid.,* p. 869

[10] Edward R. Lewis, "European Prejudices and American Politics," in *The Alien in Our Midst,* ed. Grant & Davison, p. 180

[11] *Ibid.*, p. 187

[12] Madison Grant, "Closing the Flood-Gates," *Ibid.*, p. 17

[13] Congressional Record—House (April 5, 1924), p. 5694

[14] Albert E. Wiggam, *The Fruit of the Family Tree* (Indianapolis: Bobbs-Merrill Co., 1924), pp. 6, 7

[15] Congressional Record—House (April 5, 1924), p. 5641

[16] *Boston Globe,* June 4, 1972

[17] Ludmerer, *Genetics and American Society,* p. 102

[18] Wiggam, *The Fruit of the Family Tree,* p. 174

[19] *Ibid.*, p. 182

[20] *Chemical and Engineering News* (May 8, 1972), p. 4

[21] Moya Woodside, *Sterilization in North Carolina: A Sociological and Psychological Study* (Chapel Hill: Univ. of North Carolina Press, 1950), p. 103

[22] Madison Grant, *The Passing of the Great Race* (New York: Charles Scribner's Sons, 1918), p. 48

[23] W. S. Myers, "Political Aspects of Immigration," Grant & Davison, ed. *The Alien in Our Midst,* p. 201

[24] Wiggam, *The Fruit of the Family Tree,* p. 323

[25] *Medical World News* (June 8, 1973), pp. 45, 50

[26] *Ibid.*, p. 50

[27] B. J. Mason, "New Threat to Blacks: Brain Surgery to Control Behavior," *Ebony,* February 1973; J. Brody, "Psychosurgery to Face Key Test Today in Midwest Courtroom," *The New York Times* (March 12, 1973)

[28] C. Holden, *Science,* pp. 179, 1112 (1973)

Reverse Racism:
The Great White Hoax

Celia Zitron

The failure of the United States Supreme Court majority to act on the constitutional issue in the De Funis "racism in reverse" appeal against the admissions policy of the Law School of the University of Washington has not lessened the dangerous implications of that case.

John Abt, noted civil liberties lawyer, warned in the *Daily World* magazine (March 24, 1974):

> "At stake is not only the preferential admissions policy of the University of Washington Law School but of every state-supported university at every level, graduate and undergraduate. ... The equal protection clause would thus become the constitutional pretext for the protection of privileges spawned by three centuries of white supremacy."

The appeal was undertaken in the climate of opinion created by the determination of the Nixon and Ford administrations to wipe out the gains won by the unprecedented Civil Rights movement of the 1960's. In education, as elsewhere, they have played upon the pervasive open as well as unacknowledged racism in our country to increase divisions and racial strife—useful tools for implementing an overall destructive program. The effects have ranged from anti-busing, anti-integration violence on the elementary and secondary school levels to assaults on opportunities for higher education for Blacks and other oppressed minorities.

Educational institutions, from the kindergartens through the universities, are reeling from budgetary cuts unparalleled since the depression days of the 1930's. But some white

154

organizations and individuals—including a number of those who at one time or another supported the Civil Rights movement—look upon the minimal and precarious advances of minorities as responsible for the loss of educational and professional opportunities. From its inception, the De Funis case was used as a means for justifying and promoting this approach to the problem of growing scarcity in the educational field.

De Funis, a white student, was not accepted for admission to the University of Washington Law School in 1971. (There were some 1,600 applicants for about 145 openings.) At the same time, the applications were accepted of thirty-six qualified minority students whose scores, based on college grades and national law school entrance examinations, were lower than those of De Funis. De Funis appealed to the Washington state courts on the ground that his right to equal protection of the laws had been violated. He won his appeal and was admitted to the Law School where he pursued his studies until his graduation in the spring of 1975.

However, before De Funis' graduation, the state's Supreme Court reversed the decision of the lower court. De Funis, with counsel supplied by the Anti-Defamation League of B'nai B'rith, appealed to the United States Supreme Court. At the same time that the applications of the lower scoring minority students were accepted, thirty-eight white applicants with scores lower than De Funis' had also been admitted; yet no objections were raised to their admission in the De Funis briefs. During oral argument before the court his attorneys made it clear that, in judging the applications of white students at the University of Washington or at other institutions of higher education, they were not questioning the use of criteria beyond those based on strictly observed entrance requirements. *Only in the case of preferential action on behalf of non-white students did they find a violation of the Constitution!*

Counsel for the Law School admitted that admissions were based on the use of separate lists of white and minority applicants; they pointed out, however, that this did not constitute a "quota" system. It was, they explained, an effort to apply affirmative action to counteract the effects of years of discrimination against non-white minorities. Washington State Attorney General Slade Gorton pointed out that in sixty-seven years of the Law School's existence only twelve of the 3,812 graduates had been Black; i.e. 0.5 of one percent. In 1969–70 there were eight Black students at the school out of a total enrollment of 356.

The Law School administration maintained that its affirmative action program had an "overriding purpose," to "increase the number of minority lawyers in the state and in the nation, and to provide a diversified student body that would aid both minority and majority students in their preparations for dealing with a pluralistic society."

Gorton argued that numerical scores "are not totally accurate predictions of success, nor do they solve the problem of ending the effects of racial discrimination. ...." He said the minority students would, because of their race and experience, "contribute more" to their law school class and to the bar than De Funis.

A brief prepared by counsel for the Law School stated: "The 14th Amendment was never intended to frustrate such remedial efforts." But the B'nai B'rith brief declared:

"If the Constitution prohibits exclusion of Blacks on racial grounds, it cannot permit the exclusion of whites on racial grounds. For it must be the exclusion on racial grounds which offends the Constitution, and not the particular skin color of the person excluded."

Continuing this bland disregard of reality–that discrimination against non-white minorities is on the increase–the brief continued:

"For at least a generation, the great decisions of the Court have been the same: Discrimination on the basis of race is illegal, immoral, unconstitutional, inherently wrong, and destructive of democratic society. Now that is to be

unlearned and we are told that it is not a matter of fundamental principle, but only a matter of whose ox is gored."

It is tragic that the B'nai B'rith brief made the rejection
of De Funis' application and the Law School's efforts to increase the number of non-white students a Jewish vs. Black
American issue. The brief recalled the long use of quotas
to keep the number of Jewish students in colleges and universities down to the barest minimum and charged that the
affirmative action policies like those at the Law School
would once again "set the style in excluding Jewish students." This makes the unwarranted assumption that De
Funis was excluded because he is Jewish. It adds to the
confusion created by the "quota" argument–putting the imposition of quotas on Jews both in Europe and the United
States into the same category as policies intended to open
the doors to almost totally excluded minorities.

Racism is inherent in the B'nai B'rith attorneys' basic
argument which would allow departures from strict admission rules for all but non-white applicants. It is painfully
explicit in one of their other briefs filed in support of the
De Funis appeal. As quoted in the *New York Times* magazine article "Discrimination to End Discrimination" (April
14, 1974), it stated:

"The predominance of whites in the university law school
may well be explained by a lack of inclination or aptitude
on the part of Blacks for such studies. Any observant
person knows that certain races have bents and inclina-
tions. . . ."

In its April 23, 1974, 5-4 decision, The United States
Supreme Court majority ruled that the De Funis appeal was
moot, since he was actually attending the University of
Washington Law School. But it said: "If the admission
procedures of the law school remain unchanged, there is no reason to suppose that a subsequent case attacking those procedures will not come with relative speed to this court. . . ."

Justice William O. Douglas, in an individual dissenting opinion, said that any policies which are not "racially neutral" are unconstitutional violations of the "equal protection under the law" doctrine.

Although a clear-cut decision on the constitutionality of the Law School's admission policies has been deferred, the De Funis case has already served to make some supporters of affirmative action cautious and has made the opposition more vocal and more insistent.

James Wilson, University of Washington counsel who argued the Law School's case before the United States Supreme Court, is quoted as saying (*The New York Times*, April 20, 1975):

> "I've said so far that they [the Law School] do not have to change their policies in the light of this decision and the Douglas dissent, but that does not mean that they should not study their whole program and see what they would deem appropriate. But I don't think they're compelled to."

De Funis Sets the Tone

There is no doubt that more law schools and other educational institutions will be studying their admission policies if they have undertaken affirmative action. There is a possibility that another case involving the medical profession may also be on its way to the courts. The recently established Center of Biomedical Education of the City University of New York (CUNY) is under attack by forces within and outside. That program is a six-year, tuition-free course of study which will enable its graduates to complete a medical course in two years at cooperating medical schools.

In May 1974, it was reported that the Anti-Defamation League of B'nai B'rith was preparing a brief on behalf of two white applicants who had not been admitted to the Center. In March 1975, the American Jewish Congress asked New York State Commissioner of Education Ewald B.

Nyquist to investigate charges of "reverse discrimination" in the Center's admission policy. Chancellor Robert J. Kibbee of CUNY replied that the Center was intended to train doctors for service in poor urban areas; that consideration of applicants' willingness to dedicate themselves to that service contributed to the enrollment of minority candidates. Nevertheless, there has been a backing down in the face of the attacks, a promise that "quotas" would be scrupulously avoided.

Further, in the De Funis case the line-up of forces was not one-sided. Amicus briefs were submitted by some sixty organizations. Among the supporters of this "racism in reverse" position were the major Jewish organizations—the Anti-Defamation League of B'nai B'rith, the American Jewish Congress, and the American Jewish Committee; there were also the United States Chamber of Commerce, the National Association of Manufacturers and the AFL-CIO.

However, on the side of the Law School one finds the United Automobile Workers, the United Farm Workers, and the United Mine Workers as well as the Council of Jewish Women and the NAACP Legal Defense and Educational Fund. Support also came from the legal profession: the American Bar Association (which itself excluded Blacks until 1943) and from deans and admission officers of law schools.

In colleges and universities, there is concern about the scuttling of affirmative action programs. A full-page advertisement in Section 4 of *The New York Times* (April 6, 1975), sponsored by The Committee for Affirmative Action—Universities and signed by hundreds of faculty members, called on President Ford to insure implementation of affirmative action regulations. On the other side, a quaintly named Committee of Academic Nondiscrimination and Integrity led by Sidney Hook, Nixon's favorite philosopher, has stepped up its attacks on "quotas."

It is no wonder that calls for an end to the SEEK program (organized in New York in 1966 to help promising students make up for earlier educational neglect) and attacks on the Open Admissions policy have increased. Yet these are not programs for minorities only. All applicants from poverty areas are considered for admission to SEEK. Open Admissions, adopted in 1970 in response to minority group-led demands and demonstrations for an increase in the number of non-white students, has benefited white working-class students as well. The enrollment of the first Open Admissions class was 60 percent white.

CUNY never had the space, the adequate counseling and remedial services for the large number of Open Admissions students whose education had been neglected in the lower schools—especially in the segregated, largely Black and Puerto Rican high schools. The failures and dropouts resulting from these conditions are used by self-professed defenders of "academic standards" as reasons for scuttling the program.

The entire Open Admissions program is being drastically curtailed. For the first time since the inception of the program, applications for the fall 1975 semester which arrived late, for whatever reasons, have been rejected—5,000 as of July, with 22,000 still to be processed.

There are constant complaints that Blacks and other minorities are favored in the hiring of teachers in the colleges and universities. Yet, as Tom Wicker reported in his *New York Times* column (January 14, 1975):

"Statistics from the American Council on Education show that in 1969 2.2 percent of college and university positions were held by Blacks, and 19.1 percent by women. By 1973 (the latest year for which figures are available) these percentages had grown scarcely at all—2.9 percent for Blacks and to 20 percent for women. ..."

The outcry against "quotas" is equally strident in opposition to efforts to increase the number of Blacks, Latins, Chicanos, American Indians, and Asians in the elementary and secondary schools. In a 1973 report Mark Ethridge, director of the Teacher Rights program of the National Education Association (NEA), cited figures to show that overall 211,000 additional non-white teachers would have to be appointed to the nation's public schools to "bring about parity and equity." The fight against "quotas" is led by Albert Shanker, president of the American Federation of Teachers (AFT), executive vice-president of the New York City United Federation of Teachers, the real power in the New York State United Teachers (NYSUT) and a close collaborator with George Meany on the AFL-CIO executive council.

At colleges and universities efforts to increase the number of minority students have been reduced or dropped entirely as the anti-minority drive and the economic crisis gain momentum. "Changing Criteria" is the heading of an article in the *Wall Street Journal* (March 25, 1974). The subhead explains: "More Colleges Grant Scholarships on Merit Not Need." Actually, as the article makes clear, scholarships are granted to those middle-class, mainly white students who can pay a good part of the skyrocketing tuition costs.

According to a report based on a survey by the College Entrance Examination Board, tuition fees alone–not including board, fees and other expenses–were expected to go up by 6 to 8 percent in the fall of 1975: to $2,240 a year on the average at private colleges and $576 for in-state residents of public colleges.

In New York City, the target of the attack on CUNY was the policy of free tuition for undergraduates. It was launched by Nelson Rockefeller when he was the governor of New York State. President Ford called it one of the city's main extravagances; its abolition is one of the conditions set by bankers in control of city finances. Undergraduate student fees, already a heavy burden for students from poverty areas, are scheduled to go up by 50 percent: to at least $60 annually in the community colleges and $100 in the senior colleges. On the graduate level, the increase for residents of New York City will go up from $45 to $75 a credit, for non-residents from $70 to $95.

Fightback Is Needed

At CUNY, the struggle of students and many members of the faculty continues against the ending of the SEEK and Open Admissions programs and free tuition. Students have demonstrated against tuition increases and the cut in the number of non-white students at Brown, Brandeis and Boston Universities.

The controversy around "quotas" and school integration highlighted the 1975 conventions of the 470,000-member American Federation of Teachers (AFL-CIO) and the non-affiliated 1.7 million-member National Education Association. At the July NEA convention in Los Angeles the Shanker-controlled delegation of NYSUT, a merged AFT-NEA organization, campaigned for the removal from the NEA constitution of provisions designed to guarantee representation of minorities in proportion to their numbers in the population on elected bodies and leading committees. The move was decisively defeated. At the AFT convention in Hawaii, later the same month, however, Black caucus resolutions in support of busing for integration in Boston and condemning the violence of the opposition were defeated. But there was such widespread support for the Black caucus resolutions (extending beyond the ranks of the United Action Caucus, the major opposition caucus in the AFT) that Shanker felt the need to step down from the chair to make a special plea for the defeat of the resolutions.

The fight against educational deprivation of oppressed minority youth did not begin with opposition to the De Funis appeal, nor has it ended with the United States Supreme Court decision. It is a fight for effective integrated education for all young people on every level of the educational system in preparation for skilled work, advanced study, and the professions. It needs to be allied with every group working towards these ends in the schools and universities, among students and faculty, in the teachers' unions and in the trade union movement as a whole.

The fight against the De Funis appeal assumptions should

also be recognized as an integral part of the movement against unemployment. The arguments on which it is based are also used to reduce even further the fast diminishing efforts of government departments to secure implementation of anti-discrimination court decisions, laws and regulations. It urgently requires united action of all people. Black youth are the first to be laid off, the first to have educational opportunities reduced below the present low level. Under present ruling class policies, all working-class, and even large sections of middle-class youth face a bleak future.

"Time on the Cross": A Rallying Cry for Racists!

Brenda L. Jones

For all of those who were stunned to silence when Daniel P. Moynihan's "benign neglect" memo was flushed to light; for those who cringed in expectation of what would come after William Shockley's "genetic" theories won the protective cover of "academic freedom," comes the publication of Fogel and Engerman's *Time on the Cross;* and with its appearance we may say that not for many, many years have racist concepts paraded so nakedly before the American people. This book, which purports to be a profoundly scientific exposé of the "myth" of the horrors of U.S. slavery, exposes, instead, the ignorance and racism of its authors. With their mixture of "cliometrics" with some fragmented and distorted figures of the U.S. Census Bureau pertaining to the slavery period, they have attempted to elevate racism—the thing itself—to the level of a science. Claiming to have used only "data which can be subjected to systematic statistical tests," and claiming to exclude "fragmentary evidence from *objective sources* such as impressionistic reports of *'detached observers,'* " (quotes in original; my italics—B.J.) they have come up with "findings" which, at most, insult the intelligence and offend the democratic spirit.

Using a motley assortment of figures—most of which were discredited long before Fogel and Engerman got up the gall to write this offensive document—they offer "proof" for many

TIME ON THE CROSS: THE ECONOMICS OF AMERICAN NEGRO SLAVERY. By Robert William Fogel and Stanley L. Engerman, Little, Brown and Company, Boston-Toronto. 286 pages. $8.95.

"astounding" conclusions, the major one being that slaves actually had a stake in the system of slavery and, therefore, identified their interests with those of the slaveholders. Fogel and Engerman tell us: "This will be a disturbing book to read. ... It requires forebearance on the part of the reader and a recognition that what is set forth represents the honest efforts of scholars whose central aim has been the discovery of what really happened." These two "honest" and "scholarly" gentlemen would have us forebear while they cleanse away the filthy, barbarous realities of slavery–an institution by which they, themselves, are not horrified and disgusted; they are, in fact, somewhat *annoyed* by the horror and disgust of others! This leaves open the possibility, of course, that they are not honest and scholarly, truth-seeking gentlemen as they represent themselves, but are, instead, agents of the sickness of white supremacy. It is a white supremacy of the most reprehensible kind, since it seeks to masquerade as a "friend" of Afro-Americans; a "friend" whose only wish is to "correct the perversion of the history of blacks" and to ". . . expose many myths that have served to corrode and poison relations between the races."

Very well, then, let us for a moment take Fogel and Engerman at their word and examine some of the major "scientific" findings of *Time on the Cross.*

Chapter four opens with a dictionary definition of exploitation (as if Webster's could even begin to approach a definition of the magnitude of exploitation which obtained in U.S. slavery!) based upon which the authors agree that slaves were, indeed, exploited. But the important thing, they conclude, is not that this exploitation existed; that is clear enough. But it is that "the extent of that exploitation is less clear. How *frequent* was the mean and improper use of slaves and *how far did meanness go?* How much of the income produced by slaves was expropriated from them?" (my italics–B.J.)

This is the crux of the matter for Fogel and Engerman! Further, they take issue with "current histories of the antebellum south" in which "Both masters and slaves are painted as degraded brutes. Masters are vile because they are the perpetrators of unbridled exploitation; slaves are vile because they are the victims of it. How true to life is the portrait?" They continue:

> "The posing of these questions may seem irrelevant, even malicious. . . . To haggle over the extent of the exploitation suggests callousness to the agony of human bondage. . . . Slaveholders have long been driven from the stage of American life, and the descendants of slaveholders generally do not wish to dwell on the meaner aspects of their ancestry."

Fogel and Engerman, however, seem willing to sacrifice the wishes of the "descendants of slaveholders" to the "need to arrive at an accurate historical image of the black man," since

> ". . . it is widely assumed [we are never quite sure, from their account, exactly by *whom* and just *how widely* the assumption is held–B.J.] that the plantation regime under which most slaves lived was so cruel, the exploitation so severe, the repression so complete, that blacks were thoroughly demoralized by it."

Our "friends" then proceed to reconstruct some of the most vicious and vile stereotypes of Blacks ever put forth, most of which–at least in their most overt and reprehensible form–were laid to rest many years ago. Why are they summoning up the rank corpses of such ideas, and why now? To "arrive at an accurate historical image of the black man?" Can it be possible? This book claims to be a look at history, an attempt to correct our interpretation of the past; but it is, in actuality, a major attempt to influence the present and *future* prospects of Black people, indeed, all working people, for a just and equal share in American society.

It is in view of this fact that the arguments and conclusions of this book merit discussion; not based upon them-

selves, for thusly they are not worth the computer tape they
were printed upon. Therefore, I offer the following open
letter to Robert W. Fogel and Stanley L. Engerman in response to *Time on the Cross:*

"Gentlemen":
It is anticipated that the following data will not be acceptable for your computers. This does not disturb me since,
despite your claims, objective and computable data formed
a very minor part of your own presentation.

You have attempted to cover the tracks of the vile slaveholders in the following ways:

1) *You have launched a most unprincipled attack upon
the abolitionist movement.* "What bitter irony it is," you
state, "that the false stereotype of black labor—was fash-
ioned not primarily by the oppressors . . . but by the most
ardent opponents of slavery, by those who worked most dili-
gently to destroy the chains of bondage." You base this
viewpoint upon the perusal of a long list of more or less
obscure persons who were about as vital to the abolitionist
movement as your "findings" are to scientific research. You
say of the main critics of slavery that they were "northern
and southern whites" and that "with very few exceptions
they were all racists. . . ." Yet one is hard put to find any
mention whatsoever in your book of John Brown. Was Harpers Ferry the stuff that racists were made of? Do the white
Americans who fell, side by side with their oppressed Black
brothers at Harpers Ferry, where they had gone prepared to
lay down their lives for the anti-slavery cause, deserve no
mention, no consideration in your deliberations? Do they
not compute? Your slanderous attack upon the white abolitionists who, you say, "were often more gullible and quick
in their acceptance of certain racial stereotypes than slaveholders," is extremely deplorable; but it is no less deplorable
than your suggestion that the abolitionist movement was, in
the main, a movement of white people. This is further
evidence of your lack of belief in the abilities and, indeed,
humanity of Black people. For only those who have no

ability to think or reason, who are, in fact, no more human than horses or goats, would sit back and cringe, depending upon others to fight, alone, in battle for their freedom.

You refer to Frederick Douglass only once in your work, and then, as one name in a long list of writers with whom he could, by no honest measure, be compared. You shamelessly imply that he was a part of a school of thinkers who felt that "the slave was 'too primitive' to successfully adapt to the complexities of urban production and life." You give no hint as to the reference or context to back up this contention. But, we are not puzzled by your attempt to push Douglass into obscurity along with the racist figures with whom you claim to disassociate yourself. You say that "the evidence put forward to support the contention of [slave] breeding for the market is meager, indeed." But Frederick Douglass says, "I was born amid such sights and scenes. . . . I will show you a man-drover. They inhabit all our Southern states. They perambulate the country, and crowd the highways of the nation with droves of human stock."[1]* You say that ". . . slave marriages . . . were not only recognized but actively promoted under plantation codes." You have a good deal more faith in "plantation codes" than did Frederick Douglass. He recognized that "In Law, the slave has no wife, no children, no country and no home"[2] and that the slaveholder may ". . . maintain and respect the marriage institution for himself and for his family, for all this can be done selfishly; but while he robs any portion of the human family of the right of marriage, and takes from innocent women the protection of the law, no matter what his individual responsibility may be, he is to be classed with the vilest of the vile, and with the basest of the base."[3] Further, "The right of the hunter to his prey stands superior to the right of marriage."[4] It is clear that you have misrepresented Frederick Douglass because his *true* views make a mockery of your entire presentation!

2) *You say that the slave had a stake in the slave system*

* See notes at end of article.

168

(not nearly so great, we suspect, as your own stake in maintaining the system which oppresses and subjugates Afro-Americans today) *and therefore identified his interests with those of the slaveholder.* You report an "absence of evidence of massive resistance" and that "the most proponents of this view were able to conjure up were a handful of abortive conspiracies and ineffectual attempts at 'day to day' resistance." Can it be possible that you undertook the writing of a major book on slavery without familiarizing yourself with the names and stories of Denmark Vesey, Gabriel Prosser, David Walker, Nat Turner (whose rebellion you reduce to one sentence and say that "economic motivations led to the transformation of many of the death sentences into deportation orders"). Can you really be so ignorant of the scores of rebellions and attempts at rebellion that characterized plantation life? You make no mention of the Underground Railroad. Does it, also, not compute? *You deny the resistance of the slave to his oppression. The logic you advance would imply that had it been left up to Black people, they would, even today, be happily laboring upon the plantations of the oppressors!* "Gentlemen!" More times than I can count, I have been tempted to lay down my pen so as not to afford you the legitimacy of a reply; but the grotesque and *dangerous* nature of your propositions inspire in me a sense of duty and responsibility which rises above my personal disgust.

So, to continue:

3) *You have most shamelessly and brazenly misused W.E.B. Du Bois.* In recalling his criticism of U. B. Phillips' *American Negro Slavery,* you imply that the view held by Dr. Du Bois more closely corresponds with your own thinking. Yet, one is hard put to find any difference between your views and those of Phillips. Using the very quote you have lifted out of context from Du Bois, I offer the following comparison between your view and those of Phillips:

Dr. Du Bois:

"Mr. Phillips recurs again and again to this inborn

character of Negroes. They are submissive and light-hearted. ..."

Your view:

"... freedom and slavery were not separated by sharp dividing lines and gradually faded into one another ... to some blacks, especially among the talented whose opportunities were most constricted by slavery, even quasi-freedom was worth nearly any price—and they risked everything for it. But for the average slave who in any case expected his lot to be that of a laborer, the cost of revolution, or even of flight, were not worth the gains of quasi-freedom."

May we conclude from this that those slaves craving freedom were a limited handful who somehow "measured-up" to your definition of "talented," but that the majority (I would be interested in knowing whose definition of an "average slave" you are using and what the heck is "quasi-freedom") were generally indifferent to it? You further state of the slave-master relationship that "The analogy to the parental use of force today is striking."

Dr. Du Bois:

"... ingratiating. ..."

Your view:

"Slaves shared in the benefits of large-scale purchases made by the planter. Their clothing, for example, would have been more costly if purchased individually. Perhaps an even more important benefit was the saving on interest charges. Through intervention of their masters, slaves, in effect, were able to borrow at prime rates."

Dr. Du Bois:

"... very fond of display. ..."

Your view:

"Slaves were able to earn substantial sums of money. Much of this was spent on such items of clothing as handkerchiefs and brightly colored cloth for dress making."

Dr. Du Bois:

"... an acceptance of subordination. ..."

Your view:

"They wanted devoted, hardworking, responsible slaves who identified their fortunes with the fortunes of their masters."

In line with this you proudly quote some vile person by the name of Bennet as saying:

"My negroes have their name up in the neighborhood ... for making more than anyone else and they think whatever they do is better than anyone else."

You conclude:

"Such an attitude could not be beaten into slaves. It had to be elicited."

I could go on and on, but, in short, the picture you paint of slaves differs only in date of publication from that of Phillips. Du Bois, a great man of integrity and intolerance for racial injustice and ignorance, has no place in your warped presentation.

4) I have saved for last a point which, being myself a Black woman, I find especially offensive and which, I think, places you squarely in the camp of white supremacist decadence.

You base much of the "evidence" against the sexual misuse of Black slave women upon the "Victorian attitudes" which "predominated in the planting class" even though "not all planters and not all of their overseers were men who lived by the moral codes of their day." But once again, "The point at issue here is not whether the sexual exploitation of slave women by masters and overseers existed, but whether it was so frequent that it undermined the black family. ... Are there reasons to believe that the degree of sexual exploitation which white men imposed on black women was greater than that imposed on white women?" And finally, "While some white men might have been tempted by the myth of black sexuality, a myth that may be stronger today than it was in the antebellum south, it is likely that far larger numbers were put off by racist aversions."

I regret that space does not permit me to answer all of the horrendous propositions you put forth along these lines. In the typical tradition of the social chauvinist who has never understood or been sensitive to the special problems of oppressed peoples, you make comparisons between that which can never, honestly, be compared. Attempts at comparing the white woman with the Black slave woman are absolutely absurd. That the misuse of white women existed, we are more than aware. But it was, during slavery, a form of misuse more in terms of mind than of body. During slavery more than any other period in history, she was reduced to a caricature of womanhood (a caricature she has since struggled against and continues to resist to this day). In relation to the "master," she was little more than a pampered slave, though in relation to the slave and especially the Black woman, she was a goddess. She sat in vegetable-like helplessness, sipped and cried into mint julep while *my* sisters listened for the dreaded sound of the approach of her husband (your gentlemen of "Victorian attitudes" who were "put off by racist aversions"). In addition, the white woman, sexually or otherwise abused, had recourse to protection by law; the Black woman *had no rights which white men were bound to respect.*

You claim to have taken it upon yourselves to project the "accurate historical image of the black man." Have not Afro-Americans, themselves, through many years—many decades—of struggle (in conjunction with their *true* friends) put forth their "accurate historical image"—the militancy, the determination, the thirst for true democracy, the intolerance for social injustice? Have they not pursued an active and steadfast path toward liberation? Has not the Black community produced such figures as Frederick Douglass, Carter G. Woodson, W.E.B. Du Bois and Martin Luther King? You, our scholarly "friends," obviously deny the dynamism of the whole anti-slavery movement; obviously, you are ignorant of past history. But can you possibly be oblivious to the many heroic *contemporary* struggles (none of which you ever allude to)—the Civil Rights movement, the massive anti-lynching and anti-Jim Crow struggles in the South, the sit-ins, the boycotts, the Angela Davis struggle, the struggles against discrimination in labor. Have you not heard of the recent struggle against the racist "mobocrats" of Boston who would rather destroy a school bus than let it park in front of certain schools—when that bus happens to be transporting Black children? Have not Black people, themselves, in every way possible, demonstrated what is their "accurate historical image?"

Clearly, the image you are concerned with remoulding is that of the slaveholders! But this task requires the remoulding of the entire image, political, ideological, social and moral, of the institution of slavery itself.

Time on the Cross is a rallying cry, a regrouping call for all of the racist forces who would continue to deny Black Americans their rightful place in society. It is a call for unity among those who would *replace* the "slaveholders long . . . driven from the stage of American life." People who would replace the chains of slavery with obstacles more suitable to modern times—more Jim Crow, more discrimination in labor, education, housing etc. More Shockleyism, Jensenism, Bandfieldism. Fogel and Engerman would cut the last rope restraining the racist hordes: *Come out, come out, wherever you are! You have no reason to denounce your slaveholding ancestors—they did nothing wrong. You have spent too much time on the cross!*

In conclusion, despite your major attempt to turn back the hands of time, to confuse and arouse masses of white people to racist thinking, to distort the true image of Afro-Americans, the movement for Black-white peoples' unity is alive and well; the movement for black liberation is alive and well. The two movements will join to block the overall racist offensive of which your book, *Time on the Cross,* is a major element.

References

1 Frederick Douglass, "Meaning of July Fourth for the Negro," in *The Life and Writings of Frederick Douglass*, ed. by Philip S. Foner (New York, International Publishers, 1950), Vol. 2, p. 193.

2 Frederick Douglass, "Lecture on Slavery–No. I," in *The Life and Writings of Frederick Douglass*, ed. by Philip S. Foner (New York, International Publishers, 1950) Vol. 2, p. 135.

3 *Ibid.*, p. 143.

4 Douglass, "July Fourth," p. 196.

Roll, Apology, Roll!

Earl Smith

Slavery, the worst in kind the world has ever known, institutionalized its system right here in America, the *land of the free–home of the oppressed.*

In claiming slavery to have been a humane institution, Eugene D. Genovese in *Roll, Jordan, Roll* does a grave injustice to what he himself describes as, "telling the story of slave life as carefully and accurately as possible." First, Genovese does everything *but* give an accurate account of the American system of slavery. Four centuries of Black peoples' struggle for freedom have been virtually wiped away in these 825 pages allotted to do just that. Instead, what is written is a proprietary class view of southern history, racist in content and coming from this self-styled pseudo-Marxist!

To justify his rationalizations, Genovese, like some other white historians* who write about Black people whom they know nothing about, goes so far as to take out of context the thought of the late Dr. W.E.B. Du Bois, often alluded to but never studied by "scholars" of Genovese's caliber. For instance, Genovese tells us that Dr. Du Bois admired the Christianity of the slaves because they could love their enemies, even though they had to give up their manhood in so doing. A misrepresentation, to say the least. What Genovese should have focused his book on is a statement made by Dr. Du Bois while he was the Chairman of the Sociology Department at Atlanta University:

Book Review: ROLL, JORDAN, ROLL: THE WORLD THE SLAVES MADE. By Eugene D. Genovese. Pantheon Books, New York, xxii, 825 pages. $17.50.

* Stanley Elkins, Ulrich B. Phillips, Robert Fogel, Stanley Engerman, George Rawick, C. Vann Woodward and others.

"I faced a crisis: I was using Grapsey's *Religion and Politics* as a Sunday School text. When Grapsey was hauled up for heresy, I refused further to teach Sunday School. When Archdeacon Henry Phillips my last rector died, I flatly refused again to join any church or sign any creed. From my 30th year on I have increasingly regarded the church as an institution which defends such evils as slavery, color caste, exploitation of labor and war."

Now I ask, does not this sound more like Dr. Du Bois than the statement Genovese ascribes to him on accepting Christianity, and knowing manhood had to be sacrificed to do so?

What Genovese fails to understand is the dialectical nature of religion. The slaves understood the *doctrine* of Christianity, as opposed to the institutional practices of the Church which were forced on the slaves as a means of control to keep slavery intact. By clearly understanding the Christian doctrine, the slaves used it to further the cause of freedom. Witness: Nat Turner, Gabriel Prosser, Frederick Douglass, and David Walker who, in his *Appeal* of 1829–30, blasted the Christianity of the slavocracy for its hypocrisy.

Paternalism, the other theme that recurs throughout the book, gets much attention from Genovese. Had he grasped a true understanding of the slave system, he would know that the plantation system made the need for more slaves necessary when it moved from producing for its own private consumption into a staple-producing system that was a part of the international market. Then Genovese would not have put forth the notion of benign paternalism. In trying to make it look as if the slaves themselves helped to shape the system of slavery, Genovese totally omits the obvious, i.e., that the system of slavery was defined by those who owned the means of production—the slaveholders themselves! This reciprocity between master and slave is a Genovese concoction.

Very early we are told that this southern paternalism's "insistence upon mutual obligations, duties, responsibilities, and ultimately even rights—implicitly recognized the slave's humanity." The "implicit" recognition of the slave's humanity speaks for itself. Genovese's reference to "mutual obligations," I assume, has to do with the *"reciprocity"* between the master and the slave? As this reciprocity and wonderful paternalism develop we find that

> "the mistresses, however they conformed to the image of the 'southern lady' in important respects, worked too hard under too many limitations to live up to their reputations as ethereal beings who wallowed in leisure."

"Wallowed in leisure" they did, for it was the Black female slaves (whom Genovese calls "mammies") who did the cooking, ironing, and sewing, not to mention other things, along with caring for the white children.

In trying to assert the deep *humanitarianism* embedded within the slave system, he would lead us to believe less than the truth. Genovese also distorts the documented history in lines such as these:

> "Masters who were not slaves to their passions tried to hold corporal punishment to a minimum. When possible, masters and overseers tried to control their slaves by withdrawing visiting privileges, forbidding a Saturday night dance, scheduling extra work, or putting an offender in the stocks or in solitary confinement."

That is somewhat hard to take. This racist interpretation of slavery gives a false picture of the diabolical cruelty that actually existed. A monograph put out on May 4, 1839, by the American Anti-Slavery Society, entitled *American Slavery As It Is: Testimony of a Thousand Witnesses*, gives a factual account:

> ". . . many poor slaves were stripped naked, stretched and tied across barrels, or large bags, and *tortured with the lash during hours, and even whole days, until their flesh is mangled to the very bone.* Others are stripped and

hung by the arms, their feet tied together, and the end of a heavy piece of timber is put between their legs in order to stretch their bodies, and so prepare them for the torturing lash—and in this situation they are often whipped until their bodies are covered with *blood and mangled flesh*—and in order to add the greatest keenness to their suffering, their wounds are washed with *liquid salt*."

Does Genovese not know what the cowardly, licentious slavocracy was all about, from its inception right down to Abolition? I contend that he does know.

One section in the book that I feel needs very close examination, and space limitation does not permit such here, is that on "Slave Revolts and Resistance." Genovese tells us that: "Here and there insurrectionary plots and even modest risings did occur, but no large scale or general risings took place." Needless to say, we know that the *first people to attack slavery were the slaves themselves!* The likes of Harriet Tubman, Nat Turner, Gabriel Prosser, David Walker, Denmark Vesey, Toussaint L'Ouverture and Frederick Douglass give the undisputable proof of the struggles for freedom.

Genovese has learned his lessons well from the "grand-daddy" of the racist historians, Ulrich B. Phillips. In newer language he updates the original thesis of Phillips, a thesis based on white supremacy. In portraying Black slaves as a metaphysical people who did not resist and struggle against the inhumane American slave system, we are assured that

"The assimilation [of religion—E.S.] solved the problem of how to achieve spiritual freedom, retain faith in earthy deliverance, instill a spirit of pride and love in each other, make with a political reality within which revolutionary solutions no longer had much prospect.

". . . for people who, even as slaves, were creating an incipient nation within a nation, it would be difficult to imagine a more satisfactory solution."

For Black people and whites who understand the meaning of struggle, "more satisfactory solutions" are not difficult to imagine, for those solutions are a part of the class struggle, and the racial-national struggle as well. Marxist historian Dr. Herbert Aptheker, whose research on slave revolts showed the true revolutionary zeal of the American slave, has this to say:

"The history of American Slavery is marked by at least two hundred and fifty *reported* Negro conspiracies and revolts. This certainly demonstrates that organized efforts at freedom were neither 'seldom' or 'rare' but were rather a regular and ever recurring phenomenon in the life of the Old South."

Genovese, had he read more than he wrote, would not have grabbed "facts" from here, there and everywhere to put together this virulent, racist book. *Slavery Is Slavery*, and no amount of apologies can undo the damage it has left on America.

The early ideology of the bourgeoisie posited as given, the inhumanity of the oppressed slaves. Contemporary ideologues like Genovese, in trying to stifle the fact of the unity of resistance to the barbaric slave system puts the onus on the victim; that is, on the slaves themselves. These contemporary rationalizations are in line with the current crisis in capitalism, which needs this racist history to continue its super-exploitation of Black people. Genovese as a ruling class apologist helps to keep the treadmill going, only now the exploitation is not as graphic as slavery of old; its guise now is *Wage Slavery*!

Slavery, therefore, which Dr. Du Bois called "at best a mistake and at worst a crime," pirated Black men, women, and children from Africa by *force*, and held them in slavery by *force*. It is the history of *Forced Super-Exploitation of Millions Upon Millions of Black People*. Hereafter only that history should be written which depicts the heroic struggles for freedom waged by Black people.

12*

Distorted, Superficial Historical Study

Martin E. Dann

Black nationalism, like black power, has become a distorted (and fearful) phrase in the hands of Theodore Draper. His recent book *The Rediscovery of Black Nationalism* is not merely an attempt to discredit black nationalism in particular, and Black Studies in general. It is to provide in a tendentious and presumptive way those who are unwilling or unable to understand the meaning of the black struggle for justice with the pretense of historical veracity. It is within this context that we read Draper's central thesis: Black nationalism "arose out of a frustrated American nationalism," and "emigration [i.e., *Draper's black nationalism*] satisfied the fundamentally negative need ... to renounce a country. ..." This assumption is applied to one of the central figures among ante-bellum Black abolitionists, Martin Robinson Delany: "... Delany's 'black nationalism' was based on unrequited love, on rejection by whites, rather than on a deeply rooted, traditional attachment to another nation." In an effort to deny legitimacy to the concept of black nationalism, he views it as a contrived, *ersatz*-nationalism, arising from a rejection by white society. In assuming this negative perspective he fails to see the fundamentally positive and constructive aspects of this philosophy.

Before dealing with more specific errors of fact and omission, it may be well to consider a re-definition of black nationalism. Two currents in black intellectual history converge repeatedly: a response to white racism and an asser-

Book Review: THE REDISCOVERY OF BLACK NATIONALISM. By Theodore Draper, Viking Press, New York. 211 pages with Index. $5.95.

tion of self-determination. And it is in the concept of black nationality that both reach a watershed. Both are inextricably linked and develop almost simultaneously, and both are directed toward the same goal of freedom, equality, and racial pride that had been denied to Black people. What emerges from the work of Delany (as most of his contemporaries) is the attempt to find a solution on such a multidimensional level. In the face of attempts by American society to repress any movement toward black self-determination and to crush any sign of self-defense, two distinct (but interrelated) programs appear in the early nineteenth century, and extend into our own times.

The first general program or goal is *inclusion*–the desire to be recognized as citizens, to change the basic nature of this country from racist to egalitarian, the demand for full citizenship rights, in short, to work through the system.

The second may be termed *separation-exclusion*–the response to racism, oppression and terrorism, leading to various forms of resistance, including foreign and domestic colonization, in short, to avoid the system.

The decision to take one path or another depended upon the individual's perception of these two alternatives. But it is important to remember that the choices were not mutually exclusive. The final aim of both was manhood, dignity, and self-respect–the goal with which black nationalism has become synonymous. Throughout black history the articulation of such a position has always been, in a sense, revolutionary in that it has implied changing a basically racist and exploitative American system. The ultimate question was always whether or not it was *possible* to achieve these goals within the system.

The concept of black nationality is central to the struggle for black liberation in that it attempts to define the place of Black people in this society, and seeks to move the society towards a more egalitarian structure. Whether in terms of colonization, or emigration, this concept has played a crucial role in black history, and particularly in outlining strategies and tactics for building the Black community.

Martin Delany's own history reflects the shifting nature of the problem. Clearly, as an active participant in the Convention Movement, as editor of *The Mystery* and as co-editor of the *North Star* he expressed a deep sensitivity to the problems facing the Black community, as well as a strong feeling for his African cultural heritage.

It is not surprising that the two should go together. Contrary to Draper, Black people saw themselves not simply as Americans, but as Afro-Americans, Anglo-Africans, Colored Americans, or Negro Americans. As every form of independence and self-determination was attacked, and every attempt at self-defense brutally crushed, such a distinction became crucial to survival. Directed toward the establishment of Black communities in Canada, and the expanding frontier of the West such efforts were consonant with a constantly evolving black nationalism. True, the Black community in general rejected emigration to Africa; but they never desired to cut that deepest of cultural ties. It is indeed curious that Draper obfuscates black colonization movements in Canada and the West and passes them off in a few sentences! Successful all-Black communities were established in the face of considerable white racist opposition, and it was only the intervention of government, institutionalized racism, and terrorism that prevented such experiments from being more successful than they were. They did not lack for adherents, as tens of thousands joined the movement, and nearly every prominent Black leader and black newspaper supported the settlers. Was it that Black people had rejected America (as Mr. Draper concludes), or that America had rejected its Black citizens? That is a crucial point, for we must consider black nationalism not in terms of the unfulfilled promises or ideals of this country and its institutions (which in fact have had no intention of accepting Black people any more than brown, or red people), but in terms of the reality of racism.

Let us examine some specific inaccuracies in Mr. Draper's historical perspective:

"... when Russwurm changed his mind in favor of colonization, he was *forced* to resign." There is no evidence to substantiate this charge, either in Russwurm's words, or those of his co-editor, Samuel Cornish. Neither is there evidence to support the contention that James Forten was "pressured" to come out against colonization, or that Paul Cuffe was "forced to join the anti-colonizationist opposition."

It is difficult to take Mr. Draper's historical observations seriously since they are often quite superficial. His discussion of colonization refers to these areas simply as "an escape," when in fact they were largely efforts to create more viable Black communities, and in terms of Haiti prior to the Civil War, a base of attack against the slaveholding states.

Mr. Draper minimizes the importance of Delany's *Condition, Elevation, Emigration and Destiny of the Colored People in the United States* as having been written "hastily" and in his "spare time." In fact, it was not. One can clearly see the ideas in 1848–49, and in a letter to Frederick Douglass (July 23, 1852) he refers to his book:

"I am deeply interested in this subject . . . having made them a matter of thought for more than 17 years. . . ."

In addition, Delany had written a long article on Cuba in the issue of the *North Star* of July 20, 1849. Clearly, the writing of his book represented the sifting of experiences of at least four years.

It is true that at the time Delany published his book it was not well received especially by the black press. Delany wrote to Douglass on July 23, 1852, asking why the book had not been reviewed. It was not until the publication of *The Weekly Anglo-African* in 1859, edited by Thomas Hamilton (the same man who published Delany's book on Africa in 1861), that emigrationist views were given significant support by the black press. It would seem that the resistance of the press (and perhaps the community), rather than Delany's own "second-thoughts" halted the sale of his book.

Mr. Draper's peculiar anti-Communist bias leads him into a wholly distorted view of the relationship between the Communist Party and the black liberation movement. Had he wished to make a thorough investigation, he might have discussed the Alabama Sharecroppers Union which during the 1930's had a very close relationship with the Party.

Since Mr. Draper prefers to rely on secondary sources for the bulk of his information, I doubt whether he has even attended a Falasha service. His statements about Black Jews are insulting, and inaccurate. They are Jews, Orthodox and traditional, though different perhaps from Mr. Draper's acquaintances.

Equally obnoxious is his treatment of the Black Panthers. There is little discussion of their roots, history, or program, and the chapter is so riddled with error and innuendo that one concludes Draper is more interested in ridiculing than understanding. Although he may not agree with the Panthers, he should take them at least as seriously as the FBI, the Justice Department and local police forces.

What stands out most clearly in Draper's work is his constant attempt to read "failure and hopelessness" into every movement for black self-determination, and to deny legitimacy to such efforts. It is in this context that he views Black Studies in terms of a power shift, quantitatively, rather than as a demand for relevance and a change in content, qualitatively. He simply does not understand the basic demand that white people must stop trying to determine the lives of Black people. It is this perspective that leads Mr. Draper into subtly racist caricatures of dependent Black men, unable to "pay for themselves," wanting to be "subsidized" (i.e., lazy), unable to "break the umbilical cord" (i.e., children), etc. In Mr. Draper's perspective, any expression of independence, selfhood, resistance to racism, and dignity is dismissed as a fantasy.

The place of Africa to Black Americans is not contrived, nor superficial. Indeed, as black nationalism in its broadest sense, speaks to basic inequalities and racism, endemic and institutional, as it speaks to attempts by white people to degrade, exploit, and murder black, brown, red, and oriental people, it epitomizes the only creative nationalism this country has left. The final question, therefore, is not what the limits are on Black people (in Draper's framework), but whether or not racism will continue to be tolerated. White Americans practice genocide upon and exploit black, red, brown, and oriental people here and abroad. When will it stop?

Black Youth: What Does the Bicentennial Offer?

James Steele

On the eve of the Bicentennial celebration of this nation's birth, Black youth, and indeed the entire young generation, have every right and every reason to draw opposite conclusions as to its meaning from those now being put forward by apologists for the system—the simplistic President Ford included.

A nation which was born in the revolutionary flames of the national liberation struggle against colonialism two hundred years later has become the arch-defender of every colonial, neo-colonial and fascist regime in the world. A nation whose struggle for democratic advance once inspired the world, today supports not one single freedom movement on the planet—and has not done so for more than the past quarter century. A nation whose independence was flawed from the beginning by limiting the humanity of Black people to "three-fifths of a man" today is ruled by forces which are still guided by the tenet that Black folks have no rights a white man is bound to respect.

Looking back over the expanse of two centuries of persevering struggles for peace, freedom and dignity, young Blacks correctly raise the question: of what significance to them is the Bicentennial of the "right to life, liberty and the pursuit of happiness"? Black youth, understanding that their people began pursuit of these lofty ideals more than a century and a half before Thomas Jefferson inscribed them in the Declaration of Independence, are keenly aware that two hundred years after their pronouncement the gap between "pursuit" and "realization" of happiness continues to widen for Black people. They know that the special system of super-exploitation and oppression of Black labor developed over the past 200 years is in some ways more ruthless than ever.

The Bicentennial of U.S. capitalism brings with it the imposition of conditions more brutal than any previous generation of Black young people had to face, even the shackled young generations of slavery. The present generation of Black youth is coming to adulthood precisely at a moment when U.S. society has reached a new, deeper stage of general crisis and decadence. The forces of racism and monopoly domination are attempting to make the working people, in the first place, shoulder the burden of the depression and U.S. imperialism's international defeats, particularly in Vietnam.

The monopoly corporate élite and their executive action committee—the Nixon-Ford administration, have set loose a racist, anti-democratic offense which is a parallel to the betrayal of Reconstruction. The result is a crisis of everyday living with unemployment and high prices bringing ruin to tens of millions of this country. The cutting edge of this crisis is racism. Black people are being hit the hardest. Representative John Conyers in a statement on the floor of Congress placed it this way, "Unlike the gentle rain, unemployment does not fall on everyone equally. It falls first on the poor, of longest duration on the Black, and hardest on Black youth."

Last January, the Bureau of Labor Statistics reported a 41.1 percent jobless rate among Black youth. By mid-year, reputable sources said that it exceeded 60 percent. Herbert Hill, Labor Director of the NAACP, Dr. Bernard Anderson of the University of Pennsylvania's Wharton School of Finance and Commerce and many others have predicted that if the present situation continues, by 1980 an entire generation of young Blacks will have become adults without ever holding a full-time job.

Statistics also show that Black enrollment in college dropped from 10.12 percent of the student body in 1970 to 5.8 percent. In addition, there is virtually not one university or college in the United States, predominantly white or predominantly Black, in which the rights of Black students—

minority students, affirmative action, open admissions, financial aid, hiring and upgrading of Black faculty and administrators, etc.–are not under siege.

President Ford, strictly adhering to the racist "end of permissiveness" policy of Richard Nixon (in relation to whom Ford is the political expression of the song "Me and My Shadow"), has emerged as a latter-day King George III. In the tradition of this tyrant of British colonialism, against whom the people of the thirteen colonies found it necessary to rebel, Gerald Ford is the modern epitome of "taxation without representation."

Without having received a single popular vote, President Ford has vetoed nearly forty legislative measures which would have provided some relief to the victims of the crisis. He has been particularly callous in crushing bills creating jobs–the thing that Black youth need the most. Ford has led the way in cutting aid to education, but he has had no hesitation in proposing enormous defense budgets to feed the gluttons in the financial-industrial-military complex. According to Ford's plans the military budget is scheduled to grow from the record $103 billion this year to more than $147 billion by 1980. Obviously, he, Rockefeller and Kissinger plan to be still around by then.

Consider what these vast sums of money would do toward dealing with the problems, not only of Black youth, but all youth and working people. Every Black youngster able and willing to work could be given a meaningful job rebuilding the inner-city. In a short period of time every ghetto in the nation could be transformed into a beautiful community with the best of housing, health and social services, recreation and cultural facilities and mass transportation.

Black youth could receive job-training with skills corresponding to the demands of modern industry and the scientific and technological revolution. Free education, from child-care to graduate school, could be guaranteed, and the students in such programs could be ensured employment after graduation.

This would mean more Black doctors, scientists, technicians and an overall rise in the level of skill of the Black community. Combined with a thorough fight against racism on the job, an end could be put to the widening wage gap between Black and white workers which is now growing more acute under the impact of the scientific and technological revolution.

However, with the same indifference King George III showed for the deteriorating conditions of the working masses in colonial times, President Ford has called "short-sighted" anyone who believes "that the billions spent for defense could be better spent for social programs to help the poor and disadvantaged."

Imagine the reaction of young Blacks upon hearing this. Incredible racism! The President of the United States can spend tens of billions of dollars stock-piling nuclear weapons, escalating the arms race, and playing games with the fate of the world by pursuing a strategy which could lead to a thermonuclear war and, in a matter of minutes, turn the planet into a pile of ashes. Ford can do this, but not a dime on providing jobs for millions of unemployed youth. It is for this reason that Youth United for Jobs, an organization uniting youth in struggle against unemployment which now exists in some sixteen cities across the country, has raised the slogan "Money for jobs, not for war."

Congress—No Source of Salvation

President Ford once boasted of never having done anything positive in the field of civil rights. Small wonder that he would say that on domestic policy he and George Wallace have "a great deal of similarities." Thus Gerald Ford himself used the "good name" of the Presidency to incite vigilante mob violence against Black children and desegregation of public schools in Boston; in effect, against the law of the land which he swore to uphold.

The Bicentennial is also a time of re-evaluation. In this

context, Black youth appropriately ask: In the system of checks and balances where is the check on the Ford-Rockefeller-Kissinger clique? Where is the counterbalance against the Executive Branch which has become the property of monopoly interests and U.S. imperialism generally?

Surely, few unemployed young brothers or sisters standing on the street corner or the Black child wondering how many racists will pelt his or her bus with stones, clubs and epithets, consider Congress a source of salvation. The U.S. Senate and House of Representatives combined include 535 people elected to meet the need of their constituencies and the population as a whole. The majority of the members of Congress—with the notable exception of the Black Caucus and very few others—also dance to the same tune as President Ford. On the whole, they have proved themselves to be a body of spineless demagogues.

Their track record is pitiful in relation to Ford vetoes, as it was with Nixon. From 1965 on, Congress has been backsliding on the question of civil rights. And now when the country is in the midst of the worst economic crisis since the Great Depression of the 1930's, Congress has not passed one piece of legislation which would substantially alleviate the plight of the people. The title "representative" is a travesty against the dignity of young people.

For the second year the Equal Opportunity and Full Employment Act introduced by Black Representative Augustus Hawkins sits in sub-committee. The bill has 107 sponsors but remains in sub-committee while every week thousands more Black youth become unemployed statistics.

On July 31, over 350 youth—most of them Black and unemployed—from New England, the Midwest and the South lobbied in Washington, D.C. They demanded an emergency session of Congress to deal with the unemployment and educational needs of youth. They also tried to acquaint their representatives with the Hawkins bill as well as the youth demands from the Youth Contingent Committee of the National Coalition to Fight Inflation and Unemployment. The demands include the following: create jobs for all at union wages; stop the layoffs of all workers; give priority jobs to those hardest hit (for Black and other nationally oppressed youth to their percentage of unemployment); on-the-job training with full pay; guaranteed employment after graduation; unemployment compensation for first-job seekers; extension of unemployment benefits for all.

These demands have been endorsed by more than one hundred youth, student, trade union, Black liberation, religious, civic, community and peace leaders; but only six out of 535 Congresspersons saw fit to support them. The Washington, D.C., City Council declared July 31 Youth Jobs Lobby Day, but not one Senator supported the proposals of these youth.

This is the same Congress which two days earlier voted itself an across-the-board 10 percent pay raise. It is abundantly clear that the present Congress rivals the infamous Do-Nothing Congress of the 1850's. The Democratic Party, which holds the majority of votes, has exposed itself as the tail side of the coin which Big Business flips at will. In the words of Stevie Wonder, "They haven't done nothing."

This is why the youth who participated in the lobby, and the thousands more they represent, so enthusiastically took the idea that it is high time that young people organize for mass struggle for their rights.

Many so-called experts on the inner-city talk about the despair and hopelessness of Black youth. Certainly, the objective conditions in which they find themselves produce hopelessness and despair. However, the crisis and the intensification of racism also foster militancy and mass radicalization. 1975 testifies to this fact. In the community and on the campus there has been an acceleration of militant, political activity among Black youth with working-class Black youth in the center of it. The 21st National Convention of the Communist Party took note of this in its resolution on youth: ". . . Although the deepening crisis of U.S. capitalism has dramatically worsened the conditions of the young generation, the anti-monopoly and peace struggles of the people against economic crisis, racism, Watergate and the Vietnam war have led to the development of a new level of radicalization and militant political activity among the youth."

In many of the major cities there have been demonstrations and other mass actions by Black youth demanding jobs and justice. No less than twenty major universities were the scenes of big struggles this past spring against cutbacks and elimination of affirmative action programs.

The masses of young Blacks will not give way to "despair and hopelessness," as the "experts" call it. And despite the intensive and massive ideological campaign of the ruling class aimed at sweeping Black youth away in a decadent, hedonistic and self-destructive culture of drugs, vulgarized sex, gangsterism, etc., the youth of the Black community will not succumb to these either.

On the contrary, there is another answer to the question of the Bicentennial's significance to Black youth. The answer echoes through the vacant lot where "low-income" housing was supposed to be built, through a shutdown school in which a young Black genius might have been educated. The answer echoes through the idle mills where a young Black worker might have made enough money to pay last month's rent, echoes through the streets where two out of every three Black youth, unemployed, "wonder as they wander." The answer echoes through the 350 years of bitterness, abuse and degradation.

Black youth hear the answer in the voices of their parents struggling to put them through college. They hear the answer in the laughter and the seriousness of Black auto, steel, rubber, and longshore workers, in the freedom songs of millions of Black men and women struggling for equality. The answer echoes in a rising crescendo of unity: Struggle! Keep on struggling! Keep on keeping on!

Unity and Mass Action

At this moment the historic charge for Black youth to "keep the faith" is to unite in mass action for their rights. The task is to draw upon the legacy of the black freedom movement, further developing the most successful forms and methods of mass struggle and applying them to the specific conditions of today. There is a need for a movement of Black youth comparable to the Southern Negro Youth Congress which was the first militant, politically oriented movement among Black youth in the South. There is a need for such a movement to take on the irrepressible, militant character of the sit-ins, freedom rides, voter registration projects of the Civil Rights movement and the universal content of the peace movement.

Such a movement of Black youth, while having its specific goals, could link with other youth and progressive forces in a massive campaign for the rights of all youth to a decent job with adequate pay, to quality and equality of education, to live in peace, to have a future with a creative purpose. A major aid in strengthening this unity is April 4–the date of the assassination of Dr. Martin Luther King, Jr.–which has been designated "International Day of Solidarity with Youth Fighting Racism in the United States" by the World Federation of Democratic Youth (WFDY). What better occasion to supplement ongoing grass-roots struggle than with a mass march on Washington against racism and for the right of youth to earn, learn and live? Only with mass youth unity supported by labor and other democratic forces can Black youth "fight the powers that be."

Such a mass movement should give priority to fighting for the economic well-being of Black youth, for jobs in the first place. But it should also develop ways of mobilizing and organizing the potential political power of youth. One of the reasons many elected officials think they can afford to be unresponsive to young people lies in the fact that the majority of youth do not vote. Youth, especially Black youth, must undertake to register young people and organize them. They must make any elected representative who fails to do something positive about youth unemployment, peace and detente, adequate funding to education and affirmative action in all aspects of life, "the last hired and the first fired."

There is no question that in numbers and in organization there is strength. Unity is the key. The theme of the first U.S. Revolution "united we stand, divided we fall" is applicable today. Black youth united with their allies can show the monopolists and their servants in the White House and on Capitol Hill that they will not accept another 200 years of racism and oppression.

Cashing in on Blackness: The Dilemma of Afro-American Education

Nancy L. Moore

Dr. Wilfred Cartey, Black educator and literary critic, has said that "any education, any growth of awareness demands its proper sacrifice. Such is its nature: to create a contrast so startling that the past must be abandoned in favor of the future it promises or the reality it so starkly reveals."[1]* In *What Black Educators Are Saying,* Nathan Wright has attempted to answer the question implied in the title by hastily compiling a mishmash of articles by an incompatible assortment of writers involved, however tangentially, in the formal education of Black people. The book does not reach any coherent conclusions, ideas that may be shared by the authors are not assembled and developed, and after reading the book the question remains, "What are Black educators saying?" The structure of the book, divided into five parts, seems contrived as though it were superimposed to accommodate whatever materials were elicited. The scope of each section is not clearly delimited. The ordering of topics does not appear to have logical continuity. And yet, this book is found in education classes all over the country because it is available, not because it is the best that Black educators have to offer the racial crisis in American education. Schools of education have finally been forced to deal with what Kelly Miller, then Dean of the Junior College at Howard, asked back in the twenties: "How shall we reshape our

WHAT BLACK EDUCATORS ARE SAYING. Edited by Nathan Wright, Jr., Hawthorne Books, Inc., New York, 286 pages. $3.95.

* See notes at end of article.

shattered ideals? ... to restate the case in terms of the peculiar and special needs of the Negro is hardest of all."[2] Today it is good business and happy publishing to write about the education of Black people. Many of the people represented in *What Black Educators Are Saying* are late arrivers saying what has been better said before. And all that some Black folk are saying about education may not be worth saying. The vision remains obscured, the contrast undelineated, the future unpredictable if not unpromising.

Wright prefaces the book with the intention of pursuing a theme, humanizing the schools. What is meant by this is not clear in spite of the fact that he describes the contributors as "all humanly inspired voices to which we must listen for our own growth and for the enhancement of the nation's peaceable and orderly progress." He justifies the need for change in the schools by drawing a parallel with the "built-in parental oppression" against which adolescence rebels. This is a euphemistic metaphor to describe the oppression of Black people by the dominant Euro-American culture. Also, the idea that power unconsciously abuses gives more credence to Wright's sensitivity than to his familiarity with the history of Negro education in the United States. The closing injunction of the foreword, to call upon "these beautiful brothers and sisters" for guidance and direction, rings of the preacher guiding his sheep, the readers, to a group of underemployed herders.

The articles themselves are uneven in quality. Under the first heading, "The Black Educator," are several very poor ones. Preston Wilcox, the highlight of this section fails to see the continuity of development when he speaks of Booker T. Washington and W.E.B. Du Bois. First of all, it was not so much Washington's educational model that was repressive, it was rather the monopoly of control and censorship he maintained as the go-between for funding agencies and Black intellectuals. As for Du Bois, Wilcox is projecting his perspective back in time and, also, clearly misunderstands the life work of Du Bois if he believes that Du Bois did not realize "that authentic blackness is not the replica of whiteness." Surely anyone who has read *The Souls of Black Folk* or *The World and Africa* knows that the orientation of Du Bois although scholarly, scientific, and thorough was hardly "white." Furthermore, in the article, "Does the Negro Need Separate Schools?,"[3] Du Bois does not come out the ardent integrationist that Wilcox makes him out to be. Du Bois was never willing to compromise the distinctive historical perspective and cultural values of Black folk. Another point in question is the statement that it was SNCC (Student Non-Violent Coordinating Committee) which first declared that "the problem is not in the Black community." E. Franklin Frazier treated race prejudice as a mental illness on the part of the white population.[4] Du Bois in his pioneer study *The Philadelphia Negro* concludes that the source of difficulties within the Black community is the political, economic and social environment of the dominant society.

The specific issues discussed by Wilcox are worth-while but we only get a little taste of each, not a real struggle with the possibilities and plans for actualization. One reason for this superficiality may be the neglect of earlier work. So much of what Wilcox has to say has been said before, albeit, in different words. Horace Mann Bond asserted in the early thirties that the education of Black students must center on the application of knowledge and skills to the implementation of the aspirations and survival requirements of the Black masses.[5] Du Bois' brilliant plan for a cooperative effort on the part of black colleges to research and solve many of the problems in the Black community has yet to be implemented. Alain Locke and others of the Harlem Renaissance eloquently stressed race pride and were the forerunners of Pan-African Negritude. It is an ego trip to think that the struggle is new. The present task consists of culminating a long proud history of protest and revolt. The humility with which the scholarship of those courageous pioneers, who fought great battles to free their minds for service to the people, is approached will be in itself an example of the standard of selfless service which will insure the survival of the dignity of black culture from generation to generation.

We need not be alienated from the past; we are part of a timeless army of freedom fighters.

The next article, "The New Black Dimension in Our Society," is filled with inconsistencies. Olivia Stokes is quite tired of controversy and yet, one wonders if she is not defining moral idealism as loving white folks rather than loving justice. Where Miss Stokes lumps black extremism, black nationalism, and black power together as "causing the white American to increase his fear and to run for repressive measures," she not only demonstrates her confusion but also her naiveté. The American system has always been ready to "whip the Black person into conformity" if he dare speak out against his being exploited. Her hang-up with separation is irrelevant—in the past and in the present it is clearly the condition of existence forced upon the majority of Black people. Read, for example, Henry Allen Bullock, *A History of Negro Education in the South*.[6] The admirable scholarly justification for integration, culminating in the 1954 Supreme Court decision combined with the best plans for the integration of American schools could not succeed in achieving the goal. Whites evaporated from the most promising plans and reappeared in self-segregated suburbs. The contributions which Miss Stokes states the "black middle American" can make to the crisis of "love, acceptance, and belonging" are not original. One wonders where she has been while Black citizens have done everything within their power to make the democratic process work. She advocates the teaching of Afro-American history, because "the black history should be in the mainstream of the thought of white Americans." Olivia Stokes seems to be unaware of the culmination of the legal battle in 1954 and in the civil rights legislation. Finally, Miss Stokes has a lot of self-educating to do in order to "understand the structures of American society and the racist nature in order to bring about change and eliminate the treatment projects which have been so popular in the war on poverty." If this were not the case she would not be in such a rush to make the white folks aware that "democratic, non-controversial, middle-class" Black

Americans still do exist nor would she be so condescending toward "the revolutionary activities, as valuable as these may be in the social change process." She concludes with a plea for more top level jobs for Blacks and a description of "the new black dimension in American society" as being a "fascinating, dynamic, creative, hopeful development in democracy." It sounds like an attempt to convince both herself and a white, middle-class audience that everything is cool and, as Roberta Flack sings, "Business can go on as usual."

Les Campbell, who has three articles included, makes some valid points that are quite current, but the devil is mythological. He speaks from hysteria in passages like "All devils must go. . . ." By the way, Campbell and Stokes make rather peculiar bedfellows.

Nathan Wright has contributed six of his own articles to the anthology, all but one of them editorials written for *The Newark Star-Ledger*. The exception, on Black Studies, is a speech given at the University of Houston. The first of the editorials, "Humanizing the Schools," opens with a panegyric to John Dewey, "a mighty prophet among us," and goes on to give a rather bizarre description of a "humane educational enterprise," neglecting the position that astute educators have held since before Dewey's time. That is, a humane education requires a humane society as its foundation. Education is not a panacea for the ills of a society in need of organic change. And then, it is a "legerdemain" to place the blame for "so much of the 'offbeat' and anti-social behavior in youth from middle-class homes" on the teacher "who fails to see a pupil as one to be inspired" and who is the "prime representative" of the society. Perhaps youth also sees society itself, in all of its agencies, including the socialization he receives at home, as warped and rigid. The suggestions he makes to humanize the university do not come to grips with the causes of brutality and rigidity in the schools. The proposal that students prepare test questions is interesting, but for the class to also prepare the answers "for the benefit of all" would evoke a conformity of response stifling to the imagination. The instructor isn't given much credit for having prepared his students properly or for taking into account the diverse interests and perspectives of his students. Wright's position, that no student at the college level should be failed is debatable. The awarding of a B.A. for "gumption" at the small church-oriented and black college may really have been a reaffirmation of the fact that such schools needed the students who could pay. Today, at most schools the resources are limited and the demand for education great. Should a student who belongs elsewhere be allowed to occupy the seat of one who is willing to work hard to develop the skills necessary to serve the community?

Part II, "The White Establishment," is composed of five unrelated articles. Among them is an important study, "New Literature on Education of the Black Child" by Edward K. Weaver, Dean of the School of Education at Atlanta University. Weaver's position is that the "new" literature, "in ignoring . . . [the] vast scientific literature about the Black people, has no roots, and indeed, sets out to be 'new' by deliberately operating as if it were a new field." In this manner, these writers attempt to cover up the history of inferior education for Black children which has been dealt with in so much of the black scholarship Weaver mentions; instead, the blame for miseducation is shifted from the school to the children and their parents. "Cultural deprivation has been a conscious policy of white racists and their dupes and stooges on the boards of education for more than a century." Weaver deftly castrates the assumptions basic to compensatory education theory and mocks the proposition that "the black ghetto child become a superchild, lifting himself through reading and language skills to a nobler and greater world of the future."

Lawrence Hawkins' "Urban School-Teaching: The Personnel Touch" has something to say but it's old hat. Kenneth Clark thoroughly presented the case that teacher behavior and expectations are important. Hawkins, however, overemphasizes this factor when he says that "boys and girls become largely what our professional conduct toward them causes them to become." So long as the larger society is an alien, hostile, or indifferent environment the Black child suffers and has to deal with a tremendous "disadvantage." Teachers who are committed to the social change necessary to end oppression on all fronts are teachers who are committed to the full development of the pupil's powers to make things happen. "Tea and Sympathy," in Lerone Bennett's words, are not enough.

Another editorial by Wright, "Shankerism," defines the problem as it is. Shankerism (for Albert Shanker, New York City Teachers' Union head) is the result of the need for institutions, including the unions, "to face the need for and fact of tremendous social change." True, and Wright goes on to hint at a compromise solution that seems very unlikely to be acceptable to the teachers, that is, that they be transferred out of the city or even the state if necessary to find another position. The Black community in Ocean Hill-Brownsville took a firm position toward the issue of incompetent teachers. So did Shanker and the union. In view of the entrenched power of the educational establishment this article reads like a worm pleading with a steamroller.

"A Message to the Establishment" is a dialogue between Norma Jean Anderson and Frank Kent, ex-Commissioner of Human Rights for the State of Minnesota. Dr. Anderson discusses frankly the felt need for community control of the schools but then, after asking the Commissioner what he sees his role in helping as being, lets him get pretty far away with the answer that desegregation is the antidote for disruption. She concurs, suggesting that integration might really be desirable if white students were bused into the ghetto schools. She does point out, however, "that you can't integrate learning tools" and so quality education will have to become part of the black "home school" whether or not integration takes place. Her suggestion that educational parks would correct the system of racial imbalance needs further consideration. What type of education it would offer and who would control the educational park are still fundamental questions. Discussing Black Studies on the secondary level, Dr. Anderson seems to evade the vital issue in much the same way she suspects the school system would. "Until the educators think this is important themselves, only then will they be part of the curricula. ..." What about the opinion of the Black community and Black students which she said were going to "help the institution, because we are part of the institution?" What about her own thoughts on the matter? Dr. Anderson's final confrontation with the Commissioner concerns housing, tying this in with deprivation of experience, acquisition of conceptual patterns, and the solution to the problem of integrating schools. The Commissioner does an about face, to which Dr. Anderson doesn't reply, by throwing the weight on Blacks not wanting to live among whites. Integrated schooling may, he hopes, help the Black child "when he becomes an adult and has to decide where to live ... feel a lot less sensitive about living in a community that may be 90 percent white." With only a few seconds left to the interview Dr. Anderson deserves the benefit of the doubt for not correcting this ludicrous line of reasoning in her closing statement.

The third section of the book, "The University Scene," contains a very fine article by Benjamin E. Mays. Dr. Mays presents an historically grounded case that Black Education is not a new phenomenon; it has roots and a tradition. Furthermore, it has never depended for its direction on the government and, in the case of at least one black institution, Howard University, has consistently preserved the integrity of its ideals. The federal government passed civil rights legislation only to feel that it had done enough: "Let the Negro now make it on his own, sink or swim, live or die!" Law has little value, but Mays is not disillusioned. Rather, he summons forth the will to create the substance of law. Here is a great man speaking with sobriety and the wisdom of experience and knowledge. Specific to the point of education he says, "There has never been and there never will be a substitute for academic excellence, and none for possessing skills that the community needs." If the student is without resources or skills, "he must inevitably lend himself to carrying out the directions and ideas of others." Finally, he warns us about the pitfalls of a desegregated society; it does not mean, for instance, that Black people will be a significant part of the policy-making bodies that shape education, industry, and government. Integration, however, is an issue to Dr. Mays and must be distinguished from desegregation. In his view, integration implies nothing less than the organic restructuring of the institutions and consciousness of present day society.

"Can We Look to Harvard?" by Nathan Wright, brings to mind a more basic question. When could we ever look to Harvard? Wright, an alumnus of Harvard, says he is "one that has always loyally questioned its somewhat sophisticated presumptuousness" and yet, he was dumbfounded by the social perversions manifested by police in the maintenance of law and order on the campus and the overlooking of this brutality by the Harvard administration. He is reminded of the publicly condoned police behavior in the 1967 riots or at the Chicago convention. Rightfully outraged, he is nonetheless a bit naive when he appeals that "we cannot hope to continue long as a free nation when the agents of law are implicitly encouraged to turn law into caprice." One can ask for a point of clarification here: When has this ever been a "free" nation. Mr. Wright considers Harvard "traditionally responsible." One knows, after reading a copy of "Who Rules Harvard?" to whom Harvard is responsible. Harvard has always been an elitist institution used by the patrician families and industrial sector to educate leaders and experts. Incidentally, Harvard did not have one Black full professor until 1949, and that rank was attained by Dr. William A. Hinton just before his retirement.

More to the issue, Wright makes some important observations. Policemen do face a dilemma, trying to enforce law while society makes a mockery of it. Education for adults is a vital necessity, but one of the most potent instruments for this, the public media, is the passive reflector of the brutal, sensational images of a violent culture. Mr. Wright's concluding remarks are nobly motivated, but given the miseducation of the mass of American citizens and the repressive controls internal to educational resources and institutions it is difficult to see how "illustrious, traditional institutions as Harvard" can be looked to "for continued excellence in the disciplining of the mind," if they are not engaged in challenging the nation's "questionable or archaic values." Other institutions shall rise in its place embodying not only the attainments of the mind but also the renewed values of service to mankind and the advancement of humane civilization.

Wright includes another editorial in the section "The University Scene." "The Campus Confrontation" is a didactic piece, loaded with implied and articulated "we musts" addressed to white authorities. The analysis of student protest is faulty. Black students, when confronting institutions of higher learning, are saying a lot more than "Up the quotas—or else!" The massacre of students at the black state-supported institution at Orangeburg, S.C., or at Texas Southern, makes such an explanation seem silly. And white students across the nation have not been simply protesting the "primacy of the teachers in the learning process." Theirs is a rebellion against society, exploitative industry and war.

Darwin Turner considers with acumen some of the ways the Afro-American college can minimize its limitations and maximize its unique possibilities. His suggestions include an "expanded use of materials related to Afro-American life, culture and history," "orientation to the black community," pooling resources with other educational institutions, closer relations between students and faculty, experimentation with innovations and new practices. These are useful directions but rather lack meat around the bone in Turner's exposition. One reference here would be the plan submitted by W.E.B. Du Bois to the annual conference of the presidents of Negro land-grant colleges in 1941.[7] Du Bois' model, if implemented, would set every student, faculty member and administrator at every black college in motion. Embarked on scientific study of the needs of the community, the black college could attain a relevance that the great universities could grow to envy. One thing needs be said, however, and it is well said by Carter G. Woodson in his book, *The Mis-Education of the Negro.* He recommended that "the Negro, whether in Africa or America must be directed toward a serious examination of the fundamentals of education, religion, literature and philosophy as they have been expounded to him. He must be sufficiently enlightened to determine for himself whether these forces have come into his life to bless him or to bless his oppressor."[8] A thorough political education and a vivid conception of the traditions, culture and aspirations of the folk will be a basic prerequisite to the kind of program Du Bois envisioned and Turner suggests.

Andrew Billingsley, author of the book, *Black Families in White America,* contributes the article, "The Black Presence in American Higher Education," a survey of current trends of demand and supply of that profitable commodity called Black Studies. As an analysis of the movement to establish Afro-American Higher Studies as a legitimate academic area, this article falls short. Billingsley does not establish a theoretical framework from which a basic perspective and conception can be defined. Without a criterion with which to evaluate the different structural and academic approaches to Black Studies by colleges and universities one is stuck with either the dogmatism of racial chauvinism or the relativism of Billingsley's attitude of different strokes for different folks. He states that Black Studies "at its best . . . is designed for several audiences or student bodies." These are Black students, white students, Black faculty, the Black community, the white community; in short, the whole society. This may be the long-range scope effect that Black Studies will have. However, at this time the most pressing issue is the one raised by Black students all over the land: an education that will prepare them to participate fully in the psychological, economic, political and cultural liberation of the Black community.

Billingsley is seemingly more concerned with the needs of higher education institutions, needs which may be incompatible with the rigorous discipline and political perspective required if Afro-American Studies are to become an effective means for training committed and culturally liberated Black intellectuals and technicians who are prepared to serve the Black community. The issue of structure is very important to the survival of Black Studies programs, contrary to what Mr. Billingsley thinks. When, for instance, he says that the comprehensive course envisioned by Harvard "may be an effective instrument for the study of the black experience" and "may be quickly and easily installed" he reveals either a lack of familiarity with the tremendous amount of scholarship pertinent to the study of the black experience or else he is timid about confronting a powerful and conservative institution such as Harvard. With regards to small colleges attempting to offer Black Studies, a better suggestion would be to try and develop a consortium program with neighboring schools. Another type of structure mentioned by Billingsley is the cross-listing of courses developed within the traditional departments. A "loosely coordinated program" will produce students who have loosely coordinated ideas. Also, the major problem with this approach is, as Billingsley mentions, the limitations placed "on innovation and relevance to the black experience." Programs do not have the power to appoint their own faculty and authorize their own courses. The "center" of Afro-American Studies, for example the one at the University of Michigan which is classified as an "area study," is another type of dependent structure. All professorial appointments must be "joint," that is, consistent with the philosophy and needs of the traditional departments. Such a "center" may find itself the ball in a game to see which department will employ the director of Afro-American Studies, thus weighing the academic bias of the "center." Black faculty are hired by the departments at half price, the center paying the other half, at a time when Black scholars are very much in demand. These arrangements are weak and are without excuse at wealthy institutions such as Michigan, Yale, or Cornell, where the only obstacles to autonomous departments of Afro-American Studies are the chauvinistic and paternalistic attitudes administrators hold. As a complement to Billingsley's essay, read Mike Thelwell's article, "Black Studies, A Political Perspective," in the *Massachusetts Review,* Autumn 1969.

In Part IV, "Educational Redefinition," is Dr. Wright's address on Black Studies. Dr. Wright holds his peculiar stance here as the spokesman of Black people to whites. This posture subtly distorts the character of Black Studies. Rationalizing the development of Afro-American Studies in the university he says, "the so-called 'black experience' is . . . a marginal experience through which American life can find clearer articulation and more helpful interpretation." This is a roundabout way of defining the function of Black Studies as being to enlighten white scholars. Then, too, Wright understands the motivation of Black students as being that they "want to be 'in' and not 'out' with reference to American life." Just how this objective is consistent with the cultural and political awareness of students who have inherited the SNCC legacy is not considered. Moreover, Wright caricatures "our" Black students, "who want the America of today to work," as saying, "Use us as a laboratory for developing the capacities and techniques for change which will be sorely needed for your future survival as well as ours." (p. 209) No doubt there are some who earn their way speaking in this vein, however, the main artery is carrying forth a swarm of proud, internationally conscious young people who have not forgotten the experiments of history and who have charted their path too carefully to be lured into the society's laboratory for problem cases. This "treat yourself to a nigger" reasoning is brought out again as Dr. Wright assures "us" that "our" Black students have much to teach all of us in terms of emphatic "skills" and want us to come to see them as persons determined to meet ruggedly and bravely a challenging new world." This comes off as a pernicious form of exploitation of Black students. Whether or not whites come to see them as determined or not, a generation of students is determined not only "to meet" this world, but to change it.

Other points, seemingly minor, reveal aspects of distorted perception. It is a projection of his own orientation, for example, that enables Wright to say that Black students are afforded a small measure of pride in that 60 percent of the undergraduates enrolled in Black Studies are white. To the politically aware student this apathy on the part of many Black students is a source of frustration. Wright is premature in saying that Afro-American Studies "will serve primarily a white public" in need of a cultural corrective while Black students will be involved in something called Urban Affairs and Human Development. Afro-American Studies in no way is exclusive of "hard-core human-development needs of those who reside in the center-city environment." Considering the newness of most programs and the difficulty in getting proposals for active community building funded this assumption is not warranted. A thorough comprehension of the political machinations of urban interests, and of the cultural foundation of Afro-American life, values and aspirations is basic to original policy-making in this area. A vision of the whole, of the dynamics and interrelationships in America and international society, is the surest antidote to stopgap measures that do little more than disappoint people.

Grace Lee Boggs really socks it to the parents and educators addressed by her speech, "Toward a New System of Education." She is involved in and therefore able to speak about the revolutionary struggle to change the structure of power relationships between Black and white in America. Words such as "revolution" which have become polemical gain concreteness as she describes with analytical precision the times in which we are living. She is explicit about the sacrifices that are required of individuals as institutions undergo change and she gives a vision of the way educators can participate in the reordering of values that is basic to the survival of humanity.

"On Correct Black Education" by John Churchville is a confusing piece due to the didactic rhetoric and religious bombast which enshroud whatever he was trying to get at. For example, he says that the true revolutionary knows that "only Jesus, the Son of the Almighty God, can cope with the corruption and confusion which is his, and makes him what he must be." Then, too, one cannot resist the temptation to ask what this "truth" is which Churchville claims that correct black education is based on and instills. Reading his description of the correct classroom one easily envisions a catechism class for plumbers. No doubt, this is not what Churchville means but because he does not clearly define the problems which need correcting we lose track of the meaning of the word "correct" and it seems as though he is just interested in pushing "Jesus." What is this new, antithetical "system and ruling class" which is going to replace the old and which it is the aim of correct black education to foster? The chaos of the day is the result of people seeking for alternatives to an outworn, degenerate social system. Churchville's article is representative of that chaos. He never defines what his new world will be like, only that we are to pack our bags and take off. It is highly probable that he does not really know the destination.

C. Eric Lincoln has contributed an essay which sets the current issue of community involvement in historical perspective. This is important because "the effects of the past ramify in the problems of the present and produce the terminology (and the unresolved racial dilemmas) which characterize contemporary education." Discussing the history of education and the illusory quality of "desegregation," Lincoln persuades the reader that it does not pay to depend in any sense of the word on white Americans. He asserts that Black people have been the only democrats in America; they have fought consistently to destroy the racial caste structure and to fulfill their right to a "relevant" and "responsible" education, one that does not program Black children en masse for social and economic oblivion. One of the most popular contentions now current in sociological scholarship is, as Jencks and Riesman have interpreted the Coleman Report, "that the factors determining the continuing differentials which operate to the disadvantage of Black Americans now derive from segregation by 'class' rather than by 'race,' thus implying a relatively unrestricted mobility and acceptance across class lines for those Negroes who acquire white middle-class habits and attitudes." Lincoln refuses to involve himself with the question of whether or not this new status is different from caste segregation, for "so long as Negroes, who are *racially* identified, remain at the bottom of the class structure, and their visibility operates to keep them there," one need not argue about it.

One last editorial has been placed by Mr. Wright in the final section on "Community Involvement and Action." Wright's piece is journalistic writing, meant to shape opinion rather than to provide the information by which opinions can be shaped. He takes the position, concerning the crucial issue of who shall teach and manage the nation's schools, that the neighborhood community should control the schools in which its children are educated. A perfectly valid opinion, yet there are many sticky questions to be worked out by hard thinkers before community control becomes a reality across the nation in Black communities. Without looking at the politics and economics of educational control it is exhilarating to declare, as Wright does, that "the spirit of decentralization must be accomplished." Few would disagree with the assumption that education is in danger "when schools are too largely removed from a sense of responsibility to their clientele." This has been particularly true for the education of Black children. Whites, both in the North and the South, have always exercised a great deal of community control, even if indirectly. Community control on the part of white communities has only been discovered to be insufficient since the Supreme Court Decision of 1954. A fundamental restructuring of power relationships will have to precede just expenditure of the nation's resources. The white version of neighborhood control calls for an economically suppressed Black community to support a system of quality schools independently. The other accepted version is community control without purse-string control, a hollow concession.

Moynihan's thesis attributes the great difficulty in achieving further progress for Blacks to the "disorganization of the Negro family resulting from the system of enslavement and its aftermath and the creation in the Negro of the Sambo syndrome." Samuel Allen, in a perceptive analysis of the state of the struggle, equivocates on this interpretation of black pathology. Now, there is great evidence in studies of slavery to show that Elkins' theory of the Sambo syndrome does not hold water.* Aptheker's books document the resistance and revolt of Black people against the condition of slavery. Frazier argued that Blacks were totally defined by the experience of slavery, acquiring all standards of behavior from the white master. The degree to which their behavior deviated from the white "norm" was a function of the hardships of slavery and oppression. Herskovits, on the other hand, saw in the flexibility of the Black family, its extended nature, its ability to function without a male always present, a carry-over from African culture which did not necessarily represent "the disorganization of the Negro family." Allen in trying to be "objective" has missed the black reality. Casualties have occurred, men have been emasculated—particularly among the intellectuals who have the trying situation of constantly and self-consciously confronting white standards. The remarkable thing has been the resiliency of the spirit of pride. One recalls the memoirs of Booker T. Washington who witnessed his enslaved grandfather being whipped by the master. With each stroke of the lash he uttered, "Pray master, pray." Whether hustling, leaving home to make a living, letting the welfare do its part, or hanging in there by whatever means necessary, the Black man has survived, the Black family exists, and the Black woman has not become an all-purpose neuter being. If Kenneth Clark's doll studies of self-concept in Black children say something definitive, it is a testimony to the fact that this is a white-dominated society and that dolls as

* See Ernest Kaiser, "Negro History: A Bibliographical Survey," *Freedomways,* Fourth Quarter 1967, pp. 335–45.

they knew them were white, white, white. "A doll is white" is not necessarily the same as "I am inferior" or "I am ugly." Categorical assumptions such as Moynihan's are deceptive. And we are still missing the point of "struggle" if we only try to shift the emphasis from black to white pathology. Fanon has dealt with the effects of colonization, albeit in Algeria, with more justice to the essential humanity of its victims. Alienation, he says, is never complete. About this there can be no equivocation.

Reading Rhody McCoy's speech, delivered at the University of Wisconsin, is a refreshing experience. Getting off the abstract clime of theoretical debate, McCoy tells just how it was that community control developed as a critical issue in Ocean Hill-Brownsville. Humorously, he recalls the changes the white establishment put the community through as it tried to deal with the conditions that need to be rectified in the schools. Perhaps this virtue, a sense of irony, is overdone; we never get a serious analysis in retrospect of why the movement for community control failed.

In conclusion, after reviewing a fair sampling of the articles included in *What Black Educators Are Saying,* it may be said that if this book, taken as a whole, is an adequate representation of what Black educators are actually saying, then we are in drastic need of a major revolution not only of the educational system, but also in the thinking of contemporary Black educators. Considering the inconsistency of the book it is difficult to determine the exact outlines of the issues and alternatives it does present. Dr. Wright, an influential educator who undoubtedly could have given us a more coherent picture of how Black educators view their task, fails to do so in this book. The anthology suffers from poor organization and the inclusion of several unsubstantial articles.

References

[1] Wilfred Cartey and Martin Kilson, eds., *The African Reader: Independent Africa* (Vintage, N. Y., 1970), p. 121.

[2] Kelly Miller, "The Practical Value of Higher Education," *Opportunity* magazine.

[3] W.E.B. Du Bois, "Does the Negro Need Separate Schools?" *Journal of Negro Education*, July 1935, p. 335.

[4] E. Franklin Frazier, "The Pathology of Race Prejudice," *Negro Caravan*, eds., Brown, Davis, Lee (Arno Reprint, 1970), pp. 904–9. (Forum, 1927).

[5] Horace Mann Bond, "The Curriculum and the Negro Child," *Journal of Negro Education*, April 1935, Vol. 4, pp. 159–68.

[6] Henry Allen Bullock, *A History of Negro Education in the South* (Praeger, New York, 1970).

[7] *The Autobiography of W.E.B. Du Bois* (International Publishers, New York, 1968), pp. 311–21.

[8] Carter G. Woodson, *The Mis-Education of the Negro* (Associate Publishers, Washington, D. C., 1933, 1969), p. 194.

III. The Black Image
in the Mass Media

The Power
of Black Movies
Ossie Davis

Black movies are like black power: We may not know exactly what they are, but we know they are worth fighting over. Any form of Art is a form of power; it has impact; it can effect change—it not only moves us, it makes us move. And therein lies the danger. And the opportunity. The thought of millions of Black people being moved in any direction—by Marcus Garvey, by Martin Luther King, Jr., by Malcolm X, by Paul Robeson, by Angela Davis, or by black movies—gives rise to deep concern in high places. *The New York Times* has been so impressed by the power of black movies that it wrote at least two serious but frightened editorials; *Newsweek* magazine carried the picture of *Shaft* (holding a gun) on its cover and wondered whether the whole idea of black movies was not a rip-off; the effects of *Superfly* (who snorted cocaine) on black juvenile behavior has been worried over in many places.

Like pornography, black movies make millions whether they have redeeming social values or not. What Hollywood has suddenly discovered is that there is a large, hungry Black movie audience out there, just waiting, and the scramble is on to come up with enough black product to keep it stuffed and sated. The larger a market is, the less the rules of decent and humane behavior tend to apply in its exploitation. Black prostitution is big business, black drug addiction is big business, black movie making is big business. The entrepreneur is seldom concerned with morality in exploiting his chosen market. In the capitalist Pantheon greed is by far the one sufficient power. The white and powerful kingpins of the super billion dollar entertainment industry are greedy men. If they were not, they would not be powerful kingpins.

The element of greed is basic to the decision by which they make their millions and maintain their status—and their control. They are uneasy about Black folks and our potential to do serious damage to them and to their way of life. They tremble at the gnawing prospect of black hostility and revenge being let loose to pillage and plunder. They feel threatened. They also know—these high barons of the mass media—and this is what makes them different—that they have much of the means and most of the power to do something constructive about it. They knew the power of mass media to influence men's behavior even before the Kerner Commission on Civil Disturbances told them so. Motion pictures and television (the two are really one in social impact) speak to the ghetto as no other instruments. You would think these powerful men, if only to protect the world they made, would use their voices differently. Most devoutly to be wished, of course, would be a complete reorientation of the content of all mass media poured into the ghetto.

Surely, pure self-interest would seem to dictate a more intelligent response from the entertainment industry than that which the commercials with their crass materiality teach us about what the ends of living should be; while the programs with their repetitious emphasis on blood, guts and gunfire provide us with the means to achieve those ends.

The Black audience is sizable, and contributes mightily to Hollywood's profit margin . . . passive consumers, with not enough of us in positions of power and authority in the industry to protect our interest. We scream about what we get, but in the end we accept it. And until we as a group are strong enough and smart enough to use our common strength—our purchasing power at the box office—to force change, we will continue to be Hollywood's black dumping ground—passive consumers of junk.

But what kind of films do we want? How would we change things if we were in control? What kind of fare is proper for a people wanting to prevent being super-exploited, but lacking the power; wanting to see our own deep needs responded to, but lacking the know-how to do it ourselves?

Many of the answers lie with a small band of actors, writers, directors, trying first to identify themselves as Black filmmakers and then to survive. How do we Black filmmakers see ourselves in all this? What is it we are trying to say that will make a difference? Are we just like everybody else in the industry? Are race and color mere accidents to be ignored and forgotten as one by one we drift into the mainstream on the strength of our individual success? Or are we Black filmmakers a different breed, separate and distinct, with a new rhythm, new sensitivity and energy, a new purpose, a new responsibility? Some few of us have gained a toe hold, but is that enough? Being where we are, we can stay where we are, being careful not to rock the boat, or we can grow. But how can we grow unless we experiment? And how can we experiment meaningfully in an industry where even a low budget film can cost up to a million dollars, and where, even after you've spent your million, you have no guarantee that distributors, who are white, will get it out to the motion picture exhibitors, who are white? If your picture differs too much from blaxploitation fare, how are you to guarantee that it will get a fair chance?

I believe the black experience, by and large, to be separate and distinct and that a body of Black artists should render that experience up in a manner that respects and preserves our differences, as well as our similarities, to the rest of the world. I believe we have much to learn from Hollywood, but mostly in terms of technology, financing, managerial expertise. In terms of content and style and artistic integrity we alone can and must teach ourselves.

The first consideration of the new black film must be the needs and wants of the millions who make up the Black audiences. We must be prepared to compete, to take them away from Hollywood, by our capacity to do a better job of filling their wants and needs. To do this we will need to develop black institutions to service black films: Black investors, Black financiers, Black producers, Black distributors, Black exhibitors—all of whom must share a common conviction that Black people in their taste and in their awareness are distinct; and that only by cultivating this cultural difference can we fulfill our highest commitment. This commitment, in my opinion, is simple: to use our films to change the world, and make of it a more civilized and humane place—not only for Black people, but for all people; and to this end to become revolutionary in our art and in our aspirations, realizing that the past is fast dying, and that the future can belong only to those who not only can sense its coming, but who can, even now, begin to use their skills to help construct it.

The power of black movies to affect our lives is beyond dispute. Whether that power brings life into our communities—"life lit by some large vision," as Du Bois dreamed—or whether it brings death is not up to Hollywood—it's up to us!

Black Male Images in Films

Francis Ward

Throughout its history, the Hollywood film industry has been indelibly capitalist—operating strictly by the profit motive and law of supply and demand. What the public wanted, it got; what it didn't ask for, Hollywood never attempted to give. There was no room for moralizers, a social conscience or investors (when they could be found) who might put social responsibility ahead of making money. We're talking about the great bulk of movie producers, directors, writers, distributors, exhibitors and investors (90 to 95 percent), not the small minority of so-called "serious" or "art" filmmakers who cater to a small segment of the market—a middle income, overwhelmingly white, educated or intellectual class that demands more from films besides action, lovemaking or comedy.

But neither the "art" films nor the big-time money makers ever took Black people seriously—as subject matter, actors or audience—until the current boom in black-oriented films began around late 1968 or early 1969 (it's difficult to pinpoint the beginning). Since that time, at least one hundred black-oriented films have gushed off the assembly lines from major studios in Hollywood and independent filmmakers. (For purposes of definition, a black-oriented film is one made specifically for Black audiences. It doesn't make any difference whether a handful of whites go to see it. If its subject matter, characters and/or locale are such that it would appeal primarily to Blacks, then the film would fit our definition.)

For the first time in film history, Blacks became a major audience to which the industry catered. Blacks always went to the movies but were always ignored as an audience, since they bought the same things as whites. We cheered, too, when Tarzan beat up or killed the African "savages," or when the three white cowboys killed all fifty Indians—with twenty-five shots!

Despite our new importance as an audience, however, the rules of white profit still prevailed. People had to be given only what they demonstrated at the box office they wanted. There still was no time for sermonizers, moralizers, or folks who wanted to make a serious social or political statement. If there were any such Blacks, they (like their white counterparts) could go out and make "art" films. The lesson was clear: This most capitalist of all enterprises could never commit the unredeemable sin of subverting profits with useful messages and images—particularly for Black people. Audiences may change, but the rules of the game don't.

As in the case of films for white audiences, black-oriented films quickly fell into certain categories. As more rolled off the assembly lines, they rolled right into the same categories, which have remained pretty much intact because these kinds of films still make money.

Though they weren't the first black-oriented films in the current boom, *Cotton Comes to Harlem, Sweet Sweetback,* and *Shaft* proved something the earlier ones didn't—that Blacks would pack in to see films with Black characters. Audiences for these three films were far bigger than audiences for any previous black-oriented flicks. Further, Blacks loved action in these flicks just as they always liked action in white films and television shows. Judging from *Cotton* and *Sweetback,* we also seemed to like more than the usual share of sex in our films. But there was another important element which the movie moguls were quick to recognize, seize upon and incorporate into what would soon become a formula for black-oriented films—black "victory?" (Though of dubious grammatical correctness, I add the question mark to further emphasize doubt in the meaning of the word.)

Ah-h-h-h-h! Like Archimedes shouting "Eureka, I have found it," when he discovered what makes objects float on water, the film industry found, to its profitable delight, that

Black people would pay huge sums to enjoy the illusion of seeing Blacks beat up and otherwise triumph over whites. It made no difference that the triumphs had no relation to reality, were nothing more than souped-up fantasy, or could never be approximated in the real world. The *illusion* was all that mattered. Blacks—hungry for victory in the day-to-day struggle for survival and liberation—seemed to devour any flick that showed the white man taking his lumps from the heroic, triumphant Black. It was and is still argued that these illusions provide valuable therapy for powerless Blacks who, perhaps, might be driven insane by their lack of success in the struggle, or lack of control of their or their children's destinies.

So Hollywood's formula was settled early in the game. Black-oriented films, whatever else they contained, had to have at least these elements: 1) Black-over-white "victory?"; 2) Lots of sex; and 3) Lots of action.

It turned out that the Black movie-goer really wasn't all that different from whites, for these last two elements were the same for white films. The big difference was that white films had to have white characters, and Black films had to have Blacks in them. Beyond this, capitalist economics was identical with each: Whites still created, wrote, photographed, produced, directed, distributed, exhibited and *profited* from the black-oriented films just as they always had from white films. True, there were a relatively few films which used Blacks in major positions. Gordon Parks, Sr., directed three films—*The Learning Tree* and the first two *Shaft* films. Ossie Davis directed *Cotton* and *Black Girl,* and Lonne Elder, III, wrote the script for *Sounder* and *Melinda,* which also had a Black director, Hugh Robertson. And there were the Poitier/Cosby/Belafonte contributions: *Buck and the Preacher* (Poitier and Belafonte) and *Uptown Saturday Night* (Poitier and Cosby). Some of these were the noblest efforts among black-oriented films, but whites contributed significantly to the success of each one and made money from all of them.

The key to making the black-oriented films work was the

same as what had always made white films work in tradition-minded, profit-minded Hollywood–the big "star." But the Black male stars were taken a step further. They not only had to be big. They had to be "Super!" on screen. Off screen, these inflated "heroes" were nothing more than manipulated pawns in a tricky, highly competitive, cruel game in which people were ruthlessly exploited, shifted, shafted and shunted aside–all in the name of profits.

So Hollywood, true to its ancient, profit-tested practice, started to give us the Black super-hero, in the mold of John Wayne, George Raft, Humphrey Bogart or Edward G. Robinson. About the only black makeover we haven't gotten yet is Tarzan. Maybe that's 'cause nobody has figured out how to make the natives white. After all, you couldn't very well have black "victory?" with the Black Tarzan beating up his own folks.

It was inevitable that the screen theatrics of these Black male stars and the images they projected would fit the traditional white stereotype of Black men–strong, virile, fast afoot, physically powerful and with huge, insatiable sexual appetites. The stereotype went further. They loved big, flashy cars, gaudy clothes, a harem of beautiful women at home and away; but they had little cognitive skill, except what they needed to survive in the streets. And they always cussed a lot, even to their mamas, wives and children. Their propensity for violence was always high, for you know how legendary it is for Black men to beat up their women. Sometimes–but not often–another kind of white stereotype would break through–the smooth, suave, well-educated, well-mannered, immaculately polished Black executive or professional who met all the requirements of white middle-class acceptance.

In the creation of the Black male image, the overwhelming emphasis had to be on super-heroics, super-achievement. A normal Black man who had both strengths and weaknesses wouldn't do, for it was harder (almost impossible, so Hollywood felt) to sell an ordinary guy. Whoever heard of a "regular" Bogart, or "ordinary" gunslinger? No! No ordinary or regular Black man could be made believable in his triumphs over whites. Only the super-hip, super-slick, super-strong, super-sexed, super-hyped up and inflated Black male could whip and kick around the white boys.

The "super" image of the Black male in films served three essential purposes: it gave Blacks whatever therapy they needed from films (illusions, illusions, always illusions); it had hot box office appeal (profits, profits and more profits); and it kept whites in control of the images we had of ourselves.

It's important to reassert the fact that whites created the notion of black "victory?" on screen. Whites created and wrote most of the black-oriented films. Most of those written by Blacks used white directors and producers. This amounts to a form of double oppression. We suffer daily from racism and exploitation, and then pay them millions to provide us a kind of comic relief from the oppression.

However, from the outset of the black-oriented film boom, it has worked to our detriment and to the financial benefit of whites. When Melvin Van Peebles created a character named "Sweetback" who could have any woman in town—even while on the run—beat up or outsmart any cop, outrun the fastest cars, dogs and helicopters, and run 100 miles, from Los Angeles to the Mexican border, it set off a chain reaction that gave us a deluge of cinematic "super-niggers."

Van Peebles is Black. He wrote, directed, produced and starred in his own film, and managed to get it distributed throughout the industry in a way that no other independent filmmaker has done so far. This feat earned Van Peebles millions, and also helped his image as a kind of new breed hustler/slickster who could whip a game on the white man and beat him at his own game. What most of Van Peebles' ecstatic supporters generally leave out is that his co-producer of *Sweetback* is Jerry Gross, chief executive of Cinemation, Inc., a New York-based producer of skin flicks, which distributed the film and who also made millions.

However, Van Peebles was the exception. He's had only one film, though for three years now we've been looking for his much heralded sequel to *Sweetback*. If the other sequels to the "super-nigger" flicks are any indication, Van Peebles' will probably have *Sweetback* running from Mexico to Guatemala—but not without stopping at every hacienda to have any and every available female.

Flying in on the heels of *Sweetback's* success was John Shaft, the Black private eye, super-cool, dashing, sexy, whirling dervish who beat the crime syndicate in Harlem, licked them again downtown (in the second flick) and then whipped the French-operated slave trade in Ethiopia and Paris in *Shaft in Africa*. Creator of the John Shaft series—three films and a TV series thus far, with perhaps more to come—is Ernest Tidyman, a white novelist.

By now, the race was on. Black actors with little or no talent were rushed into service to fill the sudden, overnight need for a strong, able-bodied Black male who could run and jump and make love while creating the illusion that he was a super-hero.

Up popped Fred (Pretty Boy) Williamson out of nowhere as a swashbuckling, fast-drawing cowboy, in a worthless piece of junk called *The Legend of Nigger Charley*. Williamson, once a good pro football player with the Kansas City Chiefs, says he quit the game " 'cause I got bored and wanted to do something else." He was perfect for the white exploiters. He looked good, tall, fairly muscular, trim with no fat anywhere. So "Pretty Boy" Freddy was launched as the star of a whole run of super-hero films—*Hammer*, the sequel to *Nigger Charley*, *Three Tough Guys*, *Three the Hard Way*.

But Freddy wasn't just satisfied to be a "super-nigger" on screen. He started a one-man publicity wave, dubbing himself as the prettiest guy in the country. Everywhere he went, Freddy became the prettiest, sexiest, "mos'est gor-jus nigger" you ever saw! When people objected to these acrobatics and criticized Freddy's films, his standard retort (as was Van Peebles') was how come nobody said anything when the whites were out promoting themselves, using these and other kinds of gimmicks. The simple answer was that some folks *were* objecting then, but few people listened. And even if nobody criticized the whites, that still was no reason why we shouldn't criticize him now, for most whites have never had the same kind of moral obligation to Black people that Fred Williamson, Van Peebles and other Blacks in films should have. In a word, we have a right to expect more from Freddy and Melvin than we expect from John Wayne.

But Fred Williamson wasn't the only—or necessarily the worst—super-stud, new wave, Black sex star. There was Jim Brown—the pro football immortal who wanted to become a screen immortal. His specialty seemed to be beating up the white boys, and sleeping with all the white girls. That way black "victory?" would be overwhelming, total.

This brings to mind another aspect of the Black male image in films that seems to show up more and more—on-screen sex scenes with white women. There was a time (not too long ago—remember Emmett Till in Mississippi, August 1955) when even the *thought* of having sex with white women would get a Black man lynched. But times do change —especially when change is so profitable for white exploitation. Jim Brown's scene in *100 Rifles* with Raquel Welch broke the ice. Since then, we've had Fred Williamson in a raunchy scene in *Hammer,* a long, torrid bedroom scene in *Slaughter* with Jim Brown and Stella Stevens, and the same thing in *Shaft in Africa* with Richard Roundtree and an unknown Yugoslav actress. These are samples, but not the only Black male-white female sex scenes on screen which seem to be designed to prove the ancient white stereotype that the greatest power of the Black male is in his sexuality.

Perhaps one hopeful sign concerning black-oriented films, particularly the Black male image, is that much of what I have said up to now does not apply to most major Black male actors like Sidney Poitier, Ossie Davis, Bill Cosby, Godfrey Cambridge and Harry Belafonte. Poitier, perhaps more than the others, has helped perpetuate the Black middle-class acceptability image, but none of these has catered to or accepted the super-stud, super-sexed roles which characterize the bulk of the Black male roles in black-oriented films. The fact is that for almost all of these roles, producers have gone to lesser known or completely unknown actors whom they didn't have to pay much and who wanted a chance to "make it" in films. This phenomenon probably will continue.

A second hopeful sign is that some recent black-oriented films seem to indicate that the criticism of the kinds of images we've discussed herein may have hit home to some extent. During the first four years of the boom, there were only a few really good, first-rate black-oriented films that could be commended for their honesty, seriousness, technical quality, and positive messages and images. But in the past year or so, the *number* of such films has increased a little, though the percentage is still pathetically low in relation to the total number of black-oriented films produced. We have seen *Sounder, Five on the Black Hand Side, Claudine,* and *Together Brothers* as more recent productions which seem to indicate that filmmakers may be listening and responding to the clamor for better films.

However, these few films—whatever they actually mean in terms of Hollywood responsiveness—are no reason for Black people to let up in their demands for more relevant and better quality films, with a total eradication of the Black male and female stereotyped roles.

Along with the five films just mentioned, we've also gotten *Truck Turner,* the latest, and probably worst, Isaac Hayes flick that slavishly panders to all the familiar stereotypes, and *Foxy Brown,* another in an endless series of Pam Grier flicks.

The ultimate goal with films, as with other forms of communication, is black-owned and controlled companies which can raise the necessary capital, do the production and distribution so that white influence, interference and domination can be held to a minimum. Black control of a part of any major industry in the capitalist system is still years away, especially if that control means raising wealth that can be used in the black liberation struggle. But, we must make control and relevancy in films our ultimate goals. Until then, we should continue to demand as many short-range concessions as we can. There is no time or place in the struggle for satisfaction or complacency.

The Media Image of Black Women

Jean Carey Bond

Since the 1960's, the visibility of minority people on the television screen has increased considerably. Black people, in particular, of both sexes, are now to be seen in commercials, in dramatic, comedy and detective programs. Indeed, the television industry, stirred by the civil rights activism of the sixties and pressed by groups organized to deal specifically with the media, would seem—at first glance—to have corrected a grave wrong.

But a closer look reveals a very interesting phenomenon. While the industry has responded to black demands that this segment of the population be better represented in TV fare, at the same time it is using this increased visibility as a front behind which to purvey age-old stereotypes about Blacks; as a front behind which to ridicule black behavior; as a front behind which to subtly belittle the problems the American system has visited upon Black people.

So-called black shows (I say so-called because the vast majority of such shows are conceived, written and produced by whites), and appearances by Blacks on other programs, cannot be regarded as mere entertainment and evaluated solely on that basis. What may appear to be just entertainment or just fun-filled fantasy has resounding political overtones.

Take, for example, *The Autobiography of Miss Jane Pittman,* a widely acclaimed slice of historical fiction adapted for TV from Ernest Gaines' very fine novel by that

This article is the unedited transcript of a speech delivered at the Media Women's Association Symposium at New York University on December 7, 1974.

name. In my opinion, not even Cicely Tyson's superb portrayal of Jane could obscure one of the film's covert messages. All of the men with whom Jane had been intimately associated in her long life are killed off in one way or another in the film. Her adopted son, who had been a civil rights activist, gets murdered when he incurs the wrath of the white community. Her husband, who had been a horse-breaker, is trampled to death by a snow-white stallion—a very cheap stroke of symbolism. And her close friend's son, whom Jane had helped to raise, is shot for challenging segregation policies. Hence, while *The Autobiography of Miss Jane Pittman,* a film written, produced and directed by white males, *seems* to celebrate the strength and soulfulness of Black women, at the same time it proclaims the impenetrability of white male power by Black men. This message is no less perceptible or malicious by virtue of its encasement in the protective covering of historical fact. In short, *Jane Pittman* makes clever use of a "positive" image of Black women to put down—or should I say, put in their place—Black people as a whole.

Another case in point: *Get Christy Love!* First of all, one hardly needs to cite the sexism ingrained in the role of this dusky policelady—it's so blatant. Never mind that Christy one-ups her co-workers a good bit of the time and dazzles us all with her sharp wit and supercompetence. The camera never fails to play on her glossy lips and swinging hips, and the script and camera constantly conspire in attaching sexual overtones to Christy's professional relationships with her all-white male colleagues at the precinct.

And was it mere coincidence that in the series' first episode, we found Ms. Love masquerading as a prostitute to catch rapists? I think not, seeing as how the white males who bring us the Christy Loves are extremely cosy with the image of Black women as prostitutes. Now I don't mean to knock the pursuit of rapists, nor to question the validity of karate-trained policewomen serving in that worthy cause. Nor is a put-down of prostitutes intended. But how many scenarios of funky liaisons in the nether regions of some black ghetto have been imagined by America's white male population down through the ages?

So much for the sexist content of this show. *Get Christy Love!* has an even more insidious function. This character is being used to cosmeticize one of the most notoriously repressive police forces in this country—an agency whose officers' guns are loaded with dumdum bullets; an agency that saw fit to barbecue alive six, albeit misguided, human beings (Black and white) who could not possibly have held out given the forces that had been marshaled to subdue them; an agency whose officers have whipped more Black heads for no good reason than you could shake a nightstick at. That is the reality of the Los Angeles police force. In view of that reality, *Get Christy Love!,* armed with its sexy Black goddess, is perpetrating a cruel hoax.

What about *Good Times* and *That's My Mama*? Rollicking good shows they are, so full of fun one scarcely notices the subtle stereotypes they project. If you check out the hidden agenda in each of these shows, between chuckles, you might note the following: Each of the female lead characters fully embodies the *myth* of the black matriarchy served up on a sociological platter by Daniel Patrick Moynihan to an eagerly receptive white American public. (Some Black males, of course, bought that simplistic concept too.) To the extent that this myth has taken hold in the white consciousness, it has tended to reinforce negative attitudes towards Blacks as a group because most whites—male and female—regard a matriarchal family structure as being, at best, unusual and foreign, and at worst, unnatural. The myth also gives a welcome lift to the egos of many white men who feel threatened by Black men, and who need to believe that the latter are substandard as measured against the "manhood" *they* know and cherish. Among Blacks, the effect of the myth has been, in a word, divisive.

Attending the matriarchy theme as it is played out in these shows is the suggestion that Black men are genetically irresponsible and mindlessly defiant. Black women are presented as the brakes on a car (Black men are the cars) that would swerve wildly out of control given half the chance. Now I'm aware that some white feminists, possibly even some Black ones, would see no reason to quarrel with that assessment of Black men—in fact, they would hold that men of all races are natural renegades. Given the state of the world, it might be possible to build such a case quite successfully. But the point here is that not only Black men, but Black women too, are ill-served by such stereotypes. We gain nothing from distorted depictions of our commendably active and varied roles in Black family and community life. And particularly, we gain nothing when comic or dramatic effect is achieved at the expense of Black male identity.

The decision-makers in the TV industry are quite comfortable, as sexists, with the strong, bosomy, authoritarian Black female, who is not viewed as being a real threat to *them* and *their* manhood. Rather, she is seen as being a threat to *Black* manhood—a notion that titillates their racist sensibilities. To put it another way: The sexist side of the TV idea-man dictates that one sex must prevail over the other. His racism dictates that, in the case of Blacks, it must be the female over the male. Where Black media images are concerned, then, sexism and racism are two sides of the same coin.

When you consider that the images of Black people that are projected are those with which the people who control television content are most comfortable, you perhaps can understand why many Black feminists feel compelled to focus primarily on what those images convey about Black people as a whole, rather than exclusively on what they say about Black women.

It has become crystal clear to Black people, if ever it was unclear, that only Black penetration of the decision-making chambers of the TV industry will lead to significant changes in the way Blacks and their lives are portrayed. In particular, Black women would have to be involved in the process by which programs are conceived and executed in order for more diversified and substantial images of Black women to emerge. Certainly, Black men could not solve the problem alone, susceptible as they are to the influence of sexist attitudes and other values that have been institutionalized by the dominant culture.

However, having noted this I must also point out that the gaining of access by Blacks to the power levers that shape media content is unlikely to occur to a meaningful extent—except, perhaps, on white terms. It is not likely to come because one of the most important unwritten functions of television is to sell the white American way of life and white American values to *all* the people. If Blacks, the largest oppressed racial group in the society, were to gain the power to define themselves, it would shake the very foundations of this endemically corrupt, unjust and racist system.

"Black" Shows
for White Viewers

Eugenia Collier

Television gives us far more than entertainment. It gives us images. Pictures of our universe. Impressions. Concepts injected so subtly that we accept them without realizing what we have done, without defining the direction our minds have taken. And I myself am convinced that television is one of the most potent weapons this nation has for keeping Blacks lulled, deceived, impotent.

I have expressed this view before; as a result, I have been called an alarmist, an élitist, an opportunist, and a bigot. I have quarreled with friends and have had to listen to hard words from strangers. The very vehemence of people's reactions indicates to me the grip in which our minds are held. Therefore, I want to begin this discussion by examining these issues: Is it logical to expect a television program, even light comedy, to present a philosophical stance? Does a program designed for "mere entertainment" actually give us something more?

Let me probe these questions by citing current thought on the impact of TV in general. First, the question of the influence of violence on TV has become pretty well resolved by the position, held by psychologists and others, that violence on TV does indeed exert influence on the behavior of suggestible people–for example, children and neurotics. A specific example, cited in the *Atlanta Constitution* (July 2, p. 20-A), occurred when a group of Canadian youngsters, having seen a mock hanging on TV, had "hanging parties" in which they tied ropes to the ceiling and around their necks and then jumped off chairs, depending upon their friends to cut them down when they turned blue. One boy lost his life. Second, a recent study based upon a questionnaire has indicated that the popular *All in the Family* tends to reinforce ethnic prejudices.

Here, then, are admissions that TV affects attitudes and behavior of susceptible people even when this is not its overt purpose. Certainly the white mind historically has been susceptible to violence against Blacks—not only physical violence but also the dreadful distortion of our image until neither we nor they can see us as complete human beings. A TV show that perpetuates this distorted image tightens the chains on our minds.

White critic Horace Newcomb, speaking generally and not of black programing *(Baltimore Sun,* June 3, 1974, p. B 5), points out the terrifying capacity for ill, inherent in TV's influence. He says that "there are those who are perfectly willing to manipulate all of us, to become our Big Brothers in the gentlest, mildest manner." It is obvious that the best interests of the whites in this country who control TV are served by keeping Blacks blind and tranquilized rather than aware and angry. The generalized danger that Newcomb senses becomes a deadly reality when we are speaking of black portraiture on TV controlled by whites.

Mere entertainment? For us, there is no such thing. As to the question of the inevitability of a built-in philosophical stance, I must agree whole-heartedly with Newcomb, who says in the same article, "Fictional content is very important in any culture. In ours, television has become the myth-maker, the storyteller, the passer on of old cultural ideals." But for us, the public myth has been distorted and damaging; the old cultural ideals of this country have enslaved us for centuries. And so a philosophical stance is woven into any show featuring Blacks, whether we will it or no.

For years, that philosophy was expressed by omission; Blacks were simply left out, except for occasional performers on variety shows. The inference is obvious. Then into this colorless void burst a passel of shows that testified that Blacks could be profitable if they did not rock any boats. Mainly the shows have been light comedy things and a couple of detective stories, conceived and executed *by* whites *for* whites, with a great number of Black viewers looking on and marveling how great it is that we have finally made TV. Rarely has there been a serious portrayal of Blacks. The most serious attempt was probably *The Autobiography of Miss Jane Pittman*—but even here the suffering of Blacks, their strength in withstanding it, and the significance of their struggle were muted in comparison with Ernest J. Gaines' fine novel and with reality. In the book, for example, the biographer is the Black writer, whose Self is attuned to Miss Jane's life experience. In the TV film, her life is told to a white reporter from a metropolitan newspaper. This intrusion of the urban white world gives the story an entirely different tone. In addition, some important details are omitted. We never see, for example, the terrible beating which the white master and mistress give the child Jane when she refuses to answer to the slave name of Ticey. This beating, caused by her assertion of her identity, results in lifelong infertility and thus has great symbolic value. But most white Americans have never accepted the savagery of their history, and so this important part was omitted.

Several aspects of the novel, in fact, were skewered to fit viewpoints comfortable to whites. The speech of the militant hero Ned, in which he declares that Blacks are Americans and not Africans, is presented in such a way as to overemphasize conciliation. And Ned is strangely passive in accepting death at the hands of a hired white assassin. Not only Ned but also Joe Pittman is diminished in manhood by TV. In the novel Joe's position as tamer of wild horses symbolizes his manhood. He is chief, he is in control, he prevails over nature. He is a Man, and for this he dies. On TV he tames horses as an obscure emotional compensation for the fact that he and Jane cannot have children. Thus he acts out of weakness rather than strength, and his death is not tragic but merely pathetic. And TV provides Jane with a wedding ring to satisfy white Puritan morality!

An important distortion occurs at the climax of the film. The novel ends with Miss Jane leading a civil rights march, surrounded by the people. Her triumph, then, belongs to the community. On TV she leaves the people and walks *alone* to the white drinking fountain, and faces the white sheriff who has known her for years and who *permits* her to drink. Her triumph, then, is an individual thing. We applaud Miss Jane, but the community remains not dangerous and not about to demand real change.

As I said, *The Autobiography of Miss Jane Pittman* is probably the most serious attempt to portray black life on television. But the tremendous acting ability of Cicely Tyson (who is undoubtedly one of the best actresses of our time) and the technical genius of the makeup department completely obscure the fact that once again our vision of blackness has been edited, has been warped.

So the presence of Blacks on TV has not heralded social progress but has simply demonstrated that an innocuous image of the Black community is comforting and entertaining to white viewers and therefore profitable to big money interests. *Sanford and Son, Rollout!, The First Family of Washington, Shaft, Love Thy Neighbor*—these and other network shows featuring Blacks are not *black* shows but shows created for whites. For the most part, they are conceived, written, and directed by whites—and in this time and place it is a rare white person who has the knowledge and compassion to recreate in art a believable black world.

In view of the powerful but subtle influence which TV holds upon our minds, we need to regard with dead seriousness the distinction between black shows and shows featuring Blacks for the entertainment of whites. This distinction emerges clearly when we contrast two shows on opposite ends of the existing continuum, *Sanford and Son* and *Good Times*. Ironically, both are produced by Tandem Productions. Both are highly popular comedies carried by extremely talented Black actors. But despite these similarities, there are several striking differences.

One difference—and this is crucial—is in the initial concept. *Sanford and Son* was intended to be an American version of the British show *Steptoe and Son*. According to Bill Davidson's *TV Guide* article, "The World's Funniest

Dishwasher Is Still Cleaning Up" (Vol. 21, No. 11, March 7, 1973, p. 30), producers Bud Yorkin and Aaron Rubin were considering using Italian-Americans in the proposed series when by chance someone suggested that Redd Foxx would be right for the part. The deal was made, and the British-Italian-American show became "black."

Good Times began in the mind of young Black Mike Evans, who plays Archie Bunker's neighbor, and writer Eric Monte. Monte grew up in a big-city housing project. He has also experienced the city as a cab driver, dishwasher, and hobo. The family in the series is based upon a real family, the setting is in the housing project so familiar to many urban Blacks, and the father is, among other things, a dishwasher. There is authenticity in the concept of *Good Times* that is missing in *Sanford and Son*.

A second difference is in the source of the humor. In *Sanford and Son* the comedy situation grows out of the assumption that the characters are not very intelligent but are wily in the sense of being quick to take advantage of each other. Thus, episodes center on Fred's attempts to sell a broken-down television set to his best friend, Grady's and Lamont's attempts to get rid of an unwanted woman relative who has moved in on them, Lamont's attempts to get rid of Fred's pool-playing friends who have worn out their welcome, Fred's luring Lena Horne to his house on the pretext that Lamont is a motherless little boy, Fred's renting a room to Grady in order to get his money—and on and on. Virtually every episode shows Blacks putting something over on one another.

Outside of this kind of trickery, Blacks are not very bright. Grady's lack of intelligence is a perpetual source of laughter, and the wit of the dialogue is often based upon stupidity. The mental incapacity of some Black person or other is very often necessary to the plot. For example, in one episode a woman shows up, some time after an encounter with Fred in a bar, determined (on the basis of that one encounter) to marry Fred. Unable to remember what Fred looks like, she is convinced that every man she encounters in that house is Fred. Ignorance, naiveté, and even mental aberration play a big part in many episodes.

Good Times has a different concept of what is funny. There is pain behind the laughter; one laughs *with* strong people rather than *at* weak people. And thus one's humanity grows rather than lessens. There is warmth in the humor of *Good Times*. One laughs at JJ's quips about his problems in school, but one senses a keen intelligence surviving in spite of the destructive nature of public education. One laughs at Willona's remarks about her men, but one senses a strong woman who makes the most of her assets and manages her life in spite of setbacks. Florida and James face fortune with an endless barrage of funny sayings; but as we laugh, we admire them and learn from them.

This difference in the humor is vitally important. There is an element of cruelty in the humor of *Sanford and Son;* it feeds our egos and assures us that we are superior to these people. This is the kind of humor that infuses such popular favorites as Abbott and Costello, the Three Stooges, Stepin Fetchit, Amos 'n' Andy, and Lucy. The humor in *Good Times* draws on the survival humor that has produced a good deal of black folklore–humor based largely on intelligence rather than stupidity, ability rather than incapacity, strength rather than weakness, community rather than fragmentation. And let nobody point out that Fred resembles the folk trickster Brer Rabbit; rabbits do not trick other rabbits–they trick bears!

A third difference between *Sanford and Son* and *Good Times* lies in the image of family relationships. Fred and Lamont are always low-rating each other–this is the source of much of the humor. And this low-rating seems qualitatively different from the friendly insult that is the basis of much black humor. Fred and his son do occasionally show warmth (for example, Lamont gives Fred a pool table for his birthday and arranges a surprise party), but not often. The Evans family of *Good Times,* on the other hand, is strongly structured, mutually respectful, and full of affection even when they disagree. In spite of his economic problems,

James is a strong father–strong enough to apologize to his youngest son when the occasion warrants, strong enough to take his wife's advice, strong enough to defy, when necessary, the white power structure that would break him if it could. Florida is in most respects the archetypal Black woman whose warmth and wisdom and fortitude and humor have been crucial to our survival.

A fourth difference between the two shows lies in the implied relationship with white America. In *Sanford and Son*, white America has very little part. There is a white policeman whose polysyllabic diction the Blacks cannot understand. There are occasional white individuals who flit across various episodes. But there is no pervading sense of whiteness which hovers ominously over every Black American, no sense of the ubiquitous, threatful *presence* which in some form or other shapes our destiny. We might *infer* that American racism has something to do with the Sanfords' plight, but we seldom (never) witness any Black person actually grappling with the specific manifestations of this racism.

In *Good Times*, however, the characters constantly do battle. A white principal who would permit Black children to be passed without having been taught; an education system that excludes black culture; an antiquated white racist teacher; the economic system that keeps James alternating between working two arduous but temporary jobs and spending long periods unemployed–these are some of the enemies against which the Evans family has pooled its resources. Not every episode focuses on racism, of course; the Evanses must deal with the same range of forces as everyone else. But the struggle against oppression, which is so deeply human and so indigenous to black art, is never totally absent.

These differences between the two shows have the composite effect of creating two very different images of Black people–one essentially negative, the other essentially positive. Not that the Sanford image is completely untrue. It is true, for example, that some Black people *do* often take advantage of others; but the task of the writer is to look beyond the surface reality and bare the complexities that comprise human experience. Moreover, the writer must choose, from the range of reality, those aspects whose portrayal will render us better able to deal with our world. Are Blacks made stronger by the constant reiteration that some Blacks damage each other, without the revelation of the causative psychological and economic pressures? Are whites made wiser and therefore more humane? Yet *Sanford and Son* repeats this surface reality week after week.

Good Times, of course, is not without flaws. In spite of its more positive portrayal of blackness, it still retains much of the slick. The Evans apartment has many accouterments of affluence, the characters are well-dressed, and somehow one does not *feel* the presence of great economic struggle. James' frequent disappointments in getting better jobs are too easily sloughed off, and everybody ends up laughing. A very serious flaw is the fact that Florida apparently does not work. In this respect, she resembles more closely the middle-class white housewife than the Black woman, whose life style has traditionally revolved around the necessity to work and still maintain her home. Indeed, this necessity is part of her agony and part of her strength. Without it, Florida is diminished.

A particularly irritating flaw, at least to me, is the show's treatment of black militancy. The youngest Evans child, Michael, a very bright lad of twelve, is a "militant." In the mouth of a child, the words of militant philosophy are made ludicrous. When the "militant midget" brings forth ideas that deserve serious consideration, they are made to sound ridiculous. The audience laughed uproariously, for example, when the youngster announced that he had been suspended from school for saying that George Washington was a racist and a slaveholder. Well, George Washington *was* a racist and a slaveholder, and Michael's parents, instead of insisting that he apologize to the teacher, should have hightailed it over to that school, gotten the kid reinstated, *and* raised serious question about that teacher's competency! Militancy has always existed in black thought, from David Walker and Henry Highland Garnet to Malcolm X and others. This skirting of the issue, this ridiculing of militancy, is not only irritating but actually harmful.

Essentially, however, *Good Times* gives a more positive portrayal of Blacks than any show on network TV. *Sanford and Son,* despite its great popularity, gives one of the most negative. Ironically both shows use Black writers. Indeed, Mike Evans, one of the originators of *Good Times,* has written for *Sanford and Son.* And I do feel that these writers have effected some improvements in the show during the past year. (Lamont, for example, seems more manly, and he and Fred do not try to break up each other's sexual attachments.) But by the time Black writers came on the scene, the format was so firmly established that the necessary renovation was not immediately possible. Hopefully, with more use of Black writers, the upward trend will continue and the image on this popular show will improve. *Good Times,* on the other hand, has used Black writers from the inception. And now Esther Rolle, the talented actress who created Florida, is insisting on not only Black writers but Black *women* writers.

Why, then, are Blacks so devoted to *Sanford and Son?* Many, I have discovered, are not; some find this program highly offensive. But a great number are truly devoted fans. Why? Part of the answer obviously lies in the comic genius of Redd Foxx, who has long been a favorite among the Black community. Perhaps, also it is partly that Blacks have finally emerged from invisibility in the media, and almost any semblance to black life smacks of the familiar and therefore seems desirable, as opposed to the overwhelming number of stories about white people, which depict a world essentially foreign—a world which (no matter how appealing the characters) has robbed us of so much. So even a *bad* "black" program touches off warm responses.

What, then, can be done to improve the portrayal of Blacks on network TV? Glib answers obviously will not suffice. I will merely suggest a few tentative ideas.

First, Black people are going to have to become more critical, to look with more penetrating vision at the image that enters our living rooms and our minds. Fortunately, this is already happening. Groups are even being formed in various cities to study the media and seek realistic solutions to the myriad problems. Such groups should proliferate and should, indeed, form alliances with each other for more effective pressuring.

Secondly, enlightened Blacks are going to have to speak up to the people who hold the power. White people write in to the studio and complain if they find a program not to their liking; sometimes telegrams and phone calls come in before the program is off the air. We are going to have to learn to write our support of good programs and our protest of those that distort our image. A phone call is better than nothing, but a letter beats a phone call. There are a few Blacks in strategic positions in TV—for example, Benjamin Hooks, who is on the Federal Communications Commission. The Black community must contact these people and seek their advice and practical help.

Actors and writers have a particularly crucial task: They must refuse to perpetuate a distorted image. Undoubtedly I will be accused of being over-idealistic here. Who can expect a hungry artist to do other than he is bid? But it is true that the days when a Black actor must sacrifice his dignity will disappear much faster if enough actors take a stand *now*—as indeed some have. An example is Redd Foxx himself, who once refused to play in *The Great White Hope* because of the negative image of Jack Johnson. And one of the points of contention in Mr. Foxx's recent battle with the producers of *Sanford and Son* was his objection to the Black image perpetuated on the show. Cicely Tyson and the late Diana Sands are among those Black actresses who have insisted on parts that did not demean them. The Black community should actively encourage Black artists in this effort and make known their disapproval of those who participate in the destruction of the image.

Surely there are other steps which we might take *now* to

improve the portrayal of Blacks on TV. The Black community possesses great resources—economic, intellectual, and spiritual—which can be tapped for effective change. We have an urgent need for a clearing house where ideas can be pooled and implemented. Certainly the key to the TV problem, like the key to virtually all our problems, lies in unity. Together we must take firm and often radical steps to effect a more realistic and more positive portrayal of Blacks on this profoundly influential dispenser of ideas and attitudes, American television.

The alternative is another generation of Blacks being taught subtly but effectively by slickly disguised versions of those white-created agents of black destruction, Rastus and Mandy. And as we applaud their antics, we will continually replay the pathetic drama of those Canadian youngsters—we will continue hanging ourselves and hoping someone will cut us down in time.

"Luther" and the Black Image in the Comics

Brumsic Brandon, Jr.

Let us begin with a definition of the word cartoon. A cartoon is "a drawing, often in caricature, made as a commentary on current events, or to illustrate a joke or narrative"; therefore, automatically built into a cartoon is the pointing of an accusative finger. If there is a joke, there must also be a butt of that joke. We Blacks have been either the butt of those jokes in the comics or totally ignored until quite recently. With the advent of the few black comic strips that exist today, we have taken a giant step away from being the butt of the joke and another giant step into the position of pointing an accusative finger. I feel I can best explain the complexities of making that tremendous transition by telling the story of my comic strip, *Luther*.

Having been a professional cartoonist since 1945, I was absolutely thrilled when I was invited to create a black comic strip in 1968. I had previously submitted at least twenty comic strips to various syndicates for consideration with no success. (All my earlier comic strips were constructed around either animals or white characters because there was "no market" for a black strip.) Now, at long last, my chance had come! Surely this was my glorious opportunity to right the wrongs of comics past, as I still vividly remembered them. Still fresh in my mind's eye were the bulbous-lipped, bug-eyed, ghost-fearing, foot-shuffling bumblers of comic pages gone. I could still quite clearly recall the repulsive images of *Smokey, Asbestos, Ebony White* and the like. Still fresh in my mind were the subservient attitudes and the ballooned "yassuhs" of yesterday. Now, the chance of a lifetime was mine!

Having totally rejected the images projected by the comic

LUTHER AND HIS FRIENDS

strips of my youth, and being acutely aware of the vital importance of creating a positive Black image for today, I attacked a large newsprint pad, filling page after page with cute little Black children from which I hoped to cull the nucleus of my proposed comic strip. When the pad was filled, I revisited each page and carefully selected the characters I felt could best fill my needs. It was painfully obvious that the first hurdle to clear was that of creating a group of kids who would not *look objectionable,* as had their predecessors. The best characters were redrawn and presented to the editors who had asked me to develop the strip. With surprising speed, and to my genuine delight, the characters were immediately approved. The first hurdle had been cleared!

I galloped confidently toward the next hurdle. Names! The characters must all be named, and the comic strip must be named as well. My proposal to call the strip *The Inner City Kids* was rejected because the editors, by virtue of past experience, felt the comic strip would have a more successful impact on readers if the strip were named after the main character. Therefore, the next problem was to select and name the main character. All of us agreed on a handsome little boy with a small Afro, soulful eyes and high-waisted pants. This too was resolved with surprising ease and we embarked immediately on a search for the newly selected main character's name. Even before the editors began to offer suggestions, I determined I would not agree to a name that would serve to perpetuate old stereotypes. No Willie or Hambone or Bubber or C.T.! Each name I offered was met with no editorial enthusiasm and each name offered by the editors met with my legitimate disapproval. We had reached our first impasse!

The meeting was adjourned to allow each of us to give the matter further, private consideration. I returned home, resolved to find a name that would help create a positive image. Surely the name of the character (and the strip) would be no less important to his image than his appearance!

Desperately I searched my mind for a name that would

be likely for this little Black boy already burdened with the responsibility of helping to change the Black image on America's comics pages. Suddenly, perhaps as it happens in the comics, a bulb lit above my head! I had thought of a great name for a thoughtful, intelligent little Black boy of today! Not having thought of it sooner annoyed me but did not lessen the joy of giving birth to an idea whose time had surely come. I was certain no one would object to this name, for it should strike a chord of positive imagery in the Black community and still not scare off potential white readers as well. Excitedly I met once again with the editors and proudly announced that I had come up with the perfect name for the star of the new comic strip . . . Luther! My mind perceived this as a salute to Dr. Martin Luther King, whose untimely demise had so recently saddened all our hearts. I was thoroughly convinced that Luther was *the* correct name. Certainly there could be no objection to the name Luther! One editor rubbed his chin pensively and wondered aloud, "What will the Catholics think?"

Despite his reservation, it was decided that we would proceed, at least tentatively, from there. Naming the rest of the kids was more of an evolutionary process and was done without the dubious assistance of the editors. As I set about further developing the characters with whom I had decided to start the strip, I pondered something that has long been clear to me. The Black community is not monolithic, and I wanted this fact reflected in the comic strip. It occurred to me that I could best depict this diversity by using the characters to represent various philosophical postures found in the Black community. This was a helpful device in naming the remaining characters.

Luther would be the thoughtful, inquisitive, only child of hard-working but poor parents, who is always searching for meanings. He would strive valiantly to cope with situations that would be almost always beyond his juvenile ability to comprehend.

Oreo would be, as her name implies, a white oriented little Black girl.

Hardcore would be a tough, street-wise, self-reliant youngster with a remarkable ability to survive.

Mary Frances would be a gum-chewing, finger-popping, independent female counterpart of Hardcore.

Pee Wee would be the youngest, smallest and most impressionable of the group but burdened with such a multitude of problems that simple survival would be his primary goal.

Lily would be a little white girl, and along with her brother, a conveyer of various white attitudes.

With this nucleus, I felt I could at least begin to talk about the things I had long felt were glaring omissions from the funny papers. Despite the absence of positive Black images in the comics of my youth, I read the comics. I studied them, and I remember wondering why "Skippy" and others were never concerned with the things that concerned me most. This was my chance! I busied myself outlining how I could, through this new comic strip, present a long ignored perspective to the American public. During the "riots" that followed the assassination of Dr. Martin Luther King, I began to think that some day in the not too distant future, there would be an intellectual curiosity on the part of some in the white population about the thought process that carries a human being to the point of burning down a city around himself. While I did not condone this kind of activity, I did feel a profound appreciation of the forces that drive some of us to react in such a manner. Perhaps I could use the comic strip to show in some small but repeated measure some of the factors that contribute to that kind of behavior.

At this point, in still another conference, the editors told me they felt the comic strip should be about Black kids, living in an inner city.... No problem! I had been a Black kid and had grown up in Washington, D.C. ... and that the strip should contain "no racial material." My initial reaction was to declare the mission impossible and direct my efforts toward some more achievable goal beyond some other distant horizon. Due to my wife's oft-stated confidence in

my problem-solving ability and my inherent reluctance to walk away from a challenge, I decided to see what could be done with such a frustrating equation.

It had occurred to me at some point beyond my fortieth birthday, that life is indeed a problem for *all* people and that my attention should be directed toward that cataclysmic condition that occurs when race becomes an added ingredient. Perhaps I could deal with the *human* condition and, without saying so, depict what happens when color is added. Perhaps I could rely on the reader to follow a path far beyond the road I pave in four panels.

Cautiously I tried this technique on the editors. It worked! My spirit soared! My reborn confidence surged inside me, much as hot lava within a volcanic mountain when eruption is imminent! I was convinced I could use this formula to say what I felt must be said without compromising my intellectual integrity. I prepared several strips using this technique and confidently turned them over to the editors.

The editors took over. It was their job to sell *Luther* to newspapers across the country. For what seemed an interminable time, I waited anxiously by the telephone. When the editors finally called, the good news for which I yearned was not forthcoming. Reaction from newspaper editors in the polled places was not what my editors had "hoped it would be." Two of the three editors lost interest completely. One persisted. In January, 1969, *Luther* burst into print in a New York City weekly, *The Manhattan Tribune!*

Now, five years and three syndicates later, *Luther* appears in several American newspapers and some foreign publications. I am delighted to state that through the *Los Angeles Times* syndicate, with whom I am currently affiliated, I am free to set about stating my messages in the manner I had originally intended without the "no racial material" restriction. This is not to say my problems are over. There are still many newspaper editors who are reluctant to use a black comic strip for a variety of "reasons." Many still feel one black strip is enough. Editors still cancel the use of a strip for still another variety of "reasons."

However the most important indication of whether the images I hope to project are being discerned lies in the mail I receive from the comic strip reading public. It pleases me to report that *most* of the mail I receive is most complimentary. Frequent requests arrive from people, both Black and white, who have taken a fancy to a strip that appeared on a particular day, asking for the original. This was the case with then Vice-President Ford! Others write to ask for any original. Still others write to tell me to keep "right on!" *Luther* is frequently reprinted in text books, trade publications and professional journals. Requests to reprint have come from as far away as Thailand. All this makes me feel that I am, at least occasionally, hitting the nail on the head, and it gives me great confidence that *Luther* is indeed making a contribution to the new, long sought after, Black image.

It is only fair to state that not all my mail is congratulatory or flattering ... or pleasant ... or kind ... or even signed, in some instances. There are those who take exception to my strip completely and those who take exception to a particular strip on a given day.

The very first letter I received from a reader, after *Luther* broke into print, was from a young white woman who said, in no uncertain terms, that the problems to which I was addressing myself were far too serious to have fun with. She stated further that if I were white, I was sick, and if I were Black, I was crazy. In my response to her, I indicated that we should not be so insensitive that we fail to see the truth, nor should we be so sensitive that we fail to see what humor lies therein. Her reply to my response was heartwarming!

A letter from a Black inmate in a Philadelphia prison stated that a particular strip was "quite true," and that "being black," he saw no humor in it. My response to him was similar to my response to the first letter.

In a letter from St. Louis, I was accused of not knowing very much about "colored" people because I had named a "negro" girl, Mary Frances. The letter was signed, "a Black reader."

A white woman in Los Angeles attributed a verbal attack by a group of Black teen-agers on her eighty-five year old father to *Luther's* being in the *Los Angeles Times*.

The president of a teachers' union condemned me for "defaming the entire teaching profession" because of the attitude of "Miss Backlash." (Miss Backlash is Luther's never shown schoolteacher.)

A policemen's union president wrote to the newspaper in which he had read one *Luther* strip and demanded an immediate apology (which he did not receive).

These letters also serve to inform me that perhaps more frequently than I supposed, *Luther* does hit the nail on the head. Earlier I was perplexed by unsigned letters. It has always been my policy to answer all my mail, regardless of content. It did not take me long to learn that the unsigned mail could not only be answered, but was a rich supply of material for new strips as well. In order to answer the "bashful" letter writers, I had only to have one of the kids in the strip assume the philosophical posture of the letter writer and have one of the other kids respond for me.

What troubles me now is that there are still far too many people who read the comics or whatever and draw vast conclusions from just one character. This is, no doubt, particularly true in the case of Black characters. No one supposes that *all* white sailors have one eye, smoke pipes and love spinach, as does Popeye. Not everyone believes little white boys never win at checkers or baseball because Charlie Brown never does. However there are those who feel that because there are four other kids sleeping in the same bed at the same time as Pee Wee that this is universally true. If this were the case I would happily make all the children little Black billionaires and presto . . . all Blacks would be contented as capitalist cows, instantly! It is my fond hope that one day all of us will be sophisticated enough to realize that no one character or author is competent to portray the total picture. It is from the ever increasing number of vignettes available that vast conclusions should be drawn.

My mail indicates quite clearly that a new, positive Black

image is emerging in the comics, and this new image is being accepted by the public, albeit begrudgingly by some. The mail also indicates to me that many comic strip readers are far ahead of the newspaper editors who do not or cannot appreciate the necessity for the presence of this new image. Therefore, it is important that the comic strip reading public write letters to editors about comic strips. Letters from the public carry a tremendous amount of weight. Letters are the editors' index as to whether or not a strip is being read. Luther has been dropped from some newspapers due to what editors call a "lack of readers' interest," while *my* mail indicates a considerable interest in the area serviced by that newspaper.

If the positive **Black** image is to continue to emerge and prosper (I refer to the images of *Wee Pals* and *Quincy* as well as *Luther* and any others who have not yet come to my attention), editors must be made to know that the comic strip readers dig what's happening.

Write on!

Great Themes for Black Plays and Films

John Henry Jones

One of the most avoided aspects of the history of drama and the theater is its beginnings more than 4,000 years ago along the sun-drenched banks of the Nile River in Egypt.

Dramatic origins while shrouded in remote antiquity were rooted in religious ritual and functional dances accompanied by pantomime and spoken or chanted narrative on occasions of births, deaths, marriages, battles, sacrifices, seasonal or elemental imprecations, initiations. This is a universal development of primitive societies—even today.

Humans are creatures of rhythm or measured movement. Primitive man was attuned to the rise and setting of the sun and the moon, the inexorable coming in and receding of the ocean's waves, the seaward roll of the rivers, the flapping of the wings of birds, the beat of the heart. Rhythmic movement thus became dancing. Uttered sounds of joy or sorrow became the germs of poetry. Hands were clapped, rattles and shells were shaken, sticks were beaten on logs and the ancestry of music is discernible. There were gods and spirits associated with nature to be implored and pleased. There was rain to be danced for, game to be hunted and killed for food, tribal history to be preserved, puberty rites to be conducted, preparations for battles, elders to be honored—a hundred uses which called for this dance-poetry-music-mimicry combination.

Primitive man very often disguised himself in animal skins to get near his intended food-kill. In this dramatic means of getting food lie the roots of the theatrical mask which, while not exclusively African, was used there extensively among such pastoral peoples as the Bushongo, the Yorubas, the Kasai, and the Bapende.

"In many African cultures the secret societies which heretofore had a very definite religious purpose to perform and into which the boys were initiated with great ceremony have become dramatic societies and their secret houses into which none but the initiated would be admitted have been turned into the theater for the populace."

These obvious dramatic roots are seldom if ever acknowledged by dramatic historians and are to be found in anthropological studies such as *The Dramas and Dramatic Dances of Non-European Peoples* by Sir William Ridgway or *The Drama of Savage Peoples* by Loomis Havemeyer. When it all came together as designed drama it is impossible to say; but we can put two and two together and see the theater's ancestral roots.

Sophisticated and conscious dramatic construction is first recorded from the walls of pyramids and tombs of the Fifth and Sixth Egyptian Dynasties about 2800 B.C. The pyramid texts are the earliest evidences of the beginnings of composed drama. These hieroglyphic texts contain directions and indications for actions and characters probably performed by priests. They portray among other things, the ascension of the soul or the resurrection of high personages like kings which obviously required the priest-actors to physically represent coming to life.

The trail of modern European drama leads to ecstatic rites and festivities participated in by the Greek populace, priests, and chanters of dithyrambic poetry—the unrestrained short poems to the god Dionysus. Their relating of events in the god's life was very similar to the Egyptian Passion Plays. Gradually the great stone theater of Dionysus evolved and a succession of Greek harpists, singers, performers, and writers like Arion, Thespis, and Aeschylus laid the foundation of Greek drama from which emerged European drama and the present day theater of the West.

The development of the drama from Greek tragedies, based as they were on rigid moral laws governing the family as a social unit, lay dormant during the Middle

Ages. Excepting the *Ars Poetica* of Horace there are few critical references to the period. We know of course that minstrelsy, festivals, and religious rites abounded and developed form and content that were to burst into a frenzy of dramatic action during the European Renaissance.

The New Age brought onto the European scene the Elizabethan theater of Shakespeare and Marlowe, the Italian commedia dell'arte; the Spanish plays of Calderon and Lope de Vega, the French plays of Pierre Corneille, Jean Racine and Molière; the Germans Andreas Gryphius and Christian Weiser; and Isak Bork of Sweden.

All these were harbingers of the germinating bourgeoisie whose tragedies and contradictions Henrik Ibsen so brilliantly delineated in his massive Norwegian dramas in the nineteenth century. This capsulized view of dramatic origins is crucial to our discussion since it firmly reveals drama's role as a reflector, a catalyst and, in modern times, a tool and servant of society's contending forces.

Hence from its very inception as pointed out by the noted dramatist and playwright Loften Mitchell (*Black Drama,* 1967), theater and/or films in the United States have for the most part been used to shatter, distort and degrade the image of Black Americans as human beings.

> "... In 1795 Murdock's *The Triumph of Love* ... introduced a shuffling, cackling, allegedly comic Negro servant. The *Politicians* in 1797 continued this stereotype. The course was therefore established—the course that was to lead the Black man to be represented on the American stage as something to be ridiculed and a creature to be denied human status."

On the other hand it is significant, therefore, that the first known play by a Black American was entitled *Escape or a Leap for Freedom* by William Wells Brown (1858). It told the tragic story of a slave woman, a cruel, lustful white master and her slave lover. Although it is crudely written and highly melodramatic there is the Abolitionist hero who helps them escape across the river and into Canada.

As is our entire culture, U.S. dramatic history is characterized by this dichotomized relationship. There are the countless dramatic outrages visited upon the Black American image on the stage, in films and lately TV. Examples are black face minstrel shows (Daniel Emmet's *Virginia Minstrels* and, in the theater, Dion Boucicault's *The Octaroon).*

Donald Bogle *(Toms, Coons, Mulattoes, Mammies, and Bucks)* points out that in films Blacks either played rapists (D. W. Griffith's *The Birth of a Nation);* the comic, lazy, shiftless lout (Stepin Fetchit, *Sleep 'n' Eat);* the tragic mulatto (Dorothy Dandridge in *Carmen Jones* and *Porgy and Bess;* Fredi Washington in *Imitation of Life)* or the faithful Black mammy (Hattie McDaniel in *Gone With the Wind).*

New and Provocative Material

Black world experience, though, is complex, exciting, and multiclass with all human intent and emotions. The writer and producer looking for black themes have a wealth of original ideas, eras, and characters to pick from. There are some themes, several synopses, and a few pointers for those who want new and provocative material. There is no need to arbitrarily categorize these suggestions as either for drama or film. The drama of the nineteenth century reflected the bourgeois individual's conflict with environmental conditions and then turned inward in philosophical soul searching.

Today, however, new social forces are operating. Masses are in motion challenging existing power and rationales. Thus while drama of passion and conviction on a picture frame stage still has great relevancy, the film as a revolutionary art form is a unique social force that can portray the vast panorama of today's clashing forces and the sweep of the past as well as zero in on a two-character tour de force. Through motion pictures and now television, millions of people have cultural experiences and see delineations of life that shape their thoughts and feelings. The selection of themes and media is therefore dependent upon the writer's and producer's understanding of what story is to be told to what audience.

The question in order now is what can be done to end the all-media sins of commission and omission against Black Americans—as to the truth of their experience and to their right of participation in the basic mainstreams of national life—social, economic, and cultural.

The brilliant actress and writer Ellen Holly recently came to the point (*New York Times,* June 2, 1974):

"While I fervently hope that more black films will be made and controlled by Black people, I suspect that it is a lot closer to the point to hope that more black films will be made and controlled by people of any color whatsoever who care about Black people."

Amen, with this proviso. Those who care, whether they are Black or white writers, producers, or directors, must know, understand and be committed to recreating and delineating the truth of this nation's experience vis-à-vis the condition of its Black citizens in their imposed subordinate status and forced identification.

The job for Black American writers or any writer committed to the truth is to define the hidden syndrome wrapped in the tangled skein of U.S. historical cause and effect. Identifying and unraveling the mechanics of this nation's near terminal malady would be an achievement forever heralded by unborn millions. It is a tedious job of painstakingly loosening up tight knots of manmade hatred, tying together the severed arteries of black/white communion, and finally stripping off the dead skin of fear until the nation's stated democratic aims are recognized by all as necessary for life or we shall all perish. Soul singer James Brown's formula is a good one. "Don't hate; communicate!"

A simple chronological order of dramatic interest for

black themes could be: 1) Africa—the remote past and near present; 2) the ordeal of slavery in the New World; 3) Reconstruction in the U.S.; 4) the survival and growth of Black people in the United States. A multiplicity of stories begs to be delineated from these alone.

Themes from African History

Obviously African history has a special meaning for those who claim its heritage. There are several great African queens whose lives have all the elements of human conflict that make for great drama. First of all as the historian and Associate Editor of *Freedomways* John Henrik Clarke points out (*Essence*, 5/71): "In the first African societies the woman played a major role without demeaning the man or making his role less important."

But of all the Cleopatras portrayed, none presents her as the Black woman she was. Her tempestuous and politically motivated love affairs with Julius Caesar and Mark Antony, in an effort to remove Egypt from Roman domination about 50 B.C., and her subsequent suicide after Octavius defeated Antony are well known. What a difference it would make to see this great woman in a play or film as she really was! How about the title *Cleopatra Was Black.*

The love story of the Queen of Sheba and King Solomon of Jerusalem is also well known and she is celebrated in Ethiopia as part of its national heritage. Her journey to Jerusalem to partake of Solomon's wisdom is a story of beauty and splendor that could throw much light on the history of today's troubled Near East.

Queen Hatshepsut of Egypt who reigned nearly 1,500 years before Cleopatra had a life filled with royal intrigue. She had become queen when her half brother, to whom she had been married by their father Thothmes I, ascended the throne as Thothmes II.

These are just a few of the colorful figures of antiquity whose stories lend themselves to dramatic portrayal of historical fact as do the more recent stories of Elizabeth of England, Catherine the Great of Russia, or the Empress Dowager of China.

The story of the rise and grandeur of later African kingdoms such as Ghana, Songhay, Timbuctu, and Mali is rich in dramatic potential. For here is the beginning of the modern era which saw the rise of European power, the beginning of the black slave trade in the fifteenth century, and the origin of today's great moral dilemma.

Two hundred years later the mighty drama of the life of the great Zulu chief Shaka is set against the conquest and partition of Africa by the European powers in the early nineteenth century.

Themes from the Slavery Period and the Civil War

The African slave trade was begun by the Portuguese about 1443 with the blessings of Pope Eugenius on the grounds that Africans were "pagans." In 1452 Pope Nicholas V gave Spanish King Alfonso permission to enslave the "pagans," and by 1481 England's Edward IV asked for and got papal permission. By 1660 the pretense of proselyting was discarded and there was a general scramble including the French and Dutch for control of the African slave trade and the beginning of the partition of the "dark continent."

This is an historial period that lends itself to dramatic clarification. The likes of Alistair Cooke with his selective and pro-white oriented historical dramatizations never venture into this ugly but pertinent reservoir of themes. While many Africans of this era were certainly highly organized by tribal societies and, in many cases, kingdoms of tribal peoples, there was no unifying system among the various hunting and agricultural peoples.

Great natural barriers of mountains, rivers, and forests led to the development of isolated peoples. There were indeed wars and the taking of captives among them. They were no match for the European invaders armed with firearms and looking for human chattels. And so the slave trade raged for centuries. The commerce of Europe was based on it, and gradually the rationalization of racial inferiority developed.

Colonial America at first cultivated its plantations with white indentured servants, but by 1650 the cultivation of rice and tobacco demanded, in the views of the newly emerging colonial bourgeoisie, more and more Black slave labor.

Here indeed is an era that begs for truthful dramatic interpretation. It is important to see that the concept of racial inferiority was developed step by step. The reasoning behind this trend, the thinking of the slavers and the resistance of the enslaved Africans are profoundly dramatic. What were the political, social, and human motivations that, as Earl Conrad suggests, entered ". . . into the building of a national pattern that would allow two utterly contradictory concepts–American liberty and American slavery to flourish side by side in the American soul?" (*The Invention of the Negro*, 1966).

When the British attempted to recruit slaves during the Revolutionary War, George Washington was forced to allow the enlistment of both free Blacks and slaves in the Continental Army. Here is an era rich in dramatic possibilities that would lend itself to spectacular depictions of the role Black men played in the country's birth. There is also the need for the roles of Thomas Jefferson, James Madison, Benjamin Franklin and Patrick Henry ("Give me liberty or give me death!") on the slavery question to be cleared up in the minds of today's citizens who revel in the narcissistic myths of the purity of their past.

In the early 1800's while other countries began freeing slaves and serfs, the slave power in the southern United States was expanding westward and challenging the free labor system of the North which was developing industrially.

The slaves existed in a virtual concentration-camp atmosphere. Sunup to sundown backbreaking farm labor, identification passes, and abject behavior were the rule. The law was rigidly enforced by brutal poor white officers, and armed patrols kept all slave quarters, roads, fields, and forests under constant observation. Violations brought severe physical punishment and many times death.

From 1800 to the Emancipation Proclamation of 1863 the Black slaves resisted slavery in hundreds of revolts that refute the lie of the happy slaves. The theme of Nat Turner's insurrection has already been the subject of a play by Paul Peters starring Frank Silvera. It is still a lode to mine. Frederick Douglass, Denmark Vesey, Sojourner Truth and Harriet Tubman are the classic powerful figures about whom much has been written. There are more of these unnamed giants in our history whose stories need to be searched out and dramatized.

William Branch's *In Splendid Error* which dealt with one episode in Douglass's life when he refused to join John Brown's raid on Harper's Ferry is the kind of dramatic truth needed for historical perspective today. One of the most crucial elements of the Civil War was President Lincoln's hesitation about freeing the slaves and his uncertainty about their future role in a free economy. Even in the face of serious defeats of the Union Army he talked about preserving the Union. He really believed in colonizing the slaves in some foreign land and openly advocated separation. Douglass, however, clearly saw that slavery was the cause of the war and he called for free Black troops to march south and proclaim freedom.

The reaction of the freedmen must have been one of the most profound in the nation's history. Douglass said later the nation had unchained "against her foes her powerful Black hand." Free Blacks and freedmen rushed to arms. The first troops entering Charleston, Virginia, the scene of Denmark Vesey's defeat, were led by a Black soldier carrying a banner with the word "Liberty." The Black regiments singing *John Brown's Body* were cheered by the ex-slaves. Auction blocks and slave pens were burned and destroyed.

Truly here is the stuff of a great spectacle—rough and

ready—but the ecstasy of revolution was never any tea party. Needed here is not the obfuscating pro-slavery rhetoric of Bruce Catton but an observer that will seek out the human drama of people newly freed from centuries of bondage.

The struggle around the land question just after the Civil War was the theme of Theodore Ward's *Our Lan'*, presented brilliantly Off-Broadway but watered down and misinterpreted on Broadway.

The disposition of the land is really what settled the destiny of Black Americans after the Civil War and is the basis of our condition today. Socially aware dramatists and producers have a great reservoir of themes here.

Thaddeus Stevens, leader of the Radical Republicans in Congress, had repeatedly urged the complete dismantling of slave power based as it was on the vast plantations. He eloquently advocated breaking them up into small farms. Charles Sumner, his counterpart in the Senate, declared: "A homestead must be secured to the freedmen so that at least every head of a family may have a piece of land."

After Lincoln's assassination the Black Codes were enacted under Vice-President Andrew Johnson to bar the freedmen's access to civil rights. Obviously a very complex man, Johnson's clash with the fiery Stevens would make very good theater.

Bitter struggles broke out across the South as the ex-slaves sought to secure land for themselves and played out in blood some of the most violent personal and mass dramas. Stevens organized a joint House and Senate committee to investigate Southern conditions and pass on the fitness of the restored states. Then came a series of Reconstruction Acts that divided the ten rebel states into five military districts.

Tragedy was then in the wings for the newly freed peoples. First, while they had won many political positions, they still had no economic power since Johnson, allied with the former slave owners, was busily pardoning them and restoring their property. Even the Republicans who generally supported Stevens shied away from his proposals for dividing the plantations into plots of 40 acres for each adult ex-slave. This was the famous "forty acres and a mule" proposal.

Themes from Reconstruction

The entire Reconstruction Era is pregnant with heroic themes and great figures as the battle for democracy raged between the former slave owners and their ex-slaves. Blacks and poor whites formed Leagues. Peoples' Assemblies and Conventions struck at the still powerful slave power. Claude G. Bowers, the apologist for slavery, called this period "The Tragic Era" and raged at the freedmen's attempt to bring democracy to the South.

Great Black figures like F. L. Cardozo and R. H. Cain of South Carolina and P. B. S. Pinchback of Louisiana are just a few of the Black politicians who served in Reconstruction state governments. The significance of these governments, indeed their very existence, is generally unknown and at best misinterpreted. This is more virgin territory for plays and films.

The election campaign of 1876 was the death knell for Black peoples' rights. It was so close that S. J. Tilden, the Democratic candidate, needed only one electoral vote to win. Many Blacks who normally voted Republican had been scared away from the polls by terror. Civil war threatened to erupt again. Rutherford B. Hayes, the Republican, then made a deal and an electoral commission gave him the contested states of Louisiana, Florida, South Carolina, and Oregon. Subsequently Federal troops were pulled from the South and the destiny of Black people in the U.S. was delivered back into the hands of the former slave masters.

This period more than any other cries out for dramatic interpretation. It is filled with the conflict of great historical issues and the clash of the dynamic personalities, both Black and white, who waged the bitter struggles.

Today's Black Drama

The history of Black Americans since Reconstruction is the story of survival and growth in the face of the sweeping and brutal victory of white supremacy. Many individual men and women have stood against the tide in personal conflict, often ending in death and again in monumental achievement despite the heavy odds against them.

Thus we have consciously dealt at length with historical and social frameworks that lend themselves to dramatic presentation. The writer has the problem of selection, and regardless of whether his story is based on fact or invention he must be wholly aware of his characters in relation to the times he places them in.

Much of today's black drama—searingly realistic—is confined to the milieu of the inner city. Its foremost exponents deal with the contemporary condition of Black Americans rooted deep, as we have seen, in the nation's past. Until these legacies are unraveled and understood many Black Americans will go on being ashamed of themselves and, as some do, assuming "foreign" names and dress. White fear, hatred and self-guilt will be with us as long as ignorance reigns.

The years since 1900 hang heavy with the bitter fruit of lynched Black bodies, but there is also the ripeness of the lives of valiant men and women whose triumphs and tragedies should be told. The Mary McLeod Bethunes, Mary Church Terrells, Madame C. J. Walkers, Florence Millses, Bert Williamses, Scott Joplins, Dr. J. E. Walkers, A. C. Spauldings, W.E.B. Du Boises, Monroe Trotters, and countless other giants (visit Harlem's Schomburg Center and find them) led complex lives of compelling dramatic possibilities. To these tableaux must be added some dramatic insights into the lives of Black American middle-class individuals. This yet untapped source of ideas is an integral part of Black American culture.

The novelists of the Negro Renaissance like Nella Larsen (*Passing* and *Quicksand*) or Jessie Fauset (*The Chinaberry*

Tree) created tragic middle-class figures whose conflicts were motivated by their desires or needs to become part of the forbidden white society.

What other problems and passions have motivated and driven these people–the doctors, lawyers, teachers, scholars, hairdressers, barbers, farmers, insurance salesmen, social workers, college presidents, actors, actresses–as they struggled throughout the decades of the twentieth century in the big white fog Theodore Ward wrote about in his memorable play?

The Black soldier and his loyalty, devotion, and courage in all the wars this nation has fought are completely ignored by all. Ellen Holly points out that a script by Paul Leaf dealing with the exploits of the all-Black 99th Fighter Squadron of World War II remains undone. "They shot down more German planes over Anzio than any other fighter squadron in the history of the war." They facetiously called themselves "the Spookwaffe." The exploits of white heroes Sergeant Alvin York in World War I and Audie Murphy in World War II were glorified in the movies. Who has heard of Needham Roberts and Henry Johnson of the 369th Regiment who single-handedly killed and wounded thirty-two Germans during a single engagement on the French front in World War I? They were decorated with the Distinguished Service Cross and France gave these Black heroes the Croix de Guerre, its highest honor.

Today the history of his remote heritage and immediate roots challenges the Black American artist. The purpose of the theater in the first place has always been communication. It follows then that the audience which plays an active part in all drama must be considered as a variable factor. It may like the play or not. The question is, did it get the message the dramatist or filmwriter was sending?

People created the theater out of their own needs. It's one way of getting together, bringing things down front and talking them out.

What better contribution can be made to our troubled times?

IV. People, Politics and Movements

Our Beloved Pauli

Ollie Harrington

The Bronx street where I grew up must have been the world's puniest black ghetto, one block long, and only half of it at that. On the other side of the street were the pungent Sheffield Farms stables whose sleek tenants in their warm stalls were the envy of every shivering Black kid on the block. Our hopes were aimed low: a chunk of cardboard to plug the holes in our shoe soles, a bit of fat meat swimming in gravy and on Sunday, if God's mood was up to it, chicken. Our dreams, or at least my dreams, were more daring. Visions of Miss Murray made into fine hash by the wheels of a locomotive, in slow motion and color. She was the teacher who lasciviously licked her thin lips each time she told our class that all Black kids belonged in the trash baskets. How our little white classmates giggled under the psychedelic kick of these first trips on racism. Another joyous dream, awake or asleep, was the howling death of Duffy, that blue-uniformed menace who lurked in the alley next to Belsky's candy store, hungry night stick twirling on leather thong. Duffy's stick had already put Melvin Toles into bed. He was only nine, but paralysis would keep him there for life. We didn't realize it then, probably because the jack-leg preacher over at Thessalonia Baptist had explained that Melvin was only "kind'a sprained by the Law." Each Fourth of July Duffy's fat buttocks pranced along the Grand Concourse in the Veterans of Foreign Wars parade. Duffy always carried the Stars and Stripes.

Mornings, dry or wet, a tiny flock of Black mothers stumbled in arthritic disorder over to Grant Avenue where they numbly waited for the penny-pinching white ladies who would hire them for ten hours. The men folk trudged across the New York Central tracks to Schrimer's umbrella factory or to the ice plant. Shamefaced they underbid each other for a day's work. The surplus floated back to some day-long card game or sat in squalid flats staring out of the vapor-glazed windowpanes.

Saturday nights the air seemed to vibrate. "Sportin' folks" clamored into the inevitable rent party where they stomped and rubbed bellies before settin' down to a heap of heavily tabascoed chitlins washed down with tub-fresh gin. Kids along the block lay awake waiting for the explosion of shouting, cussing, screaming and shattering glass. Often after these happenings Reverend Passley, the barber-bricklayer-undertaker (and some said, root man) had work to do in the part-time mortuary behind the barber shop. The good Reverend had only one oration which began with: "We so confused and upset all the time that we got to lash out at one another. . . ." Unfortunately the folks often lashed out with a straight razor and this inhibited the Reverend's talents considerably. Which is probably why, it was widely whispered, he preferred the ice pick which left the deceased looking more natural.

Our sources of inspiration were meager. There was Ray Mitchel the "genius" who could "put just about anything together and make a radio out of it." But to be that "deep" called for schooling and such "fool notions" were throttled at birth by the high-minded dedication of Duffy and Miss Murray. One other possible goal was fuzzily sketched by Mr. Sweet Reuban, who not only owned the corner poolroom but also a most formidable pile of gold on constant display in the open showcase of his upper and lower gums. Sweet Reuban would tip back his pearl-gray, exposing a magnificent head of conked locks and pronounce, "You little 'niggers' will never git nowhere workin' wif your hands and sweatin' all over the damn place. You ever heard of a president sweatin'?" With that he would reach into his vest pocket for the famous gold toothpick and gently dig around the nuggets with little sucking noises. But by then the predatory eyes of the oracle were focused on some other world and we knew that we'd been dismissed.

The kids disappeared one by one into the fog of other

black slums. All except Biffo, our beloved jester. Biffo found his golden hoard–all $17.50 of it–in a night-shuttered tailor shop. The widowed Polish woman who owned the shop lay in a pool of her own blood the next morning. Biffo's gravelly laugh floated up from the dark cellars and vestibules along the block for several nights. In these hastily commandeered love bowers Biffo squandered his fortune, converted into chocolate-covered nut bars, on giggling, squealing teen-age girls. Duffy followed the candied spoor and pounced, delivering Biffo to the plain-clothes men and eventually the electric chair at Sing Sing. We climbed the rickety tenement stairs to the flat of Biffo's work-gnarled father, drawn by whispered rumors of horrible burns on Biffo's skull. But he lay in a sealed coffin and we quietly crept out, leaving the huge Black father rocking wordlessly over an oilcloth-covered kitchen table.

My hopeless world was smashed by Meyer Fischer. Every morning at five Meyer and his wife Blanche rolled in the heavy ten-gallon milk containers, then tugged and swiveled the bulky bread baskets to open their unheated grocery store. They were, and always would be, poor Jews because they couldn't resist mumbled pleas for credit which was rarely repaid. Many afternoons I sat on a meal sack while Meyer, clasping and unclasping his blue-veined hands, his tiny mouth puffing vapor in the freezing cold store, told me of Black poets, teachers, Black doctors. One day he told me of an unbelievable Black man named Paul Robeson. He told me of this Black man who was not as good as white men. He had to be, and he was, ten times better. Meyer's piercing eyes refused to release my unbelieving stare. They willed me to think that perhaps there was such a Black man! And if there was it would mean that we were not trash and dirt– even though Black. It was a soul-splitting thought. It was a blow-torch burning out the foundations of existence. I, along with every child and adult on the block, was cruelly maimed by everything I'd ever seen, or heard, or even tasted. We knew that we were a tiny lepers' island surrounded by the "land of the free and the home of the brave." Even the

18

church steeple "crosstown" had its backside turned in our faces. The red-faced butcher, who could barely speak English, kept a special pile of offal for his "nigger trade." If there were ever a Nobel Prize for the vivisection of living, breathing Black kids Miss Murray should have had it. Duffy the Law was tearing out palpitating Black hearts long before Dr. Barnard left the diaper stage. And when we thought of Duffy we thought of the Stars and Stripes. We were "niggers" and we'd been so magnificently brainwashed in what that meant that the only art, the only poetry in our little "nigger" hearts was:

A chicken ain't nothin' but a bird
A nigger ain't nothin' but a turd.

The caterpillar, covered with gray-green, undulating hairs, hides its slimy ugliness inside a cocoon. When the season arrives some magic in nature opens the prison and a completely new creature emerges to rest on a leaf in God's air. Gently it folds and unfolds its breathlessly beautiful wings in the strength-building sunlight. Black children carrying their "niggerness" like lead weights on anxiety-tensed shoulders can experience this same metamorphosis. It's happening all around us. On my single-street ghetto it happened when Meyer Fischer first told me of Paul Robeson.

Five years later my "wings" had lifted me out of the tiny Bronx ghetto and set me down in a real people-sized one— Harlem. The rest of America was being cruelly ravaged by the depression but Harlem only giggled over the sounds of self-pity which the wind carried from across the Central Park lake. "Baby, if you crave to see some real, honest-to-goodness depression, come to Harlem, the Home of Happy Feet," giggled the wits on "the turf." I discovered that I wasn't any more hungry learning to draw and paint at the National Academy of Design than I would be huddled up in my room. Anyway it was free and the Academy rooms were warm. At night bunches of us milled around the sidewalk outside the IdleWyle or the Big Apple. Downtown they were still mournfully talking about the good, solid white folks who had walked into space from Wall Street's many windows. Uptown we were talking about Paul Robeson, who was singing songs which gripped some inner fibers in us that had been dozing. And he was saying things which widened black eyes and sharpened black ears, things which sounded elusively familiar. But there were a few cats in the crowd who somehow managed to own one Brooks Brothers suit. They sported frat pins (jim-crow frats) and pretended to read the financial section of *The New York Times* which they'd found on the floor of some Lenox Ave. IRT local. "That damn Robeson," they grumbled, "gon' make the big white folks mad, you just wait and see." They were right. Robeson did make the big white folks mad. But when his voice boomed, "I Hear America Singing," he blew flame in the souls of Black folk, and a hell of a lot of white folks too, where dim embers had barely glowed since the days of Reconstruction.

One blustery night the space between the bar and the lunch counter at the Harlem Moon rocked and reeled in the heat of another "Robeson debate." Hopeless fear, cynicism and outraged frustration quickly drew the lines between "Uncle Tom niggers" and "goddamn red niggers." A flat-footed, sad-eyed waiter from New Haven said to me, "Son, them students up there got so much money they don't know what to do. They requires an awful lot of service. Now if you can get together enough for one semester you can hustle your way through." It was a long story but I got there. One of the waiters in the Chi Psi house where I was installed as head–and only–dishwasher asked me, "How in the hell did a little-assed 'nigger' like you get to come to Yale?" All I could answer was, "I guess it was Paul Robeson." "What," he gasped, "you know Paul Robeson?" I lifted a tray of steaming glasses out of the suds and said, "Nope. Just know of him."

My first real job was as art editor of the *People's Voice*. Adam Powell, Charlie Buchanan and Ben Davis published that great sheet and one day Adam called me into his office. "Ollie," he said, "there's someone I want you to meet." A beaming giant of a man left his chair, thumped me on the back with a hand as powerful as John Henry's sledge hammer and boomed, "Feller, I just wanted you to know that those cartoons of yours are great." Of course it was Paul Robeson. I can't remember doing much more than gulping. What can one say to a mountain? But it was the beginning of a treasured friendship.

Paul walked into that ramshackle Harlem newspaper office one afternoon with Ilya Ehrenburg, one of the world's great writers. With them came a tiny slip of a woman, the captain of a Soviet ship which had been torpedoed and sunk in a convoy. Robeson spoke to the staff. Ehrenburg spoke and thanked all Americans, in the name of the Soviet Union, for the weapons the Red Army was putting to such good use against Hitler's killer hordes. And he made it clear that this deep gratitude included all of the people of Harlem. The little ship's captain–I believe her name was Valentina–spoke no English but she beamed as if she'd lived in Harlem all of her life. Later we discovered that she'd lost all of her clothing at sea. In two days a bespectacled Black tailor in 126th Street had made her a uniform and overcoat that must have been the pride of the Soviet merchant fleet. *Made in Harlem* and joyfully paid for by everyone on the staff, from editor to telephone receptionist.

There are many other treasured snapshots engraved in my mind. Paul, a great one for a session of "talkin' and signifyin'," sitting astride an ancient looking desk in the miniature-sized office of his publication *Freedom.* Again I was contributing cartoonist and fascinated spectator. Paul was holding forth on the wizardry of old Josh Gibson, Satchel Paige and other Black ballplayers jim-crowed out of what was euphemistically called the national pastime. Listening were editors Lou Burnham and George Murphy, with Lou exploding every now and then with a characteristic, "Amen, Amen!" Behind the desk sat a diminutive secretary whose lovely brown face was illuminated with a serenity which seemed curiously out of place in a loft on 125th Street. "One day," said Paul, "our boys are going to bust right into the Yankee Stadium dugout and teach 'em the fine points of the game." The little secretary's eyes twinkled and she asked, "Mister Robeson, shall I make a note to get a committee together this afternoon?" Paul stopped in mid-sentence and then "fell out." Lou dissolved into a laughter-shaken mass on a pile of newspapers, and George, always cool, sat shaking his head. The secretary who was there gently growing her wings was Lorraine Hansberry.

There are many other memories. A huge sea of Black folk silently filling Seventh Avenue as far as one could see. It was Ben Davis' last campaign for a seat on the City Council and it was night, drizzling. Ben had lost, with the help of the cops who somehow managed an epidemic of polling booth breakdowns that day. But the crowds waited patiently outside Ben's election headquarters in the Theresa Hotel. One of those thoroughly reliable Harlem rumors had it that Paul would sing. "Naw," said someone, "his man lost so what he gon' sing for?" An old church sister just smiled and said, " 'Cause he said he would." And then there was Robeson and the heart-filling voice singing "What Is America to Me."

Not very long ago I was invited by the satirical *Krokodil* to see the Soviet Union. In Tashkent I sat on a park-bench where I could drink in the breath-taking oriental beauty of the opera house. I was thinking of coming back the next day with my sketch pad when a little Uzbek girl came to me holding out a flower. Her oval face was so lovely, even with a missing front tooth. Of course I couldn't understand what she was saying but Yuri, my interpreter explained, "She asks if you are Paul Robeson?" Her mother appeared and suddenly it seemed there were hundreds of Uzbek children with their mothers, all carrying hastily picked flowers. I was terribly flustered but I managed to explain that I wasn't Paul Robeson but that he was my friend. And then one Uzbek mother, proud of her English said, "Here, he is our beloved Pauli."

Paul Robeson at Peekskill

Charles H. Wright

Few people had heard of Peekskill, N.Y., before 1949. Two dramatic events which occurred on August 27 and September 4 of that year attracted world-wide attention to this Hudson Valley hamlet, and its name, henceforth, became synonymous with mob violence.

Paul Robeson was the star of the Peekskill performance. Having been there before, he knew the scene well. Now, however, time and circumstances were fused in an explosive mix that would make his 1949 appearances memorable. Subsequent events suggest that Peekskill bears the same relationship to the Civil Rights Movement as Fort Sumter does to the Civil War.

In retrospect, it can be postulated that Robeson began a collision course with the United States establishment as early as 1934. En route to the Soviet Union for the first time in December of 1934, he was racially abused and threatened by Nazi storm troopers outside the Berlin railroad station. Here began his eternal war against fascism. He crossed the Russian border a few hours later, and the Russian people, by contrast, welcomed him with open arms. Thus was born his abiding friendship with the peoples of the Soviet Union. These two events changed the course of Robeson's life. He paid dearly for both of them.

Opinions differ as to when the Peekskill confrontation became inevitable. Marie Seton, author of *Paul Robeson* (Dobson Press Ltd.) is certain that the die was cast in 1947 when Robeson included the song "Joe Hill" in his concert at the University of Utah. Never before, in this area, had anyone dared sing this lament to the ill-fated labor organizer, Joseph Hillstrom, whose death before a Utah firing squad had caused an international crisis earlier in the century. Robeson must have known that there were "copper bosses" in the audience. His plaintive rendition of the song disturbed the uneasy consciences of many listeners. After a stunned period of silence, some of the audience clapped loudly. Others clenched their fists. Nothing seemed to go well for Robeson thereafter.

His concert series began to crumble almost immediately. Peoria, Ill. and Albany, N.Y. led the way. When all of the returns were in, more than eighty concerts were canceled. Public pressure forced Albany officials to relent but not before anti-Robeson forces surfaced among Catholic students in New York City and veterans' organizations in Peekskill, N.Y.

Prior to 1947, Robeson was the national champion of the rights of the working man. Nearly a dozen unions had honored him with life memberships. He appeared regularly as guest artist at their national conventions, marched in their picket lines and gave benefit concerts to support their causes. Cold War politics, a way of life in the late forties, and a compliant judiciary changed Robeson's relationship with most of organized labor appreciably. Implementation of President Harry Truman's anti-Communist foreign policy and the passage of such labor legislation as the Taft-Hartley law forced labor organizations to make difficult decisions in 1947. They either had to support a foreign policy of "Communist containment" and expel those radicals who had been so vital to their earlier organizing drives, or suffer suppression, suspension and possible destruction. This new look in labor made Robeson's brand of militant unionism unfashionable. He was no longer welcome in the halls of the conformist unions. Some groups even attempted to withdraw his life memberships. Only the "renegade" unions had the audacity to invite Robeson to their meetings in the late forties and the early fifties.

Robeson's support of the Progressive Party in 1948 aroused the enmity of the power brokers in the Democratic Party. Michael Quill, President of the Transport Workers'

Union, expressed some of the prevailing sentiment of the period. He blamed Robeson and the progressives for the loss of New York State to the Republicans in 1948. Speaking before the National Convention of the National Maritime Union in 1949, Quill predicted that Robeson might run for the U.S. Senate from New York. Such unpopular activity plus his public challenge to President Truman to support anti-poll tax and anti-lynch legislation isolated Robeson from the Democratic Party.

Aside from his unpopular political stands, Robeson engaged in other activities that increased his enemies exponentially. In 1947 he responded to a plea from Black workers in Winston-Salem, N.C. who were striking against the R. J. Reynolds Tobacco Co. He boosted their morale and raised money for their support. Some time later, a Russian radio broadcast carried an interview with Robeson in which he criticized the poor working conditions for Black workers in the tobacco industry. Local officials, already displeased with Robeson's interference in their internal affairs, seized this opportunity to discredit Robeson and undermine the strike effort. Not only was the union effort defeated, but the R. J. Reynolds Co. remains unorganized to this day.

Also in 1948 Robeson went to Hawaii in support of the Longshoremen's and Warehousemen's Union, the parent union of the sugar cane and pineapple workers. The "Big Five" took a dim view of Robeson's presence. He was accused of aiding the Communists, and threats were hurled at him from many quarters.

The rift between the United Public Workers (UPW) and their parent, the Congress of Industrial Organizations (CIO), was widened when the UPW sent Robeson into the Panama Canal Zone in 1947 in support of the Silver-roll workers. Government officials were resentful of and embarrassed by Robeson's public criticisms of the vicious racist practices against their non-white employees in the Canal Zone.

Pressure Mounts

The arrival of the fateful year of 1949 found Robeson under heavy pressure from the business community, the government and some segments of the labor force. With his recording contracts canceled, under constant surveillance by the government, barred from all radio and other public appearances of similar nature which reduced his income to only a fraction of what it had been, Robeson went abroad in February of 1949. In Europe and England he sang to sell-out audiences. Although his tour was a financial success and bolstered his ego, it was a disaster for his public image back home and his future as an American citizen.

Robeson compounded his problems by announcing from England that he would, upon his return, testify in support of the Communist leaders then on trial at the Foley Square court house in New York City. Hard on the heels of that bombshell, he appeared in Paris at the World Peace Congress, organized by the partisans of peace.

Robeson criticized the racist practices of the U.S. government and found little to choose between it and the fascist government of Nazi Germany. He labeled President Truman's Point Four Program for colonial development as a "new form of slavery," especially for Africans. His one statement that caused an international furor was:

> "It is unthinkable that American Negroes should go to war in behalf of those who have oppressed us for generations, against the Soviet Union, which in one generation has raised our people to full human dignity."*

Although *The New York Times* quoted Robeson accurately and in full, secondary waves of editorial comment quoted Robeson as saying, "American Negroes would never fight against Russia."

Revulsion against Robeson reached new heights in the

* *The New York Times*, April 21, 1949.

States. The architects of our foreign policy, only a year away from the Korean War, concluded that they had to do something about Robeson once and for all. A frantic federal officialdom summoned an impressive list of Black leaders to Washington to discredit Robeson and assure them that the Black populace would fight to preserve the system. The Black leaders, for the most part, told the uneasy politicians what they wanted to hear.

Robeson arrived home from Europe on June 16, 1949. Included in the welcoming party were twenty uniformed policemen, a sign of things to come. A few days later, Robeson spoke to a tense, overflow crowd at the Rockland Palace, New York City. Word had spread through Harlem that "Big" Paul was mad. The rank and file Black workers, uninfluenced by high-level politics and name-calling, came in droves to welcome their hero home and hear him tell off his enemies. They were not disappointed. Throwing caution to the winds, the fury of Robeson's attacks spared no one. His sharpest blasts, however, were directed toward those Blacks who had tried to discredit him. When the storm subsided, Robeson had few friends in high places anywhere in this country. Henceforth, his major support would come from the political left and the apolitical Black masses, who continued to follow him despite vilification and intimidation.

Now as never before the federal government began to close in on Robeson and the left-wing organizations with which he was identified. The State Department of the Executive Branch, both houses of the Legislative Branch and a sympathetic Judicial Branch of the government were mobilized to secure national conformity with our anti-Communist foreign policy. Robeson was cited by the House Un-American Activities Committee more than 200 times. Called before the Committee several times, he denied under oath that he was a Communist, the first time he was asked. Afterwards, he vowed never to answer that question again, believing that such questions about a man's political beliefs were unconstitutional.

Violence at Peekskill

Thus, the storm clouds hung low and were heavily charged when the Harlem Chapter of the Civil Rights Congress announced, late in July, that Robeson would give a benefit concert for them on August 27, 1949, in Peekskill. Representatives of Peoples Artists Inc. rented the Lakelands Acre Public Grounds for the affair. Immediately, members of the Peekskill Junior Chamber of Commerce condemned the concert and called for group action to discourage it. The sponsors were undeterred. Apparently, they had forgotten that it was the Peekskill Post of the American Legion that had attacked Robeson in Albany two years before. They had also issued a protest against Robeson's Peekskill concert in 1948. Even then the local press had warned against another concert.

As the date of the concert approached, the smoldering coals of anti-Robeson sentiment were fanned into flame by the actions of some members of Peekskill's Veterans of Foreign Wars, the Jewish War Veterans, the Catholic War Veterans and the Junior Chamber of Commerce. The local press and radio were used to keep the issue alive. Several groups in Peekskill and New York City warned local and state officials of the threat of violence. The anti-Robeson forces attempted to get an injunction against the concert, but they failed. Local groups tried to dissuade the veterans' groups from a showdown. They also failed. Governor Dewey was preoccupied with weightier matters, and he turned the problem over to subordinates. In the absence of any strong, meaningful preventative measures, violence became a reality.

Adding to the dangerous drift of political polarization, the Attorney General listed the Civil Rights Congress as a Communist-front organization and listed Robeson as one of its chief supporters. Public disclosures in Peekskill indicated that Peoples Artists Inc. had been labeled a "red front" organization by a loyalty group in California. The timing of these two reports was perfect for the anti-Robesonites. It gave them a cause célèbre and crowned their effort with a halo of patriotism.

The veterans' forces and their allies scheduled a parade in the vicinity of the concert site to coincide with the time of the concert. Many in military uniform carried sticks and rocks of varying sizes. They appeared to be on the best of terms with the local law enforcement officers. When concert-goers arrived they found the roads leading to the picnic grounds blocked by legionnaires. The majority were turned around and forced to run a gantlet of rocks and anti-Jewish, anti-Black, anti-Communist epithets as they fled the scene. A few less fortunate persons did reach the concert area. At-tacked from all sides, the men locked arms to form a protec-tive circle around their women and children. The attackers, frustrated by this defensive maneuver, reduced the stage to splinter wood, shredded the sheet music and set them to the torch. Eventually, the hapless group escaped from their at-tackers and fled in disorder.

Robeson never reached the picnic grounds, which was just as well. Unaware of the rising tide of hatred that was flood-ing the concert area, he arrived at the Peekskill railway station alone. He was met by a woman and two children, ages ten and twelve. She hustled him into her car and smug-gled him out of sight before he was recognized.

Robeson's son, Paul Jr., did not make it either. His wife fell ill just before the departure time, and he elected to re-main with his bride of two and one-half months. This was just as well, also. The automobile in which he was scheduled to ride was damaged by flying missiles.

The Peekskill forces were jubilant over the success of their military expedition. They congratulated themselves on providing an excellent example to the nation of how to deal with "domestic Communists."

Undaunted, a mass meeting was held in Harlem a few days later. Robeson vowed to return to Peekskill as soon as possible. The crowd responded with a standing ovation of approval and support. This Harlem decision galvanized the Peekskill protagonists into a fury of resistance against a second invasion into their territory. One of their first moves was to make sure that the picnic grounds would not be available again. Peoples Artists Inc. rented the former Hollow Brook Country Club, now a meadow, from Stephen Szego for Sunday, September 4, 1949. This meadow is located in Cortlandt, just outside of Peekskill. Apparently, some of the local citizens looked with displeasure upon Szego's actions. Shortly after signing his agreement with Peoples Artists Inc., several shots were fired at his home. Later, there were four separate attempts to burn down his house. When he tried to collect for the fire damages, his insurance contract was canceled.

Peace-loving citizens of Peekskill and environs again called upon Gov. Dewey to insure the safety of the visitors to their vicinity. Representative Vito Marcantonio and Paul Robeson called on the Governor to fire all officials who were responsible for the violence the week before. Dewey held emergency sessions with his law enforcement officers and deployed 904 men to garrison the concert site and the surrounding area. He assured the public that his men had the situation well in hand.

Favorable weather made September 4th an ideal day for the 50-mile drive from New York City to Peekskill. Thousands took advantage of the opportunity. The anti-Robeson forces were more numerous, better disciplined and more heavily armed than before. Making use of their military experience, the veterans allowed the visitors to enter the meadow with nothing more damaging hurled at them than sullen glances and racial epithets. Once the crowd was assembled, the opposition closed certain exit routes, forcing egress along prearranged corridors. Arrayed against this external force were 2,500 Robesonites who volunteered to form a wall to protect Robeson and the audience of 25,000. The majority of these men were trade unionists from such unions as the Furriers, United Electrical, Clothing Workers and the Newspaper Guild.

Soon after the concert got under way, Robeson arrived escorted by a detail of alert, unsmiling workers. He sang with his back against a tree, flanked by a formidable phalanx of muscle and grim determination. Robeson opened his portion of the concert with a chanson and "Go Down Moses" and ended with "Ole Man River." His security guards enclosed him in a protective cocoon as he left the area. Only someone with a strong suicidal bent would have attempted a direct assault at that time. The "Honor Guard" delivered Robeson back to New York intact, but his automobile was damaged by a hail of stones.

The concert ended soon after Robeson's departure, around 3:30 p.m. Violence erupted as the concert-goers tried to leave the meadow. Forced to pass along the preplanned routes, they were jeered and attacked from both sides with sticks and flying objects of great variety. The newspapers reported that 145 people were injured and hundreds of cars were damaged, some totally. Many of the injured criticized the police for inaction; others accused them of complicity in the violence. The former charge proved to be unfounded, for the law enforcement officers were quite busy writing speeding tickets for those victims who tried to flee the area. Those who did not get away were ticketed for driving with broken windshields. Subsequent news photographs of the event supported the latter charge of complicity. At its height the violence covered a 10-square-mile area and extended as far south as Yonkers. The spreading tentacles of disorder enveloped innocent people who had no idea of what was happening. One such group, returning from a visit to the shrine of Franklin D. Roosevelt at Hyde Park, sustained injury and was delayed for several hours.

The world press reported the details of the Peekskill violence in blazing headlines. Opinion from abroad was, for the most part, critical of the lax law enforcement and the mob action. They praised the efforts of the law-abiding citizens of Peekskill who did what they could to avert disaster and, failing that, deplored the inhumanity of their fellow citizens.

Domestic opinion was sharply divided. It was not surprising that under the circumstances the majority were sympathetic to the anti-Robeson forces. Robeson was described as a dupe of the Communists to foment disunity at a time when "our national security is at stake." The liberal and left-wing press, including the news sheets of the noncompliant labor unions, supported Robeson and compared the violence of Peekskill with the Nazi onslaught in Europe. This group demanded that Gov. Dewey order a full-scale investigation by a special grand jury.

Many trade unionists suffered physical injury and property damage in the Peekskill melee. A giant stone was thrown through the windshield of the car of Irving Potash, an official of the Furriers Union. He suffered the loss of sight in one eye, damage to the other, a fractured skull and crushing injury to the nose and cheekbones. Despite his injury, Potash joined labor officials from the United Electrical and other unions in street corner protests in downtown Manhattan. They called upon Attorney General Howard McGrath to prosecute those who had caused the Peekskill riots. Members of the Newspaper Guild of New York called upon Gov. Dewey to launch a full investigation of the violence and to remove all of the state and local officials responsible for it.

On September 20, 1949, 300 people boarded a train in New York City for Albany, the capital, to express their outrage directly to the Governor. A special detail of armed guards insured the safety of the train as it passed through Peekskill. Albany police restrained a crowd of nearly 5,000 who lined the sidewalks as the delegation marched to the capital. Aside from a few tomatoes and eggs, which missed their marks, there was no violence in Albany. As a matter of fact, there was very little action of any kind. Instead of the Governor, the group was received by Lawrence Walsh, the noncommittal Assistant Counsel to the Governor. He listened attentively, promised little and sent them on their way.

Eighty-three victims of the Peekskill disorder filed suit against Westchester County officials for property damages totaling $20,345, charging official negligence. Several attempts were made to have the charges dismissed. They eventually succeeded, and the federal court dropped all charges against all defendants.

Robeson and writer Howard Fast, along with twenty-six other plaintiffs, filed a civil suit for $2,020,000 against Westchester County and two veterans' groups in September of 1949. The case was in litigation until January 23, 1952, when the federal court again dismissed all charges against all defendants. Neither the investigations nor the court actions yielded any significant relief for the petitioners.

In the wake of the civil disorder, the Peekskill community became alive with rumors. Szego reported that the threat of a fascist takeover was causing many people to consider moving out of the Peekskill area. Another rumor had it that the insurance rates against property damage would be increased substantially. On September 27th, a Peekskill merchants' group announced the cancellation of their Jan Peek celebration, honoring the founders of the city. They considered it unwise to hold public assemblies at that time. Many other social and civic activities were canceled or postponed.

Robeson Continues the Crusade

The Robeson group, on the other hand, scheduled appearances for Robeson in many cities across the country. The tour became a vehicle for him to continue his unpopular crusade for peace and a nonmilitary rapprochement (détente) with world Communism, despite the growing threat of war in Korea.

When the tour schedule was published, veterans' groups in New Haven, Pittsburgh, Chicago and other cities urged that the meetings be canceled. When they failed to effect cancellation, the groups forbade their members to attend any of Robeson's appearances.

Robeson's Detroit appearance occurred on October 9, 1949. Nearly 50,000 people jammed the area of Forest and Hastings Streets, overflowing the Forest Club and forcing the diversion of traffic for three blocks in all directions. One thousand police kept watch over the crowd from the windows and roofs of adjacent buildings, as well as at ground level. Secret service and FBI men infiltrated the crowd, keeping records for future use. Members of the establishment, Black and white, were prominently absent.

Reverend Charles Hill, one of Detroit's most fearless freedom fighters, had the cooperation of many rank and file trade unionists in completing the arrangements for Robeson's appearance. They provided Robeson with a tight security guard during his stay and established their own surveillance network to find, report and deal with any signs of violence against Robeson. Detroit's officials breathed a sigh of great relief when he left the city without mishap.

The Peekskill affair accelerated many events that were already in progress and made many others possible that seemed only probable before. The activities of the nonconformist trade unions in Peekskill widened the split within the CIO. Both the purse and power of the investigative committees of the House and Senate were increased in the name of national security. Senator Joseph R. McCarthy (Democrat-Wisconsin) was already testing his anti-Communist line with which he would strangle the nation with brief and terrifying success. Freedom was threatened on all sides by a proliferation of federal, state and local legislation of dubious constitutionality.

This national conflict and controversy nearly drowned out Robeson's own statement on Peekskill. Under the heading, "My Answer," he gave his position and issued a plea and a prophecy:

"... I am well-equipped, now, although I have not always been so, to make the supreme fight for my people and all other underprivileged masses, wherever they may be. Here, I speak of those bereft of uncompromising, courageous leadership that cannot be intimidated and cannot be swerved from its purpose of bringing true freedom to those who follow it.

". . . This thing burns in me, and it is not my nature or inclination to be scared off.

". . . They revile me; they scandalize me and try to holler me down on all sides. That's all right. It's okay. Let them continue. My voice topped the blare of the Legion's bands and the hoots of hired hoodlums who tried to break up my concert for the Harlem Division of the Civil Rights Congress. It will be heard above the screams of the intolerant.

"My weapons are peaceful; for it is only by peace that peace can be attained. The Song of Freedom must prevail."

Robeson's position paper enraged his enemies more than ever, and spurred them on to more imaginative acts of violence against him. His prophecy and plea, out of tune with the times, were ignored.

Peekskill's first anniversary was more than two months away when the United States military forces entered the Korean phase of our Southeast Asian misadventure that would eventually waste millions of lives, trillions of dollars and accelerate our headlong plunge into financial and moral bankruptcy. Before a year had elapsed, the disruptive fissure within the CIO became an unbridgeable chasm, as the latter-day saints, then in power, began to exorcise the militant demons of the left. Guardians of the status quo in Birmingham, Bogalusa, and Selma were instructed and encouraged by the permissiveness of Peekskill. They bided their time and kept their powder dry.

In less than a year, Robeson's passport was canceled by a punitive State Department. Denied the opportunity to make a living at home and unable to travel abroad, he was sentenced to a slow death by economic strangulation and political repression. Robeson, as usual, would not cooperate with his enemies. Not only did he refuse to die, he lived to see all of his unpopular causes become a part of the everyday American way of life.

Despite the vindications of time and circumstance, Robeson remains a prophet without honor in his own land. One of the most glaring evidences of this dishonor is Robeson's absence from the College Football's Hall of Fame. He is the only two-time All-American so ignored. A reversal of this decision, long overdue, could signal the start of a timely re-evaluation of this controversial American and, perhaps, a change in his outrageous fortune.

The Cold War: Its Impact on the Black Liberation Struggle within the United States

Charles W. Cheng

Paul Robeson and W. E. B. Du Bois: They Refused to be Silenced

Citing the record of Robeson and Du Bois, two staunch freedom fighters, and their inestimable contribution to the world-wide liberation struggle has been already documented by others more capable and knowledgeable than myself. A chronicle of their significant role in history is not under discussion. Vital to understand, though, for this discussion is the magnitude of the government attack on these men in the 1950's. To grasp the underlying reasons for this government attack, the discussion will primarily be confined to the ideas advocated by both men. As will be seen, their public views during this period clashed sharply with official government policy.

In the case of Robeson, as he has written in his brilliant book, *Here I Stand,* his trouble with the government began as a direct result of the speech he delivered at the World Peace Conference held in Paris in 1949. Robeson, testifying before the House Un-American Activities Committee in June 1956 summarized the salient point in his speech that had angered the government:

"... I did say, in passing, that it was unthinkable to me

This is the second part of a two-part essay.

that any people would take up arms in the name of an Eastland to go against anybody, and, gentlemen, I still say that. I thought it was healthy for Americans to consider whether or not Negroes should fight for people who kicked them around.

"What should happen would be that this U.S. Government should go down to Mississippi and protect my people."[1]*

It was this audacious statement that eventually led the federal government to withdrawal of Robeson's passport. Trying to prevent him from spreading his views was obviously the major reason for this government action. On the domestic scene, NBC joined in the drive to silence Robeson when it canceled his scheduled television appearance on a show with Eleanor Roosevelt. In reality, Robeson had dared to challenge the basic assumptions of American foreign policy. In stark contrast, for instance, to the stance taken by the NAACP, Robeson declared: "It is high time for Negro leadership to take a new look at the world beyond our borders and to stop parroting the fearful wails of Washington officialdom that Asia and Africa may be lost to the 'Free World.' "[2]

Robeson was cogently raising arguments that if accepted by Black people, let alone the nation at large, would seriously call into question the underpinning of American foreign policy: "The era of White Supremacy, the imperialist domination of the East by a handful of Western nations, is rapidly coming to an end. ... We, the Negro people of the United States, and of the Caribbean as well, are a part of the rising colored peoples of the world." [3] This, indeed, was dangerous thought. Not only did he project the linkage of the black struggle at home with the international struggle for freedom, but he pointed out that the Cold War policies at home and abroad came from people who were responsible for the maintenance of racist ideology:

* See notes at end of article.

"The upholders of 'states' rights' against Negro rights are at the same time supporters of the so-called 'right to work' laws against the trade unions. The reactionary laws which have undermined the gains of Roosevelt's New Deal–the anti-labor Taft-Hartley Act, the anti-foreign-born Walter McCarran Act, the thought control Smith Act, all were strongly backed by The Dixiecrats in Congress."[4]

It was statements like these that produced the situation whereby the white press boycotted Robeson's *Here I Stand* when it was published. This was as late as 1958. Of course, during the height of the red fever, with the government accusing him of subversive activity, he was subjected to mob violence. In 1949, for instance, he gave a concert in Peekskill, New York, under the most explosive circumstances. The concert was held, but at its conclusion, mobs overturned cars, rocks were hurled, windshields broken, and many people injured. It seems certain that this outbreak, and a similar one a week earlier, were not simply directed at Robeson because he was Black. After all, he had performed throughout America in the past and had not been subject to such terrorist action. Rather, this mob violence can be attributed to a combination of his being Black and the fact that as a Black person he had spoken out against the Cold War practices of the government. People in attendance at the concert were considered reds, pinkos, Communist dupes, or "integrationists." Jack O'Dell has provided an insightful summary of the meaning of Peekskill:

"Paul Robeson had been able to hold his concert that day and thousands of people had demonstrated by their presence a willingness to uphold freedom of speech in general and the right of this great artist to perform in particular. Nevertheless, the violence we confronted at the end of that day confirmed the fact that the hysteria in the country was still very much with us, aided and abetted by the government itself."[5]

Despite the mob violence, and the government's repressive acts directed against Robeson, some Blacks sang the tune of the Cold War. Jackie Robinson testified before the House Un-American Activities Committee indicating Robeson did not represent the views of the majority of "loyal" Negro citizens. And, when the local Washington, D.C., branch of the NAACP was about ready to condemn NBC for canceling Robeson's television appearance, the former lobbyist for Alpha Kappa Alpha sorority, Thomasina Norford, intervened, persuading the branch not to take such action. As one reporter for the *Afro-American* said: "The best job insurance a government employee can have today is to be fighting commies and fellow-travelers—and Robeson is a popular whipping boy."[6] (Ms. Norford was then working for the government.) Now it would be misleading to conclude that Blacks were in any way behind the persecution of Robeson. As Robeson himself has written, "white folks on top" were responsible for the witch hunt and the repression he was subjected to. It need only be noted that the atmosphere of the country had reached such a state of red frenzy that some Black citizens also became "dupes" of the Cold War philosophy.

Another thunderous voice that joined with Robeson in protesting the foreign policy of the United States was Dr. W.E.B. Du Bois. As a crusader for the rights of his people all his life, Du Bois was totally familiar with what level of resistance and force the federal government had employed in blocking the advancement of human rights. But, he was not prepared for the intensity of the attack directed against him when he, like Robeson, continued to speak out on the relationship between U.S. style imperialism and the plight of Black people in the United States. He maintained his consistent advocacy for peace. As some have said, he remained an apostle for world peace. His association with the world peace movement would lead to his being indicted by the federal government as an alleged criminal. One could argue that his dismissal from the NAACP, at the urging of Walter White, Executive Secretary for the NAACP in 1948, came about because of his opposition to the Cold War policy being pursued by the Truman Administration. By Du Bois's own account, however, this was not the reason cited when he was dismissed. But it does not seem idle conjecture to conclude that his radical peace notions might be embarrassing to an organization that would soon end up endorsing the foreign policy of the United States. Commenting on his leaving the NAACP, Du Bois prophetically wrote:

"... the relations of American Negroes to the working people of America and the socialist and Communist movements of the world have got to be matters of grave and present consideration. The whole world is confronting these problems, while the NAACP, the greatest organization among 20 million of the most advanced group of Negroes in the world, has no program or leadership; no experts, no commentators or leaders but can only answer each problem with the parrot-like call, 'No Discrimination.' This was the slogan of the last generation. It is desperately inadequate today."[7]

He then perceptively added: "What shall their [Negroes'] attitude be toward socialism and Communism, and especially toward the Soviet Union and China who above all nations fight the very color bar which we try to get rid of."[8]

Ideas like these prompted the American Labor Party to solicit Du Bois to run as a candidate for the U.S. Senate from New York in 1950. Du Bois accepted the ALP nomination, his first try for public office at the age of eighty-two. In announcing his senatorial candidacy, Du Bois delivered a salvo against the present course of historical events. He called for the seating of the People's Republic of China in the United Nations, the immediate end of the Korean War and the resumption of the free flow of trade between east and west. Stressing the connection between civil rights and the Cold War, he trenchantly said:

"To stop this program of reason and progress, the allied

and associated political profit makers, called the Republican and Democratic parties, have adopted the last tactic of despair. They have made not only truth, but civil rights a casualty of war. They have turned your attention from progress and peace to hate and war. They are making it illegal to think progress and advocate peace or progress. Every path to reform, like taxation of great wealth, effective rent control, river development and forest planning are all called communistic or socialistic and their promoters threatened with disgrace, jail or loss of livelihood."[9]

Significantly, during the zenith of the red hysteria, Joe McCarthy riding high and the Korean police action occurring, Du Bois became actively involved in the World Peace Appeal, familiarly known as the Stockholm Petition. The petition was aimed at outlawing atomic weapons. In this country the petition was promulgated by the Peace Information Center, an organization in which Du Bois was a prime participant. Eventually, the U.S. State Department ordered the Peace Center to register as an agent of a foreign power. The peace petition was deemed alien to the United States government. Refusing to comply with the State Department's order resulted in Du Bois's indictment. An indictment that saw him handcuffed and brought before a United States Court to face criminal prosecution. Of this indictment, Du Bois declared: "It is a curious thing that I am called upon to defend myself against charges for openly advocating one thing all people want–peace."[10] Nevertheless, Du Bois also realized the meaning of his indictment with regard to the struggle of Black people. Behind the indictment rested the intent of the government to silence American citizens, particularly those who are Black, from daring to question or to speak against the actions of the United States on the international scene, especially those actions that perpetuated colonial subserviency and were directed toward crushing socialism in the Soviet Union and China.[11]

Understanding the underlying reasons for the criminal

charge can be discerned in the response of the *New York Herald Tribune* to the indictment. This response more than likely exemplified the viewpoint of the federal government. On February 11, 1951, the *Tribune* wrote:

"The Du Bois outfit was set up to promote a tricky appeal of Soviet origin. . . . 'A lot of men and women of good will throughout the world,' to quote the petition's bland phrasing, were snared into signing without quite realizing that this thing came straight from the Cominform."[12]

The *Chicago Defender* expressed a similar view in saying, "Dr. Du Bois has earned many honors and it is a supreme tragedy that he should become embroiled in activities that have been exposed as subversive in the twilight of his years."[13] At about this time friends of Du Bois had laid plans for the celebration of his eighty-third birthday. However, when the charge was publicly announced in February 1951, the hotel canceled the contract for the affair. Scheduled speakers withdrew and many sponsors asked that their names be withdrawn. After some search, the birthday party was held in an overcrowded cabaret setting in Harlem.

As the indictment proceeded many believed the NAACP itself might come to the assistance of Du Bois. True, the NAACP adopted a mild resolution implying that the charges against Du Bois could be construed as an effort to "silence spokesmen for full equality of Negroes." Quietly though, the NAACP urged its local branches not to touch the case, according to Du Bois. Certainly, the NAACP resolution fell short of outright support for Du Bois. More, however, might have been expected from this organization considering the dedication, devotion and commitment Du Bois had contributed in the struggle to advance his people. Much of this contribution had come during the time he helped to build the NAACP. But, as already seen, the defense of Du Bois was too great a risk for an organization that, for whatever its reasons, came down on the side of the government with respect to the Cold War.

On the other hand, Du Bois did not stand entirely alone and isolated. He himself cited the black papers, the *Pittsburgh Courier* and the *Afro-American,* as well as columnist J. A. Rogers for forthrightly coming to his defense. Indeed, the *Pittsburgh Courier* in saying, "the handcuffs on Du Bois are meant to serve as a gag on any Negro leadership that is disposed to 'shoot the works' for freedom. [These are] times that beckon the Uncle Toms among us," reflected a point of view shared by many but not, of course, shared by the dominant forces in society pushing the Cold War. Even after the trial, however, which proved his innocence, he remained a victim of Cold War demagoguery. Truman Nelson has sharply underscored the extreme irony of this persecution after the trial was over:

"... he was still tainted in the eyes of the rotten center, the lynch mob. The soaring crescendos of the African liberation movement exploded like fireworks. ... Across the river from the tower of the Empire State Building lived the man who had prophesied it and helped make it. Nobody asked him; nobody put in a ten cent call to have him explain it. Now he was in exile."[14]

In some ways, both Robeson and Du Bois were in forced exile. It is of crucial importance to emphasize that these two renowned, courageous, undaunted and indefatigable foes of racial injustice became the chief targets for government persecution within the Black community. Standing up against race discrimination within the United States was to be expected from prominent Black leaders. But, persuasively challenging the intentions of American foreign policy was another matter, particularly when Robeson and Du Bois were projecting the interrelatedness between the Cold War and the suppression of Black people at home. Respected and highly regarded Black leaders were now labeled as "subversive." Uppity Blacks who dared speak out against America's Cold War had to be put in their place. More importantly, Robeson and Du Bois served as reminders to other Blacks of exactly what remissive measures the federal government was prepared to take against anyone, especially Blacks, who would not be silenced into acquiescing to the second massive red scare in the nation's history. Paul Robeson probably came close to representing the feelings of both Du Bois and himself when he candidly declared before the House Un-American Activities Committee:

"Because my father was a slave and my people died to build this country, I'm going to stay right here and have a part of it, just like you. And no fascist-minded people like you will drive me from it. Is that clear?"[15]

Overcoming the Cold War Legacy

"Now it should be incandescently clear that no one who has any concern for the integrity and life of America today can ignore the present war. If America's soul becomes totally poisoned, part of the autopsy must read Vietnam."[16]

Dr. Martin Luther King
April 4, 1967, Riverside Church

Dr. King's now famous speech *A Time to Break Silence* delivered at Riverside Church was appropriately titled. Although Dr. King was specifically addressing himself to the Vietnam War, his sweeping condemnation of the Asian holocaust spearheaded by the United States also constituted a clear break by a major civil rights organization (Southern Christian Leadership Conference) with the Cold War policy launched in 1946 (the Student Non-Violent Coordinating Committee had also taken a stand against the war). From many quarters, Dr. King, like Robeson and Du Bois, was denounced for moving SCLC into the ranks of the peace movement. Still influenced by its earlier support for the Cold War, the NAACP's Roy Wilkins adopted the stance that the Vietnam War was not "a proper sphere for public analysis or criticism," at least not by a civil rights organization.[17]

Significantly, breaking the silence came over the Vietnam War–a war that stemmed from the Cold War policy. For, it was the foreign policy espoused and implemented by the Truman Administration that directly led to American intervention in Vietnam.

"It is also essential to remain aware of the fact that the global perspective of the United States between 1946 and 1949 stressed the decisive importance of Europe to the future of world power. When the United States looked at Indo-China they saw France and through it Europe and a weak France would open the door to Communism in Europe. But for no other reason, this meant a tolerant attitude toward the bloody French policy in Vietnam."[18]

Thus, it is not at all surprising that in July of 1949 Dean Acheson would send a memo to a State Department official who was chairing a committee to assess American policy in Asia, categorically stating, "You will please take as your assumption that it is a fundamental decision of American policy that the United States does not intend to permit further extension of Communist domination in the continent of Asia or in the Southeast Asia area."[19]

But, it would be incorrect to leave the impression that not until the Vietnam War did Blacks speak out in opposition to American foreign policy. As already indicated, Du Bois and Robeson vigorously protested the Cold War policy. Many Blacks joined with them. However, the general purpose in this discussion has been to assess the impact of the Cold War on the black liberation struggle. The writer is persuaded that the foreign policy pursued by the United States tended to retard the freedom movement within the United States.

It has been noted that the Truman Administration became more occupied with containing Communism both at home and abroad, and one consequence was that the civil rights report "To Secure These Rights" was never implemented. This seems a far cry from the hopes, expectations and aspirations of Black people at the end of World War II. One commentator writing in *March of Labor* in 1951 reminds us of the failures of the Truman Administration up to that time:

> "If we had effective civil rights laws, an FEPC, end to Jim Crow in jobs and political freedom in the South, the 1948 election results would have been different."[20]

On the labor scene, the CIO which had been in the vanguard of fighting for Black workers, devoted much of its time and energy to a "red purge" within its own ranks, and this purge resulted in an eroding of the commitment by the CIO to fight for Black worker rights specifically and civil rights in general. The CIO purge itself was led by men like Walter Reuther, who were supporters of the Truman Doctrine and the Marshall Plan. The age-old NAACP endorsed the Cold War, failing to acknowledge the connections between billions to contain and defeat Communism and the continued racist and economic oppression of Blacks at home.

Robeson and Du Bois, for emphasizing this interrelatedness between American foreign policy and the plight of Blacks were officially persecuted by the government. Carlton B. Goodlett and Carl Bloice in their essay on Du Bois described the essence of this connection:

> "Du Bois recognized that foreign policy is a mirrored image of domestic policy. A nation whose majority white citizens could not treat with equity, justice and equality, Black neighbors and citizens living in the same hamlets, cities and states throughout the nation could not develop a foreign policy involving international relationships reflecting equality and justice with two-thirds of the people of the world who are people of color."[21]

Although this discussion has not treated the rise nor the influence of McCarthyism, it seems safe to conclude that the effects of his histrionic Communist witch-hunting undoubtedly resulted in the silencing of many who might have been counted on to speak out for racial justice.

These happenings suggest that the black movement received a momentary setback during the postwar years. While this is the case I argue, it is not to be construed that there was no black movement during this critical period.* Despite its backing of the Cold War, the NAACP won many landmark legal cases aimed at smashing legal segregation. These outstanding legal victories were climaxed by the 1954 Brown decision, banning school segregation.

On the political front many Blacks participated in progressive movements. As already indicated, Blacks were active in the Wallace campaign. In 1949, under the American Labor Party, a Black person ran for Manhattan Borough president for the first time. Neither was Black labor silent, for in 1951 the National Negro Labor Council was founded. At this founding meeting William Hood, Recording Secretary of Ford Local 600, UAW-CIO, declared:

"We come here today because we are conscious at this hour of a confronting world crisis: We are here because many of our liberties are disappearing in the face of powerful war economy and grave economic problems facing working men and women everywhere."[22]

Thus, it would be a serious error to underestimate the contribution made by Blacks during the Cold War period. For many gallant and important struggles were waged under the most severely repressive circumstances. Yet, even today, because of the Cold War syndrome many authoritative writers conspicuously or unconsciously ignore this critical period in the historical development of the black liberation struggle. Joanne Grant, for example, in her book *Black*

* For a good analysis and review of developments within the black liberation struggle during this time, see J. H. O'Dell's "A Rock in a Weary Lan'," *Freedomways* Vol. 11, No. 1, 1971.

Protest 1619 to Present (1968), does not provide any documents on this period. John Hope Franklin and Isadore Starr, in editing *The Negro in 20th Century America* fail to include any serious documentation of the Cold War period. Further, Franklin's popular *From Slavery to Freedom* in a section dealing with reaction to the struggle for Negro rights during the postwar period does not discuss the government's attempt to silence Du Bois and Robeson. He simply, like so many others, tends to avoid dealing with the question of how the official policy of anti-Communism affected Blacks. Instead, he offers the view that resistance to equality can be mainly attributed to whites who opposed integration. None would deny such an analysis, but by itself such a view is insufficient in that it does not take into account other powerful economic and political forces operating during the postwar period.

Here the contention is that the political and economic forces chiefly responsible for creating the Truman Doctrine, the Marshall Plan—hence the Cold War—were equally responsible for creating an atmosphere that led to the second national red scare—a "red scare" that overshadowed the drive for human rights in this nation. Ironically, this drive for human rights was accelerated in part by World War II; for Blacks once again found themselves carrying the gun to make the world "safe for democracy." Only this time, countries in Africa and Asia were revolting against colonial rule. In short, the postwar period was seemingly a ripe moment in history for an upsurge by Blacks to force this nation into the second Reconstruction. But, the nation, specifically the federal government, slowed the momentum. Interests of Black people were considered of secondary importance in the fight against world-wide Communism.

A change in the freedom movement lull would not be dramatically altered until the Montgomery bus boycott in 1955–56. To some, Dr. King's Montgomery campaign marked the first massive confrontation, outside the legal route, against state institutionalized racism since the Cold War began. Others will even argue that McCarthyism and the Cold War had a paralyzing effect on the freedom movement. Not until the 1960's in any event would the freedom forces throughout the country become unleashed from the Cold War albatross. And, as already mentioned, it was as late as 1967 before Martin Luther King made his speech at Riverside Church. (Malcolm X was also another leading Black leader who linked international events in the Third World with the black liberation struggle in the United States.) There is then some truth in the argument that the Cold War created a paralysis in the freedom movement.

In this cursory account, I have sought to treat a thread in American history that affected the black liberation struggle. That thread has been the direct relationship between American foreign policy and the protracted struggle for human rights in this country. This contemporary thread has had a pivotal impact on the development of the struggle for freedom in this nation. Like the Cold War, the Vietnam War resulted in a curtailing of federal government action to combat racism and poverty. In essence, then, our foreign policy today still remains a shackle on the liberation struggle in this nation. There is much to learn from the Cold War period in planning tactics and strategies in the years ahead.

Hopefully, issues have been raised that will arouse others to critically review these crucial years in such a way as to enhance our understanding and awareness of how racial justice can be secured in this "land of the free." W.E.B. Du Bois's message of twenty years ago is as pertinent today as it was then:

"You as voters and intelligent citizens must force peace on the professional soldiers and the business leaders who make fortunes on war and murder, and you must let the world know this is your simple and unwavering program. The abolition of poverty, disease and ignorance the world over among women and men of all races, religions and colors. To accomplish this by just control of concentrated wealth and the overthrow of monopoly. To insure that income depends on work and not on privilege or chance.

"That freedom is the heritage of man and by freedom we do not mean freedom from the laws of nature, but freedom to think and believe, to express our thoughts and dream our dreams, and to maintain our rights against secret police, witch hunters or any other sort of modern fool or tyrant."[23]

References

[1] Paul Robeson, *Here I Stand*, Beacon Press, Boston, p. 42.

[2] *Ibid.*, p. 86.

[3] *Ibid.*, p. 84.

[4] *Ibid.*, p. 29.

[5] J. H. O'Dell, "A Rock in a Weary Lan'," *Freedomways*, New York, Vol. 11, No. 1, 1971, p. 43.

[6] "Which Way Are They," *Afro American*, April 8, 1950.

[7] W.E.B. Du Bois, *The Autobiography of W.E.B. Du Bois*, International Publishers, New York, 1968, p. 337.

[8] *Ibid.*, p. 337.

[9] W.E.B. Du Bois, Press Statement, September 24, 1950, p. 6.

[10] Carlton B. Goodlett and Carl Bloice, "W.E.B. Du Bois—Apostle of World Peace," *Freedomways*, Vol. 5, No. 1, 1965, p. 190.

[11] Truman Nelson, "W.E.B. Du Bois as a Prophet," *Freedomways*, Vol. 5, No. 1, 1965.

[12] W.E.B. Du Bois, op. cit., p. 369.

[13] *Ibid.*, p. 370.

[14] Truman Nelson, op. cit., p. 57.

[15] Robeson, op. cit., p. XIX.

[16] Martin Luther King, "A Time To Break Silence," *Freedomways*, Vol. 7, No. 2, 1967, p. 106.

[17] Robert S. Browne, "The Freedom Movement and the War in Vietnam," *Freedomways*, Vol. 5, No. 4, 1965, p. 472.

[18] Gabriel Kolko, *The Roots of American Foreign Policy*, Beacon Press, Boston, 1969, p. 94.

[19] *Ibid.*, p. 95.

[20] Russ Nixon, "Congress vs. the People," *March of Labor*, February 1951, p. 20.

[21] Goodlett and Bloice, op. cit., p. 189.

[22] Ewart Guinier, "Cooperation—not Permission," *March of Labor*, December 1951, p. 10.

[23] "Some Unpublished Writings of W.E.B. Du Bois," edited by Herbert Aptheker, *Freedomways*, Vol. 5, No. 1, 1965, p. 123.

Black Women in Freedom's Battles

Augusta Strong

Where is tomorrow born?
How does the future start?
On a winter working day.
In a Negro woman's heart. . . .

The day was December 1, 1955, when Rosa Parks, a working
woman, took a seat on a bus in Montgomery and refused the
driver's request to move to the back and give her seat to
a white passenger.

The story has been told many times over and simply and
movingly in the verse of Eve Merriam:

Where there's a place to sit, I'm entitled to ride,
And the Supreme Court is standing up right by my side.

Long ago, another day
Conductor Harriet Tubman on her way:
Not a track, not a marker was found
When her railway to freedom ran under ground.

Now what is the sound the future makes?
Not a threat. Not a shout.
But not a bus rolls out.

No one could have realized they were sharing in a
momentous event. The handful in the bus were privileged to
witness the opening of a new echo which would see the
revolutionary awakening of the long-oppressed Blacks of the
United States. Mrs. Parks was taken off the bus and jailed.
By that night a committee of women were protesting the
arrest, calling upon local leaders for action. Three days
later, the idea of a boycott of buses had taken hold, and a

new young clergyman, Martin Luther King, Jr., was elected president of the association formed to organize to achieve their goals, which at that time were very modest.

Ten months later, a United States Supreme Court ruling struck down segregated travel on all municipal facilities, and the seemingly timeless façade of segregation in the South had received another in a series of mortal wounds. The Rosa Parks incident was over, but a new era of struggle had begun—a struggle that was to extend from the South to all parts of the nation.

It is an interesting circumstance that a woman and a women's committee gave the impulse to this new revolution of our day. Whatever impelled her—whether tiredness, frustration, suppressed anger, overlong humiliation—at that moment she became, as many other courageous women have, a center from which spread widening circles of social consciousness and resistance to oppression.

Despite the image that has been kept alive in the public mind of the Black woman as a patient matriarch or carefree harlot, there are countless stories, far more dramatic of their role as inspirers, instigators, collaborators, and as leaders in the cause of freedom.

There is another image that can be drawn from the lives of the famous and those unknown women who have participated in every movement toward liberty in this country from colonial days to the present. There are many, from Phillis Wheatley, born a slave, whose ode to George Washington voiced the joys of liberation for all men, to Fannie Lou Hamer of Ruleville, Mississippi, who today is leading one of the most advanced movements on our scene for political freedom.

If one could make a composite picture of these heroines, what would it show What kind of woman?

A woman of lowly birth, perhaps a slave like Sojourner Truth who never slept in a bed until, at thirty, she ran away from slavery; a woman who knew hard labor for long hours, like Harriet Tubman who as a girl did a man's work in the fields; a life nourished on hardship and despair, like Phillis

Wheatley, kidnaped at the age of seven from her mother, sold into slavery, whose fame and genius came to an early end in a life swallowed up in indifference and poverty; a woman who is fearless of loss of status or earning ability, like the young women who followed in the wake of the Union armies to teach the freedmen and their children. She would know the meaning of sacrifice—the sacrifice of personal happiness, insofar as it might have been achieved; the sacrifice of personal interests; familiarity with scorn, danger, violence and mistreatment. She would be a wife, mother, grandmother—a family person—who might live to see her children stolen, sold, jailed, beaten, murdered, cheated, discouraged.

Her modern prototype would be Fannie Lou Hamer, one of twenty children born to her parents in rural Mississippi . . . at work in the cotton fields when she was six years old . . . her education and wisdom derived from the harsh experiences of her life . . . but challenging the "white only" rule of Sunflower County where Blacks have had a perpetual majority of population, but have never yet been able to be represented by legislators of their own choosing. Mrs. Hamer has brought to dramatic life the struggle for the right to vote, carrying to every observer as she speaks throughout the country the full significance of that fight. "You are not free up here until I am free down there," is her message to the nation.

People have taken countless paths in their quest for freedom . . . some ways devious and obscure, some pioneering; some sanctioned, though seldom aided, by laws and legislatures; some illegal and inseparable from violence. Each one holds its own hazards. Blacks have traveled them all.

Pre-Civil War Period

The first recorded petition made by an individual Negro to a legislature is the appeal of a woman, dated 1661, in Dutch, addressed to the government of New Netherlands, seeking freedom from slavery for the adopted son of Reytory Angola who ". . . with the fruits of her hands' bitter toil, she reared him as her own child, and up to the present supported him, taking all motherly solicitude and care for him, without aid of anyone in the world. . . ." The petition happily was granted.

One of the more curious outrages of slavery was that sometimes the road to freedom meant buying one's self. Usually it was the male who took on additional work, if permitted by his master, which over the years earned him a sum to purchase liberty. In other instances, those who most ardently believed in freedom had to purchase slaves in order to free them. There is preserved the petition of Jemima Hunt, "free woman of color," in 1810 who contracted to pay ten pounds a year for ten years to a Virginia slave owner to secure the freedom of her husband, Stephen, father of the children whom she supported through her daily labors. Many women who had escaped from slavery sent money to a third party to purchase a son, daughter, sister or brother. Other free Black women in the North formed organizations for the purpose of raising funds to buy and liberate slaves; a few women devoted their lives and most of their earnings to this work.

From the beginning of the organized anti-slavery movement, Black women were active participants and leaders. While the movement was interracial, such centers as Boston and Philadelphia and other areas also had All-Negro Ladies' Anti-Slavery Societies. They were represented in national and international gatherings, became accustomed to facing hostile mobs, circulating petitions, and effectively agitating against slavery.

Women were among the leaders of the New England Freedom Association, founded in 1845 by Blacks to assist fugitive slaves. Though their purpose was illegal, they boldly published their aims:

". . . to extend a helping hand to all who may bid adieu to whips and chains, and by the welcome light of the North

Star, reach a haven where they can be protected from the manstealer. An article of the Constitution enjoins us not to pay one farthing to any slaveholder for the property they may claim in a human being. . . . Our mission is to succor those who claim property in themselves, and thereby acknowledge an independence of slavery."

One of those who became famous and was widely regarded as a heroine for her daring exploits was Ellen Craft who with her husband, William, in 1849 made her way out of Georgia by a ruse. Since her color did not betray her identity, Ellen was able to travel disguised as a Southern gentleman. Using money they had saved (through William's working nights and Saturdays after his master was served) they traveled the public conveyances and stayed at first-class hotels. Ellen carried her arm in a sling to account for the fact that she did not sign the register at hotels, for neither of them could read or write. Posing as her valet, her husband was able to remain constantly at her side during the risky experiments. After their escape the Crafts traveled widely for the Anti-Slavery Society for a number of years, talking to audiences in the United States and in Europe.

While the abolition of slavery remained the principal concern of the freedom movements of the pre-Civil War era, there was also continuous action around other issues. National and state conventions were called during the 1830's and 1840's which sought equal education, the right to vote and to serve on juries, the right to enroll in the militia, to bear arms in the navy, to be eligible for settling on public lands, and the repeal of oppressive "black laws." At these gatherings, women were always present as delegates, and occasionally as leaders.

One of these conventions, representing Garrison's view of the Constitution as "a covenant with the devil and an agreement with hell," meeting in Cleveland in 1854 with a Black woman, Mary E. Bibb as vice-president, proclaims in surprisingly contemporary terms:

"That no oppressed people have ever obtained their rights by voluntary acts of generosity on the part of their oppressors. ... That if we desire liberty, it can only be obtained at the price which others have paid for it. ... That we are willing to pay that price, *let the cost be what it may.*"

The Ladies' Anti-Slavery Society of Delaware, Ohio, in an address to a State convention of men in 1856, with eloquent rhetoric urges united action for freedom: "It was a Spartan mother's farewell to her son, 'Bring home your shield or be brought upon it' ... and we pledge ourselves to exert our influence unceasingly in the cause of Liberty and Humanity." The militancy of their words was echoed by other groups of women throughout the nation who followed eagerly the gallant attempt of John Brown and his seventeen followers to seize the Harper's Ferry arsenal and free the slaves of the surrounding area. When Brown and his men were condemned to death a tremendous wave of indignation and sympathy found expression in Black communities—meetings, demonstrations and resolutions paid tribute to the idealistic leader and letters of solidarity poured in.

A typical one, adopted at a meeting of The Colored Women of Brooklyn, was addressed to the martyr, while he was under sentence to be executed a week later:

"We a portion of the American people ... offer you our sincere and heartfelt sympathies in the cause you have so nobly espoused. ... We consider you a model of true patriotism, and one whom our enemy will yet regard as the greatest it has produced ... We shall ever hold you dear in our remembrance, and shall infuse the same feelings in our posterity. ..."

From Frances Ellen Watkins Harper, poet and an indefatigable traveler and lecturer for the Abolitionist cause, came a pledge to never desist from the cause of freedom.

Writing to John Brown in prison a few days before his death, she wrote:

"Although the hands of slavery throw a barrier between you and me, and it may not be my privilege to see you in your prison house, Virginia has no bolts or bars through which I dread to send you my sympathy. . . . You have rocked the bloody Bastille; and I hope that from your sad fate great good may arise to the cause of freedom. Already from your prison has come a shout of triumph against the giant sin of our country.

"I have written your dear wife, and sent her a few dollars, and I pledge myself to you that I will continue to assist her. Send my sympathy to your fellow prisoners. . . . If any of them, like you, have a wife or children that I can help, let them send me word. Yours in the cause of freedom. . . ."

Frances Harper, born of free parents, in Maryland in 1825, was a striking woman of handsome features and commanding voice and was then one of the best known woman poets of her day.

Orphaned early in life, she attended a School for Colored Children run by an uncle and aunt, but went to work at thirteen, and was largely self-educated. She left Maryland to teach school in Ohio and in the North where she came into contact with the Underground Railroad. She was engaged as a permanent lecturer for the anti-slavery movement, traveled and spoke, attaining wide popularity both as lecturer and poet. Fellow anti-slavery workers spoke of her as a "good and glorious" speaker. Her poems, moral and didactic, in the fashion of her day, are eloquent in their denunciation of slavery and in honor of those who have given their lives for freedom. She was still a woman in the prime of life when the Emancipation Proclamation was signed, and she greeted it with these enthusiastic words:

It shall flash through the coming ages,
It shall light the distant years;

And eyes now dim with sorrow
Shall be brighter through their tears.

Her last poems were published in 1900, when she was seventy-five years old, and she remained a figure in the freedom movement until her death in 1911.

John Brown's conviction that the slaves themselves must be armed and rise against the system had a following among the anti-slavery workers. One of them, Charles Remond, advocated an appeal for insurrection before the 1858 Massachusetts State Convention of Negroes. He proudly proclaimed himself a traitor to a government which condoned slavery, and declared that he would rather stand over the graves of his mother and sister than to feel that they might be violated at the whim of a slaveholder.

The sister of whom he spoke was as fiery an Abolitionist as her brother, a familiar figure on lecture platforms of the Anti-Slavery Society, for whom she lectured in the North and abroad in England, Ireland and Scotland where she was received with friendship and sympathy. During the Civil War she came to England, like other Abolitionist leaders, to win the support of the British for the liberation struggle of the slaves. Though British textile mills were closed and workers unemployed because of the disruption of cotton farming in the South, she spoke against British support of the Confederacy:

"Let no diplomacy of statesmen, no intimidation of slaveholders, no scarcity of cotton, no fear of slave insurrections, prevent the people of Great Britain from maintaining their position as the friend of the oppressed Negro, which they deservedly occupied previous to the disastrous civil war."

Sarah Remond numbered among her antecedents a grandfather who fought in the American Revolution, a father who was an immigrant from the West Indies. She was born of free parentage in Salem, Massachusetts, was well educated and well read. She continued her education after the end of the Civil War, obtaining a medical degree in Florence, Italy, at the age of fifty-six, and working there as a practicing physician until her death.

The two most famous of all anti-slavery fighters are Sojourner Truth and Harriet Tubman whose long lives spanned the century of rebellion, war, and Reconstruction. Like the prophets of Biblical history, they roamed about the country in the performance of their mission; both were women who exercised leadership through personal authority and the claim of divine inspiration. Their only school was slavery; their teachers, the bitter experiences of their lives.

The Role of Harriet Tubman

Harriet Tubman escaped to freedom from a Maryland plantation, returning again and again to lead others out of slavery. She made nineteen trips into slave territory, and personally conducted 300 slaves through the Underground Railroad to the North, taking some of them as far as Canada to escape the slave-snatchers. She became known as "the Moses of her people," and the slaveholders placed a price of $40,000 on her head. Her methods combined a practical knowledge of psychology and astute planning. She never permitted a fugitive to turn back, sometimes propelling the faint-hearted forward at gun point, lest they fall back and betray the route the others had taken. She herself set the example of overcoming obstacles for the timid, and was always the first to advance into any dangerous situation to assure her followers.

"General Tubman," as John Brown called her, was considered the equal of any man in courage, physical stamina, and militancy. In the first thirty years of life she endured the most oppressive kind of brutal treatment; through life she suffered the effects of a skull injury from an ironweight flung at her head by an overseer when she was ten years old.

She was a friend and associate of the leading anti-slavery fighters—John Brown, Frederick Douglass, Gerrit

Smith, and Thomas Wentworth Higginson who called her "the greatest heroine of the age." William Grant Still, leader and historian of the Underground Railroad, said of her work: "Her like, it is probable, was never known before or since." Only the accident of an unexpected illness prevented her joining John Brown at Harper's Ferry, and it was Brown who bestowed on her the title "General" in genuine admiration and gratitude for help in securing recruits for his plan and in mapping his campaign.

During the Civil War, she served as a guide for Union forces, relying on her years of experience in the back country of the South as a conductor of the Underground Railroad, led scouting and raiding parties into Confederate territory. We get a glimpse of General Tubman in action from a contemporary Boston journalist reporting on the Union Army in South Carolina in 1863:

"Col. Montgomery and his gallant band of 300 black soldiers, under the guidance of a black woman, dashed into the enemy's country, struck a bold and effective blow, destroying millions of dollars worth of commissary stores, cotton and lordly dwellings, and striking terror into the heart of rebeldom, brought off near 800 slaves and thousands of dollars worth of property, without losing a man or receiving a scratch. It was a glorious consummation."

It is no small credit to her generalship that in her recollections of the victory, Harriet Tubman noted that nearly all of the able-bodied males among the slaves they freed joined the Union Army. In her declining years seeking compensation for her wartime services, her claim to the U.S. Government indicated that she had commanded eight or nine scouts "under directions and orders of Edwin M. Stanton, Secretary of War, and of several generals."

Frederick Douglass's estimate put her above the great leaders of his day: "Excepting John Brown . . . I know of no one who has willingly encountered more perils and hardships to serve our enslaved people than you have. . . ."

The Role of Sojourner Truth

Sojourner Truth, freed from slavery at the age of thirty by the New York State statute of 1828, similarly had been spared none of the hells of slavery. She saw her parents helpless, as all but one of her ten or twelve brothers and sisters were sold; she saw her aged and crippled mother and father turned out of the only home they knew in their sick old age. As for herself, first sold at the age of twelve, she belonged to five different families in succession; she watched her children taken away to the auction block, and through her life bore the stripes and scars of her masters' beatings.

Her anti-slavery fervor was always closely allied with a crusading and mystical belief in God and his powers. "Oh, God, I did not know you were so big!" she cried out when she succeeded in running away from her last master, unwilling to wait until he freed her under state laws. Her first public appearances were as member and leader of a fanatical religious cult, involving whites and Blacks, important to mention here because it culminated in sensational murder charges of which she was cleared. Much of the information on her life comes from a two-volume work, the *Narrative of Isabella,* written to vindicate her at the time by a white sympathizer in 1835.

Once the cult in which she had passionately believed was dissolved, she never again confined herself to a single organization. She was well into middle age, in the 1840's when she adopted her name which she felt suited her new role as itinerant evangelist: "I am to travel up and down the land, showing the people their sins, and being a sign unto them." God's work, she saw, had many outlets, and throughout her long life she was continually to find new crusades.

In the two decades before the Civil War, she rapidly became a legendary figure, and a second narrative of the life of the extraordinary ex-slave was published in 1850. She made her way to New England and sought out the Abolitionists—Douglass, Garrison, Harriet Beecher Stowe, and Wendell Phillips were her associates. She was in demand as a speaker for many gatherings, and frequently she would appear at public meetings unannounced and unwanted. She was accustomed to dealing with hostile crowds, was at times attacked and beaten by ruffians, and occasionally arrested. Nothing deterred her. If there was a cause more unpopular than anti-slavery in the 1850's, it was the cause of women's rights. Sojourner Truth championed both causes with fervor.

On the speakers' platform, her deep-throated voice and powerful singing cast a spell over her audiences. Her wit was like a fork of lightning, striking at contempt and complacency: "If the first woman God made was strong enough to turn the world upside down, all alone–these together ought to be able to turn it back and get it right side up again; and now they is asking to do it, the men better let them," she said to thunderous applause at a women's rights gathering.

Her name was honored throughout the anti-slavery movement, and when she visited Abraham Lincoln after the signing of the Emancipation Proclamation, she was told by the President that he had heard of her for many years. During the Civil War she was a constant visitor at the soldiers' camps and frequently spoke at meetings to raise welfare funds for them. After the establishment of the Freedmen's Bureau, she worked among the ex-slaves in the Capital.

Well over seventy, she saw that the freedom she had agitated for had been won–but mostly in name, for none of the fruits had been garnered. Poverty, oppression, misery, filthy dwelling places, illiteracy accompanied the new status, as it had the old. She drew up a petition to Congress requesting, for the freedmen, land in the West, schools, homes and buildings constructed by the Government. She took to the road, traveling through fifteen states collecting signatures on her petition: "America owes to my people some of the dividends," was her insistent argument. "You owe it to them, because you took away from them all they earned and made them what they are."

Ten years later, shortly before her death in 1883, she still held to her ideas, giving moral support to a movement to settle Blacks in the West, and remarking prophetically:

"These colored people will bring the whites out of Egyptian darkness into marvelous light. . . . They will teach the slaveholders the truth that they never had and never knew of. . . . These colored people are going to be a people. Do you think God has had them robbed and scourged all the days of their life for nothing?"

With the progress of the Northern armies in the Civil War, educators and organizers (women as well as men) came South in large numbers, much like today's Freedom fighters, to live, work, and organize and help ex-slaves consolidate the gains of freedom. Typical of the scores who volunteered to serve even before victory, was Charlotte Forten, granddaughter of a Revolutionary War veteran. Born in Philadelphia, she was a graduate of the State Normal School of Salem, Massachusetts. In a letter to Garrison's *Liberator*, describing her arrival on St. Helena's Island where she and two other young women conducted a school, she writes:

"I did not realize that I actually was in South Carolina! And indeed I do not quite realize it now. But we were far from feeling fear, and we were in a very excited, jubilant state of mind, and sang the John Brown song with spirit, as we drove through the palms and palmettos. Ah, it was good to be able to sing that *here*, in the very heart of Rebeldom!

"I wish some of those persons at the North, who say the race is hopelessly and naturally inferior, could see the readiness with which these children, so long oppressed and deprived of every privilege, learn and understand."

Miss Forten, who later married into the anti-slavery Grimké family, was following a family tradition. Her grandfather James Forten, a free man, educated by the Quakers in Philadelphia, had helped raise a force of Negro volunteers to defend the city in 1812 from the British. A businessman of means, described as a "merchant prince," he was one of Garrison's principal backers in the launching of the *Liberator* and throughout his life a militant organizer for Negro rights.

Post-Civil War Period

Education and freedom have been closely intertwined in the Negro's efforts to improve his status. Thousands of women in the teaching profession, like Charlotte Forten, raised their voices for equality in the schools and in society beginning in the post-Civil War period. Teachers' associations, mostly women, continually pressed for Federal intervention and support to insure standards in education of Black children, equal salaries for Black and white teachers, and the right to enroll in schools of higher education in the South. This activity continued at an accelerating pace up to the sweeping Supreme Court decisions of the past two decades which brought them closer to their demands.

The next few decades to the turn of the century were a period of intensive organization; there were widespread protests against revived Ku Klux Klan activities; Congress was pushed into investigations which revealed the extent of the conspiracy to enslave the Negro anew. While militant action was suppressed by terror, a number of organizations came into being to try to ameliorate the situation through education, through self-help efforts among the Negro group, through appeals for legislative redress. It was an era of the founding of a number of the Negro organizations which exist today.

Some remarkable women leaders emerged, mostly from the tiny Black middle class, who had had the advantages of education and felt that through this means some of the goals of the race could be attained. Others, despairing of help from the white rulers on the basis of the Constitution and justice, determined to wrest what could be gained by trying to meet the white man on his own grounds—like Madame C. J. Walker and Maggie Walker, remarkable business pioneers, who sought ways to found enterprises which would ease the economic strain their people faced.

Still others like Ida Wells Barnett followed the tradition of the anti-slavery leaders. She edited a crusading newspaper, the *Memphis Free Press,* and was driven out of town by local hostility. She lectured widely, speaking out against lynching, exposing conditions among Blacks in the South. At a meeting with President McKinley, she demanded the punishment of lynchers, indemnity for the widows and children of the victims and national legislation for the suppression of lynching. A few years later, with Dr. W.E.B. Du Bois, she became one of the founders of the Niagara Movement, predecessor of the NAACP.

Her spiritual descendants in our day would certainly include the indomitable Los Angeles editor, Charlotta Bass, who as a penniless girl borrowed the fifty dollars to purchase the decrepit holdings of the *California Eagle* and developed it into the most politically advanced of all black newspapers of our day—and heroic Daisy Bates, veteran of the first and hardest of public school integration struggles in Little Rock, Arkansas, in 1954.

One of the earliest exponents of the salvation-through-education philosophy was Lucy Craft Laney, born a slave in Macon, Georgia, who became one of the first graduates of Atlanta University in 1873. Working against incredible difficulties and hostility, she secured an old shack, and opened a school which became Haines Industrial Institute to train boys and girls for vocations, and a few of the superior students for teaching. Out of Haines came other notable educators, Mary McLeod Bethune, the founder of Bethune-Cookman, and Charlotte Hawkins Brown, founder of Palmer Memorial Institute. All of these were private institutions. Their founders faced local terror, scrounged for pitifully small sums of money to keep their doors open for their poverty-stricken students, cleaned, cooked, taught and disciplined—and sent out class after class of young men and women dedicated to the bootstrap operation of "Lifting as we climb."

The Era of Mary Church Terrell

The most outstanding woman of the era was Mary Church Terrell, an organizer, lecturer, writer, and demonstrator to her last days. Her ninety years encompassed the period from the signing of the Emancipation Proclamation to the 1954 Supreme Court schools' decision—and through all her adult years her energy, her versatile abilities and, later, her enormous prestige were generously devoted to various movements for freedom.

She was born into a well-to-do family and was graduated in 1884 from Oberlin, the third Black woman in the United States to receive a college degree. She was one of the early members of the Women's Equal Suffrage League, a friend of Susan B. Anthony and Carrie Chapman Catt, and an advocate both of women's and Negro rights among her own people. Under her leadership the National Association of Colored Women was formed as a merger of the scattered women's groups in the country, with the aim of uniting women to work for civil rights, the right to vote, for the education of youth and the protection of mothers.

She was one of the earliest members of the NAACP. She organized the national sorority of Negro college women, Delta Sigma Theta, with basic objectives paralleling those of the National Association of Colored Women and with emphasis on training leaders among women. Sent as a United States delegate to the International Congress of Women in Berlin, she spoke eloquently of the plight of Black women. She took part in the international peace movement, beginning shortly after World War I. Brilliant and courageous, she associated herself with innumerable causes—the fight for the first Fair Employment Practice Act, the anti-poll tax legislation, the organization of Blacks into trade unions. She took part in countless demonstrations, marches, conferences. Characteristically in the last year of her life at eighty-nine, she headed a committee of Washington, D.C., residents to demand the desegregation of Capital restaurants, an action which led to favorable ruling by the Supreme Court.

With Mary Church Terrell, an era ended, just at the dawning of a new day of direct and open confrontation of mass movements with the entrenched institutions of oppression. A younger generation, born to renewed hope, learned to work in new ways—and the leaders in the fight for freedom are legion—the names of many of the women, known only to the companions who fight by their sides in the sit-ins, the pray-ins, the marches, the demonstrations, the jails.

A History of Courage

The years have brought from every period, every necessity, its heroines, whose names may be known only locally or transitorily, but whose labors have speeded all the many movements toward freedom. Many have heard of Crispus Attucks, but few until recently knew of the Black woman, Deborah Gannett, who, the record shows, served as a soldier in the American Revolution. Disguised as a man, using the name Robert Shurtliff, she fought with the Fourth Massachusetts Regiment of the Continental Army for seventeen months from 1782 to 1783. At the end of her service, she was awarded a stipend by the State and her deeds cited as "an extraordinary instance of female heroism." Few know that in the period before the Civil War women slaves also paid the penalty of death or lashing for taking part in slave rebellions or conspiracies against the system of slavery. Or, how many have heard this school integration story: When seventeen-year-old Ann Eliza Hammond attempted to attend a high school, furious citizens of the community stoned the building, contaminated the school's water supply with manure, and set the school on fire. The young girl was arrested under a vagrancy law, and her penalty set as a lashing on the naked body up to

21*

ten stripes. Merchants refused to sell food to the school; doctors would not treat its ill patients. Finally the schoolteacher who had insisted upon taking Black girls into her finishing school for young ladies was seized and thrown into a jail cell with murderers, thieves, and prostitutes. The school was closed forever, and humanity and education took a backward step—to last for many decades. The year was 1833; the place was Canterbury, Connecticut; the teacher, Prudence Crandall, a Quaker, whose courage was matched by that of Ann Elizabeth and her nineteen Black fellow students.

They were the prototypes of the brave young women of the 1950's and 1960's, who faced infuriated mobs in pursuit of an education. "When we walk out, horns are blown and pistols fired," said one of Prudence Crandall's students; just as more than a century later the hoodlums of an Alabama town hurled abuse at Autherine Lucy, first of her people to attempt to enroll in the University of Alabama.

The names of other women of courage and conviction form another chapter in the freedom story—those who rose from the ranks during the hunger years of the 1930's. Those were the days when the famous Scottsboro case electrified the world, and tens of thousands demonstrated in our cities to save the lives of the nine innocent youths sentenced to die on a framed charge of rape. The names of Mother Patterson, whose son was one of the victims, and Williana Burroughs are unforgettably linked with this struggle against injustice. The radical working-class movement, in the van of Scottsboro, developed local and national leadership. Claudia Jones, a Communist, was one of the best known of these valiant women; she suffered imprisonment and later deportation for her activities. Others, like her, were in the Unemployed Councils, the newly born CIO, in Harlem, and the black ghettos of the big cities fighting racism, police brutality, and racial oppression in all areas of life.

Their tradition is as old as slavery, as enduring as the fight for freedom, and every struggle has its heroic women. Out of oppression and agony they arise to challenge and to help destroy the tyrannies that create them.

Black Union Power in the Steel Mills

George Powers

Richard Clay is a native of Montgomery, Alabama. Twenty-seven years ago he gathered up his meager belongings and headed north. In Chicago he heard people say, "Jobs are plentiful and wages high."

After a two-year stretch at the Chicago stockyards at miserable pay, Mr. Clay landed a job in a steel mill. Steel mill management herded newly hired Blacks into the "yard" department as laborers. Some time later, a friend told Mr. Clay that there was an opening in the pipe mill. He applied, and to his surprise, was hired. He held down that job until a few months ago when he took his company pension.

About ten years after Clay, Sr., entered the steel mill, his son Richard Clay, a young Korean War veteran, followed his dad into the same plant. Not much had changed regarding job opportunities for Black workers in the steel mills during that ten-year period. Young Clay, like his father, was saddled with a low-paying job with little promise of any advancement. But there was one difference. Richard, Jr., was of the "new breed." He took great pride in his black heritage, manhood, union membership and his principles. Nobody was going to push him around!

Unity and Struggle Spell Progress

Young Clay and a group of Black union brothers decided to challenge the steel corporation's racist policy of job discrimination. As he recalls it, "We were successful in securing the support of 'good union men' among the white workers in the mill. Thus, a coalition was formed!"

This group made a careful survey of the whole mill—shop by shop, department by department and came up with the indisputable evidence: there were practically no Blacks or Chicanos or other Latin Americans on skilled jobs. The report was presented to a local membership meeting where action was voted to demand an end to company discrimination because of race.

The plant management was furious. Young Clay promptly took the next step. He requested a transfer to a better job in one of the shops. When management turned him down, he filed charges of discrimination with the State and later the Federal Fair Employment Practices Commission. There followed a frustrating period of red tape, investigations and briefs but the company was found in violation of federal anti-discrimination laws. The Commission ruled that Clay was entitled to the job for which he had applied. During the long delays he was subjected to severe pressure, intimidation, harassment, and "disciplines" (time off). But Brother Clay stood pat and determined. They failed to turn him around.

This militant action won by Clay and the coalition of Black and white union men was fully supported by the local union. It inspired new courage in many others to dare to stand up for their rights to better jobs. The door had been pried open for other Blacks and Chicanos to follow through to better paying jobs. Today, Black union men as well as Spanish-speaking brothers are working as boilermakers, welders, machinists, carpenters, riggers, millwrights and cranemen.

In the steel melting departments of most mills, as high as 50 percent of the work force today are Blacks and Chicanos. They work as first and second helpers on open hearths and electric furnaces; hot ladle men and charging crane operators. In many rolling mills they make up a substantial percentage of the work force.

This changed situation in the mills is also reflected within many of the local unions. Black steelworkers are becoming actively involved in the affairs of the union and in its leadership. They, along with Spanish-speaking union brothers, function effectively as top grievance committee-men on a department level and as officers and Executive Board members.

The general lessons to be learned from these activities are invaluable:

1. To achieve progress, Blacks, and other discriminated groups of mill workers need to get themselves together around their common needs.

2. To exercise maximum power, a coalition with white union brothers is necessary. A go-it-alone policy can only lead to disunity, and ineffectiveness.

3. The main target—racism—has to be identified, and the struggle directed against the enemy. *The corporation is the enemy, not the union.*

Steelworker Leaders Speak for Solidarity

In another mill employing about 9,000, 60 percent of the workers are Black, another 15 percent are Spanish-speaking, and the rest, a variety of European ethnic origin or descent. The president of the local steelworkers union is an impressive looking Black man of fifty-five, with thirty years of service in the mill. He declares proudly, "I am the president of all union members, not just Blacks."

Another outstanding leader of Mexican descent, in this local union who has established a sterling reputation in the local union as well as in his community, strongly agrees that Blacks and Spanish-speaking workers have to be on the ball to guard their rights, but he strongly warns against "polarization of workers." He says, "The labor movement is not perfect, but its principles of unity, solidarity and brotherhood are of tremendous significance. True, some members don't live up to these principles. All the more reason why Chicanos and Black people should press even harder to preserve them."

The experiences in steel mills in Pittsburgh, Chicago, Cleveland and Birmingham verify the report in *Freedom-*

ways (Second Quarter, 1971) by Carl E. Farris of the experiences of striking steelworkers in Georgetown, South Carolina. He describes the victory won by the Black and white union men as a result of their united action and the active support of the Southern Christian Leadership Conference. Black liberation organizations could gain much if they gave more attention to developing a working relationship with Black unionists in basic industries.

"Basic Steel" (the aggregate of America's largest steel corporations: U.S. Steel, Bethlehem Steel, Republic Steel, Jones & Laughlin, Youngstown Sheet and Tube, etc.) employs about 560,000 production and maintenance workers. Of these, nearly 30 percent, or about 165,000 are Black. The corporation's notorious racist employment policy has traditionally enforced brazen discrimination against Black employees. In this, the companies have been aided (and in some mills still are), by phony local "progression and regression charts" designed to exclude Blacks, Chicanos and Puerto Ricans from promotions. These charts (local agreements signed by department superintendents and union grievance committeemen) establish departmental "home rule" procedures which are discriminatory; so is the system of so-called "labor pools" where there are five and ten pools in each mill instead of just one pool.

In a number of steel mills where Black steelworkers are on the move, and where these practices have been militantly challenged, the company eliminated them.

The New Challenges

Now that our country is caught in the grip of an economic depression, sharply intensified by the Nixonian wage freeze, Blacks and Chicanos face new threats to their hard-won rights and security in the mills. A stark example of this is in Mayor Hatcher's city of Gary, Indiana, where the federal government acknowledges a 35 percent unemployment rate (primarily affecting Blacks).

It has been said that these mass layoffs are due to "stock piling" and "foreign imports." While these play some role, the fundamental fact is that America and the steel industry especially are in a major economic depression which continues to deepen and spread world wide. After years of grabbing up huge profits at the expense of workers' living conditions, poor peoples' starvation at home; robbing the Asian people, and destroying many of them, as well as our own youth in the "dirtiest war" our country has ever fought, the entire capitalist economic system is going through one of its historic crises. Not satisfied with looting and destroying the homeland of millions of Asians, our government has permitted the big corporations to loot the federal treasury of taxpayers' money to guarantee the super-profits of the billionaire corporations, banks and Wall Street gamblers. Thus our "free enterprise" system is proven to be neither free nor enterprising for the American people.

All talk of wage freeze and ending inflation are tricky words aimed at putting the entire burden of this corporation-made depression upon the shoulders of the working people and the nation's unemployed. There is a real danger that if labor and the people do not stand up and fight back, tens of thousands of steelworkers now on layoff will never be called back to work. "More production with fewer men" is what is meant by more "productivity" talk.

A drive to mechanize and automate the steel mills has been under way for some time. The Basic Oxygen Furnace will completely replace the present old open-hearth methods of steel production, where as much steel can be produced in one hour as the old methods produced in eight. The continuous casting process will also be installed which will eliminate molds, mold prep departments, soaking pits and much of the transportation work. The United Steel Workers Union says, "In 1960, 461,000 workers produced 99 million tons of steel. In 1969, 141 million tons were produced with only 428,000 workers." And much more of the same looms in the near future.

Taking full advantage of the layoffs (as a club over the

heads of the workers on the job), steel management is tightening the screws on the men, particularly the Black and Spanish-speaking workers. In the crafts and shops, Black boilermakers, welders and other mechanics are more often sent to work on down turns (where mills are down for repairs for one eight hour turn). This work provides little or no incentive earnings. White craftsmen, on the other hand, who enjoy more seniority are for the most part given the gravy jobs with high incentive pay.

The corporations must not be permitted to succeed in their efforts to wipe out the gains Black steelworkers have made in the past few years by their heroic struggle and sacrifice. The new, ominous developments in the mills will require new tactics of struggle, in which the unity and co-operation between organized Black steelworkers and black liberation movements like SCLC can be decisive.

Pages from the Life
of a Black Prisoner

Frank E. Chapman, Jr.

To enter prison at the age of nineteen is no extraordinary event for thousands of young Black people in the ghetto–it merely happens every day. The day I entered the Missouri State Penitentiary was November 3, 1961. To me it wasn't just another day because I entered those gray walls with a sentence of life and fifty years for murder and armed robbery. Elsewhere I have told the story of how this came about, so here I will tell about my experience in prison and my current effort to secure my freedom.

I was brought to prison in a train along with fifty other inmates. When we arrived at the train station, we were picked up by a bus which transported us inside the prison. Upon arrival we were all taken past an iron gate into a large room. We were lined up and told to take off all our clothing. After we were all naked, the guards told us to bend over so they could inspect our rectums, then we were told to open our mouths so they too could be inspected. After this ordeal we were all given a pair of overalls and taken into another room to be photographed and fingerprinted. All this took several tedious hours.

We arrived at prison at noon. However, for the foregoing reasons, we were not assigned and taken to cells until around 6 o'clock in the evening. The cells were just large enough to accommodate two men and were about 7 ft. wide and 11 ft. long, and 10 ft. high with one set of double-decker bunks. They were located in a building called the "Reception Diagnostic Center." We were to be kept here for about thirty days before being released into the general prison population.

During my thirty days in "Reception" I brooded quite a

lot about what life could be like if I were in prison. Jail is not something one can adjust to overnight. However, the most disgusting part of my stay in "Reception" was having to sit in a room and listen to the prison officials lecture about the prison rules and codes of conduct. At one such lecture the warden said, "In here every son-of-a-bitch has to shift for himself, so if one of you young fresh punks go out there playing tough and get a knife hung in you, don't come crying to me. This is a penitentiary for *men*!" We knew nobody cared whether we lived or died in here so the warden's remarks only added insult to injury.

While in "Reception" I also talked with a caseworker. He asked me what did I want to do while in prison. I replied, "Get an education." The caseworker wanted to know why I wanted an education. My answer sort of shook him up. I said, "I think my coming here is the greatest mistake I ever made in life and if I can't learn from it, then there is no purpose in me living." He asked me, did I want to live. To me the question seemed very silly so I refused to answer. I just sat there and gave him a bitter stare. After a moment or two, he said, "I think you are a very bitter young man." He was right. I was bitter but I still wanted an education and I wanted to know if he could help me. The interview ended on this note: "Be a good boy, Chapman, bring us ten or maybe fifteen years, and maybe you'll go free on parole. I'll tell the classification board you want to go to school."

When I went up before classification for assignment to the general population, they assigned me to the garbage detail. I protested stating that I wanted an education. I was told, with arrogance, that I would be a garbage worker and if I didn't like that, I could be disciplined.

In 1961 there was only one cell block in the general population for Black inmates and it was called A Hall. A Hall is a tall gray stone medieval-looking structure that was built about 133 years ago. Black inmates were housed in here and forced to live with roaches, rats, and six men to a cell—only big enough to accommodate two men. In the winter we would nearly freeze, and in the summer the heat was always intolerable. I was forced to live in A Hall for nearly four years, and these were some of my most miserable years in prison.

When I first hit population I worked on the garbage detail for about sixty days. During this period I wrote letters to the educational director, requesting that I be assigned to the school. Finally I was called down to the school and given a Stanford Achievement Test; shortly thereafter I was enrolled as a student in the eighth grade.

In school I studied hard and made good grades. But I couldn't find in school an education that would give me my purpose in life, so I would go to the prison library and check out books on philosophy. Most of these books were too deep for me but I would get a dictionary and try to read them anyway.

One day while browsing in the library a white prisoner who worked in the library asked me if I wanted to read a very good book. I said yes and he gave me *Les Miserables* by Victor Hugo. This book told the most moving story of human oppression I had ever read. In reading it I was moved to tears and anger on several occasions. When I finished this book, I asked myself over and over again, "Why, why does man have to suffer such abuse and persecution at the hands of his fellows?" I did not know, yet I swore that before I die I would have the answer, no matter the cost.

In school I was learning about science, man's conquest of disease and human suffering. I noticed that science often stood in opposition to ignorance and superstition, thus I decided to study science. In reading science books I learned that the language of science is mathematics, so like a man dying from thirst plunges into water, I plunged into mathematics.

I began with textbooks that contained sections on arithmetic and algebra. I was very much fascinated with algebra, for it was like learning to speak some unknown tongue. I progressed rapidly because I was eager to learn and no one could stop me. Finally, I came upon a book in the prison library called *Mathematics for the Million* by Lancelot Hogben and it was such a happy accident because this was just what I wanted, a book that covers the whole field of mathematics and written for laymen like myself. I fell in love with this delicious little book (I think it contained about 600 pages) because everything I wanted to know was here, and the author had written it in such a way that it read like an exciting mystery story. I found myself copying down Hogben's brilliant satirical comments on white supremacy, mysticism, and the relation between science and society. After reading Hogben's book, I was convinced that science alone had the key to the riddle of the universe.

After Hogben I ventured to take a look at the classical mathematicians and scientists. I went to the liberary and tapped the *Great Books of the Western World;* I read Euclid, Archimedes, Descartes, Pascal, Newton, Galileo, Copernicus, Ptolemy. I also became interested in modern physics and cosmology. I wrote Professor Robert L. Carter at Missouri University inquiring about plasma physics. I studied the atomic theory, and became familiar with the works of Dr. Albert Einstein. I think the best book I ever read on physics was *The Evolution of Physics* by Infield and Einstein.

It is very difficult for a person of my temperament to study knowledge for its own sake. I was seeking a purpose in life, therefore as far as I was concerned, I would have to know something about every significant branch of human knowledge. So I began to study books like *Science for the Citizen* by Lancelot Hogben, outlines of science by authors like Sherwood Taylor and J. Arthur Thomson. In these books I learned something about all the major branches of natural science. Also I read the philosophers who supposedly based their positions on natural science, e.g. Herbert Spencer, John Fiske, and others of the evolutionist school; and the philosophers who claimed they were in tune with the discoveries of modern physics, e.g. Ernst Mach, Henri Poincaré, Sir James Jeans, Alfred Korzybski (the semanticist), Moritz Schlick (the Vienna School), and others. Many times I got lost in this maze of science and philosophy, but I would always find my way again.

At this point I want to say something which I think is very important. In studying science I became interested in the idealist and materialist arguments of Western philosophy. It seemed to me that idealism was in league with superstition and prejudice in that it tried to reduce science to uncertainty and opinion by denying the existence of the material world or by putting mind over matter. But I couldn't be satisfied with my own opinion of idealism without any further inquiry so I undertook a more serious study of philosophy. I began with Frederick Paulsen's *Introduction to Philosophy*, after that I read several standard histories of philosophy. Now I settled down to the classics, reading with great interest Plato's *Dialogues*, works of Aristotle, Lucretius' *On the Nature of Things*, B. Spinoza's *Ethics*, Rene Descartes's *Discourse on Method*, Francis Bacon's *Novum Organum*, Berkeley's *Dialogues*, Kant's *Critique of Pure Reason*, Hegel's *Phenomenology of Mind and Science of Logic*. I considered Aristotle and Hegel the greatest speculative thinkers of all time but was sorely disappointed because neither was a materialist.

Philosophy made me even more sensitive to human problems because it probed the very nature of human existence. And yet there was a contradiction: Philosophy, which supposedly stood above the natural sciences, justified rather than addressed itself to the problems of human slavery. So in my quest for freedom and humanity, I learned from philosophy that human bondage (greed, egoism, catch-as-catch-can competition, racism, etc.) is not an objective social fact but a state of mind-subjective evaluation. According to idealist philosophy, my own suffering in prison had nothing to do with my *objective* surroundings, to be sure I learned that my *objective* surroundings were merely events in my mind and that I had absolutely no way of knowing what lay outside my mind. Consequently, I found myself imprisoned once again—imprisoned within the confines of my own thought processes, locked up in my own narrow experiences. Hegel's words, "A great mind is great in its experience," offered no consolation. My mood was amply depicted by Goethe's "Ultimatum":

"No mortal mind can Nature's inner secrets tell
Too happy only if he knows the outer shell."
For sixty years to this I've had to hark,
I curse the sentiment, but keep it dark,
Not shell nor kernel Nature does possess
Is everything at once and nothing less.

I refused to accept the idealist bifurcation between appearance and reality. I knew knowledge was positive, and I firmly believed that through positive scientific knowledge man could become master of the universe and create a world free of hunger and disease. In my opinion science accepts the unknown but not the unknowable. Also I felt that any school of philosophy which taught that no mortal mind could know Nature's inner secrets was catering to superstition and ignorance.

By this time I had had about enough of philosophic controversy. I now wanted to know how the vast store of human knowledge could be used to change the world, to improve the quality of human life. Also I wanted to share my knowledge with my Black people, and I was beginning to realize that I knew a great deal about Western culture but next to nothing about my own black culture. On several occasions Black brothers in the prison came to me because they respected me, and asked me questions about black culture and I was unable to answer them. I felt badly about this because, after all, and in spite of my learning, I was a Black man.

Also my contacts with the Black Muslim brothers intensified my desire to learn about black culture. I remember quite vividly, an incident with the Muslim brothers that more or less embarrassed me. I had attended one of their meetings in the prison yard, and the brothers asked me would I teach them black history; they told me that they felt I was the only Black brother qualified to do this. I stood up and told them that I was very sorry but my ignorance would not permit me to do this; however, I said they could rest assured that I would prepare myself for the task. They all clapped and I left the meeting very much embarrassed and ashamed of myself.

I had a very difficult time getting books on Black Studies literature on Black people. However, during this period because at this time the prison library didn't have any (1963) I was attending prison high school and I was offered a job to teach seventh and eighth grade science and history classes. I accepted the job at once. Shortly after I got the teacher's job, I asked the civilian instructor (a Black man named Nathaniel Burgher) to bring in from the public library, books on black history.

I never will forget the first book I read on black history. It was entitled *World's Great Men of Color* by J. A. Rogers. I was absolutely astonished by the brilliant cultural achievements of Black people extending back 6,000 years! After Rogers, I read W.E.B. Du Bois's *Black Folk: Then and Now*. I was very much impressed by the scholarship and erudition of Dr. Du Bois. My chest swelled with pride just to know that a Black man like W.E.B. Du Bois existed. I became a disciple of Dr. Du Bois at once, making it my solemn duty to read every book he had in print. I read *Souls of Black Folk, Dusk of Dawn, Darkwater, The World and Africa,* one right after the other.

I was inspired by the writings of Dr. Du Bois to make a study of the contributions of colored people to the development of science and mathematics. I presented the results of my inquiries in a book I wrote entitled *Science and Africa.*

In studying black history, I became more and more absorbed in the struggle for black liberation. From 1964 to the present I have been a devoted student of the current struggles for black liberation. In the struggle of my people for freedom, I saw the need for science and I wanted to contribute whatever I could in this regard. So I read, as often as I could, the works of Black authors. Here I will only name those authors who impressed me the most: O. C. Cox's *Caste, Class and Race,* E. Franklin Frazier, Arna Bontemps, Saunders Redding, Horace Cayton, John O. Killens, Richard Rives, Peter Abrahams, Kwame Nkrumah, Richard Wright, Ernest Gaines, Ernest Kaiser, Alphaeus Hunton, Lorraine Hansberry, Paul Robeson, Frederick Douglass, James W. Ford, Harry Haywood, Frantz Fanon, Malcolm X, and others whose writings are a great inspiration to me.

This just about concludes my intellectual biography, save for one item. In doing my research for my book *Science and Africa,* I came into knowledge of the Marxist historians J. D. Bernal, Dirk J. Struik, Benjamin Farrington and Bernhard J. Stern. I was so impressed with their materialist interpretation of history that I felt it was necessary for me to check their sources. Thus I was reading the writings of Marx and Engels. I must say, in all honesty, that this was one of the happiest moments of my life. At last I had found a philosophy in Dialectical Materialism that truthfully and courageously tackled the all-important problems of human bondage from the standpoint of science. As far as I am concerned, Karl Marx is one of the greatest scientific humanists that ever lived. I became a Marxist because I hate human slavery, and Marx was the only philosopher who put his knowledge and his wisdom to the service of oppressed humanity. Once again I was ashamed, I was ashamed for having accepted all the lies and vile slander about Karl Marx at face value. In all my reading I had never read a 20th century Western philosopher who had a kind word for Marx. Even Bertrand Russell, in his monumental work on the history of Western philosophy, rarely passes up an opportunity to belittle Marx and make his work seem trivial. All the so-called authorities discussed the ideas of Marx in a most artificial and disgusting manner, but in my opinion these so-called authorities were mere pygmies throwing pebbles at a giant.

And this concludes my intellectual autobiography, which is a brief summary of my activities over a nine-year period. For the sake of brevity I left out my academic activities so

I will just state here that I have currently earned twenty-one college hours at Missouri University through the prison college training program which began in 1969.

II

This second part of my autobiographical notes will deal with my experiences as a Black prisoner. I don't have the time and space to tell it all so this will be just a general discussion.

First of all, in prison a person is subjected to the most savage conditions, and one is simply not allowed to function as a human being. From 1961 through 1964 I was living in a cell with five other men. We all had to use the same toilet and washbowl. There was absolutely no privacy. Sometimes when I would be trying to study, the radio would be blasting and people would be talking very loud about pimping, shooting dope, selling dope, homosexuals and so on.

Prison officials have absolutely no regard for convicts as human beings. When a guard talks to you, he talks to you in a most degrading manner and tone. He says, "Hey, boy, where do you think you're going? Get against that wall! Put your hands up! Empty your pockets! You want to go to the hole for not shaving? Get a shave, you son-of-a-bitch! I see we are going to have to beat this nigger's ass for being smart! Hey sunshine, get your ass over here!" In most cases an inmate's conduct record depends on the whim of the officials. A "good" inmate is simply an obedient slave of the state.

Shortly after my imprisonment, the prison officials began to regard me as a "bad" inmate. Why? Well, it began with my assignment as an inmate teacher in the prison school. In my history classes I taught black history right along with Western history. In order to do this effectively, I used film strips from the public library (most of these were on Africa), *The Negro in Our History* by Carter G. Woodson, and some Negro History Bulletins. Also I organized a discussion group on world affairs; every two or three weeks we would discuss some major problem such as the Congo Crisis, the

22*

Vietnam War, World Population and Hunger, Cuba, Red China and so on. In the discussion group I used material I managed to get from the United Nations *Scientific American* magazine, and I used an assortment of pamphlets along with current literature on the problem being discussed. The civilian teacher, Mr. Burgher, thought I was doing an excellent job and he always gave me Excellent (Grade E) on my work report. Work reports are for the purpose of reporting an inmate's progress to the Parole Board and prison authorities. Nevertheless, my classes antagonized some of the white inmates in my class because . . . notions of white supremacy were under persistent attack. So, some of the white inmates began telling prison officials that I was using the prison school to brainwash people in Communism and "Black Racism."

Due to the enthusiastic support I was receiving from Mr. Burgher, the accusations made against me by white inmates were not taken too seriously at first. However, this was quickly altered by my activities on the prison yard. I had accepted the teaching position offered me by the Muslim brothers, consequently I would go to the yard every Saturday and Sunday and lecture on black history. On many occasions I had as many as fifty Black brothers (both Muslim and non-Muslim) sitting and listening attentively to my lectures. This really frightened the racist prison authorities.

I could see that the racist guards had cause for alarm so I tried to avoid a crisis by going to the prison chaplain and asking him to help us in getting a place to conduct our Black Studies program. I explained to him that if we had a place to study and lecture, then we wouldn't have to make a spectacle every weekend on the yard. The chaplain agreed with me and he promised to take the matter up with higher officials.

But before the chaplain could do anything, the officials swept down upon me without warning. It happened like this. It was noon and I was walking down the school hall on my way to lunch. When I got near the principal's office, I was stopped by a guard. The guard asked me to step into the principal's office and when I stepped into the office, he quickly shut the door behind me and locked it. I shouted, "Hey, what's going on?" He replied, "You'll know soon enough!" I was locked up in the room alone for about thirty-five minutes (that is, the entire lunch period).

When I was released from the room, I saw Major Poiry, a senior guard, coming toward me down the hall with a large box. The major was confiscating all my books and papers. I inquired, "Why are you taking all my books and my personal papers?" The major said, "All this stuff will be taken to the warden's office for inspection, and you are to return to your cell for transfer."

I was transferred to the prison industries. I was barred from the school and prison library permanently, and the warden ordered burned all my personal papers which consisted of all my research notes on books I was writing and a manuscript copy of my book *Science and Africa*. I have never been so disgusted and mad in all my life. No one could have convinced me that the warden was so ignorant and stupid.

After this incident I was constantly harassed by guards and labeled a Black Muslim agitator; and yet for seven years I had had no serious conduct violations (I have never had a fight with another inmate during my entire stay in prison): My crime was that I was Black and I was helping other Black inmates.

I started studying civil and criminal law so I could combat the official harassment with suits in the courts. I filed a civil rights suit in the Federal District seeking an injunction and/or restraining order forbidding the warden to further deprive me of my constitutional rights and practice racial discrimination under cover of state law. Although I had ample grounds for action on the part of the court, my civil action was erroneously dismissed without prejudice because I failed to exhaust a phony grievance procedure set up by the warden after I had filed my complaint.

Also I was getting more and more impatient with the calculated racist insults and senseless guard brutality. So I and other inmates got together and began writing letters to our state representatives and to Congressman William Clay complaining of racism. Most of the letters were answered and on one occasion we were visited by a Black woman state representative. But matters were still not getting better; thus I began to think in terms of something more dramatic.

Two incidents made me decide in favor of more militant and dramatic action. One involved me and the other one involved a mentally deranged inmate. The incidents were as follows:

First Incident: It was January, 1969. I was sick with Asiatic Flu and running a fever of about 101. I attempted to check into the prison hospital but was refused because I was not sick enough. In a few days I was so sick I had to stay in bed in my cell. The inmates nursed me and got food for me. Finally, one night, I got so sick that I asked the brothers in my cell row to raise hell to get the guard back there. The guard came back to talk to me and I told him I wanted to be checked in the hospital. He said he would call "control center" and tell them I was very sick. The guard called around 1:00 a.m. but I was carried to the hospital at approximately 3:00 a.m. The reason for the long delay is that the guard at "control center" had refused to call the hospital because he didn't feel an agitator like Frank Chapman could be sick! A Black inmate who worked at "control center" named Elmer Hendricks intervened in my behalf and talked the superior officer of the shift into taking me to the hospital. When I was checked in the hospital that morning, I was told that I had a temperature of 102 and that I had begun to suffer from pneumonia. While in the hospital I wrote an indignant letter to the Director of the Missouri Department of Corrections.

Second Incident: A Black inmate named Theodore Taylor was going insane as a result of cruel and unusual punishment. He had been kept in solitary confinement for a year.

After these two incidents, I began to draft a petition to the U.S. Department of Justice and the Missouri Human

Rights Commission to end racism and guard brutality in the Missouri State Penitentiary. I conferred with other inmates on how to go about getting signatures on the petition. We decided to have several copies made up and to distribute them in the cell blocks for signatures. After we procured about 256 signatures, I signed my name as the author of the petition and dropped it in the mailbox.

The warden would not permit the petition to be mailed, and he tried to intimidate the signatories with threats of punishment if they would not remove their signatures. He also tried to get some of the inmates to lie and say I forced them to sign the petition against their wills. As a result of these pressure tactics, many inmates became violently mad and there was talk of burning down the penitentiary.

Truthfully speaking, I felt the penitentiary really needed burning down, but I knew a rash outbreak of violence would only hurt our cause at this point so I advised the brothers to be cool and not be provoked into doing something that would justify more guard brutality and possibly a mass killing.

But the officials were so bent on teaching us a lesson that they came over to our cell block and attacked an inmate without provocation, thereupon some Black brothers attacked a white guard. In a matter of seconds, our whole cell block was up in rebellion and there were demands to see the warden. The associate warden of custody came over to check us out.

When the associate warden entered the cell block, I told him that Black people are tired of being treated like dogs and that we want an end put to racism. He said, "Are you the spokesman?" and I replied that this was no time to try and play tricks on us ... that we were dead serious about the rotten conditions we were being subjected to. He said, "Well, will you have a conference with the warden right now?" I told him I would not have anything to do with the warden. He said that he was serious and that if we got a committee of say five inmates, we could go see the warden right then. We held a brief conference among ourselves and decided to form a committee of five to meet with the warden.

We met with the warden in the officers' assembly room. The warden called the meeting for one purpose–to line the ringleaders up. We knew this so I told him quite frankly that regardless of what he did to us, there was going to be trouble if the racism and brutality were not stopped. We didn't cause the trouble, I said, the prison officials started the trouble.

The warden asked me to drop the petition. I refused. After about forty-five minutes or more of discussion, the agreement reached was that the committee would meet again with the Deputy Director and other officials the next day. Meanwhile we were asked to return to our cells.

We returned to the cell block and told the brothers that all the warden agreed to was another meeting. I told them no matter what happened, we should stick to the demands of the petition. I said that the Ku Klux Klan-minded guards had the full backing of the warden and that the warden refused to recognize the legitimacy of our demands. At this point the brothers began shouting, "Let's strike!" I responded to this by pointing out that whatever we do, we must stick together and carry the fight for our constitutional rights through to the finish.

The next morning about eighty Black inmates refused to go to work. There was no violence on the part of the inmates, just a passive protest. Nevertheless the warden, determined not to treat us as human, called in the state troopers and ordered them to shoot in our cell block, which they did.

After the shooting we peacefully returned to our cells. As soon as everyone was safely locked in his cell, two guards came to my cell, armed with a shotgun and a club. I was handcuffed and taken to the maximum security unit and put in solitary confinement.

I was kept in solitary confinement from February 1969 to November 25, 1969, a period of nine months. During my stay in solitary confinement I was subjected to the most savage and degrading treatment imaginable. I was thrown in strip cells with nothing but a concrete floor and toilet, totally naked. I was threatened with a club beating every time I left my cell. Nevertheless, I continued to protest vigorously against the outrageous conditions. I filed suits in the federal courts, daily protested to prison officials in spite of their silly threats of violence, and even went on a thirty-day food strike for better medical care. But I was not alone in these protests. Beside me stood many courageous inmates, both white and Black. During my stay in solitary confinement, I learned something about man's ability to resist slavery and shame, even under the most degrading conditions. I couldn't help but admire the fighting spirit of man in the face of adversity.

While in solitary confinement the warden allowed me to have some of my books, and all my law books. I began to study law more seriously. There was a juvenile named Robert Henderson in solitary confinement with me. He had been illegally committed to prison. I led a legal motion in his behalf and he and several other juveniles were released from prison early this year.

The struggles and bitter experiences I have had in prison are very valuable to me. Only when you see man at his lowest can you appreciate him at his highest, therefore I consider these experiences a most worthy contribution to my understanding and love of oppressed humanity. I have seen how people who extol the so-called dignity of the individual can mercilessly reduce other men to a bestial existence. I have seen with my own eyes that human love and kindness cannot be abolished by even the most insensitive tyrants. I have learned in the dirt and blood of battle, that it is better to have a brain of passion, than a passion of the brain. And, above all, I have learned to love life and to love more the endless struggle for a better life.

When I entered prison at the age of nineteen, I was a wretched slave. But now, nearly ten years later, I am a man, a man whose heart aches for freedom for himself and his oppressed people. I know the cynic will smile at my remarks, yet I care nothing about his smile because I speak the truth!

I want to go to college (currently I have earned twenty-one college hours), I want to be a historian of science in Africa, and that is not all. I also want to help my Black people in whatever way I can to win their freedom. I feel that only knowledge and adequate formal training will enable me to be an effective person in the struggle for black liberation.

III

This third and final part will deal with my legal struggle for freedom. My legal struggle is based on the following facts, namely:

1. On May 6, 1959, I was committed to the St. Louis State Hospital by Circuit Court order, and at the request of the Chairman of the State Mental Health Commission, for observation and diagnosis. On October 23, 1959, I escaped from the State Hospital and fled to Chicago.

2. At the time of my arrest for murder first degree and armed robbery, I was in fact an escapee from a mental institution. My mother informed my court-appointed lawyer, Mr. Joseph Noskay, of the fact that I was an escapee yet he failed to mention it to the court and he let me plead guilty. However, according to law, I was legally incompetent to plead guilty.

3. There is no record to show that my plea of guilty was, in fact, voluntary, and there is every indication that I did not have adequate and effective assistance of counsel.

These facts constitute the gist of my case. The established constitutional rule since 1956 is that "the conviction of an accused person while he is legally incompetent, violates due process...." (See Bishop v. United States, 350 U.S. 961, 76 S. Ct. 400.)

My lawyer, Mr. Arley R. Woodrow, has filed a legal motion seeking my discharge from custody since I have been detained under this illegal conviction for nearly ten years. However, even though there is no legal reason why I shouldn't be discharged, the authorities are reluctant to grant me my freedom. In a sense it has nothing to do with the merits of my case, but my skin color and political beliefs. I am no longer being held in jail for a crime against the state. I have become a political prisoner.

In my current quest for freedom I am going to need the help of all those who believe in social justice, if I am ever to be free again. However, it is not I alone who will benefit from such help because there are brothers like me throughout America whose lives are becoming permanently deranged by our bureaucratic prison system. I don't like to make dark and frightening predictions, but in all sincerity I believe that unless something is done about the wretched conditions in prison, there is going to be (in fact there already is) a lot of senseless bloodshed. I have spent ten years of my life in these human junkyards so I want very strongly to contribute what I can to help improve things.

In conclusion, my legal struggle cannot be separated from the overall struggle for social justice in our country because I am one among many. I am typical of the injustice in our country.

Confronting Monopoly and Keeping the Movement Moving

Jesse L. Jackson

We are aware that a wide range of opinion in our country is beginning to question seriously whether or not what has been called an "energy crisis" is indeed real or contrived. Given the large number of layoffs of workers in key industries, the soaring prices of gasoline and fuel oil, which are really pushing the general inflationary spiral ever higher, and the inconveniences being imposed on the average consumer trying to purchase gasoline, many people are rethinking and taking a new look at the officially proclaimed "energy crisis."

Under pressure from this newly emerging public opinion, congressional committees have begun to search seriously for the facts and call some of the major oil companies to account on this matter. This should result in a valuable body of information being *accumulated* regarding the tremendous, though hidden, power of the oil industry monopoly in this country. None of us should be surprised if before long, the so-called "energy crisis" takes its place among the major scandals of the Nixon Administration. After considered judgment and weighing the facts, we at Operation P.U.S.H.* have taken the position, over the past five months or more, that there is no energy crisis. There is only a shortage of the supply of oil and other fuel being allowed on the market. This conclusion is really quite inescapable from facts that are already public knowledge. Tanker ships in the ports of our country, loaded with oil, that have no place to

* People United to Save Humanity.

unload; refineries that are operating below capacity; increases in the exportation of oil from the United States to Japan and Western Europe; hundreds of oil wells in the Gulf of Mexico and elsewhere that have been tapped, oil discovered, and then closed for future use; the continued sending of 165,000 barrels of oil per week to Vietnam and Cambodia and the exorbitant increase in profits that the major oil companies have made in 1973 as compared with just one year earlier—these and other facts confirm our position that there is really no energy crisis.

Due to the heavy propaganda that has accompanied this hoax, the public has been made to feel guilty about wasting fuel and other energy. We have been admonished to turn down the thermostats in our homes to 68, eliminate Sunday driving, and adopt other forms of austerity. One not so distinguished Congressman from Michigan has even managed to get a bill passed that will eliminate the busing of schoolchildren, under certain circumstances, on the grounds that this would serve to save a considerable quantity of gasoline. Yet, the facts are that home owners use only 19 percent of all the energy used in this country, and that there is more energy *wasted* by industry and commerce than is *used* by home owners. Seventy percent of all energy used is used by commerce and industry, and nearly one-third of that is waste. Yet it is the consuming public that is being given a guilt complex about allegedly wasting energy. This is a carefully designed propaganda campaign by the big oil companies and spearheaded by an Administration that has no credibility.

When a P.U.S.H. delegation of gas station operators from five states visited energy czar Simon's office in Washington in late February, we put three questions to his representatives. We asked what his office would do if they caught refineries burning up gasoline; what their program is to deal with the problems of workers who are being laid off from their jobs; and, thirdly, we asked if his office operates from the premise that it is dealing with a *monopoly*. Their replies to these questions were evasive enough to suggest that the so-called energy czar lacks any real authority to deal with this energy hoax in any basic way. In their view each of these questions involves the responsibility of another department of the federal government other than their own. Consequently, the energy czar's office busies itself Simon-izing the public mind and selling the oil companies' propaganda.

In the so-called energy crisis we see more evidence of the law of monopoly operating than the law of scarcity. Less than two dozen oil and gas corporations control the majority of refineries, pipelines and retail gasoline outlets, and at least four of them own the largest coal-producing enterprises. The monopoly is real while the energy shortage is artificially created. Yes, we charge that Exxon, Gulf, Texaco, Standard Oil and a handful more are a monopoly and it is the responsibility of the federal government to act in the public interest to break up this monopoly "with all deliberate speed."

The Right to Work

In first taking this position last November, we at Operation P.U.S.H. were confident that the working people and small business people in our country, who are the most directly affected by this hoax, would soon get over the initial shock of the suddenness of the propaganda barrage, and begin to organize to resist the inevitable lowering of living standards, which this situation was bringing on.

The first encouraging signs of resistance came from the independent truck drivers who held their stall-ins on some of the major highways in our country protesting the drastic price increase in diesel fuel, oil and the difficulty in obtaining adequate supplies except under "white market" conditions; i.e., whites control this illegal market, not Blacks. These independent truckers were right and deserved public support because they were acting in the best traditions of non-violent resistance to exploitation and robbery. After all, these small businessmen were fighting for their lives and the livelihood of their families in the face of price-gouging by these few giant corporations that control the market and the source of supply. The compromise reached by the truckers was not a victory for them, for it really split their ranks. It was a compromise with the Administration that allows for passing on the increase in the price of diesel fuel to the average consumer in the form of a "surcharge." This does not solve any problems; on the contrary, it aggravates the problem of inflationary prices. It is unfortunate that the truckers stopped short of winning a roll-back in prices.

Not only are independent truckers trying to survive this squeeze by the oil monopolies but also the small retail gasoline dealers who independently own or lease their stations. In Chicago these Black and white dealers in the inner city are coming together, with the help of Operation P.U.S.H. to resist going out of business by joining with consumers. These small retail gasoline station dealers are being squeezed out by the monopolies because they can't survive the limited supplies of gasoline being allowed them under the new regulations enforced by the Federal Energy Office in the Nixon Administration. At the same time brand-new stations are opening up in the ghetto, owned directly by Shell, Texaco and others, with an unlimited supply of gasoline and offering free car washes because, as new stations, government regulations allow them unlimited supplies. While the monopolies are destroying their competitors and while thousands of small retailers are going out of business others who manage to survive are being forced to cut back drastically on the number of people they employ. The unemployment picture is most serious.

Recent visits to our P.U.S.H. satellites in Detroit, Philadelphia, Greenville, S.C. (a major textile center), and elsewhere, sharply focused our attention on this problem. Philadelphia had over 100,000 unemployed at the end of last year, before the effects of the energy hoax were being felt. Increases in unemployment in that city are especially severe among the youth aged sixteen to twenty-four, as well as among blue collar and service workers. Institutionalized racist patterns in hiring and upgrading continue to linger on in that city. Regarding jobs in the city government, 58 percent of the Black employees of the city and 55 percent of the Spanish-speaking employees are confined to jobs in the lower paying brackets—under $10,000 a year. By comparison only 17 percent of the white workers employed by the city are in these low-paying jobs. Blacks and Latins make up well over 40 percent of the population, yet hold only a handful of the top jobs in city government. With segregation officially ended in the South there is no longer any substantial difference in a Philadelphia, Pa., and a Greenville, S.C., today. This also means that the conditions are right for nationalizing our Civil Economics Movement.

It is also clear that Detroit, the capital of the auto industry in our country, is not likely to escape the devastating effects of this energy hoax. Car production is already down 30 percent from last year. Six plants were recently scheduled to be closed in one week. In making adjustments to the myth of an energy crisis, the auto manufacturing corporations have created their own set of myths which the public is supposed to swallow. Their myth is that the size of an automobile body determines how much gas is used, so the current layoffs are in connection with the shift to small car production. *Big* motors in *small* cars will use just as much gasoline as a large automobile. The auto manufacturers are using the energy crisis to maximize their corporate profits at the expense of the consumers just as other sections of the monopoly are doing. Producing smaller cars, using less steel, less plastics and fewer workers, while they boost the prices of small cars, all add up to a new profit boom for them. It is also an opportunity to introduce new technology which displaces workers from their jobs. Black workers, whom we saw doing welding operations on auto parts in the Budd (automotive) Plant in Philadelphia have been replaced by computerized technology doing the same welding operation in the General Motors Vega plant in Lordstown, Ohio.

This whole economic picture is a challenge and an opportunity to the Detroit working population to give leadership to the entire country in resisting another depression. Just as Detroiters and workers in Flint sparked the great sit-down strikes in the 1930's, the great need today is for a mass movement of creative protests against the threat of a new depression. Through mobilized direct action, we can turn the negative situation into a positive one. This centers upon winning national recognition and acceptance of the right of every person to a job at socially useful work with decent wages as a human right that working people will not silently give up under whatever false pretense.

Our Commitment is to Life

During this energy crisis hoax our commitment is to protect workers' jobs and living standards. Our national P.U.S.H. program includes practical immediate steps designed to expand employment for the unemployed, help unorganized workers on low-paying jobs get organized, and encourage workers with jobs to resist further layoffs.

"Work-ins" and other forms of creative mass protest are needed and needed *now!* Also, there should be a moratorium on all bill payments for the unemployed for the period of time they are out of work and until such time as they are recycled back into the economy with fulltime jobs. No man or woman should have to lose home, furniture, or have their children pulled out of school because of layoffs. No job, no income, no bill payments! This is only simple justice.

Finally, as a matter of principle we insist on the private and public sector of the economy adopting the "quota" principle in hiring–in which Blacks and Spanish-speaking workers are employed at all levels of decision-making in proportion to their size in the local population. This is the only formula for beginning to seriously redress the long historic racist hiring practices that have been the tradition of American industry and government. Obviously, the best conditions for fully implementing the quota principle are a full employment economy in which the right to a job is considered a human right.

The economic issues which are the New Agenda of our movement are of particular significance to the youth—both the students as well as those in the labor forces. Down through the years, socially conscious university students characteristically show one of two tendencies. One tendency affecting many is to waste themselves in social protest, often dropping out of school under the rationale that they are getting involved in the movement. In this tendency, they abandon the opportunity to basically prepare themselves for leadership and for making a maximum contribution to the freedom struggle. But they do so under the rationale that they are "too busy" in protest demonstrations to find the time for academic work. The other tendency one encounters among students is that of getting immersed in theory at the expense of being involved in concrete action. This is what Dr. Martin Luther King, Jr., called "getting bogged down in the paralysis of analysis." So they find themselves in a kind of self-imposed impotence. For they become so theoretical that they never take the time to learn where the masses of people are in their thinking, they just concern themselves with where they think the masses of people ought to be. Yet, the record shows that the men and women revolutionary leaders whom we admire the most, whether we are speaking of the Castros, Nkrumahs, Du Boises or Martin Luther Kings, each took the time to prepare for leadership responsibility and, in their everyday practical work, used the scientific ideas of their age as a guide to action.

Because the entire Western world and especially the United States are now in the throes of a far-reaching crisis, this student generation is confronted with yet another psycho-cultural problem. Many have come through the drug scene, which was really a form of attack upon their ability to think. These students must now find the ways of getting beyond certain other diversions and entering, full force, into the struggle for *social* change. Changing hair styles or changing our name or religion are merely symbols of identity and, however dramatic and emotionally satisfying, they have little to do with the struggle to change the real world and guarantee a more civilized social existence for ourselves and our families. So while in recent years we have invested a great deal of time in studying "Black History," and that is good, we must now direct our energies toward studying the black future and that means for us, as it does for all people, studying the world of work and wealth and the relationship between these two.

Here in the U.S. one of the great assumptions popularly accepted is the idea of a kind of automatic improvement in the living standards and opportunity of each new generation. Yet, that assumption can no longer be held as valid today in the face of the deteriorating living standards which millions of people are experiencing as a result of rampant inflation and mounting unemployment existing side by side.

The future summons the youth of today to resist being deluged and thrown off course by the contemporary culture which glorifies "the corner" and non-work. The degenerate movies attempt to make heroes of social parasites and teach violence and other inhuman acts. The authentic Afro-American Experience is in the world of work, not in hustling and freeloading on those who do work. We may live in a slum, but the struggle to improve our condition starts with not allowing the slum to live in us.

When we organized Operation P.U.S.H. a little over two years ago, our stated objective was to help effect and direct a transformation of the Human Rights Movement from emphasis on Civil Rights to one on Civil Economics. This became necessary because of the festering economic problems which our communities face and because the largest of the corporations which make the major decisions affecting this economy have not been civilized enough to guarantee an expanding quality of life for the millions of Blacks, Chicanos, Puerto Ricans, Indians and poverty-stricken whites. We, in P.U.S.H., have developed the double-edged techniques of organized mass consumer boycotts and negotiations directed at affecting the policy of major corporations. We are committed to opening up opportunities for those who have been historically left out. Consequently, our organ-

23*

ization has consistently advocated that there must be serious corporate responsibility for the quality of life in our country to match the level of corporate influence that exists. We know this is a reasonable idea, and yet experience has shown that reasonable ideas have to be fought for with tenacity until they are accepted as a matter of principle, and the most effective way to get a just idea accepted is to build a mass movement behind it. Yet, we take up this battle confidently because it is clearly an idea whose time has come. We're talking about making America a better place for all to live in, and this is quite consistent with the entire history of our freedom movement. For the most part, the changes of the past two decades have been basically attitudinal changes and psychological changes. Admittedly, changes in mind precede changes in matter and for that reason our self-expectations have been on the rise. The self-pride of Afro-Americans has noticeably increased; our ambition level has changed as new opportunities, long denied, have opened up. Our performance has shown signs of great growth and yet untouched capabilities. Significant changes in the attitudes and behavior of the white population have also occurred in this period. In the course of struggle they have exhibited a capacity to respond in a healthy way, however slowly, to social change.

In spite of all we hear today about an "energy crisis" with reference to oil and other natural resources, it's time for us as a society to recognize that the greatest waste of energy is the waste of human lives, resulting from poor education, unemployment and the limiting of opportunity and the human energy expended in the struggle to win rights that any civilized nation would take for granted and never contest. It will take serious comprehensive economic planning to deal adequately with the problems of this society. And the cost of comprehensive economic planning to develop people and the quality of life is to be measured against how much it will cost *not* to do it.

Let us not deceive ourselves, the United States today is in the grip of a civilizational crisis. And the choice confronting all of us is either to mobilize to go forward, in continued progress, or to go backward because we failed to mobilize our best efforts. The desired objective is *Full Employment in an Expanding Economy,* not mounting unemployment in an economy shrinking and falling apart. This is a struggle for the New Detroit, the New Philadelphia, and the working populations of our great industrial cities are the key to its success.

Revealing the Dialectics of Black Liberation

Ernest Kaiser

The writings of leading Black progressive thinkers and activists over the last twenty-five or thirty years have developed the black liberation question to new levels of analysis and understanding. These writers, armed with a Marxist philosophy, do not confine their writings solely to black liberation; but they have given us William L. Patterson's *We Charge Genocide: The Crime of Government Against the Negro People* (1951, 1970); Roscoe Proctor's pamphlets and articles in *Political Affairs;* Claude Lightfoot's *Ghetto Rebellion to Black Liberation* (1968), *Black America and the World Revolution* (1970) and *Racism and Human Survival* (1972); and Henry Winston's *Strategy for a Black Agenda: A Critique of New Theories of Liberation in the United States and Africa* (1973) plus innumerable pamphlets and don't forget the white Marxists: Gus Hall's pamphlet *Racism: The Nation's Most Dangerous Pollutant* (1971) and Herbert Aptheker's *Political Affairs* articles and many books.

James E. Jackson is an important member of this group of Black Marxist writers. He joined the progressive movement in 1931 when he was sixteen years old and in college. He has been an activist in the working-class and national-liberation movements for forty years and is now the National Education Director of the Communist Party, U.S.A. Jackson was a founder of the Southern Negro Youth

Book Review: REVOLUTIONARY TRACINGS IN WORLD POLITICS AND BLACK LIBERATION. By James E. Jackson. International Publishers, New York, ix, 263 pages. $9.50 (cloth); $3.50 (paper).

Congress of the thirties and forties, led the tobacco workers' strike in Richmond, Va., in 1938, worked with the Detroit auto workers and held leadership positions in the Communist Party in the South in the forties and fifties. He is also a Marxist-Leninist theoretician, a teacher and writer. His first two books *The View from Here* (1963) and *U.S. Negroes in Battle, From Little Rock to Watts* (1967) grew out of his editorials and critical reportage as editor-in-chief of *The Worker* newspaper in the late fifties and sixties. The author of many pamphlets and articles such as "The Meaning of Black Power," "National Pride–Not Nationalism" and "A Fighting People Forging Unity," it was his ground-breaking article "New Features of the Negro Question in the U.S." in the late fifties that showed with great documentation that self-determination for Blacks in the southern black-belt states had become anachronistic and no longer viable at all. His argument is spelled out in full in *Revolutionary Tracings* in a report "On the Theory of Black Liberation in the U.S." and in "Separatism–A Bourgeois Nationalist Trap."

Today it is very clear that self-segregation or withdrawal or go-it-alone policies are a trap to prevent Blacks from solving their many and pressing problems; that unifying the Black communities for struggle is good, but that the Blacks-organized labor alliance must be built at the same time since the U.S. Blacks have migrated up to 70 percent into the cities and are 85 percent working class and 30 percent of the total working class; that Black people cannot get their freedom alone; that the working class (Black and white) is the decisive class in bringing about social change in a capitalist society because of its direct relationship to the means of production; and that the struggle for black equality and freedom is really a specialized part of the working-class struggle. In line with this and especially valid for our time and the struggle in our country, there is Lenin's concept of the wide range of relations between the oppressed Black people's movements and the white U.S. working-class movement of the oppressing people; that each movement must be helped to identify its cause and goals with that of the other; and that the convergence and mutual reinforcement of these two movements are essential for the victory of either; and especially so when 85 percent of U.S. Blacks are of the working class; and that the hostility, distrust and prejudice of each of these two groups for the other, built up and kept alive for many decades by the ruling class to facilitate the dividing and exploiting of both Black and white workers, must be overcome for the mutual benefit and advancement of both groups.

All of this is especially apropos at this time when Black intellectuals and activists are writing polemics in black journals as advocates of a "new" Communism-Socialism or of the old separatist black nationalism (*New York Times*, April 28, 1975). The Black nationalists are hopelessly wrong and the "new" Communists-Socialists are away out in left field talking about overthrowing capitalism and imperialism while ignoring the existing movements (white and black) already fighting the ravages of capitalism. This is sheer dreaming and rhetoric; revolutionary phrasemongering with programs doomed for defeat. There is no understanding here of Leninist tactics of struggle, of the need to organize and unite the people, to form alliances and coalitions, however temporary and wavering, that will advance the black struggle. Some of the "new" Communists-Socialists have disavowed their previous black nationalist hatred of all whites. But the Black nationalists continue to try to make Marxism-Leninism a white racist doctrine thus revealing that they are totally ignorant of this philosophy which is the very opposite of white racism. It's a skin thing with the Black nationalists, as Henry Winston says in his book. They hate all whites of whatever philosophy and want to have nothing to do with them. The nationalists also say that virulent white racism existed before mercantilism and capitalism. Thus they fly in the face of Frank M. Snowden's *Blacks in Antiquity* (1971) which documents exhaustively that people of the ancient world belonging to different ethnic groups respected each other before the introduction and widespread use of racism as a rationale for black slavery which was the economic basis of mercantilism and capitalism. But the nationalists' assertions won't wash. Historical truth is rapidly coming to the fore to refute the falsifiers and distorters.

James Jackson's "A Talk to Teachers of Marxism" (*Political Affairs*, April 1974) shows that he is a great Marxist teacher. Only a master of Marxism-Leninism could do what Jackson has done in his latest book *Revolutionary Tracings*. He has pulled together selected speeches, memos, reports, articles in *The Worker, World Magazine, Daily World, World Marxist Review* and his many articles in *Political Affairs*, some of which were reprinted as pamphlets, and has made a book covering all important aspects of world politics and black liberation. All of the issues I have raised about black liberation have been more than adequately explained. And much more. Covering the period from 1952 to 1974 Jackson denounces as criminal the advice of the petty-bourgeois radicals of *Monthly Review* magazine and the adventuristic advice of I. F. Stone to the black liberation movement. Their advice seems to be in essence: form the Symbionese Liberation Army and wage guerrilla warfare inside the black ghettos against Black collaborators and informers. Jackson also points to the writings of James Boggs and Frantz Fanon as petty-bourgeois departures from Marxism-Leninism which have a disorienting effect within the broad left movement.

Jackson finds the main source of Mao Tse-tung's errors in the one-sided experience of the Chinese Revolution which developed through a 22-year civil war. Maoism, a mixture of Trotskyism, bourgeois nationalism, petty-bourgeois revolutionism and crude opportunism, is now, he says, the gravest deviation and attack on Marxism in its 124-year history. He compares the progress of the 12 million people of color in Kazakhstan, in the Soviet Union under socialism, with the pitiful progress and degradation of U.S. Blacks under capitalism. The Southern Negro Youth Congress, which he helped found, worked for the southern Blacks' right to vote and for full political representation in the 1930's and 1940's long before the freedom movement and the Voting Rights Act of the 1960's enabled millions of Black southerners to vote. Jackson's running commentary and analysis of the black liberation movement of the 1960's is particularly valuable. He calls for a continuous fight against racist ideology and propaganda in scholarship and elsewhere as Ted Bassett, Claude Lightfoot, Herbert Aptheker and others have waged for years. And a fight for socialist clarity among Black workers, Black youth and Black intellectuals.

Finally, Jackson explains that Lenin's great work *Imperialism,* with its theory of the uneven development of capitalism, showed the road to national liberation of colonial peoples; it explained why there were colonial peoples, how these colonial peoples were coupled to the working class and the importance of the national liberation struggle in the world revolution. And in his piece on Africa, he points to the Asian-African bloc plus the socialist countries pressuring (later barring) South Africa in the U.N. This is a profoundly learned, clarifying book that should be widely read and studied. The erudition is handled well. Such apt quotations and clear explanations! Very rarely does he let his alliteration get out of hand as in "the desperate antediluvian denizens of Dixiedom." This is also a fighting book pointing the way to correct struggle and to eventual but sure socialist liberation. His speech in the debate with Senator Edmund Muskie at Colby College, Maine, his essay "Lenin and National Liberation" and his speech on Engels, Marcuse and Angela Davis are classic statements summarizing the experiences of the U.S. working class and of the working class of the world.

American Indian and Chicano History and Culture

Ernest Kaiser

The Indians of the Americas have struggled against extermination, removal and starvation over hundreds of years by waging war, signing treaties and other means. They have needed and have produced great warriors, leaders and heroes by the score. This great, gallant and courageous people consisting of hundreds of tribes have survived although the attrition over the long years has been terrible. More than 75 million Indians have been exterminated throughout the Americas. Some tribes have been destroyed completely by the cruel and inhuman treatment of the white imperialist Americans. America's colonial Indian policy of destruction of all Indian organizations, denial of all self-rule, constant violations of treaties which were only to trick the Indians, suppression of all Indian cultures including their religions and the theft of almost all Indian lands was really a policy of liquidation of Indian properties and Indian life, that is, genocide. (See John Collier's pamphlet, *America's Colonial Record,* 1947.)

Dale Van Every, author of *Disinherited: The Lost Birthright of the American Indian* (1967), in a review of Alvin M. Josephy, Jr.'s *The Indian Heritage of America (New York Times Book Review,* Oct. 6, 1968) says that Josephy's book describes the development and progress of these first Americans' cultures from the early beginnings through the hunting and agricultural stages to the building of cities and pyramids. There were "the mound-builders culture in the eastern half of the Mississippi Valley . . . and the introduction of the horse in the Far West which revolutionized the life of the Indians of the plains and mountains in the space of a single generation." But this Indian progress, says Van Every, suffered a "sudden and total catastrophe when the arrival of the white man deprived Indians not only of their lives and lands but as a people of every hope for the future. In human annals there is no other record of the destruction of an entire race along with the violent subjugation of two whole continents. A macabre glare is cast across the process of extermination, enslavement and dispossession by the circumstance that by far the most murderously effective weapons wielded by the whites were alcohol and pestilence. We may speculate on what heights Indian culture might have reached had it not been suddenly obliterated by alien onslaught, but we can never know. For the Indians, from the log houses on the Mohawk to the tepees of the plains to the pyramids of Mexico to the palaces of Peru, the world had come to an end."

About 1,200,000 American Indians were massacred in the U.S. alone. The U.S. Indian population dropped to 300,000 around 1900. It has built up to about one million excluding Alaska today. Henry Steele Commager, in "A Historian Looks at Our Political Morality" *(Saturday Review,* July 10, 1965), states the Americans' rationalization for their bloody, brutal history:

"The conquest and decimation of the Indian didn't count— after all the Indians were heathens—and when that argument lost its force, there was the undeniable charge that they got in the way of progress. The students of my own college [Amherst] celebrate Lord Jeffrey Amherst on all ceremonial occasions, but few of them remember that Lord Amherst's solution to the Indian problem was to send the Indians blankets infected with small pox! How many of us, after all, remember what Helen Hunt Jackson called a 'Century of Dishonor'? Or there was slavery; it was pervasive and flourishing, and slaveholders defended it as a moral good. Somehow slavery didn't count, either, because it was nature's way of bringing the African to

Western civilization, or because it was all so romantic (only recently have we developed a sense of guilt here). . . .

"So, too, with what, in other nations, would be called imperialism, but with us was called 'westward expansion' –manifest destiny working itself out in some foreordained fashion. . . .

"For we were very sure of our own virtue, and we read history to discover that we were a peculiar people. Our history books exalted everything American. They contrasted our Indian policy with the wicked policy of the Spaniards–that was part of the black legend–conveniently overlooking the elementary fact that the Indian survived in Mexico and South America but not in the United States. They painted slavery as a romantic institution, or perhaps as a kind of fortunate accident for the Africans. . . . We forget Reinhold Niebuhr's admonishment that 'the more we indulge in uncritical reverence for the supposed wisdom of the American way of life, the more odious we make it in the eyes of the world, and the more we destroy our moral authority. . . .' "

Many tribes were removed from their homelands and their lands taken by whites in the nineteenth century. After the passage by Congress of the General Allotment Act of 1887, Indian lands were cut down by 1930 from 139 million acres to 47 million acres. This destruction and scattering of the tribes had a devastating effect on Indian life and culture. Diseases ravaged the tribes, but the U.S. government was indifferent to this. The terrible hunger, deprivation, disease, illiteracy, suffering and death of Indian men, women and children on the reservations and in the city slums are their current and continuing plight. There are hundreds of claims against the federal government by Indian tribes and tribal groups requiring payment for lands taken from them–some pending for twenty years. In the late 1950's and early 1960's the Senecas of New York State were fighting in the courts to prevent their arable land from being flooded by the

Kinzua Dam, and the New York State Tuscaroras were fighting in the courts to prevent the building of a reservoir on a large part of their reservation. The Iroquois later picketed the White House and said that they would take their grievances of confiscated lands and destitution to the United Nations as an international problem. (Canada, likewise, entered into treaties and agreements with Indian tribes, says Collier, in *Indians of the Americas,* but unlike the U.S., she made her agreements with thrift and foresight and adhered to them with rigid faithfulness. The result was that Canada had few Indian wars. Collier should have added that Canada with its cold climate, large area and very small population did not develop industrially as rapidly as the U.S. and did not have the pressure to rob the Indians of their lands.)

The coastal Quinault Indian tribe recently closed 25 miles of scenic Pacific Ocean reservation beach in Washington State to all whites (*New York Times,* Aug. 26, 1969). They objected to littering, thefts of Indian fish nets drying on the beach, removal of driftwood, defacing of legend-ridden rocks and destruction of Indian clambeds by land developers. The Indians have built strong organizations such as the large, 34-year-old National Congress of American Indians, a moderate organization representing two-thirds of the 600,000 Indians on the reservations in 105 tribes and in more than 20 states, and the National Indian Youth Council which grew out of the discussions at the American Indian Chicago Conference of 1961. Others are the American Indians United and the United Nations of Pan-American Indians Movement. These are developing leadership toward unity in their fight for Indian rights. Indians are demanding fishing rights on rivers through fish-ins, self-determination and political independence–that is, Red Power. Dick Gregory was convicted and served time in jail for participating in an Indian fish-in in the State of Washington. Senator Edward M. Kennedy, speaking at the annual 1969 meeting of the National Congress of American Indians in Albuquerque, N. M., repeated the late Robert Kennedy's

1968 criticism of the federal government's Indian policies as a national disgrace. He called on President Nixon to convene a White House conference on Indian affairs to map major reforms of a policy that takes away Indian land, destroys Indian families and keeps them in poverty and encourages prejudice and discrimination against Indians by leaving the public uninformed and misinformed about Indians. Senator Kennedy also called for the establishment in the Senate of a select committee on the human needs of the American Indian. Interior Secretary Walter J. Hickel, who had said earlier that the federal government should do less for Indians, was booed and jeered repeatedly when he addressed the NCAI (*New York Times*, Oct. 8, 9, 1969). At this meeting, young Indian leaders came to the fore advocating a new, harsh militancy for Indians.

The Chicano people (Indians, mestizos, mulattoes and zambos, Spanish and Negroes), descendants of Geronimo, Cochise and other great leaders, are today more than 300 million on a land area extending from the U.S. throughout Mexico, Central and South America. They are still struggling to retain and regain their lands and to recoup and keep their many cultures and ways of life. The more than eight million Mexican-Americans of New Mexico, Texas and California are struggling today in the Chicano community for land, for self-determination and nationhood, for the Spanish language, for Chicano studies programs on college campuses, for support of the farm workers' movement, for better jobs in the cities where 70 percent of the Chicanos now live, for independent Chicano political power, community control of education, ties with Latin America and publication of a Marxist periodical on the Chicano revolutionary movements. See Stan Steiner's *La Raza: The Mexican-Americans* (1970), Julian Samora's *La Raza: Forgotten Americans* (1970), Patricia Bell Blawis's *Tijerina and the Land Grants: Mexican Americans in the Struggle for Their Heritage* (1972), *Toward Chicano Liberation* (1972), a pamphlet, Armando B. Rendon's *Chicano Manifesto* (1971), *A Documentary History of the Mexican Americans* (1971) edited by W. Moquin and Charles Van Doren, M. S. Meier and F. Rivera's *The Chicanos: A History of Mexican Americans* (1972) and P. D. Ortego's *We are Chicanos: An Anthology of Mexican-American Literature* (1973).

Let no one say, as Herbert Spencer and his American disciples did, that all of this killing, destruction and enslavement of millions of Indians and Africans can all be put down as the price of progress even though the price was terribly high. But, as William Z. Foster says in *Outline Political History of the Americas* (1951):

"... in reality, the consequences of the conquest have been revolutionary for the Indians, inasmuch as it fundamentally undermined their old tribal communalism and literally catapulted them into the higher, feudal-capitalist regime. ... The normal course of evolution of Indian society has been rudely interrupted and sort of telescoped. Consequently, the Indians in this hemisphere will not experience the characteristic centuries-long development through slavery and feudalism, that societies have previously known in many parts of the world. They will, so to speak, skip these stages and will go with the peoples wherever they live through capitalism to socialism."

Foster also counters what he calls two misconceptions: first, the Indians, despite the decimation, agony and destruction, are not vanishing. They number in the many millions and their population is increasing rapidly. Second, while many Indians (in the U.S. and elsewhere) have continued in their old tribal ways isolated from capitalist life, the vast bulk of the Indian masses in this hemisphere exist in a capitalist environment and are basically subject to its economic and political laws. Their society has been changed to a capitalist basis. They are developing class differentiations; they have produced proletariat that worked the mines, plantations and cattle ranches as slaves, peons and wage workers. The mestizos have developed a large petty bourgeoisie of intellectuals, merchants and handicraftsmen. The

Osage Indians of the U.S., one of the rare cases, have even a few wealthy, landowning Indians. Even the most isolated tribes must adopt a commodity economy more or less in order to get the things that they must have.

Foster says that the looting of the American hemisphere especially in the early colonial period, gave great impetus to the bourgeois revolution and the development of European capitalism in general. The great amounts of gold and silver mined in Latin America were a tremendous factor in European capital accumulation which was necessary to give birth to the factory system and the industrial revolution. As Karl Marx states in *Capital* (volume I):

> "The discovery of gold and silver in America, the extirpation, enslavement and entombment in mines of the aboriginal population, the beginning of the conquest and looting of the East Indies, the turning of Africa into a warren for the commercial hunting of black-skins, signalized the rosy dawn of the era of capitalist production. These idyllic proceedings are the chief momenta of primitive accumulation."

"Slave trading, the profits from slave products, and African trade in general, were very important in the British economy," said J. A. Rogers in *Africa's Gift to America* (1961). Marx also said that "the population and wealth of England, after slumbering for seven hundred years, began to develop itself under the influence of slave-acquired capital." Eric Williams, in *Capitalism and Slavery* (1964), has documented how the eighteenth-century slave trade, centered in Liverpool, provided the foundation of nineteenth-century British capitalism. Marx described the capitalist basis of the American slave system thus: "Those who carry on their own business with Negro slaves are capitalists."

"The development of the colonies of all the nations," says Foster finally, "opened up a whole series of new markets for budding European capitalism. The ensuing American political revolutionary struggles also gave a big push to the struggle of the rising capitalist class in Europe against feudal-clerical reaction. The new hemisphere, particularly the U.S., itself was destined to play such a decisive role in shaping world capitalism, so that today it has finally become the center and main stronghold of the world capitalist system."

The Indians' contributions to the U.S., according to Allan Harper's monograph, in foodstuffs and drugs alone are phenomenal. Four-sevenths of the total agricultural production of the U.S. consists of economic plants domesticated by the Indians and adopted by whites. Whites appropriated the Indians' canoe, snowshoe and toboggan, built their roads and canals over the Indians' trails, emulated the Indians' methods of warfare, fishing and recreation, copied and adopted the Indians' clothes for life in the forest. The Indians taught whites how to live with the outdoors, quickened their imagination and became an important subject for American literature. They have also contributed to American music, literature, theatre, law, medicine, psychology, folklore and mythology and folk arts and crafts, language, cookery and modern clothes and hair styles. The three-record album *Authentic Music of the American Indian* includes war dances, honor songs, social and folk songs, ceremonial songs and chants of over 20 western tribes (Sioux, Apache, Hopi, Navajo etc.) performed by the Indians. These contributions have usually been overlooked or ignored. But the Indians' indelible and ineradicable marks on the American land and people are everywhere. American literature is replete with poems, stories and novels about Indians usually stereotyped as noble savages, Tontos or brutish beasts. The same themes are in the films, newspaper stories and TV programs about Indians. The Americana Hotel in New York City has moved the stereotyped figure of the wooden Indian from the fronts of cigar stores to the entrance of its spacious wooden Indian room. Most of the truth about Indians is still confined to the several Indian museums and Indian wings of general museums throughout the United States. Claude Lightfoot's "Social Development of the American Indians" *(Political Affairs,* April 1975) and Wilfred Wille's "Amerindian Heritage" *(Political Affairs,* December 1975) spell out in rich detail the North and South American Indians' great contributions to American and world civilization and the need for a Marxist interpretation of American Indian history from the pre-Columbian period into modern times. Although neither writer mentions William Z. Foster's *Outline Political History of the Americas* (1951), this book is a Marxist interpretation of Indian history although the pre-Columbian period is omitted since it starts with the age of discovery and exploration.

Every schoolboy used to know and thrill to these lines from the "Hiawatha's Childhood" section of Longfellow's long poem *The Song of Hiawatha:*

By the shores of Gitche Gumee
By the shining Big-Sea-Water,
Stood the wigwam of Nokomis.
Daughter of the Moon, Nokomis.

Hiawatha, whose life is recounted in the poem, was an Indian folk hero and warrior who performed miracles for the tribes and helped them in many ways. The poem is based on Indian tales and stories. The Black composer Samuel Coleridge-Taylor wrote a very successful oratorio *Hiawatha* based on Longfellow's poem. Thurlow Lieurance's Indian love song "By the Waters of Minnetonka," Edward MacDowell's *Indian Suite* and Anton Dvořák's, "From the New World" symphony with its Indian and Negro themes and feeling are often heard in live vocal and orchestral concerts and on recorded radio concerts.

Stephen Vincent Benet's poem "American Names" shows his love for the sound of Indian and other names:

I have fallen in love with American names,
The sharp names that never get fat,

24*

The snakeskin-titles of mining-claims,
The plumed war-bonnet of Medicine Hat,
Tucson and Deadwood and Lost Mule Flat.

Benet mentions Bleeding-Heart-Yard, Painted Post, Nantucket Light and Wounded Knee. But this poem also contains this vilely racist couplet:

And a blue-gum nigger to sing me blues.
I am tired of loving a foreign muse.

New York Times art critic John Canaday takes the opposite view. He expresses his boredom as a child with *The Song of Hiawatha's* Gitche Gumee and his dislike for what he calls the unloveliest sounds ever invented—the Indian names of lakes and small towns of Rhode Island and Connecticut and the Chinook word "potlatch." This view was a part of his review of a major art show: a large group of carvings by Northwest Coast American Indians in the 1969 "Man and His World" exhibits at Montreal, Canada (*New York Times,* Aug. 10, 1969). Canaday praises the art of the Kwakiutls and other tribes highly. He also points to fine Indian art in the Metropolitan Museum of Art's recent "Art of Africa, Oceania and the Americas" exhibit, in the Paris Musée de l'Homme's then current Indian art show, in Seattle's 1962 Century 21 Exposition collection, in a 1968 Vancouver show and in New York's Museum of the American Indian collection. He admits that these do not add up to very much. Indian art is still very much neglected. The Cleveland American Indian Center, the first American Indian center in the State of Ohio, was opened in September 1969. Frederick J. Dockstader's *Indian Art in North America: Arts and Crafts* (4th printing) describes the various tribes' shell and quill work, pottery and weaving, deer and buffalo hide painting, carved stone pipes and tomahawks and many different masks from every region of the United States and Canada. Olivia Vlahos's *New World Beginnings: Indian Cultures in the Americas* (1970) is popularized study of the historic cultures of the North and South American Indians.

With a four million dollar Rockefeller Foundation grant, New World Records in New York City will produce 20 albums (100 records) from 1976 through 1978 of American music from the earliest beginnings to the present. An early release is a disc of American Indian music recorded by an Indian musicologist on reservations in Oklahoma, New Mexico, Arizona and New York as well as records of jazz, ragtime and a reconstruction of the early 1920's black musical *Shuffle Along* taken from various old recordings by the original participants and assembled into a unified whole for the first time.

The white publishing houses have put out more and better books on Indian literature. Some of these are Hettie Jones's *The Trees Stand Shining: Poetry of the North American Indians; Four Masterpieces of American Literature;* Shirley H. Witt and Stan Steiner's *The Way: An Anthology of American Indian Literature,* short stories of American Indians; and Louise K. Barnett's *The Ignoble Savage: A Study in American Literary Racism, 1790–1890* (1975) about the Puritan image of the Indian as a child of Satan. Also the left-wing International Publishers' *Voices from Wah'Kon-Tah: Contemporary Poetry of Native Americans* (1975) edited by Robert K. Dodge and Joseph B. McCullough. But the American Indian Historical Society felt that it was necessary to organize The Indian Historian Press in 1969 to publish their own books counteracting the terrible textbooks and non-textbooks misrepresenting Indian cultures, degrading Indian peoples and spreading misinformation about Indian life and culture.

Vine Deloria, Jr., points out in *Custer Died for Your Sins: An Indian Manifesto* (1969) that American Indians hate the proliferating anthropological studies of them because they reinforce and justify taking more Indian land to bring civilization to the poor savages instead of doing something positive to improve the Indians' wretched conditions. A lot of books and some unpublished dissertations have been written about the many U.S. Indian nations or tribes. They are history, anthropology, social and political science and novels. But relying on usual available sources, these books are written for the most part from the viewpoint of the white American conquerors of the Indians. Anthropologists have studied and restudied intensively all phases and aspects of Indian life and culture. With more and more grants, the anthropological studies have increased. But these studies have been and still are a dodge, a substitute for doing something tangible to improve the Indians' conditions. So the Indians naturally hate these studies just as Blacks hate the mountains of sociological studies of them which substitute for meaningful actions to improve the conditions of Blacks. The Indian Historian Press has published a few books. *The Indian Historian,* a magazine, was started in 1967 by the Historical Society. But the Press is in an economic bind now and will probably go under if it doesn't get financial help.

Other recent books of value on Indian history, life and struggle are *Chronicles of American Indian Protest* (1971) compiled by the Council on Interracial Books for Children, New York City; Virgil J. Vogel's *This Country Was Ours: A Documentary History of the American Indian;* W. Moquin and Charles Van Doren's *Great Documents in American Indian History;* Dee Brown's *Bury My Heart at Wounded Knee: An Indian History of the American West;* Robert Burnette and John Koster's *The Road to Wounded Knee;* Stan Steiner's *The New Indians;* Alvin M. Josephy, Jr.'s *Red Power: The American Indians' Fight for Freedom;* the Indian William Meyer's *Native Americans: The New Indian Resistance;* K. Kickingbird and Karen Ducheneaux's *One Hundred Million Acres* (1973), about Indian lands stolen from the Indians; and G. L. Heath's *Red, Brown & Black Demands for Better Education,* about Indians, Chicanos and Blacks.

Travels
in the Soviet Union
Manchild
in the Land of Lenin
Clarence J. Munford

In 1922, under the guidance of Lenin, the Union of Soviet Socialist Republics was formed as a unique kind of federal state. It was the first state in the history of mankind in which all peoples, regardless of race, color or nationality, were equal and able independently and freely to determine their own destiny. Today the 250 million citizens of this fraternal family consisting of all races and over a hundred nations and nationalities live and work together in astonishing harmony. Their labor and working-class power have created a socialist economy in which the entire national income is utilized in the interests of working people.

It was no great surprise to me that a large share of the national income in the Soviet Union goes for expanding production in industry and agriculture. Like others, I had read and heard very much about the land of Lenin. I had heard tell fabulous tales about its twofold resurrection from ruins, once after the Civil War and foreign capitalist intervention, and once after the Nazi holocaust. I had heard that racism had been wiped out and that harmonious assimilation is far advanced. I had read the statistical reports. I knew that one of ten families in the Soviet Union is an "internationalities family"—family unions that Americans would designate inter-racial or inter-ethnic. I had learned that these mixed marriages are the consequence of enlightened Soviet policy, especially of the affirmation of woman's equality, and I had seen the divorce figures showing that mixed marriages prove more lasting than one-nationality marriages.

Yet it is one thing to read about and study a society that lies far yonder, and another to see for oneself how wealth may be used to improve the people's material and cultural standards. Above all, it was important for me to see for *myself* how the Soviet Union's many non-white, non-European citizens were faring.

Who am I? No one outstanding. Just the manchild of Black worker parents from Alabama and Louisiana whose wanderings north from Jim Crow took them first to a small racist Ohio steel town, and finally, like so many others, to Cleveland, the industrial "mistake on the lake." I was a boychild who became a stripling and then a man in Cleveland's dreadful eastside Hough ghetto, a fellow who, like many of his compeers, hustled for an education and who, after various, not always purposeless meanderings, is roosting now in his late thirties in an Ontario university trying to teach Black Studies. Who am I? Just a manchild who knows that racist America is *not* the promised land.

Anyway, it was time for me—a Black American—to go and observe at first hand the rising real wages of the Soviet Union's Brown people I had heard reports of. The moment had come to verify for myself the increasing expenditures for social security and public health services of the U.S.S.R.'s Asian citizens. It was with a critical eye and a sensitive ear that I set out then, at the beginning of October 1973, to test the educational, scientific and cultural advances of Soviet Central Asia and the Caucasus, but mostly to see whether it is possible for a society to solve the racial-national question.

On my itinerary I crisscrossed three of Soviet Central Asia's five Union Republics, a journey spanning thousands of miles. It took me deep into the Caucasus Mountains and to the shores of the Caspian Sea, cheek by jowl with the Shah's Persia. It took me to the legendary cities of Tashkent, Samarkand, Bukhara, Dushanbe, Penzikhant and Ashkhabad, Arabian Nights oases strung across golden desert sands. It threw me into challenging, person-to-person contact with real people, with Uzbeks, Tadjiks, Tatars, Kara-Kalpaks, nationalities of which little is heard in the United States, and even with Soviet Germans. I penetrated to the very heart of ancient Central Asia and saw a rejuvenated land. I came away with the firm realization that the peoples of the Soviet Union have indeed solved the racial and national questions. I would like to share some of my experiences and impressions with the readers of *Freedomways*, for there are vital lessons for Black Americans to learn in Soviet Central Asia. Soviet Central Asia provides the most positive and relevant kind of proof for Blacks in this country that socialism and socialism alone eradicates racial discrimination. The example of the Brown people of the Soviet Union indicates the road to salvation for Black people from their lifelong crucifixion under monopoly capitalism. The future of American Black people is writ at the foot of the Pamirs.

Industrialization in Soviet Asia

Production is the cornerstone of social living. Fifty years ago the peoples of Soviet Central Asia realized that if they were going to bring to life the Leninist principle of voluntary state alliance of equal peoples they had to make it in production, and in productivity of labor. They not only made it, they were a thundering success.

Before Soviet power was established, productive forces in the region languished at one of the lowest levels on earth, and some of the most degrading social relations of production to be found anywhere tormented the people. Soviet power came in a purifying storm and the Central Asian Republics made a breathtaking leap from backwardness to progress. The people were determined that the earth should rise on new foundations and rise it did. Compared with 1922 the volume of industrial goods increased 228-fold in Uzbekistan, 500-fold in Tadjikistan, 130-fold in Turkmenia, 381-fold in Kirghizia, and 558-fold in Kazakhstan. In the lifetime of one generation the five Union Republics of Soviet Central Asia have become highly industrialized countries with a well developed agriculture and advanced science and technology.

I tasted this tremendous achievement by going right into Central Asia's factories and talking with Uzbek, Tadjik and Tatar workers directly.

Even in Moscow, before setting out for Central Asia, I got a presentiment of the new world of work relations I was about to enter, work relations light years removed from those known to most Americans. I glimpsed some Moscow textile factories in passing. I was struck by the fact that the factories of one of the world's largest and busiest capitals show a humanized aspect. Moscow factories looked so clean, so unassuming and so un-factory-like, so unlike the horrible, dark, filthy and forbidding premises in which American workers, especially minority workers, must toil, that the manchild began to wonder—had he finally found a society in which labor is indeed being transformed from an onerous burden into a truly creative activity for the individual?

Tashkent, the capital of Uzbekistan and a metropolis of a million and a half, reinforced this impression. This city, more than a thousand miles distant from Moscow, closer to Afghanistan than to Russia, was ravaged by a terrible earthquake in 1966, a short seven years ago. Now it is one gigantic construction site. No phoenix ever rose from ruins more swiftly or more gracefully than Tashkent. All the fraternal nations and nationalities of the wide Soviet land pitched in to rebuild the stricken city.

From Tashkent we winged south and west, until we came to Samarkand, in the Middle Ages a city of khans and conquerors, now a modern industrial center of 600,000.

Here I toured my first Central Asian plant—the Samarkand Silk Factory. Its name is a concession to the past. Actually the enterprise's 3,000 textile workers—mostly women and mostly youthful—now turn out nylon and other artificial fabrics to meet modern consumer needs. Only one small department still manufactures natural silk fabrics. Although the productivity of the average workers in the plant is understandably lower than in fully automated Soviet textile factories, these Uzbek, Tadjik and Tatar women workers approach the productive standards of similarly equipped textile mills throughout the country. They now produce in a single day the same amount as in the whole of 1935. They know that improvements in output result in better wages and higher living standards for themselves, their children, husbands and sweethearts. These Asian women have long since freed themselves of the parasites who siphoned off the fruits of their labor as owners' profits.

Right now there are three categories of wages in the U.S.S.R.: a) piece wages, b) time wages based on hours of work, and c) time wages plus bonuses. The last is the most widespread system and predominates at the Samarkand Silk Factory. Thus each worker's pay is based on his productivity. The enterprise's annual gross social product is subdivided and allocated in a manner that is grasped by every worker. There is no hocus-pocus by management, no one tries to pull the wool over the eyes of the workers. A fund is set aside to replace means of production consumed in the course of the year and to finance enlarged production the next. The remainder is divided into a fund for workers' remuneration and a fund for cultural and social expenditures. The sum for workers' remuneration contains employees' wages and bonuses and a special emulation fund shared out annually and based on yearly performance. There are job norms for all work places. Through their trade union the workers have a large say in the allocation of funds realized from the social product. When I was visiting, the minimum monthly wage in the Samarkand Silk Factory was 90 rubles, the maximum 230 rubles. The factory average was 130 rubles. But a factory worker pays less than 7 rubles a month for a two-room apartment with kitchen and bath, electricity, water and gas. Since 1926 there has been a single rent rate in effect throughout the Soviet Union. Tenants pay 13.2 kopecks a month per square meter of living-room space (100 kopecks to 1 ruble). No rent is charged for the kitchen, bathroom, corridors and other auxiliary premises and large families pay 15 percent less than the standard rate. Government taxes are almost nominal (10 percent of wages). Medical care is free, accessible and good.

Women as Leaders

However, women not only work in the Samarkand Silk Factory, they also run it. Although a few departments have male chief engineers, the secretary of the party committee and the factory's head engineer are women. The party secretary, the plant's first lady, is a charming Uzbek woman in her mid-forties. Workers themselves, the women who head the enterprise keep a sharp eye on the well-being and cultural advancement of the workers. It is their duty to see to it that the plant provides them with the facilities to enjoy leisure time. The factory has a library (and it is much used, as I discovered), a drama group, various sports clubs, a literature group and a chess club. Fifteen percent of the workers are members of the Trade Union's "Communist Schools." These schools teach the workers the principles of Scientific Communism while giving them the opportunity to learn advanced skills. Naturally, social life centers around the work place and the factory is spotlessly clean. There is no speedup, no slave-driving foreman. The work pace I observed was relaxed and free of the pressures that cause nervous disorders in American workers.

From a personal standpoint the high point of my visit to the factory was a brief encounter with a young Tadjik woman operative. In passing, I noticed her standing at her machine which she had decorated with fresh flowers—a widespread habit of Soviet workers. She glanced at me, took a second look, returning my smile. Then suddenly came a spontaneous, unrehearsed act of friendship and attraction. She snatched the bouquet of flowers from the vase on her work machine and sped toward me. Shyly, warmly, with trepidation she held the bouquet out to me and then fled back to her work place. Here was an act extraordinary in a factory work situation. For the first time I sensed the Soviet workers' deep friendship and solidarity with Black Americans. For years they have been schooled in the best traditions of internationalism and brotherhood, and here in a small way I encountered the result of that teaching. My enchanting acquaintee was not exceptional. Themselves Brown people, Soviet Central Asians—Uzbeks, Tadjiks, Tatars and others—feel they march shoulder to shoulder with Black Americans. This was evident in the wild welcome they gave Angela Davis upon her visit to Tashkent the year before. Aglow, stammering tongue-tied thanks, the manchild stumbled away, clutching his bouquet of flowers.

The next plant toured was much larger. It is located in Dushanbe, capital of the Tadjik Union Republic which borders Uzbekistan on the southeast. Across the mountains lie Afghanistan, Pakistan and China. Before the October Revolution there were only a handful of miserable enterprises in the country and the proletariat was minuscule. The Tadjik working class formed only after the Revolution when state enterprises were set up. The Civil War was very bitter in this part of the Soviet Union. For years White Guards raided over the border from China and Afghanistan, and the armed struggle dragged on long after it had ended in other parts of the country. After the Civil War many young Tadjiks were sent to other parts of the Soviet Union to be educated. They returned to train those who remained behind. Even the aged went to school. Those were difficult, raw years, but illiteracy was eliminated and the people acquired higher work skills. Aid in the form of machinery and trained personnel poured in from all over the Soviet Union, and the year 1929 marked the real beginnings of the Tadjik working class. Great difficulties were experienced in convincing backward Tadjiks of the superiority of collective labor. Beliefs rooted in Islam also stood in the way of progress. Women who discarded the veil were often murdered by reactionaries. It was a tough struggle to persuade women to join the labor force. It was an even tougher struggle to prevent chauvinist males from standing in their way.

The enterprise I entered is a textile mill constructed during World War II at a juncture when many industries were moved from the west to Central Asia to escape the Nazi invaders. Sprawling over 146 acres, the mill employs 8,500 workers of all races and nationalities. Last year more than 1,930,000 yards of cotton fabrics spun from its looms. The domestic market absorbs the cottons and only velvets are exported. Six thousand looms with 267,000 spindles operate around the clock. In one highly mechanized shop there is one machine maintenance man for every eight operatives, but the plant-wide ratio is 650 to 7,850. The whole complex nestles in lush parkland with buildings scattered among apple trees. Most Americans would find it a most improbable setting for a textile mill. It gave me the impression of a small, serene, self-contained town.

Production and the Unions

This graceful setting conceals the most modern techniques. The production process in this mill is almost fully automated. Workers need only oversee the procedure and supervise the workings of machinery. I saw no humans turned into appendages of machines, only machines lightening labor, and I noted the leisurely pace at which automatic machines were tended. Workers spontaneously broke away from their machines, came over and welcomed us, spoke to me of friendship and peace, and then moved away with slow dignity—masters in their own house. There was no one to harass them, no one to hurry them back to work. Production norms are negotiated between union and management with the union always having the final say. No agreement is valid unless it bears the signature of the head of the mill's trade union committee.

Production is continuous. The looms spin without stopping. There is never a break, so the plant runs on the shift system. Actually there are two shift systems—one section of the plant lays on three shifts a day, the other only two at the moment. The shortfall is due to a shortage of labor. An additional two thousand hands are needed, a shortage that will be filled by labor-saving investments combined with enlivened recruitment. Further mechanization and automation are under way, designed to free workers to staff third shifts in departments now limited to two.

Meanwhile the available hands work a forty-hour week. Those who work six days a week have a seven-hour day. The working day lasts eight hours for persons on a five-day week. Operatives begin a shift by working three hours steadily, with a fifteen-minute rest period midway, then break off for a forty-minute lunch or dinner interval, returning to complete the remaining three and a half or four and a half hours. The last stint is interrupted by another fifteen-minute break.

The trade union committee, headed by a competent, no-nonsense Tadjik woman, shows unstinting concern for the workers' health and well-being. Meals are taken in a well stocked canteen and cost only 40 kopecks. But night shift workers pay nothing at all. The food is hearty and the portions are large. Work places are kept spotlessly clean and safe working conditions are an overriding rule. Before it can harm the lungs of workers all cotton lint is sucked up by automatic vacuum devices. In one shop, rather than walk, women charged with replacing empty spindles ride up and down the line of spinning machines in small, comfortable buggies. The harmful effect of din is recognized and noisy, old-fashioned looms are being phased out in favor of quiet, pneumatic machines. So far 2,000,000 rubles have been laid out this year for the new machines. No worker ever need fear being ousted by machinery. He can always count on being reassigned to a new task in keeping with his skills, or having his skills upgraded.

The plant is equipped with excellent recreational facilities to accommodate vacationing workers and those merely out for a leisurely weekend. There is no absenteeism other than for illness. The plant's own kindergarten and pioneer camps relieve working mothers of most of the burden of child care. The mill has two libraries and two large halls set aside for concerts and other cultural events. The evening school is well attended. Astonishing to an American is the way the plant's system of transportation works. Buses carry workers from their doorstep to the job and home again. There is none of the nerve-wracking scurry of U.S. workers left to their own resources to get to and from work.

I found essentially the same working conditions, the same respect and concern for working people in the great oil city of Baku, the capital of the Azerbaijan Union Republic, a country situated in the Caucasus bordering on Iran. Though Uzbekistan and Tadjikistan are Central Asian lands, while Azerbaijan is in Asia Minor, in regard to the ruling class status of workers they are the same. A quick side trip to an offshore oil field in the Caspian Sea linked to the mainland by a giant causeway resting on trestles (Baku itself anchors a peninsula which juts out into the Caspian), and a frank discussion with some of the oil workers confirmed my findings.

Education of the Young

This manchild was not foolish enough to leave Central Asia without sampling the system of education. I simply could not overlook the schooling of Soviet citizens knowing as I did that people, human beings, are the most dynamic ingredient in the forces of production. Lenin's great love and solicitude for children are the precious heritage of the Soviet Union. I had heard tell that a deep-reaching cultural revolution was the very basis for the buildings of socialism in the U.S.S.R. So I went in search of kindergartens, schools and universities.

First the kindergartens, the homes away from home for millions of Soviet children between the ages of three and seven. Although these child care centers release countless mothers for gainful employment, their purpose is to provide for the physical, moral and aesthetic education of very young children.

In Samarkand, the desert oasis, I found a combined nursery and kindergarten for babes from six months to seven years. Like most such centers it was open for at least twelve hours a day. But it also had a special section, a five-day kindergarten, where the children spend only weekends at home, going home on Friday night or Saturday. Regardless of the section in which a tot is enrolled, his parents pay only a tiny fee. The State bears the burden of the cost.

I watched the little ones learning to work and to become independent. Each child is assigned regular duties. The older children see that the younger ones keep their room tidy, make their own beds and put away toys after play. Others help their teachers to set and clear tables at meal-times. Several times a week, or every day, if necessary, a doctor or medical nurse examines each child and records his temperature. A woman physician heads the kindergarten I saw. By the time a child enters school a precise medical case history has been compiled.

What fascinated me most about the kindergarten in Samarkand is the way art and music are used to impart socialist values. We watched the little ones singing and dancing at their music lessons. Then I remembered the allegation of some American New Leftists that the Soviet Union is not training "revolutionary successors," that it neglects the ideological moulding of the young. How hollow and ludicrous that claim now seems! It is slander, rubbish of the worst kind. Here in remote Central Asia I found pre-school children surrounded by pictures, displays and lessons about Lenin's life. They recited poems about Lenin to me, sang songs about Soviet power and were learning to live in comradely friendship with children of all races, colors and nationalities. I looked in vain for disturbed children.

Primary and secondary schools continue the training in the finest traditions of the working class. I was invited to Tashkent's School No. 110 by its principal, a beguiling Uzbek woman who voiced special affinity for Black Americans. I met tranquil, purposeful youngsters from seven to seventeen years, and it was a wonderful, inspiring experience. They have absolutely no drug problems and the school officials do not know what a "dropout" is.

25

In Dushanbe I had a bit more time. I spent it in a Tadjik-language high school. The city's population of 600,000 is served by seventy-eight secondary schools. The one I checked out has 1,500 pupils. In a room adorned with revolutionary flags and pictures of Lenin as a child and as an adult, the principal, a Tadjik woman, welcomed us and told us something about the school and its close-knit community of teachers and pupils. She herself is the proud mother of six children. Four have already completed higher education and are working, while the two youngest are still in university. Though she was too modest to mention it, we discovered that she wears an Order of Lenin awarded by her country-men for her services to the people. The math teacher, another Tadjik woman, wears the medal of an Honored Teacher of the Republic. In all, forty nationalities are represented on the teaching staff. There are two vice-principals, both men, both married, one with five and the other with two children. The spouse of one is studying to be a physician; his colleague's wife is employed at the local textile mill.

Tadjik is the main language of instruction, but Uzbek runs a close second. Russian ranks third. Each child is taught in his native tongue by teachers trained in local teachers' colleges. Tadjik, Uzbek and Tatar boys and girls learn German and English from teachers of Tadjik nationality in beautifully equipped language labs. The curriculum includes a sound grounding in mathematics, biology, chemistry, physics and social science.

I watched a 7th grade physics lesson in progress. The youngsters were very advanced for their age and I was astounded at the neatness and precision of their notes. When I looked in, the history class was busy learning how fascism was defeated in the Great Patriotic War (1941–1945). The 9th grade has more girls than boys, but all wear red ties to show that they are Young Pioneers, active helpers of the Young Communist League and the Communist Party. Girls predominated in the home economics room with only a few lads. I was told that most boys prefer shop, but the choice is left to the youngsters and there is frequent interchange. There is no pressure on the girls to confine themselves to endeavors traditional for women and vocational counseling is both competent and sympathetic to individual preferences. An air of intimacy reigns in the school library; there I found Tadjik translations of the works of progressive American writers.

Before departing we were given a special treat: to the accompaniment of native instruments, a small troupe of very tiny Tadjik girls performed an enchanting and graceful national dance—a ballet of stylized hand and shoulder movements.

Extracurricular Activities with a Purpose

It is the task of education in the Soviet Union to train children ideologically, to give them a dialectical, materialist concept of the various phenomena and processes in social life. It must reveal to them the inevitability of society's transition from capitalism to socialism, and it must impart the ideals of Communism. The Young Pioneers' Organization, uniting nearly all children from ten to fourteen, is a great help in accomplishing these lofty aims. In Baku, the oilman's capital, I got a look at one of this organization's out-of-school centers—a Young Pioneers' Palace.

Young Pioneers' Houses and Palaces arrange competitions, reviews, exhibitions, rallies of young technicians and naturalists. They take charge of festivals dedicated to the outdoors and organize hikes. Young Pioneers' Palaces have special sections specializing in physics, chemistry, mathematics, history, literary criticism, and more. It is the duty of Palace instructors to arrange visits by writers, poets, scientists, actors, leading workers and war veterans, while at the same time introducing youngsters to the arts of singing, dancing, drama, painting and sculpture.

A large, stately building houses the Baku Pioneers' Palace. I counted no less than eleven voluntary hobby interest groups. Though the size of each activity group is limited, for obvious reasons, to fifteen to twenty youngsters, the only restriction on a child's participation is passing marks in school; a youngster with poor marks is expected to spend more time at homework than with hobbies. In any case, there could be no question about the seriousness of these young buffs. Each pursues his hobby with passion, developing it to the fullest potential. After graduating from secondary school, many of the pioneers, I was told, go on to develop their skills professionally—today's bird watcher, tomorrow's ornithologist. They get a good start, for each group is instructed by a qualified teacher. For instance, the astronomy workshop—in many ways the most interesting in the Baku Palace—is led by a math teacher who, though self-taught, has become famous in his own right as an astronomer throughout the Soviet Union and abroad. His young charges, mostly boys from the 6th to the 10th grade, were busy grinding their own lens for a telescope with 0.01 micron accuracy. When finished, the telescope will weigh more than a ton. Manipulating lathes and other machinery, these youngsters manufacture sophisticated instruments and regularly photograph and study the moon and stars with them. In the radio shop teenagers from fourteen to seventeen handle sensitive radio transmitters. Not only are they competent Morse code telegraphers and short wave radio operators, but they also have built all their equipment themselves. A proud map display traces a network of radio contact with hams from all over the globe. Although this was Azerbaijan and not Russia, we even found a ballet group, the youngest a tender four years. There proud little lads added a masculine flavor to a roomful of future prima ballerinas—they were not intimidated or embarrassed by the girls in the least.

In Tashkent I met Komsomols and in Samarkand had a delightful evening with university students who entertained us with a musical variety group. Today the Leninist Komsomol—the Young Communist League of the Soviet Union—has a membership in excess of 23 millions. I was invited to sit on the presidium at a Tashkent branch meeting. It was thrilling to see the Komsomol at work teaching its members to be purposeful, to show initiative and to study and work well. This branch, like others, gives voluntary assistance to building projects, sending its best members to construction sites.

Samarkand has six institutes of higher learning and one university, founded in 1927 with just 60 students and a single professor. Now it numbers 15,000 students, 11 faculties, 65 professorial chairs. The entire teaching faculty is more than 700. The library contains two million volumes. Thirty nationalities are represented among the student body, but since this is Uzbekistan, the majority of students are Uzbeks, Tatars and Tadjiks with a leavening of Russians and other nationalities. No racial or ethnic friction upsets the tranquility of the university.

My host was the International Friendship Association, a student body most of whose participants are enrolled in the Foreign Languages Faculty. The Faculty specializes in English, German and French. The languages of instruction are Uzbek, Tadjik and Russian. Foreign language training is topnotch. I had fluent discussions in English with students who have never in their lives set foot out of Central Asia. Others speak excellent French and German. The more outstanding students win special scholarships of which there are three at graduated levels, the highest being the Lenin Scholarship. With or without a scholarship, all students are paid stipends and no student pays more than 30 kopecks a month for dormitory accommodation.

Higher Education

Soviet universities are composed of separate faculties. A student matriculates in the faculty of his choice for five years and then must pass a taxing state examination for a diploma. Postgraduate study is not unlike that in the United States. The second degree, known as the Candidate of Science, is awarded at the end of three additional years of study and successful defense of an academic thesis. The Doctorate of Science is the highest degree. Both Candidate of Science and Doctor of Science are academic degrees which qualify one to teach in institutions of higher learning. The Doctorate of Science resembles both the American Ph.D. and the German *Habilitation,* but, unlike the latter, is granted in recognition of outstanding contribution to science and not for any prescribed academic dissertation. Thus the author of any particularly brilliant book or article may be recommended for a Doctorate. Academic rankings among the teaching faculty at Samarkand University are very like American rankings. The lowest grade is that of Instructor, a scholar who holds a diploma and who, in most cases, is preparing to defend a thesis for the degree of Candidate of Science while teaching. The middle rank is Candidate of Science. At the top is the Doctor of Science. There are several hundred Instructors at Samarkand University, 76 Candidates and 43 Doctors of Science. The most reputed Faculties are Biology and Mathematics. The Faculty of History specializes in Uzbek history, but also gives its students a firm grounding in the general principles of historical materialism. Scientific Communism is one of the subjects of the state exam all Soviet students must pass at the end of five years. I was informed that each faculty in Samarkand includes specialists who teach dialectical and historical materialism to students of the faculty in a manner specially related to their subject. However, these specialists are themselves trained in the main universities in the capital city of each Union Republic —e.g., Moscow, Kiev, Tashkent, Alma-Ata, etc. Only there can separate Faculties of Philosophy (Marxism-Leninism) be found.

Scientific research, teaching and scholarship all merge in the Soviet Union's great Academies of Sciences. In Moscow sits the headquarters of the All-Union Academy of Sciences, but each Union Republic has its own Academy. In Dushanbe, capital of Tadjikistan, we were invited to the Tadjik Academy by the Director of its History Institute. He received us in his study where he remarked with modest pride that his colleagues were churning out scientific books and articles at the "rate of a conveyor belt." The Academy has its own publishing house. Altogether the Tadjik Academy of Sciences has 3,000 members.

The History Institute is a working collective of 130 scientists. Research is divided among seven subdivisions. The brunt of the work is carried by the archaeological division, the pre-Revolutionary division which handles the history of Tadjikistan up to the October Revolution, and the Soviet division which studies the period from 1917 to the present. The latter is by far the most important division. It is headed by a woman historian and recently published a pioneering five-volume history of the Tadjik people which sold out immediately. In addition, there is a division of art history, a division devoted to Tadjik culture, an ethnographic division, and a restorations laboratory. With this elaborate set-up there is no danger that the history of this Brown Central Asian people will ever be lost or ignored. Accustomed as I am to struggling to teach Afro-American history on a shoe-string budget, I was floored by the facilities available to my Tadjik colleagues. I was one flabbergasted manchild. The archaeological division stages expeditions to remote parts of Tadjikistan. There are ample funds for research trips both within the Soviet Union and abroad. The Institute has a wide network of international contacts. Its members appear prominently at international conferences.

The director likened the staff to an "international brigade," for it is a multi-national body of historians, all enjoying equal rights. Current research programs include the history of the working class in Tadjikistan and the development of the now flourishing Tadjik intelligentsia. The chairwoman of the Soviet division is researching the Tadjik people's share in the Great Patriotic War against Hitler. Of great interest to me personally is the work on the history of the establishment of collective farms in Tadjikistan. We learned there was a gap in time between the collectivization of farms in the rest of the Soviet Union and in Tadjikistan. Collectivization in this Moslem country began in 1928 but dragged on for a decade. The process finished only in 1937. First attempts took the form of mutual aid teams and remained stuck at that stage for quite a while. Fierce class struggle roared back and forth throughout the countryside. At first collective ownership was restricted merely to land, tools were exempted, farm animals and implements remained private property. But at that stage it did not matter, for there were very few tools in existence in backward Tadjikistan anyway. Today 90 percent of all farms are collective farms and most have modern equipment.

Museums and Political Education

Everyone knows the Soviet Union is filled with monuments to Lenin and the world is familiar with the great Lenin Mausoleum on Moscow's Red Square. Overlooked by many foreigners, however, is the large Lenin Museum situated close by the mausoleum, an incomparable collection of mementos from the life of the leader of the first victorious proletarian revolution. The museum houses graphic and visual displays of the history of the Bolshevik Party, the working-class movement, and the Soviet Union since the October Revolution. A walk through it is as good as a short, concentrated course in political education—the history of the class struggle in Czarist Russia and Leninist strategy and tactics unfold before the viewer.

Although the Moscow museum is a must for foreign Communist Party delegations and representatives of the national liberation movements, what even fewer foreigners seem to know is that each one of the fourteen other Union Republic capitals has its own Lenin Museum, exact replicas of the Moscow collection supplemented by unique reminders of the local revolutionary past (e.g., Lenin with the leaders of the Peoples of the East etc.). The love for Lenin and the desire to learn from him carry over into remote Central Asia. There the Lenin Museums, magnificent edifices, serve the ideological needs of the working people and their children. Soviet Central Asia's Lenin Museums are priceless schools in the principles of Scientific Communism. Tashkent, Dushanbe, Ashkhabad, Frunze, Alma-Ata—each has its Lenin Museum and into each one stream Uzbeks, Tadjiks,

Turkmen, Kirghiz, Kazakhs, Tatars and Kara-Kalpaks, workers, collective and state farmers and intellectuals. I observed rapt Central Asian schoolchildren, whole classes, being guided on political lecture tours through these museums. Once I came upon deaf-mute children, a little silent band enjoying a lesson about Lenin and the struggle against capitalism in *sign language.* Some Lenin Museums even have foreign language guides who give expert commentaries in English, German, French and other tongues. The layout is modern and attractive. For easy comprehension the display is divided into sections corresponding with distinct periods in Lenin's career (e.g., 1895–1903).

All in all, it is awe-inspiring proof of the Soviet Union's determination to realize Lenin's legacy concretely. If ever he is fortunate enough to revisit the land of Lenin, this man-child will make a beeline to a Lenin Museum.

Everywhere I went in the Soviet Union I found the same concern to preserve alive the memory of the Revolution and the centuries-long fight against oppression. For instance, the most striking work of art in all of Azerbaijan is the huge, sparkling monument in Baku to *26 Bolshevik Commissars,* among them Shaumyan and Japaridze, butchered in 1918 by British and Turkish imperialists and Azerbaijanian counter-revolutionaries. While in Baku, I attended a superbly danced ballet whose plot would stun Americans–it depicted the anti-feudal class struggle in medieval Asia.

The People–Educated, Wise, Unforgettable

What more need I say? That the land of Lenin is gorgeous? From all I have said that is obvious. That the Soviet Union's non-white citizens have made the leap from poverty and illiteracy to well-being and advanced culture? Everything I saw testifies to that. That the national question has been solved and that racism is just a bad memory? No one who actually sees Soviet Central Asia can honestly think otherwise.

Naturally I registered kaleidoscopic impressions, some more lasting than others. I remember Tashkent, for instance, shimmering in the sun, limpid and resplendent in reconstructed elegance. Along its boulevards, umbrellaed by leafy trees, stroll folks for whom the horrid memory of the earthquake is beginning to fade. I remember its graceful fountains and its gracious people, mostly one remembers the people—it is they who are truly unforgettable. The Uzbeks are a hearty, handsome people, strong stock cradled in Asia's midriff, the kind of people who, once they were rid of their exploiters, were able to make the arid steppe bloom and the desert surrender its secrets. An engaging and spontaneous people now preparing to reverse the flow of the rivers to water the desert. I remember their heartfelt sympathy for bleeding Chile, their pain at the thought of the fascist murders going on there, their solidarity with valiant Vietnam, their determination to aid the embattled Arab peoples and fighting Black Africa (Guinea-Bissau, Angola, Mozambique).

Tashkent is noted for its great open-air market with fixed stalls and concrete canopy for all-weather service. There on a Sunday morning I made instant friends with collective farmers vending fruits and vegetables. Shoppers elbowed one another good-naturedly, the crowd ebbed and flowed, people milled about at a row of haberdashery stalls—a riot of color and animation. Above the roar I heard what sounded like haggling, but do not be misled. There were no wheeler-dealers here, no slick young men on the make, no private enterprise greed. The goods on display in the haberdashery stalls are state-owned and the stalls are run by employees of the state. I wandered across to the pomegranate counter and ran upon an ordinary looking Uzbek collective farmer. He was a collective farmer all right, but he also turned out to be a foreign language specialist. We conversed in French, his much more fluent than mine. I came away feeling there is more to be learned about real social equality in the Tashkent marketplace than in all the leaden volumes of bourgeois sociologists back home.

One evening I wandered into the hotel bar in Dushanbe, the number one hotel, and was immediately approached by two truck drivers, one Tadjik, his partner a *Volksdeutscher* (German), born and raised in the Soviet Union. They patted my back, shook my hand, and insisted that I drink a fiery toast with them to peace, friendship and international workers' solidarity—at their expense. Not only did they make me welcome, these two workers were themselves well at ease. The bar was filled with ordinary Tadjik and Tatar working men taking their pleasure. Thunderstruck I remembered that this was the most exclusive hotel in the Union Republic capital. It was the equivalent of Black workers hanging out at the bar in the Waldorf-Astoria, not only being served but actually being able to afford the expense!

When the manchild left the land of Lenin, he left knowing that at the foot of the Pamirs, in remote Central Asia, he had indeed read his own people's future. For the first time he knew where the "promised land" lay.

The Sixth Pan-African Congress: Agenda for African–Afro-American Solidarity

Anthony Monteiro

Pan-Africanism has historically been a strategic focus of the anti-racist and anti-colonial forces among the nationally and racially oppressed of Africa and the Americas. The First Pan-African Conference was held in 1900, organized by Henry Sylvester-Williams. From 1919 to 1945 there were five Pan-African Congresses organized and inspired, in the main, by Dr. W.E.B. Du Bois. The barbarity of colonial oppression in Africa during this period required that they all be held either in Europe or the United States.

Prior to the Fifth Pan-African Congress, the Pan-African movement, though orienting upon the aspirations of millions dominated by colonial and racist oppression, remained a movement of progressive intellectuals. This being the case, the main outlook of the first four Congresses called merely for the reformation of the colonial system. Not yet a mass movement, Pan-Africanism did not fully appreciate the place of masses in making history. The lesson that the fundamental element of the anti-colonial and anti-racist struggles is the working people awaited the Fifth Congress' deliberations. This recognition became critical to the Fifth Congress and, in fact, was the central aspect of its outlook. At this Congress, which was by far the most important to that point, the center of gravity of Pan-Africanism was placed as the African continent and its people. This Congress held that the working people must lead the movement to liquidate colonialism, to end racism. In its "Declaration to the

Colonial Peoples of the World," the Manchester Congress declared:

> "The Fifth Pan-African Congress, therefore, calls on the workers and farmers of the colonies to organize effectively. Colonial workers must be in the front lines of the battle against imperialism."

Continuing, it said:

> "The Fifth Pan-African Congress calls on the intellectuals and professional classes of the colonies to awaken to their responsibility."

Here, anti-imperialism was established as the essence of the struggle against colonialism; hence, Pan-Africanism's guiding political position. The first stage of the anti-imperialist struggle was viewed as the struggle for political independence, laying the foundation for the struggle for social and economic emancipation, for the African peoples' total control of their natural and human resources. The Declaration, therefore, held that "... the struggle for political power by colonial and subject peoples is the first step towards, and the necessary prerequisite to, complete social, economic and political emancipation." Henceforth, Pan-Africanism became a movement rooted in the working people of Africa and the West Indies, the racially and nationally oppressed of African descent in the United States, which at the same time joined itself with all the oppressed in an alliance against oppression. It stood for self-determination for the nations of Africa and the Caribbean, for advancing democracy and equality for Afro-Americans. Thus, it recognized imperialism—that socio-politico-economic system of exploitation and domination which serves the interests of the large corporate wealth in the capitalist countries—as the common enemy of the oppressed and exploited of every continent. Pan-Africanism, further, was placed by the Manchester Congress within the orbit of the global movement for liberation. For this reason, "Colonial and Subject Peoples of the World—Unite."

Kwame Nkrumah stated that the Manchester Congress adopted socialism as its political ideology. Nourished by the continent-wide rebellion that erupted in Africa after World War II, Pan-Africanism very rapidly established bonds of struggle with the peoples of Asia, engaged in intense anti-colonial battles; and to use the formulation of Amilcar Cabral (martyred leader of the African Party for the Independence of Guinea-Bissau and the Cape Verde Islands), it became an historic associate of the world community of Socialist states.

The historic period following World War II would have, as a dominant feature, the accelerated intensification of the national liberation struggles in the colonial world. This would then occasion the deepening of the crisis of the world imperialist system; hence, the rapid deterioration of the system of classical colonialism on a world scale. The new strength and combat capacity gained by the patriots of the Third World, who joined the armed struggle to destroy fascism during World War II, would now be applied to the battles for political independence. This crisis of imperialism brought forth a shift in the center of power of world imperialism. Imperialism, based in the United States and rooted in the corporate monopoly wealth of this country, became politically, economically and militarily dominant. Its might became critical to the maintenance and resuscitation of all the imperialist nations and therefore fundamental to the continuance of colonialism. In fact, the colonial powers could absorb the tremendous blows delivered them by the national liberation fighters only if they could depend upon economic and military aid flowing from the United States. Hence, the United States imperialists who themselves had no vast colonial possessions, became central to maintaining colonialism, whereupon world imperialism became increasingly dependent upon the United States. In the United States, therefore, was established the racist, anti-Communist counterrevolutionary bastion of world imperialism, the main source of global oppression and war.

Though committed to the salvation of imperialism in

general, the United States at the same time perfidiously pursued its own interests. These interests were expressed in the offensive struggle to establish a new form of colonialism and oppression in the Third World. This was a struggle with its imperialist allies over the redivision of the colonial world based upon neo-colonialism. Neo-colonialism preserves foreign domination and control of the wealth of Third World countries, while at the same time recognizing the limited sovereignty of those countries. Under these circumstances social exploitation is intensified and the economies of the newly independent countries are more securely attached to and dependent upon those of the capitalist countries. Thus, the tremendous wave of struggles for political independence was met by the organized efforts of imperialism to maintain the relationships of inequality and to preserve the newly independent countries as economic and political adjuncts of imperialism through neo-colonialism. The process of neo-colonial aggression was coupled with the policy of strengthening classical colonialism in southern Africa. Basic to this policy was the strengthening of Portuguese and South African fascist colonialism. Corporate investment and military aid were placed as decisive in maintaining a colonial beachhead for imperialism in Africa.

By 1966 the majority of African nations had achieved political independence, opening the door to the second stage of the struggle for socio-economic development. In the struggle for the total control of their labor and their natural resources the peoples of Africa faced, more directly, the enemy crystallized in the American, European and Japanese multi-national corporations. The completion of the second stage required renewed efforts by the African masses to destroy imperialism in Africa. This historic task demanded the pursuance of a noncapitalist, socialist-oriented path of development. However, so long as classical colonialism, based upon governmental power being held by fascist regimes, remained in southern Africa, the independence of all African nations would be jeopardized. Therefore, the struggle against classical colonialism became one with the struggle for freedom from neo-colonialism. The two phenomena, themselves derivatives of imperialism, became objects of the anti-imperialist struggle.

Centrality of U.S. Imperialism

Contemporary Pan-Africanism, dating from the Manchester Congress of 1945, as opposed to its predecessors, developed under conditions which were quite favorable for the anti-colonial and anti-neo-colonial struggles. The crisis gripping imperialism had widened the struggle against colonialism and racism and placed them upon an offensive footing as well. The centrality of United States imperialism demanded that the struggle for emancipation focus more sharply against it. Though the other imperialist powers, like Great Britain, France, Japan, Belgium and West Germany, remained as oppressors of African people, without the United States their capacity to oppress was considerably weakened. This fact necessitated that Pan-Africanism which is based in the United States direct its efforts against the monopoly corporations here that plunder Africa and against the imperialist foreign policy of the United States government. From this standpoint the deliberations and conclusions of the Sixth Pan-African Congress, held in June of 1974, in Dar es Salaam, Tanzania, must be applied in the United States in such a way as to reverse the posture of the United States in Africa.

The Sixth Congress occurred in the historic period when the forces of class and national liberation are unquestionably shaping events. Standing upon the shoulders of the past achievements of Pan-Africanism as demonstrated in the achievement of political independence by forty-two nations, and occurring within the midst of the collapse of Portuguese colonialism, occasioned by the victories of the patriots of Guinea-Bissau, Mozambique and Angola, this Congress would be called upon to exceed its predecessors in establishing Pan-Africanism as an instrument of liberation. Thirty of the forty-two independent nations of Africa, including the majority of the liberation organizations of southern Africa, were in attendance. As well, delegations attended from the nations of the Caribbean, including Socialist Cuba. This was the first Pan-African Congress to be held on the African continent, the first to have delegations from independent African nations and the first to be addressed by heads of state. The speeches of Julius Nyerere, President of the United Republic of Tanzania, and Ahmed Sekou Touré of Guinea were both adopted by the Congress as guiding documents. At this Congress were represented the two trends of socio-economic development which exist among the independent nations of Africa. Hence, there were nations pursuing a socialist-oriented course to social development and others where capitalism represented the dominant trend. The struggle to determine the course of development, to strengthen sovereignty and to liquidate all remnants of colonialism and imperialism in each nation sharpened the social contradictions. Moreover, the Sixth Congress occurred at a time when the continent is the arena for the unfolding of two historic processes, that for political independence and for social and economic development.

The political outlook of the Congress was anti-imperialist. The General Declaration, which was the main political document of the Congress, held "The universality of imperialism implies the universality of the anti-imperialist struggle." This formulation is the basis of the internationalism adopted by the Congress. Julius Nyerere in his opening address urged that the Congress recognize that Pan-Africanism is part and parcel of a global struggle. He stated, "For although this Congress movement was made necessary by racialism, and was itself originally confined to Black people, our particular struggle for dignity has always been one aspect of the world-wide struggle for human liberation." He called upon the Congress to deliberate with the recognition that the Congress takes "place in the context of a world-wide movement for human equality and national self-determination." Touré, in further elaborating the organic character of the anti-imperialist struggle, held:

"The universal nature of imperialism dictates that the struggle against imperialism should be of a universal nature, and this realization, far from submerging our specific responsibilities in confusion, increases them and bestows on us giant status by giving to the consequences of our acts world dimension."

The outlook of Touré and Nyerere was a confirmation of the position of Amilcar Cabral, who in 1971 called attention to the fact that the struggle against Portuguese colonialism was not directed against the Portuguese people. At that time Cabral sent greetings to the anti-fascists and anti-colonialists of Portugal, "who by defending the interests of their own people and ours are effectively opposing the colonial military machine, thereby furthering the common struggle and strengthening the bonds of solidarity which unite our people." The point is that the struggle against oppression ends neither at the lines that divide people nationally nor racially. This understanding in no way belittles the struggle against racism, or for unity of Black people against racism. Rather it places as the cornerstone of the fight against racism the unity of all anti-racist forces. Moreover, this position demonstrates that the struggle against racism is organically linked to the struggles against imperialism.

Noting that the Sixth Pan-African Congress is "called upon to develop in a period which is extraordinarily favorable for the progress of the revolutionary forces on our continent and the world," the Declaration states that this necessitates Pan-Africanism becoming anti-imperialist and revolutionary. For these reasons Pan-Africanism "inscribes itself within the context of the class struggle." Calling for vigilance on this matter the Declaration continues, "Not to be conscious of this would be to expose ourselves to confusion which imperialism would not fail to exploit." The Congress recognized the class struggle as elemental to the struggle for national liberation and against racism. Based upon a scientific analysis, the Congress identified imperialism as a class phenomenon, based upon the class interests of the corporate monopolies in the capitalist countries. Further, the Sixth Congress, as with the Fifth, understood that the majority of the oppressed in Africa and the Americas belong to the classes that constitute the working people. Finally, the Congress recognized that the total liberation of the peoples of Africa and of African descent is to be found, as the Declaration holds, in "building societies based on the power of the exploited working masses," i.e., socialist societies.

Surely, this perspective is a smashing repudiation of narrow black nationalism, black capitalism and cultural nationalism. Those who would appropriate the African revolution to justify these positions, the Congress forthrightly rejected. Marcelinos Dos Santos, while addressing the Congress, brought the experience of FRELIMO to the delegates by quoting his President, Samora Machel, on the nature of the enemy and the struggle. Samora Machel in a speech entitled, "Establish Peoples' Power to Serve the Masses" held:

"... we always say that we are struggling against the exploitation of man by man, of which Portuguese colonialism is today the principal expression in our country. In other words, this means that our objective is to overthrow the power of the exploiting classes in Mozambique, represented chiefly by the colonial and imperialist bourgeoisie, and to destroy the colonial state. ...

"... There are nationalists–some naively, because they do not have a developed class consciousness, and others because they are involved in exploitation–who think the purpose of our struggle should be to establish black power instead of white power. ... For them our struggle should be a struggle between black power and white power, whereas for us the struggle is between the power of the exploiters and the people's power."

Dos Santos in elaborating upon the position of Machel told the Congress:

"In our historical circumstances a superficial or emotional analysis could easily lead to identifying the enemy on the basis of race or skin color, thereby deforming the nature of our fight. For us the enemy is the system of exploitation."

The overall thrust of the Sixth Pan-African Congress has profound and long-term meaning for the struggle for black liberation and against racism in the United States. The documents of this Congress are a weapon in the hands of Black liberation fighters in the struggle for freedom. If accepted, the decisions of the Congress aid in developing a scientific posture in the fight by Afro-Americans against oppression. These documents point to the enemy as imperialism—for us in the United States, the imperialism rooted here. Moreover, they correctly place the relationship between the struggle for national liberation (i.e., black liberation) and the class struggle. This is achieved by giving to the enemy a class identification. Herein is the source of rapid ideological development among Black liberation fighters; here is the basis for placing black liberation on a similar footing with the majority of humanity.

However, these documents are likewise a source of bringing clarity to the peace forces in the United States, which are now called upon to see their role more accurately in struggling against imperialist aggression in Africa. The struggle for peace is directly related to the struggle for self-determination and against imperialism. The question of the struggle against United States imperialist aggression in Africa raises sharply the interconnection between the fight against racism and for peace. This understanding would certainly elevate the ideological posture of the United States peace movement, but also deepen its mass influence, especially among the racially oppressed.

In summary, its meaning to the struggle for black liberation is as follows: firstly, the Sixth Pan-African Congress laid the foundation for the reanimation of the black liberation struggles predicated upon anti-imperialist principles.

Secondly, this is the basis for internationalizing the black liberation struggle and coordinating its activity with the world-wide struggle for liberation. Thirdly, it rescues the anti-imperialist heritage which Dr. Du Bois left to Pan-Africanism from those who would transform it into a monument to separatism and narrow nationalism. Finally, it lays the basis for resuscitating the movement for solidarity with Africa based upon anti-imperialism.

The decisions of this Congress deserve the widest and most serious consideration and discussion. Moreover, they should be seen as a source of action and organizing, of redoubling our efforts to facilitate the most rapid achievement of independence and social progress on the African continent.

Historical Source Book and Literary Testament

Keith E. Baird

Dr. Kwame Nkrumah was not only a politician and states-
man. It is true, of course, that he led his country Ghana to
independence, attained in 1957, and that until his deposition
from the Presidency in a military coup in February 1966 he
was actively engaged nationally and internationally in the
leadership of the Ghanaian nation. But Dr. Nkrumah was
also a scholar and political theorist who dedicated his intellectual talents to the promotion of the freedom of all African
people. He wrote in the course of his busy life no less than
a dozen books and several pamphlets ranging in scope from
an account of his own involvement in the independence
struggle of his country (*Ghana: The Autobiography of Kwame Nkrumah,* 1957), to a "Philosophy and Ideology for De-
colonization and Development with particular reference to
the African Revolution" (*Consciencism,* 1964) and a devastating critique of international capitalist control and exploitation of African labor and resources with particular attention to the activity of United States corporate financial
organization (*Neo-Colonialism: The Last Stage of Imperialism,* 1965). The present work, published posthumously,
brings together a number of key writings by Dr. Nkrumah,
some published for the first time, which trace chronological-
ly their author's development as a political activist, and as
a principal theorist of African freedom and self-determination. Many of the selections are from previously published
books, but the brief comments preceding each both provide
lucid explanation of the related historical events and demonstrate the consistency of the author's political thought.

Book Review: REVOLUTIONARY PATH. By Kwame Nkrumah. International Publishers, New York, 235 pages. $4.25.

As early as 1942, while still a student in the U.S.A., Kwame Nkrumah was moved to record his reactions to the imperialist oppression of the African people. "I was so revolted," he wrote twenty years later, "by the ruthless colonial exploitation and political oppression of the people of Africa that I knew no peace. The matter exercised my mind to such a degree that I decided to put down my thoughts in writing and to dilate on the results of some of my research concerning the subject of colonialism and imperialism." It was not until 1962, however, that the jottings begun at that time, and completed in 1945 in London, were published in that city as the book, *Towards Colonial Freedom*. In its Preface, from which the preceding quotation was taken, Dr. Nkrumah informs us that the book was printed exactly as it was originally written. "No changes or additions were made," he writes, "and nothing was added or taken from it. The views I expressed then are precisely the views I hold today concerning the nature of imperialism and colonialism. Furthermore, most of the points I made then have been borne out to the letter, and confirmed by subsequent developments in Africa and Asia." Dr. Nkrumah does, however, confess to a certain modification in his views between 1945 and 1962; whereas at the earlier date his ideas on African unity had been limited to West African unity as a first step, by 1962 he had come as a result of actual experience to "lay greater stress on the vital importance to Africa's survival of a political unification of the entire African continent." Here we have not a change of outlook, but an extension of horizon.

The first steps along Nkrumah's "revolutionary path" are indicated by the title of the book's first section, "The Struggle for National Liberation." Included in this section, for example, is the text of a "Declaration to the Colonial Peoples of the World," approved and adopted by the historic Fifth Pan-African Congress held in Manchester, England, in October 1945. This Congress was held under the joint sponsorship of Dr. W.E.B. Du Bois and Dr. Peter Milliard, a Guyanese physician. In this Congress for the first time there was strong worker and student participation, and most of the two hundred delegates attending came from Africa. Written by Dr. Nkrumah, the Declaration affirmed the right of all colonial peoples to govern themselves, and called upon the organized masses of the "colonial and subject peoples of the world" to unite for effective action towards their complete social, economic, and political emancipation. "It was no surprise when the Congress adopted socialism as its political philosophy," Dr. Nkrumah comments with evident satisfaction. In this section, too, are selected editorials from the *Accra Evening News*, the newspaper founded by Dr. Nkrumah; the text of the "Motion of Destiny," a masterpiece of forensic virtuosity and parliamentary punctilio, in which the Legislative Assembly of the then Gold Coast requested from the United Kingdom independence within the British Commonwealth; and an extract from the "Midnight Pronouncement of Independence" of March 5-6, 1957.

By a logical progression in Dr. Nkrumah's theory and practice, "National Liberation" is followed by "Socialist Construction and the Struggle for the Liberation and Unification of Africa," which is the title of the second and largest section of the book. Here one finds, *inter alia*, the text of the Secret Agreement signed by Patrice Lumumba and Nkrumah in Accra, August 8, 1960; the significant "Speeches at the Party Ideological Institute, Winneba," February 1961 and February 1962; portions of Nkrumah's dramatic "Dawn Broadcast" of April 8, 1961, in which he responded to insistent rumors of corrupt practices by high functionaries, and announced dire penalties for nepotism and other forms of official misconduct; his speeches before the Organization of African Unity (OAU); and extracts from the book that evoked U.S. State Department outrage and protest, *Neo-Colonialism: The Last Stage of Imperialism*.

Following upon the coup in February 1966, Dr. Nkrumah lived mostly in Guinea on the invitation of its president, Ahmed Sekou Touré. From the capital, Conakry, he made a series of broadcasts which were beamed to Ghana. The full texts of these broadcasts were published in a book, *Voice of Conakry.* It is in the third and final section of *Revolutionary Path,* the section entitled, "Class Struggle, and the Armed Phase of the African Revolution" that some *Voice of Conakry* texts appear. In these broadcasts, as Dr. Nkrumah declares in his Introduction to *Voice of Conakry* (Panaf Publications, London, 1967), he was determined "to expose the counter-revolutionary nature of the 'coup' and at the same time to show how the blow struck against progressive Ghana was also an attempt to set back the pace of the wider African Revolution for total liberation and an All-African Government."

Dr. Nkrumah was an uncompromising Pan-Africanist. He was also an uncompromising socialist. Thus he does not accept the general notion of a "Third World." In an essay entitled "The Myth of the Third World" included in the third section, Dr. Nkrumah declares that today the "Third World" is neither a practical political concept nor a reality. "It is," he says, "merely a misused expression which has come to mean everything and nothing. If we are to achieve revolutionary socialism then we must avoid any suggestion that will imply that there is any separation between the socialist world and a 'Third World.'" In similar fashion, Nkrumah sought to have political leaders and thinkers eschew the term "African socialism" in favor simply of "socialism." He asserted that the realities of the diverse and irreconcilable social, political and economic policies being pursued by African states today have made the term "African socialism" meaningless and irrelevant, and gibed that "African socialism" has now come to acquire some of its greatest publicists in Europe and North America "precisely because of its predominant anthropologist charm." Dr. Nkrumah acknowledged that "the basic organization of many African societies in different periods of history manifested a certain communalism and that the philosophy and humanist purposes behind that organization are worthy of recapture." He insisted, however, that "what socialist thought in Africa must recapture is not the structure of the 'traditional African society' but its spirit, for the spirit of communalism is crystallized in its humanism and in its reconciliation of individual advancement with group welfare." It is in this third section, indeed, the greater part of which represents his writing done since 1966, in exile, that Dr. Nkrumah is most patently Marxist-Leninist in his expression. As is implied by the section heading, "Class Struggle, and the Armed Phase of the African Revolution," African liberation is by no means completely effected–even where independence from colonialism has been achieved. "In fact," says Nkrumah, "independence must never be considered as an end in itself but as a stage, the very first stage of the people's revolutionary struggle." Independent African states, then, must be ever watchful that imperialists and their "local stooges" do not re-subjugate them. It is in the context of world revolution, in which he saw nonviolent methods as now anachronistic, that Dr. Nkrumah viewed the Black Power movement in the United States and arrived at the conclusion that "Racial discrimination is the product of an environment, an environment of a divided class society, and its solution is to change that environment. This presupposes the fact that it is only under socialism in the United States of America that the African-American can really be free in the land of his birth."

Revolutionary Path is both an historical source-book, a companion and guide to its author's previous works, and a literary last will and testament. Many of the introductions to the documents were written by Dr. Nkrumah while in an advanced stage of his ultimately fatal illness. He dictated the conclusion to the book in October 1971 in a clinic in Bucharest, Rumania, where he was undergoing medical treatment, and where he died six months later, on April 27, 1972. Kwame Nkrumah was a maker as well as a recorder of history. In this his last work one may trace lineaments of his character: his great personal courage, his self-confidence, his unswerving commitment to human freedom and dignity in Africa and the world over. It is evident from Dr. Nkrumah's acts as well as from his words that he had a profound sense of history, and of his own role in its development. He died far from his native land, an exile. One suspects, in reviewing this documentary account of his life and work, that history will both absolve and vindicate him.

Paradise Lost: Some Observations Directed Toward the Bicentennial of the U.S.

J. H. O'Dell

Born during the Industrial Revolution and the Age of Enlightenment in 18th century Europe, fully a product of the capitalist epoch in world history, the United States of America as a society has always expressed in exaggerated form all of the contradictions characteristic of the capitalist world order. The leaders of the U.S. Revolution of 1776 were the first to raise the enlightened, democratic demand of popular individual freedom which was crystallized in the Bill of Rights of the Republic's Constitution. Yet this was the last industrial country to abolish human slavery on its national territory. The United States was a sanctuary for millions of the poor from Europe who flocked to its shores, and at one and the same time a slave pen for millions of Africans dragged here in chains and a prison house for the captive peoples of the Mexican Republic and the sovereign Indian nations conquered by the United States in wars of aggression.

The United States was the first to proclaim, in its Declaration of Independence, that "governments derive their just powers by consent of the governed," yet it was one of the last to achieve universal adult suffrage for its citizens (with the Voting Rights Act of 1965), and today it has the lowest voting rate in national elections of any industrial country in the world. It was the first to proclaim to the world that "Life, Liberty and the Pursuit of Happiness" were the natural endowments of mankind, and yet today it stands as one of a mere handful of societies in the world whose government has never ratified the International Agreement Against Genocide adopted by the United Nations.

And so, at the end of two centuries of this Republic, whirlwinds of revolutionary change are testing the capacity and relevance of its institutions. For this is the kind of period which only matures in the fullness of time, as the tumultuous procession of events and developments cause past injustices and present demands to surface at one and the same time, demanding a redress all at once. Much that was ignored before now compels attention and adds its weight to the demands of the present.

In the last two decades, history and revolutionary struggle have overturned that time-honored adage: "The sun never sets upon the British Empire." It was inevitable that the sunset of the British Empire would usher in its wake the twilight of the American Way of Life. Only the conscious action of the peoples of the United States directed towards becoming part of the progressive stream of world history during this period could have prevented the present crisis. But that potential for conscious action was effectively aborted by the class in power after the Second World War by offering "full employment" to a Depression-scarred generation, and McCarthyism for all dissenters. The United States, alongside Britain, stood against the tide of history. Therefore Britain and America, the two English-speaking pillars of the capitalist world order, the two countries who spearheaded the ascendancy of the capitalist mode of production in world history and its Industrial Revolution, have now entered a stage of decline and descending line of development.

The rosy dawn of the capitalist epoch broke over the British Isles as they became the "workshop of the world" for the two centuries following the Cromwellian Revolution of 1640. And Britain's child, the United States of America, became the premier country of developed capitalism following its Civil War. Aided in its primary accumulation of wealth by the African slave trade and the plunder of Asia,

Latin America and the Caribbean, Great Britain became the self-styled model of "civilized" institutions; the United States, the self-proclaimed paragon of "Democracy." The competition between them sometimes led to the point of war. Despite this they shared responsibility, through the Anglo-American tradition, for spreading (usually at gunpoint) the Protestant Ethic and the virtues of the capitalist profit system of production to those "inferior peoples" in the tropical climates who were, and are, a majority of the world's population.

The United States Revolution of 1776 made a distinct contribution to the Age of Enlightenment in the Western world by breaking with the feudal tradition of a church-state and effecting a constitutional separation of the two. Yet, the class that led the revolution adopted its own kind of state religion—namely, the belief in the sacredness of private property; a religion conveniently designed to serve the class interest of those who owned the most basic properties: the mines, factories, landed estates, slaves and financial institutions which served as the means of economic production.

The doctrine of white supremacy became one of the cardinal dogmas of this state religion, whose basic assumptions were preached not only from the pulpits of the white Christian churches, but from such professorial sanctuaries as Oxford, Princeton, Harvard, Johns Hopkins and other intellectual centers of the "Free World."

With this ideological base intact, the captains of industry dispatched their armies across the North American continent, seizing the land and natural resources and acting out the ritual of annexation. The European immigrant poor were offered "citizenship" in the New Order as their piece of the "American Dream" in return for their services to the uncrowned royalists of the Free Enterprise system.

Under this state religion the London Stock Exchange was wedded in holy matrimony to the New Orleans Cotton Exchange as the power of capital was internationalized around the principle that those who control capital shall rule the world.

The leaders of the United States Revolution of 1776 were the first to articulate the liberating idea that "All men are created equal." This struck a mortal blow at the "divine right" presumptions of kings and feudal lords. Yet, instead of this idea becoming the guiding ethic to secure equal rights and opportunities for men and women in this society, it has been used to promote the mythology that at least all *men* enjoyed equal rights. The purpose of this distortion was to conceal the basic class character of American society and the laws of exploitation operating, which create mass poverty and enormous private wealth in one and the same process. When today a farm laborer, working in the apple orchards in New York State, cannot afford to buy apples for his family, while the Vice-President of the United States, Nelson Rockefeller, describes his private gifts to political associates, amounting to millions of dollars, as nothing more than "sharing a bowl of apples"—that is a mirror of a system of economic tyranny.

Of all the countries of Western civilization, the United States of America is the society in which the idea of *private property* has been carried to such prodigious extremes that today, two hundred years after the founding of this country and on the eve of the 21st century, the very concept of "social property" has not yet entered the language of this society.

In the ascendant period in its history during the last century, the United States pioneered in the establishment of a free public school system supported by public taxes and achieved a level of literacy which compared favorably with the most advanced countries of the world. Today "the little red school house" of American folk tradition, in the urban crisis setting, increasingly takes on the character of an institutional extension of the prison system, wherein armed guards and dope are far more in evidence than education and learning. A strategic dimension of our struggle for a civilized society in the future is the effort to rescue a whole generation of our children from the chaos and nihilism being programed through the public schools.

Apropos of this group of children: are not the millions of

children in Vietnam and Cambodia, who are running fearfully, napalm-scarred, through the wasteland and devastation which American bombs have made of their national homeland—are not these *our* children just as surely as the children we have fathered and mothered here in this jungle of epidemic selfishness? What of our legal and moral obligation to rebuild Vietnam? The official leaders of the United States have turned a deaf ear or responded with sophistry to the demands by the Afro-American and Indian communities that reparations be made for past injustices. We have cavalierly been told that these demands represent "racism in reverse." Well, what about Vietnam? We owe the answer to this question to ourselves as much as to the Vietnamese. For the peoples of the United States are not going to solve any problems, in any fundamental way, until we as a society are prepared to confront the true history of this country—face up to the carnage and despoliation that have been the legacy of this capitalist republic. We must understand the full implications of a system which is destroying our children here at home with dope and killing babies in Southeast Asia with napalm. The martyred Afro-American national patriot, Martin Luther King, Jr., called it "the greatest purveyor of violence in the world today."

United States share of world industrial and agricultural production
1949—46 %
1970—23 %
1980—15 % (estimate)

We see in these statistics a portrait of the decline in the relative importance of the United States in the world economy. Two factors have contributed to this decline. It will be recalled that in 1949 most of Asia and Africa were still under colonialism and much of Latin America had been held back by its economic relations with the United States to a pre-industrial stage of development. By 1970 the colonial empires had been reduced to only one-tenth of their former size; such were the successes of the independence movements. In the meantime the industrial output of these former colonial countries has progressed considerably. The other major factor in the world economy is the rise of the Socialist world community since the Second World War with outstanding achievements in the development of productive forces in both industry and agriculture. As a case in point, this sector of the world economy now produces more oil and steel annually than is produced under capitalism in our country. A large and significant part of the world economy no longer rests on capitalist relations nor on capitalism's system of colonial relations. The most important new feature of the world economy is the tremendous output of the Socialist world and of those former colonial countries that are developing economic production along noncapitalist lines. Much of the American national arrogance and of the relatively high standard of living in this country rested upon the economic realities of 1949, but those realities have now been altered and the process is irreversible. The peoples of the United States can maintain and improve their standard of living to the degree that they are prepared to enter into peaceful, constructive trade and cultural relations with other peoples of the world, and reorganize the political economy of our country to serve the needs of our people and support rising living standards. Another element in this picture, of course, is the restoration of the economies of Western Europe and Japan which have now become major competitors of the United States in the world market. It is notable that in 1974, for the first time in history, the United States actually suffered an absolute decline in national productivity.

The "American Century" proclaimed so ambitiously in the late 1940's is *over,* having lasted all of twenty-five years. Usually the projection of a century of time involves a span of one hundred calendar years, but the "American Century" of United States domination in the world economy lasted twenty-five years (1945–1970). Such is the speed with which time telescopes events today, and the laws of social development put the stamp of finality on those class ambitions which run contrary to the progressive historical process.

Looking towards the 200th anniversary of the birth of the United States, it is of no less importance that we understand the internal contradictions shaping the features of the present crisis of this republic. The *laissez-faire* capitalism of the 18th century has succumbed to monopoly in industry, agriculture and finance. Select any area one wishes—food, oil, automobile, steel, finance—and one will find the lion's share of the market and of the profit, in the grip of a few large business institutions. This is not a new development* by any means, but it is a process which has been carefully concealed from the people of our country by the diet of "free enterprise" propaganda. This pattern of monopoly control is so firmly established in the economy of our country today that it determines the character of the military budget and revenue sharing.** In fact, the government itself (local, state and national) is in debt to a financial oligarchy of banks and insurance companies to the amount of 500 billion dollars. The interest and debt servicing charges paid out annually from the federal budget on this debt are around 31 billion dollars. This means simply that over a 15-year period, at current interest rates, the Chase National Bank, Morgan Guaranty Trust and other financial monopolies will collect almost as much in interest as the debt itself. Such is the magnitude of the "rip-off."

The other side of this process is revealed in the fact that during this entire decade of the 1970's the richest 20 percent of the population has been getting a bigger share of the national income than at any time since the end of World War II, while the share of national income received by the working- and middle-class population has been getting smaller

---

* The world capitalist economy, of which the United States is a part, evolved from *laissez-faire* to monopoly during the long Depression 1873–1896.

** Some 62 multi-national corporations receive the bulk of the money appropriated through defense contracts. As for revenue sharing, of the 38,000 administrative units of state and local government, which are, in theory at least, eligible to receive General Revenue Sharing Funds, only a mere handful get this tax money filtered back to them.

during this same period. It should be self-evident that such problems cannot be resolved through arguments over school busing.

A Bridge over Troubled Waters

The main weight of social progress in the United States over the past twenty years has been carried by the Afro-American community. Were it not for the emergence of the general democratic mass movement for citizenship rights during the decades of the 1950's and 1960's, it is very likely that by now we would be observing the 200th birthday of the United States under the conditions of a fairly developed fascism. The development of such a system of repression was obviously a strategic part of the timetable of the class that holds power in our country. The Watergate revelations underscore this beyond a shadow of a doubt. However, they miscalculated; they did not count on "Black Americans" coming from the hinterland of Montgomery, Alabama, building a movement for justice and human dignity of sufficient moral weight and momentum to take command of the center of stage and open up a new chapter in the political evolution of the United States.

This socially significant role coincides with the period in which we became a predominantly urban, wage-earning, working-class population. The relative weight of the rural population among Blacks has dramatically declined since World War II, and the relative weight of the urban population, both in its working-class and middle strata components, has dramatically increased. We have gainfully employed numbers in such industrial sectors of the economy as steel, maritime, auto, shipbuilding, urban transit, textile, as well as in the urban social services (postal, sanitation, hospital, teaching). This transformation of the Black community from a predominantly rural Southern population to a nationally distributed, urban, working-class population found its major expression in the mass-action struggles of the civil rights era of our Freedom Movement.

27*

The mass mobilization, mass movement form of protest demonstrations reflects the predominantly working-class character of the Black community, even though these struggles have not as yet become *industrial strike* forms centered in the factories, mines, etc., where we are working. A major by-product of this sociological transformation of this national community—a reflection of the victories won by the civil rights movement in opening up opportunities and ending segregation—is the significant growth of the middle class often called the "Black Bourgeoisie." In reality they are the higher income group of the working class, the character of whose work is primarily *mental* rather than physical labor (the civil service, teachers, lawyers, architects, engineers). The term "Black Bourgeoisie" is a misnomer when applied to this group, for while it may describe their attitudes and life style of relative affluence, they are nevertheless not owners of wealth-producing property and exploiters of labor and, therefore, are *not* members of a bourgeois class. It is important to clear this up conceptually, so that we do not make the mistake as a movement of alienating them from active participation when, in fact, there are many examples expressing their readiness to be a part of the Freedom Movement. As an aggregate, notwithstanding exceptions to the rule, they identify with the freedom goals of our movement. They have generally a more literate knowledge of Afro-American history than do other strata and are a potential force for embracing ideas which go beyond the limits of the capitalist system in the United States.

The "Black Bourgeoisie," on the other hand, small as it is, thrives and grows on the exploitation of labor, as do all members of the capitalist class. However, they can be considered a more progressive sector of that class by virtue of their marginal position in the business sectors of the economy,* and therefore their dependence upon the growing pros-

---

* The minuscule share which Black-owned businesses receive of the total gross receipts of American business (0.8 of 1 %) is much smaller than the share of the total U.S. personal income received by Afro-American workers.

perity of the Black community for their own prosperity. The "Black Bourgeoisie" *per se* is a minute section of the Black population; and in this period, when the movement is increasingly turning a critical eye and making demands upon the larger political economy, the influence of the "Black Bourgeoisie" ideologically actually decreases rather than being on the upswing.

This is not to ignore the fact that there do exist some petty hustlers who have been riding the upsurge of "Black consciousness" of recent years and hope to capitalize on this growing Afro-American consciousness by selling wigs, knit caps, and ornamental jewelry, leaving an impression that "Black Capitalism" is on the upswing. But this is largely a chimera, because basically the Black community is more critical of the capitalist system today than at any time in our history—except perhaps the decade of the thirties and the Great Depression. And as our emerging program of demands pressed on this political economy (jobs for all at full time, socially useful work; the right to the best medical services available, regardless of income etc.) grips the social consciousness of ever-growing sectors of the Black population, all else will fall into its proper relationship because this will become the material reality and our jack-leg hucksters will fall by the wayside, as their irrelevance becomes clear.

An example of the all-class character of our liberation movement today, with its emphasis on mass action around economic issues, is Operation P.U.S.H. (People United to Save Humanity), under the leadership of Rev. Jesse L. Jackson. In preserving the involvement of all classes of the Afro-American community and stressing mass action as the primary way of educating and mobilizing the larger community, P.U.S.H. continues the experiences gained from the civil rights era of our movement. Its emphasis (as well as other black organizations) on jobs as a right, the right to medical attention for all regardless of income, housing, quality education for all children, and other such issues involving the living standards of the working class represents the ascendancy of the interests of that class as the primary concern on the agenda of our movement. Like all significant movements in the 200-year history of the Black community, P.U.S.H. draws upon the spiritual reserves and organizational strength of the Black church. In seeking to unite the Black community in this period of crisis around the themes of economic generation *and* spiritual regeneration, the leadership of P.U.S.H. nevertheless rejects any provincialism which would isolate our community from other sectors of the United States population who have a common self-interest in struggling for some fundamental changes in the present political economy. Consequently, P.U.S.H. as an organization actively pursues a strategy of coalition with Latins, Native Americans, sections of organized labor, and others who are engaged in organized movements.

Nothing has higher priority among the concerns of our Movement than does the present critical state of the economy. Unemployment has already reached Depression levels in Black and Latin communities and continues to grow unchecked each day. So far no program has come from the Rockefeller-Ford Administration designed to even stabilize this situation much less prevent it from getting worse. The median income gap between Black and white families is growing wider with each passing year, while the purchasing power of the average American family, according to government statistics, declined in 1973 compared to 1972. This is a profoundly sick economic picture. Perhaps the outstanding symbol of this harsh economic reality is the fact that one-third of the dog and cat food sold in the ghettos of America is eaten by humans, according to the Senate Sub-Committee on Hunger and Nutrition.

The biggest monopolies in every sector of the economy are not missing the opportunity to use the climate of rampant recession to further tighten up their game of securing the maximum profits, just as they did during the "Energy Crisis" hoax a year ago. Many readers will recall that just a few years ago one of the major actions of our Movement was to picket chain stores in the ghetto demanding the hiring and upgrading of Blacks in decision-making positions and demanding that these companies use the services of black-owned institutions like banks, insurance companies etc. This was one major focus of our economic thrust. It is clear now that we were in a race with time and cold economic reality. As a case in point, food chains like A & P (The Great Atlantic & Pacific Tea Company is its official name) are closing down a large number of their stores now located in the ghetto and fleeing to the suburbs. In the stores that remain they are introducing a computerized system of pricing which eliminates whole groups of employees, such as stock clerks, as pricing throughout the store is eliminated and a computerized price panel is established at the checkout counter.

Black, Chicano and Puerto Rican workers are heavily concentrated in those industries whose corporate decision-makers have been dismantling industry and carrying it to Taiwan, South Korea, South Vietnam, and other parts of the world where the American military presence protects them in their drive to obtain maximum profits from low wages. We are referring particularly to the electrical and clothing industries and the flight of capital from our country amounting to two billion dollars alone since the Nixon gang removed restrictions on the flight of capital overseas last year. In addition there are strong tendencies in the right-wing Administration to bow to the wishes of the big plantation landlords and commercial farmers, in their effort to get the Bracero Bill in Mexico renewed, allowing for hundreds of thousands of Mexican farm workers to cross the border and be used as non-union labor in California and Texas—a definite blow at the already depressed living standards of all farm workers who are trying to organize and win the elementary right to collective bargaining.

Nor is there much help or hope being spread these days by the economic soothsayers who make up the President's Council of Economic Advisors. These pretenders to the throne of economic knowledge are not sticking their necks out to predict *anything*, such are the uncertainties clouding the picture. While it is obvious they are not much help, the comedy of their role is that neither are they allowing themselves to be set up to be the fall guys just in case this stuff goes berserk. Apparently, for them the world beyond their cubby hole of Keynesian* prescriptions is a world of economic theory and experience that does not exist. Such is the dismal state of affairs in the economics profession, which has so often been called "the dismal science."

More than seventy years ago at the turn of this century, the prophet and sage W.E.B. Du Bois set forth in his book *The Souls of Black Folk* a certain proposition: "The problem of the twentieth century is the problem of the color line—the relation of the darker to the lighter races of men in Asia and Africa, in America and the islands of the sea."

Dr. Du Bois was right in his analysis, as our Freedom Movement faced the long night of the twentieth century in those early years. Now that question he defined so eloquently has been resolved. The absolute and relative decline of Western Europe and the United States, the end of their domination and institutional influence in the world, as phenomena which had been enforced over the past four and one-half centuries, have in this current century resolved "the problem of the color line." The evidence of that resolution is all around us. From the shores of the vast subcontinent of India to the isles of the Georgia-South Carolina seacoast men and women of color now stand in positions of power and authority once ruled by the minions of "Master Race" colonialism.

The problem for the remainder of the twentieth century is the problem of capitalist relations—the problem by which the ownership of the means of production by the few amounts to life and death authority over the means of survival for the many. In our country this problem of capitalist relations takes the form of the "Divine Right" of General Motors, U.S. Steel, Lockheed, Standard Oil and the like to determine what is produced and how much; who may

* Based on theories of the English economist, John Maynard Keynes.

424

work and who may not; how they as corporations can be assured of maximum corporate profits from the consumer's pocketbook and government subsidies and in return pay little or no taxes. This is the problem of capitalist relations which the march of historical events has placed on the national agenda of our time. And the problem is as international as was the problem of the color line, as there is a growing impoverishment for large sections of the working population in all those countries who continue to live under capitalist relations.

It will come as a surprise, no doubt, for some to learn that even this formidable problem of capitalist relations has been resolved by a large section of the human family. Around the world there are organized societies that have come to grips with the struggle to abolish capitalist relations ". . . and to institute new Government, laying its foundation on such principles and organizing its powers in such form, as to them shall seem most likely for their Safety and Happiness . . ." *(Declaration of Independence)*. These societies are no longer plagued with the triple-headed monster of mass unemployment, rampant inflation and the shortage of raw materials and energy. Each of their nationally planned economies is in turn being phased into a coordinated effort across national lines to increase the possibility of growth and development of the whole.

Now that we in the United States are being liberated by historical events from the assumptions of world leadership, we are in a good position to learn from the body of experience that has been created by other peoples in resolving the problem of capitalist relations. And the moment is favorable for doing so. For just so long as we avoid the overriding prerogatives of the capitalist class in the United States—just so long will we be obliged to make repeated adjustments and accommodations to the general social ruin and accompanying moral deterioration which the present political economy is generating.

In summary then, the United States as a society is in a state of advanced social decay and stagnation. Because of this, the present political economy is unable to guarantee either a civilized future for the young generation or a life of spiritual and material quality and fulfillment for the present adult generation. So as we approach the 200th anniversary of the formal establishment of this Republic, a new Declaration of Independence is needed—one that declares our determination to free ourselves from the rule of monopoly. This is central among the truths that we hold to be self-evident.

An Authors Who's Who

Keith E. Baird, a long-time contributing editor of *Freedomways* magazine, is a teacher in the Black Studies Department of the State University of New York at Buffalo. An outstanding linguist, he edited Ogonna Chuks-orji's *Names from Africa: Their Origin, Meaning, and Pronunciation* (1972).

Dr. Arlene P. Bennett is a medical clinician in Philadelphia and was formerly a medical consultant on minority affairs in New Jersey.

Jean Carey Bond, a contributing editor of *Freedomways* magazine, is on the staff of the *Bulletin* of the Council on Interracial Books for Children. She is the author of two children's books: *A Is for Africa* (1969) and *Brown Is a Beautiful Color* (1969) and co-authored with Pat Perry "Is the Black Male Castrated?" in *The Black Woman: An Anthology* (1970) edited by Toni Cade.

Brumsic Brandon, Jr., a syndicated cartoonist and essayist, has been contributing cartoons to *Freedomways* magazine for 15 years. He has published five Luther cartoon books such as *Luther's Got Class* and *Outta Sight, Luther!*

Dorothy Burnham, a member of the Board of Directors of Freedomways Associates, Inc., from the magazine's beginning in 1961, is a teacher and adviser in the Science Department of Empire State College of the State University of New York.

Frank E. Chapman, Jr., who served 13 years in the Missouri State Penitentiary until his release in 1975, is a brilliant Black writer who has published several essays in *Freedomways* magazine. A section from one of these essays, "Science and Africa," was reprinted in Claudia Zaslavsky's book *Africa Counts* (1972).

Charles W. Cheng, now in the Dept. of Education, U.C.L.A., has been active in the teachers' union movement. He has also worked on his doctorate at the Harvard Graduate School of Education.

John Henrik Clarke has been associate editor of *Freedomways* magazine since 1962 and is a professor in the Department of Black and Puerto Rican Studies at Hunter College of the City University of New York. He is editor of *American Negro Short Stories; William Styron's Nat Turner: Ten Black Writers Respond; Malcolm X: The Man and His Times; Harlem: A Community in Transition; Harlem, U.S.A.* (Seven Seas Books, 1964); *Harlem: Voices from the Soul of Black America;* and *Marcus Garvey and the Vision of Africa.* Clarke has written innumerable articles and short stories for magazines and newspapers and *Rebellion in Rhyme,* a book of poetry. His work is found in many anthologies. A writer on African history, he contributed a chapter to *The Horizon History of Africa* (1971), and additional material to new editions of John G. Jackson's *Introduction to African Civilizations* and Joel A. Rogers' *World's Great Men of Color.*

Eugenia Collier is a professor of English at the Community College of Baltimore, Md. She has published essays, book reviews, poetry and short stories in several magazines. She has co-edited three books, one being *Afro-American Writing: An Anthology of Prose and Poetry* (2 vols., 1972) with Richard A. Long.

Martin E. Dann has done graduate work in history at the City University of New York. He edited *The Black Press, 1827–1890: The Quest for National Identity,* published in 1971.

Ossie Davis is the well-known actor, playwright, director, writer and social activist. He has been associated with *Freedomways* magazine from its beginning in 1961 and has written many articles for it.

Loyle Hairston, a contributing editor of *Freedomways* since 1970, writes essays, short stories and reviews books. His short stories and essays have been published in *American Negro Short Stories; Harlem, U.S.A.; Harlem: Voices from the Soul of Black America* and *William Styron's Nat Turner: Ten Black Writers Respond,* all edited by John Henrik Clarke.

Ollie Harrington, cartoonist and writer, in 1972 visited the U.S. from the German Democratic Republic for the first time in 21 years. His "Bootsie" cartoons appear regularly in the black press and his political cartoons in the *Daily World* in New York City. A portfolio of his political cartoons, *Soul Shots,* was brought out by the *Daily World* in 1972 with an introduction by another Black artist, Elton C. Fax. His book of cartoons *Bootsie and Others* was published in 1958 by Dodd Mead. Harrington's earlier illustrated children's books such as Ellen Tarry's *The Runaway Elephant* (1950) and *Hezekiah Horton* (1942) and later his humorous cartoons were used to illustrate Philip Sterling's *Laughing on the Outside* (1965), an anthology of black humor.

James V. Hatch is an associate professor of English at the City University of New York as well as an editor, poet and playwright. His books are *Black Image on the American Stage: A Bibliography of Plays and Musicals 1770–1970* (1970), and *Black Theater, U.S.A.: Forty-Five Plays by Black Americans, 1847–1972* (1974), edited with Ted Shine.

Rev. Jesse L. Jackson is the national president of Operation P.U.S.H., a black civil economics organization, and an outstanding Black U.S. leader. Rev. Jackson began writing a weekly syndicated column for the *Los Angeles Times* early in 1977.

Brenda L. Jones now teaches at Seton Hall University in New Jersey. Her book reviews have appeared in several issues of *Freedomways*. An activist in the youth movement, she has attended international conferences.

John Henry Jones, formerly an assistant editor of *Medical World News,* a McGraw-Hill publication, is now on the staff of the American Cancer Society. A founder of the Harlem Writers Workshop, his essays, book reviews and short stories have been published in the magazines *The Harlem Quarterly, Accent* and *Freedomways* and in several black newspapers as well as in *Harlem, U.S.A.,* edited by John H. Clarke. Jones and his wife Lois L. Jones published *All About the Natural,* a book about black hair styles, in 1971.

Ernest Kaiser, an associate editor of *Freedomways* magazine, has been a member of the staff of the Schomburg Center for Research in Black Culture of the New York Public Library for many years. He was an adviser and wrote ten introductions for the 141-volume Arno Press series "The American Negro: His History and Literature." He was consultant and an editor for the one-volume *Encyclopedia of Black America* to be published by McGraw-Hill and is an editor with Herbert Aptheker (the main editor) and Sidney Kaplan of the 3-volume *Correspondence of W.E.B. Du Bois: Selections 1877–1963* (1973, 1976, 1978?). Kaiser is author of *In Defense of the People's Black and White History and Culture* (1970), and co-author or co-editor of *Harlem: A History of Broken Dreams* (1974) with Warren J. Halliburton and *The Negro Almanac* or *The Black American* (1971, 1976) with Harry A. Ploski. His essays, book reviews and bibliographies have been published in *William Styron's Nat Turner: Ten Black Writers Respond; Harlem: A Community in Transition; In Black America 1968: The Year of Awakening; Black Expression; Black Titan: W.E.B. Du Bois; Twentieth Century Interpretations of Invisible Man; Black American Reference Book* and in other books and many magazines.

Anthony Monteiro is executive secretary of the National

Anti-Imperialist Movement for Solidarity with African Liberation (NAIMSAL). An outstanding speaker and writer, he is the author of the booklet *Africa and the USA: The Peoples Must Unite* (1975) and *Africa Demands Freedom Now.*

Nancy L. Moore received a Ph.D. in education from the University of Mass. Now program supervisor, Office of Federal Programs, S.C. State Dept. of Education.

Carlton Moss is a writer, film critic and director affiliated with the production of educational films. His article, "The Negro in American Films," appeared in *Freedomways,* Vol. 3, No. 2, Spring 1963.

Dr. Clarence J. Munford is associate professor in the Department of History, University of Guelph, Ontario, Canada. His essays have also been published in *Political Affairs* and *Black Scholar.*

J. H. O'Dell, a long-time associate editor of *Freedomways,* has written many essays and editorials for the magazine. Some of these essays have been published in *Violence in America: A Historical and Contemporary Reader* (1970), edited by Thomas Rose; in *Black Titan: W.E.B. Du Bois* (1970) and in the forthcoming book *Paul Robeson: The Great Forerunner.* O'Dell is also one of the editors of the latter two books on Du Bois and Robeson. He has been closely associated with Rev. Jesse L. Jackson and Operation P.U.S.H. and has taught at Antioch College, Washington, D.C., for the last several years.

Thomas J. Porter is now Acting Director, Afro-American Studies, Ohio University, Athens.

George Powers worked in the steel mills for 25 years and was a steel union organizer in Pennsylvania, Kentucky, Maryland and Missouri. Until his recent death he wrote and lectured as a member of the Frank London Brown Historical Association, Chicago.

Earl Smith, formerly community organizer in Freeport and Brentwood, Long Island, is currently on the f   of the University of Connecticut, Storrs.

James Steele is the national chairman of the Young Workers' Liberation League.

Augusta Strong, who died on September 1, 1976, was a long-time contributing editor of *Freedomways* magazine, a linguist, teacher and writer.

Francis Ward is a reporter on *The Los Angeles Times* and is one of the founders of Kuumba Workshop in Chicago, Ill. His articles have appeared in *Black World, Black Scholar* and other publications.

Jim Williams, actor, essayist and poet, is an ad salesman for the Black women's magazine *Essence* in New York City. His poetry and other essays on the black theater have appeared earlier in *Freedomways,* one of which was later published in two books.

Charles H. Wright, M.D., is chairman of the Board of Trustees of the Afro-American Museum in Detroit, Mich. His book, *Robeson: Labor's Forgotten Champion,* was published in 1975. Dr. Wright has also written for the stage and TV.

Jacqueline Lee Young is presently a teacher of children with special problems in Brooklyn, New York, and was formerly an early childhood teacher.

Celia Zitron was formerly a teacher in the New York City public high schools. She was dismissed by the New York City Board of Education during the McCarthyite period in 1951; in 1973 the Board acted favorably on the appeal of 33 teachers—including Ms. Zitron. She is the author of *The New York City Teachers' Union: 1916–1964: A Story of Educational and Social Commitment.*